In Pursuit of the Great Peace

SUNY series in Chinese Philosophy and Culture

Roger T. Ames, editor

In Pursuit of the Great Peace

Han Dynasty Classicism and the
Making of Early Medieval Literati Culture

Zhao Lu

趙璐

Cover art: (1) A rubbing of the "Great Peace": A design based on the rubbing with the word "Great Peace" substituting the original words on the aforementioned drawing. Designed by Lala Zuo. (2) A rubbing of the Classics with three scripts: A redrawing of the rubbing of Santi Shijing from the Palace Museum, People's Republic of China. Redrawn by Lala Zuo.

Published by State University of New York Press, Albany

© 2019 State University of New York

All rights reserved

No part of this book may be used or reproduced in any manner whatsoever without written permission. No part of this book may be stored in a retrieval system or transmitted in any form or by any means including electronic, electrostatic, magnetic tape, mechanical, photocopying, recording, or otherwise without the prior permission in writing of the publisher.

For information, contact State University of New York Press, Albany, NY
www.sunypress.edu

Library of Congress Cataloging-in-Publication Data

Names: Zhao, Lu, 1985– author.
Title: In pursuit of the great peace : Han Dynasty classicism and the making of early medieval literati culture / Zhao Lu.
Description: Albany : State University of New York Press, [2019] | Series: SUNY series in Chinese philosophy and culture | Revision of author's thesis (doctoral)—University of Pennsylvania, 2013. | Includes bibliographical references and index.
Identifiers: LCCN 2018035997 | ISBN 9781438474915 (hardcover : alk. paper) | ISBN ISBN 9781438474922 (pbk. : alk. paper) | ISBN 9781438474939 (ebook)
Subjects: LCSH: China—Intellectual life—221 B.C.–960 A.D. | Classicism—China—History.
Classification: LCC DS747.42 .Z453 2019 | DDC 931/.04—dc23
LC record available at https://lccn.loc.gov/2018035997

10 9 8 7 6 5 4 3 2 1

To Kelsey and Sarah

Contents

List of Illustrations	xi
Acknowledgments	xiii
Introduction	xv

1. Toward a Zeal for Classicism: Intellectual Transitions from 74 BC to AD 9 China — 1
   - The Search for Heaven's Will in Emperor Xuan's Period — 3
   - Toward the Great Peace: Emperor Yuan and the Restoration of the Kingly Way — 12
   - The Six Classics: Complete and Fundamental — 20
   - Restoring the Original Six Classics or Getting Rid of Them: Two Paths of Innovation — 28
   - Concluding Remarks — 45

2. The Conflation between Heaven and the Classics: The Rise of Apocrypha (*chenwei* 讖緯) — 49
   - Discovering the Heavenly Nature of the Classics — 50
   - Forming a Tradition: The Sociopolitical Background of the Emergence of the Apocryphal Texts — 63
   - A Case Study: Liu Xiu's *Feng* and *Shan* Sacrifices — 74
   - Concluding Remarks — 78

3. Apocrypha, Confucius, and Monarchy in Emperor Ming's Reign (AD 58–75) — 79
   - *Xuan sheng*: The Dark Sage — 80
   - *Su Wang*, the "Uncrowned King" — 85
   - Zixia and Confucius: A Political Analogy — 89
   - Concluding Remarks — 97

4. Finding Teachers versus Making Friends: The Gradual Departure from Classicism in the First Two Centuries AD	99
How to Succeed in the Han: Sketching the Han Official Recruitment System	101
How One Learned Classical Knowledge in the Han: Schools and Curricula	103
Ma Rong and His Friends: A Case Study of Horizontal Relationships	125
Concluding Remarks	134
5. The Radical and the Conservative: Zheng Xuan, He Xiu, the *Scripture of the Great Peace*, and Their Stances on the Classics	137
Zheng Xuan and His Scholarship	140
He Xiu and His Return to the Gongyang Tradition	151
The (Re)emergence of the *Scripture of the Great Peace*	159
Concluding Remarks	169
Conclusion	171
Han Intellectual Communities and Their Features	171
The Matter of the Great Peace	174
The Production of Innovation and Its Driving Force	175
The Impact and Legacy of Classicism	177
Appendix 1. The Chinese Classics	181
Appendix 2. The Origin of the Old Script / New Script Controversy	185
Appendix 3. The Contrast-Debate Model and Its Critique	189
Appendix 4. The Assumptions of Confucian Empire and Its Problems	199
Appendix 5. Apocryphal Texts: A History of Superstition and Adulation	209
Appendix 6. *Chen, Wei,* and Apocrypha: A Matter of Definition	213

Notes	217
Bibliography	285
Index	313

Illustrations

Charts

1.	The Transmission Line of the *Changes*	10
2.	Hou Cang and His Disciples	19
3.	Liu Xiang and Liu Xin's Learning	40
4.	Liu Xiang and His Alliances	41
5.	Liu Xin and His Enemies	43
6.	Liu Xin and Li Xun's Affiliates	44
7.	Family Transmission Lines 1	108
8.	Family Transmission Lines 2	109
9.	Transmission Lines of Old Text Traditions	111
10.	The Huan Family and Their Disciples	114
11.	Transmission of Knowledge in Ma Rong and Zheng Xuan's Time	121
12.	Partisans and Their Affiliates	127

Tables

1.	A Literal Translation of Apocrypha Titles Quoted in Chapter 2	51
2–3.	Two Theories of the Five Phases	61
4.	Ages and Reign Years of the Eastern Han Emperors	100

Acknowledgments

Although many guides to writing acknowledgments tell me to keep them concise without strong emotive language, I find it impossible to do so and do justice to the people to whom I am in debt. Even with that said, the thanks I give and how much these people contributed to my book is still understated.

First, I express my deep gratitude to Paul R. Goldin, my PhD advisor. Through writing my dissertation and turning it into this current form, I have benefited from his insightful and carefully constructed arguments, succinct and clear writing style, upright work ethic, and a witty sense of humor. While granting me great liberty in choosing my topic, Paul always provided me with concrete guidance, helpful critiques, and practical suggestions. Without his constant and generous help, I would not be able to finish the dissertation, not to mention turning it into a book.

Special thanks to Nathan Sivin for his unfailing mentoring. A polymath, Nathan has taught me Chinese medicine, astronomy, Daoist studies, writing skills, German, and even how to format my dissertation. More importantly, his broad academic curiosity and vision of breaking down the boundaries between specialized fields continues to inspire me. This book took shape based on his vision that historians should account for as many aspects of history as possible in their research. It also took shape via weekly discussions with him, via his careful examination of every single word of my drafts, and via his belief in the importance of serving a larger audience.

I would also like to thank Randall Collins, my dissertation committee member. I have greatly benefited from his erudition in world intellectual history as well as his expertise in sociology. His sociological view shaped the theoretical skeleton of this book, and his suggestions based on a comparative perspective never failed to stimulate me and improve this project.

As a nonnative speaker of English, this book would be barely intelligible without many people's help with my writing. Besides Paul and Nathan, my deepest gratitude goes to Sarah A. G. Basham and Kelsey Seymour, my language partners. They have patiently read through countless drafts since I started writing my dissertation until the final version. They identified any part that was unclear and always offered me means of clarification. Their criticism, ranging from my choice of word to the structure of a chapter, helped to bring this book to another level. Most importantly, they never settled with me on writing a "good enough" sentence because I am not a native speaker of English; they always urged me to strive for excellence.

Along the way, I became indebted to many people with whom I have had the honor to work and without whom the path would have been much darker. Michael Nylan gave me enthusiastic encouragement as well as practical suggestions that decisively turned the project around. Anonymous reviewer A's meticulous comments have greatly improved the quality of the work. Anonymous reviewer B's comments not only increased the readability of the manuscript but also put my decade-long anxieties toward English at ease. My editor Christopher Ahn bravely took on the project, and Chelsea Miller and the rest of the SUNY Press team vigorously pushed the project forward ever since. Zuo Lala visualized the central argument of my book and created the main image for the book cover, a stone stele of the classics with nothing but the Great Peace. Adam Smith and Barbara Hendrischke insightfully pointed out many logical fallacies in first drafts, which set straight the project in the very beginning. Constance A. Cook, Chang Chia-Feng, and Hon Tze-ki have provided tremendous moral support through the whole process. I am particularly thankful that Connie practically cornered me into sending my materials to SUNY. I am also very grateful for the timely support of Mark Csikszentmihalyi and Michael Puett.

I thank the International Consortium of Research in the Humanities (IKGF) at the University of Erlangen-Nuremberg and its director, Michael Lackner. Both have provided me great liberty to pursue my project as well as the stimulating environment where I had the chance to meet most of the aforementioned people. I am especially grateful for Michael's unceasing help, generous mentoring, and faith in me.

Last but not least, I thank Academia Sinica for allowing me to reprint a revised version of the article "To Become Confucius: Political Legitimacy and Han Apocryphal Texts in the Case of Emperor Ming (r. AD 58–75)," *Asia Major* 28.1 (May 2015): 115–44. I am particularly indebted to Lee Jender's prompt support.

Introduction

Scriptures are an intriguing phenomenon in both the ancient and modern world. From the Talmud, Bible, and Qur'an to the Chinese classics,[1] they seem to provide unfailing guidance for the people who are devoted to them.[2] More than that, they have been responsible for forming communities, shaping social identities, and stimulating intellectual innovations throughout history. If anyone doubts the role of scriptures in the modern world, they could look to the curriculum of Sunday schools in America, the reading lists that Chinese teachers make for their students to understand Chinese culture, and what the adult-to-be will read in their Bar or Bat Mitzvahs. In the ancient world, from the innovation of the codex to Eusebius's library, from the formation of Medieval European countries to the Muslim Conquests, scriptures played an indispensable role.[3]

This book concentrates on people who established their careers on reading and interpreting scriptures, their production of knowledge based on scriptures and their impact on society. It will focus on those who mastered a corpus of texts labeled "classics," or *jing* 經, in the Han dynasty (205 BC–AD 220). This is a conscious choice. Students of China have long relished the stimulating debates between thinkers from the time of Confucius to the dawn of the first Chinese empire; we have also been fascinated by the flourishing of literary writing, the booming of Daoist movements, and the spread of Buddhism in the third century AD. The period in the middle, however, remains a dark tunnel. The untamed and subversive Confucians and other thinkers entered this tunnel, and litterateurs and promoters of Daoist and Buddhist religions emerged from the other end. We know very little about the transformation process *in* this tunnel.

Previous scholarship can only take us so far; it has long focused on the controversy between the so-called "new script" and "old script" groups of texts. As the labels suggest, the "new script" was a classical corpus whose transmission was clearly recorded; it was written in the characters of the last two centuries BC in China. The "old script" refers to several texts that had no active transmission line, and which were probably written in scripts no longer commonly used. Modern scholars have treated the compilers of these two groups as mutually hostile schools with opposed agendas. Many also equate Han classicism with a corrupted version of Confucianism due to political pressure and treat classicism as reactionary political propaganda, an obstacle to innovation.[4]

According to this narrative, the intellectual landscape from 100 BC to AD 200 is a grim one: two groups of bigoted pedants upheld twisted, fossilized Confucian doctrines for their political benefits. This caricature results from assuming that certain key words in primary sources always had the same meanings. Many also accept early scholars' vehement disparagements of each other as objective assessments. Recently, Michael Nylan has questioned the significance of the old script versus new script controversy, and Michael Loewe has expressed doubts that "Confucianism" has a single authoritative meaning.[5] Although such historians have cast old models away, the intellectual world of early imperial China and the nature of classicism are yet to be refined.

We poorly understand the transformations that took place in this nebulous three hundred years. For instance, many search for the root of second-century Daoist movements more often in books centuries older, such as *Laozi* 老子 or *Zhuangzi* 莊子, rather than in the immediate intellectual context. Scholars try to explain the blooming of literary writing by the decline of classicism instead of investigating the particular routines of literati life that classicism had already shaped. Meanwhile, they make classicism a state-promoted ideology responsible for smothering the lively intellectual atmosphere of the third and second centuries BC and look elsewhere to account for the exciting innovations of the second century AD. In this framework, the so-called apocrypha (*chenwei* 讖緯), a corpus of texts peculiar to the Eastern Han dynasty, was merely a maladroit fabrication woven by superstition and propaganda.[6] Worst of all, with few exceptions, we see classicism, literature, and Daoist religions as three separate story lines and seek to reconstruct each while disregarding the others.

This book attempts to explore the mechanisms that connected these trends. I believe that the key to understanding how these heterogeneous fields worked together, as well as the actual role of classicism, is to explore how the people then used written words to navigate their lives. Classics are not created from nothing; they are products of transmission and interpretation.

Traditions of classics are first of all interactions between people. They evoke emotions and alter participants. Literati made conversations, discussed common concerns, and solved crucial problems of their times. These routines decided their own and their families' welfare, social status, and success. They became immersed in the existing knowledge of their time, whether poetry, ancient wisdom, or revelations from Heaven; tried to exhaust their resources; and competed with each other. From time to time, writings that can be classified as philosophy, literature, or religion did highlight certain periods, but behind them were generations of literati who produced them in the process of adopting, negating, combining, and adjusting each other's ideas. Concentrating on them will shed light on this nebulous period and solve many problems.

This work thus will examine the dynamic between scholars, the classics, intellectual innovations, and political reality. Through the constant appropriation of the classics, intellectual innovations took place among these communities, thus gradually forming the political and literati culture that became fundamental to imperial China. This culture and many elements of classical hermeneutics inspired Daoist sects after the collapse of the Han dynasty.

The next question is how we can sort individuals' intellectual backgrounds, their writings, and their relations to others to generate a constructive narrative of intellectual competition and innovation. Randall Collins's interaction ritual chains theory (IR theory) is particularly useful for this purpose. IR theory assumes that during positive personal contacts, individuals are inspired by attention, generating emotional energy (EE). The accumulation of EE not only leads to further contacts and the recharging of EE, but also makes the central topics and objects of those interactions "sacred objects," which certain groups of individuals come to consider special and essential. In Collins's *The Sociology of Philosophies*, the application of IR to the intellectual world predicts ubiquitous patterns of scholarly innovation rather than the static transmission of knowledge.[7] These innovations are primarily due to competition for attention in coteries. In order to receive attention from colleagues, scholars need to prove that their approaches to significant topics are important. The significance of the topics and the plausibility of their approach are based on the appropriation of sacred objects shared by their intellectual communities. This theory reveals the driving force for innovations and their origin *inside* scholarly groups. Hence IR provides us with a theoretical basis to focus on the internal dynamics of intellectual communities as the primary stimulus of change in Han classicism. It also allows us to link the scholarship of individuals or single innovations together as elements in series of changes.

The analysis starts from local situations. In the case of Han classicists, their daily routine of learning, memorizing, and ruminating on their master's lectures on the classics are rituals in the sociological sense. As Randall Collins argues, an interaction ritual needs the following: "1. a group of at least two people is physically assembled; 2. they focus attention on the same object or action, and each becomes aware that the other is maintaining this focus, and 3. they share a common mood or emotion." These three ingredients predict the cumulative result of a repeatable situation. This makes better sense than solely emphasizing verbal chants, dress code, and other symbols and their meanings throughout history. The symbols are subject to human attention and emotion.[8]

On the other hand, the three components give rise to a long-term process; they produce, keep, and renew attention paid and the emotions attached to symbols. The mutual focus and shared emotion intensify cumulatively and trans-situationally. Focus and emotion are carried by bodily motions, speech, and other events and information. This adds to the feeling of membership in a group with moral obligations to one another. Collins explains this process as follows: "in the series of IRs, participants are filled with emotional energy (EE), in proportion to the intensity of the interaction."[9] The level of emotional energy accumulated from previous IRs decides whether a given person will choose to participate further in the IRs. EE is a trans-situational feeling that can ebb away or be recharged by participating in IRs.

Members of intellectual communities compete to become the center of conversations. These struggles take the shape of "my ideas are new," "my ideas are important," and "my ideas are true." Their ideas or innovations result from new combinations of old ideas, or opposition to them. As Collins points out, intellectuals "of each generation operate within a lineup of existing intellectual factions, which gives a limited number of moves that can be made by recombining, negating, and abstracting existing ideas."[10] In other words, new ideas respond to old ones. Therefore, so-called "intellectual transitions" or "paradigm shifts" result as such innovations accumulate.

The Han transmitters of classics are not an exception. The interaction of students in their daily activities drew attention to the sacred objects that they held in common—the classics and their master's understanding of them—reinforcing their group solidarity. Students not only learned a worldview from this process but became emotionally committed to their identifying symbols. Members of various traditions competed over whose traditions better explained the classics and were more capable of answering contemporary questions. They defended the classics, their master's teaching, and their worldview by arguing that their competitors distorted the classics or made huge mistakes in their commentaries, losing the original and true meaning of the classics. However, through defenses, they created new knowledge as well. Indeed, they were not just to iterate, but to invent.

In classicists' commentaries, a few fundamental ideas drove the miscellaneous exegesis. This book investigates one of them, namely, the vision of the ideal society, one of the most crucial concerns during early imperial China. It will explore how the study of the Confucian classics increasingly came to shape early imaginations of an ideal empire and transformed the intellectual communities of the Han empire. Through constant competition among scholars over finding the right way for this new empire, classicism led to innovations in the understanding of dynastic cycles based on the mandate of Heaven. It did so by studying various commentarial traditions, prophecies, and religious writings. These men strove to be erudite advisors to the destined emperor, who worked to achieve the Great Peace, the perennial goal of a society striving to accord with Heaven.

Behind the search for the Great Peace, we will witness a transformation of literati culture that ended the proliferating discourses among Warring States thinkers and perpetuated the transmission of what had become classics by the end of the first century AD. The literati who served as bureaucrats around the first century BC gradually became classicists who depended on social networking while traveling. Classicism dissolved in this traveling culture, as literati started to envision a broader inventory of knowledge than the classics. This new intellectual fashion gave birth to a peripatetic and epistolary scholarly culture marked by the use of calligraphy and poetry in the social life of newly mobile teachers and disciples throughout imperial China. At the end of this book, we will see, at the end of the second century AD, the pursuit of erudition and the multiplication of interpersonal contacts led to a new period of proliferating discourses, which facilitated literary writing and various religious communities.

The primary sources for this book range from dynastic histories such as Ban Gu's 班固 (AD 32–92) *History of the Han* (*Han shu* 漢書) and Fan Ye's 范曄 (AD 398–445) *History of the Later Han* (*Hou Han shu* 後漢書) to compilations of fragments or integral writings from Han dynasty texts, such as Ma Guohan's 馬國翰 *Jade Box Mountain House's Collections of Lost Books* (*Yuhan Shanfang jiyi shu* 玉函山房輯佚書) and Yan Kejun's 嚴可均 *Comprehensive*

Collection of Great Antiquity, the Three Dynasties, Qin, Han, the Three Kingdoms, and Six Dynasties Prose (*Quan shanggu sandai Qin Han Sanguo Liuchao wen* 全上古三代秦漢三國六朝文). The most obscure corpus is the so-called "apocryphal texts," or *chenwei* 讖緯. This corpus emerged in the first century CE as explanations of the classics, purportedly revealed by Heaven. Apocrypha contain anecdotes, instructions for rituals, and miscellaneous visions of the cosmos, history, and the Great Peace. They can provide invaluable evidence to fill the gaps in our knowledge of the connections between Han dynasty classicism and various Daoist cults after the Han dynasty.

This book provides a radically different angle in reading apocrypha. I will discuss apocryphal texts and orthodox commentarial traditions together with literary works and early Daoist writings to show intellectual and social transitions. I will show that so-called "Confucians" and "Daoists" actually had much in common in Eastern Han (AD 25–220) written culture. Solely dividing scholars as members of one or the other "schools" does not accurately reflect their ideas or social groupings.

The first chapter deals with how, in the late Western Han (206 BC–AD 9), groups of literati, as part of their struggles to establish the Great Peace, contested the understanding of the classics. Heaven's mandate, ancient sages' words, and an ideal society were the beams of their intellectual architecture. The chapter climaxes in a vital debate on whether the dynasty should rely on the classics or directly rely on Heaven's messages. The second chapter explores an innovative response to the debate: the formation of apocryphal texts and its relationship to literati's knowledge about the classics at the beginning of the Eastern Han. The corpus states that the classics contain Heaven's messages, and literati could help their readers decipher them. Behind the intellectual transitions, the first two chapters also reveal the social relationships between the groups that embodied the transitions. We will find that groups formerly considered disparate were in fact well connected.

The next two chapters touch on two sides of a coin: the emperor and the literati. The third chapter surveys the interaction between politics and culture, arguing that Emperor Ming (r. AD 58–75) adopted apocrypha to depict himself as a latter-day Confucius, claiming that he could bring on the Great Peace. The fourth chapter uses social history to explain how in the first two centuries AD the recruitment of the Han bureaucracy led to the flourishing of Eastern Han local academies. These academies encouraged more travel, more frequent contacts among literati, and greater accessibility of texts, which changed literati's understanding of classics and literary works. A new trend of erudition emerged from such a context. These two chapters reveal the social mechanism based on which intellectual innovations and exchanges took place.

The last chapter shows responses to these changes: important second-century commentators, in pursuit of the Great Peace, adhered to the spirit of ancient texts rather than following them to the letter. Meanwhile, others departed from classicism more radically. In this chapter, we will see how one of the earliest Daoist scriptures, the *Scripture of the Great Peace* (*Taiping jing* 太平經), was tightly connected to the world of the classics. Paradox is central to my argument: intellectual dissimilarity often comes from similar assumptions and close social relationships. We would not realize this unless we look at what people do in addition to how ideas spin.

Chapter 1

Toward a Zeal for Classicism

Intellectual Transitions from 74 BC to AD 9 China

Sometimes we assume that we are more normal than we actually are, especially when it comes to beliefs. Words like orthodox, heterodox, conservative, radical, and hater imply a spectrum in which we sit in the sweet middle spot and others fall on the less normal, and hence less correct, range. Words like pagan, Pharisee, and zealot from biblical traditions embody this spectrum. Was Judas a good or bad person? The New Testament Gospels and the Gospel of Judas would give you opposite answers.[1] Nevertheless, both seek to convince you that their ideas are the norm; both compete over the middle spot in the spectrum.

At the end of the first century BC in China, Liu Xin railed against his colleagues and insisted on adding several texts to the canon of the Five Classics. While his colleagues were still outraged by this extreme move, an incident added more fuel to the controversy: Liu's enemy Li Xun 李尋 (fl. 15–5 BC) convinced the emperor to depart from the classics in general. A similar spectrum seems to have formed: Liu Xin and Li Xun fell on two poles of the spectrum, and the others sat in the middle as the normal ones. But from the perspective of Li, was not everyone conservative, and from that of Liu, was not Li too radical and others too conservative? If so, how do we make sense of the different spectra in their minds?

This chapter tells the story of radicals and conservatives in first century BC China, except they are more than radicals or conservatives. I see them as intellectual contenders who reacted to concerns of their contemporaries in the way that they thought was the best approach. Simply put: they lived to prove that their ideas were better than others'. This perspective emancipates us from the two notorious spectra, that of Confucianism and that of old script / new script texts. The first spectrum puts the original teachings of Confucius, Mencius, and Xunzi in the middle and judges the

1

literati by how faithfully they conformed to the middle point. The second divides the literati in two segregated, mutually hostile parties, one promoting a version of the classics written in contemporary script and the other supporting those in the ancient script. These kinds of views highlight the conformity to certain beliefs but obscure the driving concerns of and the agency of individuals. Moreover, our perspective reveals layers of thought as well as social connections invisible in these spectra.[2]

Therefore, this chapter tells the story in a more label-free way. Up to the first century BC, the classics started out as merely one of the weapons in the intellectual arsenal of literati. However, in the beginning of the first century AD, they became the paramount canon, disrespect for which could cost a person's life. This turn paralleled a political turn: the Han empire was facing the consequences of overexpansion and needed a less aggressive state policy.[3] Most literati during that time believed that the previously failed policies endangered the imperial house's heavenly granted right to rule and put the empire at the edge of a precipice.[4] A new policy might well be the last chance for the imperial house before Heaven shifted its mandate to someone else, so the court needed to choose this policy wisely.[5] Since, to most of them, Heaven was the ultimate agent that would decide the fate of the Han dynasty, the literati extensively elaborated on Heaven's will.

The imagination of an ideal society, namely, the Great Peace (*taiping* 太平), emerged from this context. If Heaven evaluated human rulers based on their subjects' welfare, the best policy to keep Heaven satisfied was the one that could bring the maximal degree of welfare to the people. Therefore, generations of scholars competed with each other to set out the right or the ideal way to rule. Most of them gradually turned their attention to following the steps of the ancient sage kings. And the classics became the focus as the records of these sage kings' speeches and deeds.

In this chapter, we will focus on the imagination of the Great Peace and examine the competing voices around it, which eventually led to the rise of classicism. From hindsight, classicism stood out in history, and classicists were certain to win the favor of the emperors. But after closely examining the debates between the literati, we can see that the promoters of the classics barely dominated, and they were constantly faced with challenges from rivals. Even the promoters themselves starkly disagreed with each other. This chapter thus not only introduces how devotion to the classics became a good idea to most of the literati, but also how seemingly opposite or outlandish ideas could result from the same context. Behind these ideas, we will see the patterns of intellectual innovation in first century BC China.

We will start with the intellectual atmosphere in Emperor Xuan's court (r. 73–49 BC), for it disclosed a concern, namely, anxiety about Heaven's will, which shaped the changes of literati thought on the classics for the rest of the Western Han dynasty. The literati and the emperor openly expressed their anxiety about Heaven's will and sought means of dealing with it. Dominant literati like Wei Xiang 魏相 (?–59 BC) and Bing Ji 丙吉 (?–55 BC) brought the classics, or chunks of classics, into this conversation not as manuals for moral cultivation but as one expeditious way of fulfilling the urgent need to restore the disturbed cosmological order.

The next generation of dominant scholars, including Liu Xiang 劉向 (77–6 BC) and several disciples of Hou Cang 后蒼 (fl. 72 BC), searched for a way to relieve the intensified anxiety. The government of the ancient sage kings, or the Kingly Way, became the paragon for the Han dynasty to follow, for it was in harmony with Heaven. The classics, putatively written by the sage kings to record the ideal government of the Golden Age, became the media for the literati to imagine and realize sagely rule in their own troubled times.

The latent sparks of the two preceding generations fueled the dramatic changes in the last years of the Western Han. The desire to harmonize with Heaven was the foundation for further intellectual innovations, which had an impact throughout the first two centuries AD. Building on the focus on the classics, two different paths of innovation cast doubts on the existing transmission lines of the classics. Liu Xin, on the one hand, suspected that the received versions of the classics were not the complete, original classics of the sage kings. Accordingly, he combined obscure and ignored versions of classics and commentarial traditions to restore the classics. Li Xun 李尋 (fl. 15–5 BC) and Xia Heliang 夏賀良 (?–5 BC), on the other hand, emphasized Heaven's will in an effort to depart from the sages and overrode the classics with the revealed text, the *Scripture of the Great Peace*. These two ways of innovation—combination in order to complete the old material and a shift to new material—marked the last years of the Western Han dynasty. They also prepared the ground for the apocrypha, a corpus of commentaries that reveal heavenly secrets hidden in the classics.

The Search for Heaven's Will in Emperor Xuan's Period

In 78 BC, a bizarre incident attracted the court's attention: a dead willow tree in the imperial garden revived itself with words on its leaves: "Gongsun

Bingyi 公孫病已 will be established."⁶ A scholar called Sui Hong 眭弘 (?–78 BC) reported to the court about the implication of this omen:

> 漢家堯後，有傳國之運。漢帝宜誰差天下，求索賢人，禪以帝位而退。自封百里，如殷周二王後，以承順天命。⁷

> The Han house is a descendant of Yao, and it has the fate to pass down the throne. Now the Han emperor should search in the world to seek out a worthy and abdicate the throne to him. Then he should retreat and grant himself a fief of a hundred square *li* like the descendants of the Shang and Zhou dynasties, in order to conform to the mandate of Heaven.

The court was outraged by this blunt claim: the mandate of Heaven had moved away from the Han dynasty. This speech was particularly disturbing because the dynasty was suffering from the policy of overexpansion from the previous emperor, Emperor Wu, and the current ruler was a young boy being manipulated by Huo Guang 霍光 (?–68 BC). During this troubling time, the mandate of Heaven was a sensitive issue; for people in the first century BC, a dynasty's destiny desperately hung on the favor of Heaven.⁸ The current difficulties of the empire inevitably aroused literati's anxiety about the mandate.

Four years later, when Emperor Xuan succeeded the throne, his announcements and policies continuously reflected this anxiety. After the political instability and the backfiring of Emperor Wu's previous aggressive policies, Emperor Xuan needed to turn the empire in another direction.⁹ However, no one knew what this transition would bring to the empire. The uncertainty of the future overlapped with the uncertainty of Heaven's will. What if the Han dynasty had already lost Heaven's favor and the new direction only worsened the situation? As a successor to the Han throne, our new emperor was also anxious about his position. He was a grandson of a crown prince whose princely status was terminated by Emperor Wu. In the early years of his reign, he behaved as a figurehead overshadowed by Huo Guang.¹⁰ It was crucial for him to live up to what others expected of a legitimate emperor.

Emperor Xuan's concern for Heaven's will was revealed in his sensitivity to omens, auspicious and inauspicious. His predecessors had already mentioned omens and Heaven's will, but he brought the significance of omens to another level. Taking them as Heaven's constant evaluation of his rule, he actively responded to them. When auspicious omens such as phoenixes (*fenghuang* 鳳凰) or sweet dew (*ganlu* 甘露) were reported, he sent out edicts modestly pointing out his careful work as well as his respect for Heaven. When earthquakes or other disasters took place, he took them as warnings about his faults. In a case where an earthquake damaged an ancestral temple of the Han, Emperor Xuan linked the warning particularly with the fate of the dynasty.[11]

Since Emperor Xuan believed Heaven constantly evaluated his government, we might ask what he thought Heaven's standards were. In explaining his faults, he stated that he failed to "harmonize the living" (*he qun sheng* 和群生), and he "did not brightly lead the people" (*dao min bu ming* 導民不明). What did he think he was supposed to do? He put it in a confessional form: "I have not been able to carry forward the magnificence of the previous emperors, harmonize and pacify the people, follow Heaven and Earth, and regulate [according to] the four seasons."[12] He did not stress moral cultivation but emphasized regulating the human order in accordance with Heaven and Earth.

The emperor's anxiety resonated in his successors and became one of the driving concerns in the intellectual world of the first century BC. Generations of scholars sought to alleviate this anxiety in their own ways. The first generation was in line with Emperor Xuan and used the cosmological order as a tool of governance.

Curing the State: Cosmology as a Political Weapon

Since the fourth century BC, generations of scholars emphasized the importance of an orderly cosmos in ruling a state.[13] During the mid-first century BC, officials brought this issue into the center of state policy. In Emperor Xuan's court, high officials such as Bing Ji 丙吉 (?–55 BC) and Wei Xiang 魏相 (?–59 BC) stressed that the human realm was part of the cosmos, and they turned to the balance of *yin* and *yang* as well as the harmony of *qi*.[14] Bing Ji's famous story illuminates this point. During a trip, Bing Ji witnessed two events: several people fighting, and a cow sticking out its tongue and gasping for breath. As an imperial chancellor, he did not take care of the melee, an apparent illegal activity. Instead, he was worried about the cow's bizarre behavior, for it was an omen that indicated irregular activity in the cosmos. For Bing Ji, keeping *yin* and *yang* in balance was the job of the highest Han officials.[15] He did not diminish the importance of laws and regulations, but he unprecedentedly prioritized the cosmological order before laws and regulations for running the empire.[16]

Wei Xiang drew a more specific blueprint in presenting principles of *yin* and *yang*:

陰陽未和，災害未息，咎在臣等。臣聞《易》曰：『天地以順動，故日月不過，四時不忒；聖王以順動，故刑罰清而民服。』天地變化，必繇陰陽。17

Now *yin* and *yang* do not harmonize with each other, and disasters have not stopped. The guilt [for these] lies in us. I have heard from the *Changes* that "Heaven and Earth act based on smooth [progress]. Therefore the sun and moon do not behave excessively, and the four seasons are free from error. When the sage kings act based on smooth [progress], the penalty is fair and the populace is thus convinced." The changes of Heaven and Earth always follow *yin* and *yang*.

Like Emperor Xuan, Wei Xiang points out that under his administration, *yin* and *yang* have not harmonized with each other. Quoting from the *Changes*, he argues that *yin* and *yang* are the foundation of the changes of Heaven and Earth. He goes on to explain the fundamental role of *yin* and *yang* for the empire and the human realm: "I think *yin* and *yang* are the base of the kingly undertaking, and the mandate of the myriad creatures. Since antiquity none of the sages or the worthies have failed to follow it. Purely following Heaven and Earth and observing the previous sages are the duties of the Son of Heaven."[18] Echoing Emperor Xuan's speech, this claim holds that *yin* and *yang* are the foundation of the empire and it is the emperor's job to maintain their relationship.

Yin and *yang* and *qi* in Bing Ji and Wei Xiang's cases are two oft-repeated concepts in cosmology from the late Warring States period on. In their understandings of the cosmos, *qi*, a fluid but materialistic substance, permeates the universe. *Yin* and *yang*, the oppositional aspects of *qi*, form the basic generational process of the cosmos. Human society, the political state, and even the human body as microcosms are linked to Heaven and Earth by *qi*. Correspondingly, they are not only subject to but also influence the overall cosmological process.[19] Based on this cosmology then, if a state, as an intermediary between Heaven and individuals, intends to function well, it needs to keep the various microcosms and the cosmos as a whole functioning regularly.[20]

This cosmology was hardly limited to Wei Xiang and Bing Ji's time.[21] Neither was forming it into a political philosophy of his invention. Dong Zhongshu 董仲舒 (179–104 BC), for example, had already mentioned similar ideas: "When the legal penalty does not hit the target, deviant *qi* (*xie qi* 邪氣) is created. When deviant *qi* accumulates below, resentment and hatred are stored above. If what is above and below do not get along, *yin* and *yang* will be in disorder, and bizarreness and disasters will occur."[22] In this case, Dong Zhongshu warns that the imbalance of *yin* and *yang* will cause catastrophes that are portents. The "deviant *qi*," shaped by the royal abuse of punishment, accumulates and brings hatred to the empire.[23] We can see that Wei Xiang's theory of *qi* echoed that of Dong Zhongshu. The link between earthquakes and an inharmonious populace mentioned in Emperor Xuan's early edict also reflects, though inexplicitly, a similar cosmology.

However, for Dong Zhongshu, the emperor's virtue is the essential factor that affects the cosmological processes; the ruler needs to constantly rectify his mind. Dong argues that achieving the balance of the cosmological order starts with the emperor's moral reflection. In order to solve the problem of deviant *qi* and the imbalance of *yin* and *yang*, he does not emphasize the need to understand the cosmos. Instead, he considers virtue the solution. In Dong's case, the balance of the cosmos and the harmony of *qi* are the result of the ruler's moral perfection.[24] Although harmony with the cosmological process is crucial for the welfare of the state, the means of adjusting and maintaining it is the moral rectification of the ruler. That is to say, for Dong Zhongshu, morality commands cosmos.

In contrast, in Wei Xiang's statement, the ruler's virtue is no longer the crux of adjusting the cosmological order. Instead, a better understanding of the cosmos and the tools to manage it are essential. Wei Xiang attaches certain trigrams, namely, Zhen 震, Li 離, Dui 兌, and Kan 坎, to East, South, West, and North, respectively, a relationship found in the "Explicating the Trigrams" ("Shuo gua" 說卦) commentary of the *Changes*.[25] The four trigrams also symbolize winter, spring, summer, and autumn.[26] People need to use the trigrams in a timely order, otherwise natural disasters will occur.[27] He argues that the ruler should respect Heaven and follow *yin* and *yang*. When the cosmological process is normal, natural disasters will disappear. In this condition, people can prosper. Then there will be no hatred or dissatisfaction.[28] In Wei's theory, inharmonious *qi* is caused by the ruler's failure to follow the correct cosmological order, not by his lack of virtue. He then gives his proposal for recruiting officials:

願陛下選明經通知陰陽者四人，各主一時，時至明言所職，以和陰陽，天下幸甚！²⁹

> I hope your majesty selects four people who are enlightened in the classics and comprehensively know *yin* and *yang* and puts each of them in charge of one of the four seasons. When the season comes, the one responsible for it should announce what trigram should be in charge, in order to harmonize *yin* and *yang*. All-under-Heaven will be very fortunate.

In other words, the welfare of the state does not depend on the ruler's moral rectification but on officials with experience in dealing with *yin* and *yang*.

Wei Xiang's proposal was accepted by Emperor Xuan. In fact, Wei Xiang and his successor Bing Ji had taken the path to the highest position in Emperor Xuan's court, from Grandee Secretary (*yushi dafu* 御史大夫) to Grand Chancellor (*chengxiang* 丞相), two of the three most privileged official positions, known as the Three Ducal Ministers (*san gong* 三公).³⁰ They had training both in Han law and in the classics: the *Book of Changes*, the *Rites* classics, and the *Classic of Poetry*.³¹

In solving the problem of ill-omened earthquakes and a dissatisfied, restless populace posed by Emperor Xuan, Bing Ji and Wei Xiang did not give any suggestion that could radically change the legal and administrative foundation of the Han dynasty. Instead, they added the cosmological order on top of this foundation. For them, to be in tune with the cosmic order, the ruler must give the populace an environment in which to prosper and employ the people in a timely manner. Only then can the cosmos function well, and the empire last. It was in this context that the *Book of Changes* came to interest the literati in the court.

The *Book of Changes* as a Means of Searching for Heaven's Will

There are, explicitly or implicitly, several allusions to the *Changes* in Wei Xiang's proposal. How, then, was the *Changes* relevant to Wei Xiang's points? What kind of text did Wei Xiang and his contemporaries perceive the *Changes* to be? It is well accepted that the hexagrams found in the received version of the *Book of Changes* were originally used for divination in the Eastern Zhou period (770–256 BC).³² The received version contains strata of commentaries on prognostication. Among these strata, a "Commentary on the Attached Statements," or "Xici zhuan" 繫辭傳,³³ already circulated in the early Western Han dynasty. And it explains how humans can penetrate Heaven's will:³⁴ Heaven and Earth change over time, and Heaven produces images to show what is auspicious and inauspicious in this constantly changing world; the sage follows the changes of Heaven and Earth and imitates Heaven's image in order to understand the way of Heaven.³⁵ As Willard J. Peterson mentions, in dealing with the changing world, the "Commentary" "is an attempt to persuade the audience that they can best do so by accepting the guidance of the *Changes*."³⁶ The "Commentary on the Attached Statements" points out that by using the *Changes*, cosmological processes are intelligible. Human beings can thus adjust to these processes in accordance with the cosmos.³⁷

During Emperor Xuan's time, when Heaven's approval of government became a central intellectual issue, the *Changes* became an essential tool.³⁸ Its unique usefulness derived from the intimate relationship between its images, especially hexagrams, and heavenly omens and other signs from Heaven. According to the commentaries, thanks to the ancient sages, people were able not only to translate Heaven's language into something they could understand but to also make Heaven's regulation of the cosmos intelligible. For this reason, the literati increasingly used the *Changes* to understand the functioning of Heaven during Emperor Xuan's reign.³⁹

It was in this context that experts on the *Changes* became important figures among literati in the court. Particularly, Shi Chou 施讎 (fl. 51 BC), Liangqiu He 梁丘賀 (fl. 59–48 BC), and Meng Xi 孟喜 (fl. 73–49 BC), taught by the same teacher, Tian Wangsun 田王孫, monopolized the transmission lines of the *Changes* there. Shi Chou took the Academician position (*boshi* 博士) for the *Changes* in Emperor Xuan's reign.⁴⁰ Liangqiu He received Emperor Xuan's favor for his interpretation of omens and later became the Chamberlain for the Palace Revenues (*shaofu* 少府) from 59 to 48 BC. Around 51 BC, his teaching was established as an official tradition after an imperial conference about the classics at Shiqu 石渠 Hall.⁴¹ Although Meng Xi was not appointed as Academician, due to his reputation for changing his master's teaching, his reading of the *Changes* was well recognized by his contemporaries, and some of his students took the position of Academician.⁴²

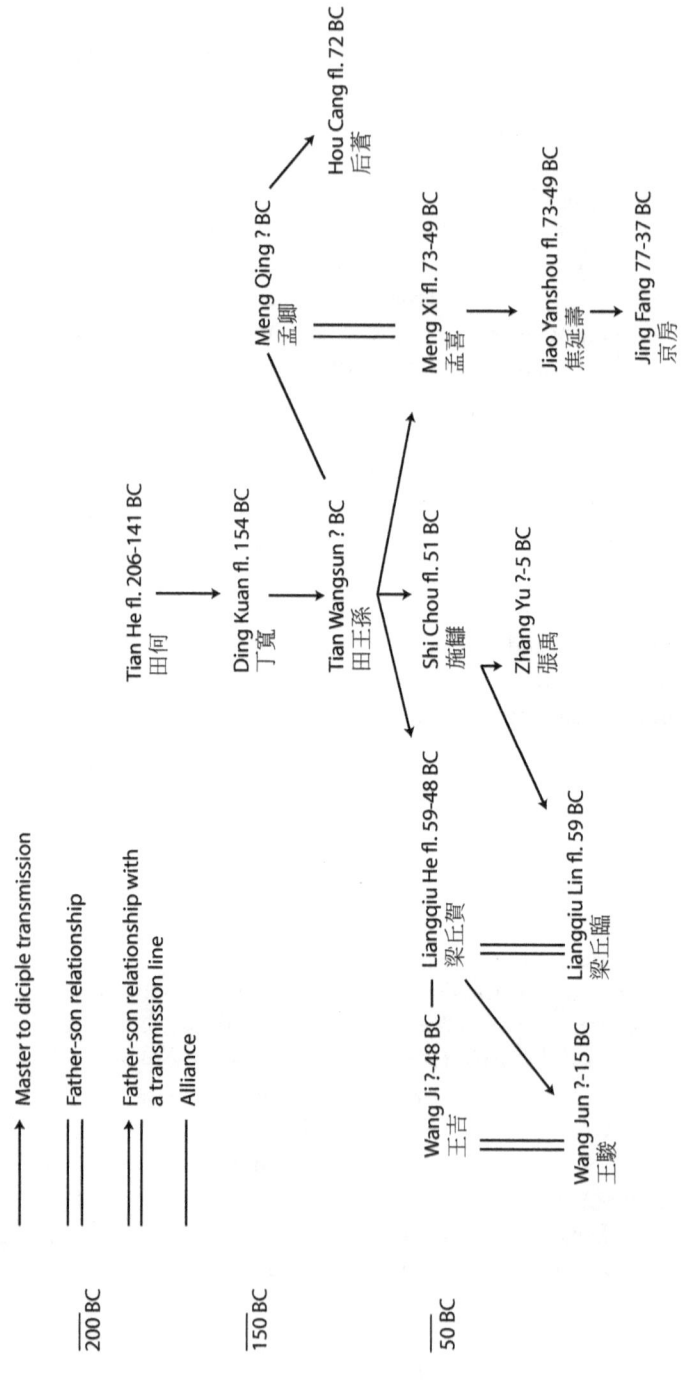

Chart 1. The Transmission Line of the *Changes*

Although the three masters' works are lost, surviving fragments from Meng Xi's work can still give us a rough impression of their scholarship.[43] In a manner similar to Wei Xiang, Meng Xi uses Kan, Zhen, Li, and Dui as the four major trigrams that explain the changes of the seasons. Like Wei and others, he matches them with the timely fluctuation of *yin* and *yang qi*.[44] We can infer that based on Meng's reading, the *Book of Changes* appears to be a guide for understanding the cosmological process as well. The trigrams of the text, the ebb and flow of *yin* and *yang*, and the changes of the seasons correspond with each other. Therefore, for many of Wei's contemporaries, commanding the first implies mastery of the other two.

An example reveals the unique position of the *Changes* at the time in contrast with the other classics. Meng Xi's father Meng Qing 孟卿 was a transmitter of the *Rites* and *Annals*. However, instead of teaching his son based on his own expertise, Meng Qing sent his son to Tian Wangsun for the *Changes*. He reasoned that the *Rites* was overwhelmingly voluminous, and the material in the *Annals* was varied and haphazardly combined.[45] Meng Qing did not feel the need to master all the knowledge of the Five Classics to make a synoptic teaching as later generations did. For him, his son only needed to master one classic, definitely not one that contained too much irrelevant information.[46]

To survive and expand their social lives, members of an intellectual community need to be involved in the shared concerns of their group. If a member wants to succeed, however, this is not enough. In an intellectual community in particular, one needs to convince others that his own ideas are plausible. What criteria establish plausibility? Among others, one's idea should solve in a new way intellectual problems shared within the community with tools familiar to members of that community.

In the case of the *Changes*, we can clearly see this innovative process. Literati like Wei Xiang and Bing Ji shared Emperor Xuan's anxiety over understanding Heaven's will. In order to resolve the anxiety, they turned to existing knowledge, in this case the *Book of Changes*, because it had been a text in accordance with the "heart of Heaven and Earth."[47] But they modified it with other contemporary, well-accepted theories, such as the cosmology of *qi*. In this way, their interpretations would be more suitable to address the anxieties or concerns of their contemporaries. In the case of Wei Xiang and Meng Xi, concepts such as *qi* and *yin* and *yang* moved to the center of their interpretations, and the *Changes* transformed from a divinatory guide to an expedient manual for regulating seasonal changes.

At this moment, Emperor Xuan and many literati around him did not see the need to rely on the Five Classics, or to closely follow the ancient kings' government. They only wanted to quickly alleviate Heaven's discontent. This attitude soon changed. In the following sections, we will see that later generations still built their arguments on Heaven's will, but instead of using the *Changes*, they adopted the whole ancient classical legacy. Their restoration of an ancient ideal, the Great Peace, was a Heaven-approved enterprise, given precedence by the ancient sage kings as recorded in the Five Classics.

Toward the Great Peace: Emperor Yuan and the Restoration of the Kingly Way

Indeed, Emperor Xuan was not interested in looking back in history or cultivating his virtues to save the empire. His successor Emperor Yuan differed. A conversation between Emperor Xuan and Emperor Yuan when the latter was Crown Prince reveals these two emperors' differences toward government:

> 嘗侍燕從容言：＂陛下持刑太深，宜用儒生。＂宣帝作色曰：＂漢家自有制度，本以霸王道雜之，奈何純任德教，用周政乎！＂⁴⁸

> Once when he was waiting upon [Emperor Xuan] at a banquet, [the Crown Prince] said, with a composed bearing, "Your Majesty is too severe in applying the laws. It would be proper to employ Ru masters [in your government]." Emperor Xuan changed color and said, "The Han dynasty has its own institutes and laws, which mix the way of the hegemons and the Kingly Way. How could I trust purely in moral instruction and use [the kind of] government [exercised by] the Zhou [dynasty]?"⁴⁹

Despite his anxiety about Heaven's will, Emperor Xuan did not think that he needed to significantly change the dynasty's political tradition in order to win over Heaven. In other words, for him, a complete restoration of the Zhou polity was not what Heaven wanted. Moral cultivation and Zhou institutions thus seemed impractical and would harm the dynasty.

However, the future Emperor Yuan had his reasons. The conflict between him and his father was more than a clash of different personalities or beliefs. It resulted from their different understandings and solutions to the same problem: the Han dynasty's reception of the heavenly mandate. What if fixing the cosmological order was not enough? What if Heaven was demanding a better society than this current mixture could provide? The new emperor had reasons to think so; as in his father's reign, in the early years of Emperor Yuan's reign, earthquakes and eclipses continued to trouble policymakers. If Emperor Xuan's policies were not enough, what else did Heaven want the new emperor to do? This question urged the literati to look deeper into history and the classics for Heaven's will. The concept of Great Peace (*taiping* 太平) thus became the center of the literati's attention.

The Great Peace as an Increasing Need for Governance

The term "Great Peace" was present since the beginning of the Han dynasty, and it indicated the peaceful state of a society.[50] One of the earliest examples is from Lu Jia's 陸賈 (ca. 240–170 BC) *New Speeches* (*Xin yu* 新語):

> 聖人因變而立功，由異而致太平，堯 、舜承蚩尤之失，而思欽明之道，君子見惡於外，則知變於內矣。[51]

> Sages establish their accomplishments by change. They transform bizarreness into the Great Peace. Yao and Shun adopted Chiyou's errors, and they thought about the way of respect and brightness. When gentlemen see the evilness outside, they then know the changes inside.

Lu Jia is describing how sages transform the currently bad government into a good one. Judging from the context, the word "bizarreness" (*yi* 異) indicates bizarre omens caused by bad governance. Sages are the ones who can fix the chaos and help the realm revert to an orderly state. Accordingly, the Great Peace indicates a state free from natural disasters and bizarre phenomena.

During Emperor Wu's time, Gongsun Hong brought up the Great Peace in the context of recruiting Academicians:

> 故教化之行也，建首善自京師始，由內及外。今陛下昭至德，開大明，配天地，本人倫，勸學修禮，崇化厲賢，以風四方，太平之原也。[52]

> Therefore, in practicing the teachings and transformation, from inside to outside, one should start with establishing the primary good in the capital and work outward. Now your majesty

illuminates the ultimate virtue, spreads the great brightness, matches Heaven and Earth, and takes human relations as essential. You advocate learning, fix the rites, promote transformation, and encourage the worthies in order to cultivate the Four Directions. This is the source of the Great Peace.

Gongsun Hong argues for a top to bottom process of cultivation. With good officials in the court, cultivation can be extended to the whole empire.

The Great Peace was also increasingly connected to the ancient sage kings. Dong Zhongshu also mentions a means of achieving the Great Peace in answering this query from Emperor Wu: "The teachings of the three kings derive from different sources, but they all have shortcomings; others say that the Way is something that lasts and does not change. Are these two sayings different?"[53] Dong Zhongshu answers: "The Greatness of the Way originated from Heaven. Heaven does not change, nor does the Way" (道之大原出於天，天不變，道亦不變). For Dong, the ancient kings' Way is in accord with each other and Heaven. However, the Han empire, as successor to the Qin, is suffering from a bad ethos, and the Kingly Way is lost. Although the Way is unchangeably one, rulers need to practice it differently based on different situations. Dong then points out that the recruitment of worthy and righteous people is the way to illuminate the Kingly Way and thus establish the Great Peace. The ideal society thus finds its precedence in the ancient Kingly Way.[54]

What, then, is the three kings' government or the Way of the Great Peace like? Dong Zhongshu elaborates:

古亦大治，上下和睦，習俗美盛，不令而行，不禁而止，吏亡姦邪，民亡盜賊，囹圄空虛，德潤草木，澤被四海，鳳皇來集，麒麟來游，以古準今，壹何不相逮之遠也！安所繆盭而陵夷若是？意者有所失於古之道與？有所詭於天之理與？試跡之古，返之於天，黨可得見乎？[55]

It was in great order in antiquity. The above and below were in harmony. The customs were beautiful and flourishing. People acted before they were commanded; they stopped before they were forbidden. There were no evil or deviant officials. There were no robbers or thieves. Prisons were empty. Virtue even reached plants. The bounties covered the Four Seas. *Fenghuang* came to assemble, and *qilin* came to travel. Using antiquity as a standard to see today, aren't they too far away from each other? How could they differ and deviate from each other like this? Maybe there is some way we failed in the Way of antiquity and there is something we departed in the principle of Heaven? If we try to follow the traces of antiquity and return to Heaven, could we see it?

There were no evil behaviors in the world of the ancients. People were in harmony and knew what was good and evil. Even plants benefited from good governance, and auspicious animals abounded. For Dong, the ideal state of a society happened in the past. It did not emphasize the pursuit of advanced technology to raise the standard of living, nor did it depend on the people's right to express different opinions about the government. In fact, in this ideal realm, people did not have different opinions at all because they are all cultivated by the ultimate Way. Dong Zhongshu points out that this is not a utopian illusion but something achievable even in the present. If this is true, then why has the Han still not achieved it? Dong Zhongshu gives his reasons: the Han empire fails to follow the ancient path and Heaven's will. Without understanding the rationale of Heaven, people will deviate from the Way; without examining the ancient kings' government, people will not have any model to follow.

None of these appeals for the Great Peace received much attention from the court before Emperor Yuan. When Wang Ji 王吉 (?–48 BC), a Grandee Remonstrant (*jian dafu* 諫大夫) during Emperor Xuan's time, proposed to reemphasize moral cultivation and the ancient sages' way in order to establish the "foundation of the Great Peace" (*taiping zhi ji* 太平之基), Emperor Xuan disapproved of this proposal for being eccentric (*yukuo* 迂闊).[56]

During Emperor Yuan's reign, the situation changed. Liu Xiang 劉向 (77–6 BC), a great erudite and a relative of the imperial family, explained to the emperor why the dynasty had to have the Great Peace.[57] In a proposal in 43 BC, he started by depicting the ideal society governed by the sage kings. He argued that since the worthies were in the court, the whole country was in a harmonious state during the rule of the ancient sage kings, namely, Huangdi 黃帝, Yao 堯, Shun 舜, Yu 禹, Tang 湯, King Wen 文王, and King Wu 武王. There were no struggles or litigation, and people showed respect and humility to each other. Liu Xiang claims that this state also affected other states and even the animal world. What is more, the harmony in the human realm influenced Heaven, and Heaven accordingly sent auspicious omens to human society.[58]

However, Liu Xiang continues, as the Zhou dynasty reached King You and Li's time, the continuum of the Golden Age was broken. Harmony was absent in the court, and the worthies were not in power. As reflected in the *Poetry*, many inauspicious omens such as solar eclipses appeared. Liu Xiang points out, according to the *Annals*, it was even more so in the period of Spring and Autumn, an era scarred by regicide.[59] Based on this observation, Liu Xiang gives a general principle of the development of history:

由此觀之，和氣致祥，乖氣致異；祥多者其國安，異眾者其國危，天地之常經，古今之通義也。[60]

Based on this, harmonious *qi* leads to auspiciousness, and deviant *qi* leads to bizarreness. The state of one who has much auspiciousness will be safe, and the state of one who has much bizarreness will be in danger. This is the regularity of Heaven and Earth, and a principle throughout history.

Like Dong Zhongshu and Gongsun Hong, Liu Xiang takes those "above," or the court, as the center responsible for the welfare of the whole state and even the entirety of human society. As with Lu Jia and Dong Zhongshu's theory, omens derive from the human realm. Liu Xiang's theory of *qi* also resembles that of Lu Jia and Dong Zhongshu, in the sense that human beings are the primary agents that affect the formation and circulation of *qi*.[61] Harmony and discord in the court could generate *qi* that leads to auspicious or inauspicious omens, respectively. What is even more crucial for a state is that the omens reveal whether it is on the road to prosperity or extinction.

Liu's idea of the Great Peace resembles Lu Jia's and Dong Zhongshu's in many ways. First, the Great Peace appears in an ordered society characterized by harmony. Hatred, dissatisfaction, and the irregular *qi* they provoke are absent. Second, this order is in accord with Heaven, as auspicious omens demonstrate. Third, starkly unlike Emperor Xuan's attitude, Liu believed that the sages of antiquity once achieved this state or could have achieved it. Therefore, emulating them is the way to achieve the Great Peace.

Liu Xiang then went further than his predecessors to point out the necessity of achieving the Great Peace. He saw deterioration over time, and at his time the Han dynasty was at the most abysmal point in history:

是以日月無光，雪霜夏隕，海水沸出，陵谷易處，列星失行，皆怨氣之所致也。夫遵衰周之軌跡，循詩人之所刺，而欲以成太平，致雅頌，猶卻行而求及前人也。初元以來六年矣，案《春秋》，六年之中，災異未有稠如今者也。夫有《春秋》之異，無孔子之救，猶不能解紛，況甚於春秋乎？[62]

Therefore, the sun and moon lacking light, snow and frost falling in summer, water boiling out of the sea, hills and abysses moving around, and the planets failing to move regularly are all caused by *qi* due to resentment. If one follows the declining path of the Zhou and adopts what is criticized by the authors of the *Book of Poetry*, but desires to achieve thereby the Great Peace and produce Elegantiae and Hymns, it is like walking backward but seeking to catch up with someone. It has been six years since the reign period of Chuyuan (48 BC). In these six years, disasters and bizarreness were more frequent than any given six years in the *Annals*. With bizarreness as described in the *Annals* but without Confucius's rescue, this crisis cannot be resolved. How about a situation that is [even] worse than in the *Annals*?

In the most recent six years (48–43 BC), the Han dynasty had received inauspicious omens more frequently than any given six years of the Spring and Autumn period, which signaled the imminent revocation of the mandate of Heaven. Yet it still practiced the opposite of any remedy, the hegemonic rule that leads to dynastic decline. Moreover, at the moment, the dynasty did not have any sage like Confucius, who could not even save the less degenerate time, the Spring and Autumn period. Liu Xiang diagnosed the Han to be in a much more critical condition than the previous generation did.

To Liu Xiang, achieving the Great Peace was not the icing on the cake but a life or death matter for the dynasty. The Han ruler would either manage to follow the path of the ancient sages or not, and in the latter case the dynasty would perish like the Qin. In a letter to Emperor Cheng 成, Liu Xiang mentions, "The heavenly mandate is broadly bestowed, and it is not bestowed on just one surname." With this rationale, he retells the story of the Han's establishment: Gaozu 高祖 thought his virtue was worse than that of the Zhou but better than the Qin. He picked Guanzhong 關中 as the capital so he could rely on the Zhou's virtue and the Qin's geographical advantage. He further points out that "the length of a dynasty takes virtue as its measure."[63] That is to say, Gaozu, as the founder of the Han dynasty, relied on both the Qin and the Zhou, a "mixture of hegemonic and kingly ways."[64] However, the longevity of a dynasty is determined by the latter, not the former. Therefore, prolonging the Han's grip on Heaven's mandate is dependent upon virtuous rule, and that, Liu Xiang points out, is exactly the responsibility of Gaozu's successors.

In Liu Xiang's narrative, the already condemned Qin dynasty became the exterminator of the Golden Age. Not only did they not govern righteously, but they even broke the continuum of the Kingly Way from the Three Dynasties, leaving the newly established Han dynasty in a difficult position.[65] Like many others, Liu Xiang believed the ancient sages' path was the Kingly Way. The evil Qin dynasty, however, destroyed all the practices of the Kingly Way so that later generations had no model to follow.[66]

Thirty years after Sui Hong's incident, Liu Xiang evoked a fin de siècle sentiment again, and thus introduced the sage kings to the core of Han policy. Before alleviating the anxiety, he intensified it: the Han dynasty was about to collapse. The ancient sage kings' government and the Great Peace became the only remedy for the troubled empire. Liu Xiang reminded his contemporaries that they should not compare the contemporary reign to reigns in the Han dynasty but to the reigns of the Golden Age, when the Great Peace prevailed and the skies proclaimed the human realm's harmony with Heaven. Adopting his predecessors' theory of omens and the Great Peace, Liu Xiang used Heaven's mandate to tie the Han dynasty and the Kingly Way together.

Liu Xiang was not alone; he belonged to a network of scholars connected by friendship and master-disciple relationships. At Emperor Yuan's court, he was recommended by Xiao Wangzhi 蕭望之 (114–47 BC), one of the emperor's former teachers. The emperor relied on them together with another former teacher of his, Zhou Kan 周堪 (?–ca. 43 BC) (see chart 4, page 41). Xiao and Zhou also received teachings from the same master, Xiahou Sheng 夏侯勝 (fl. 72–51 BC) (see chart 2). Through this chapter, we will see increasingly more people connected to their intellectual community.

Liu Xiang answered this vexing question: If Emperor Xuan's policy was not enough for Heaven, what else should one do? The Han turned to the ancient Kingly Way. Now the concern focused on where the Han dynasty could find the Kingly Way and how they could imitate it, especially when most of them believed that the Qin eliminated the practices of the Zhou government. This context eventually caused the classics to reach the heart of imperial China for the first time and triggered further intellectual innovations in understanding the classics.

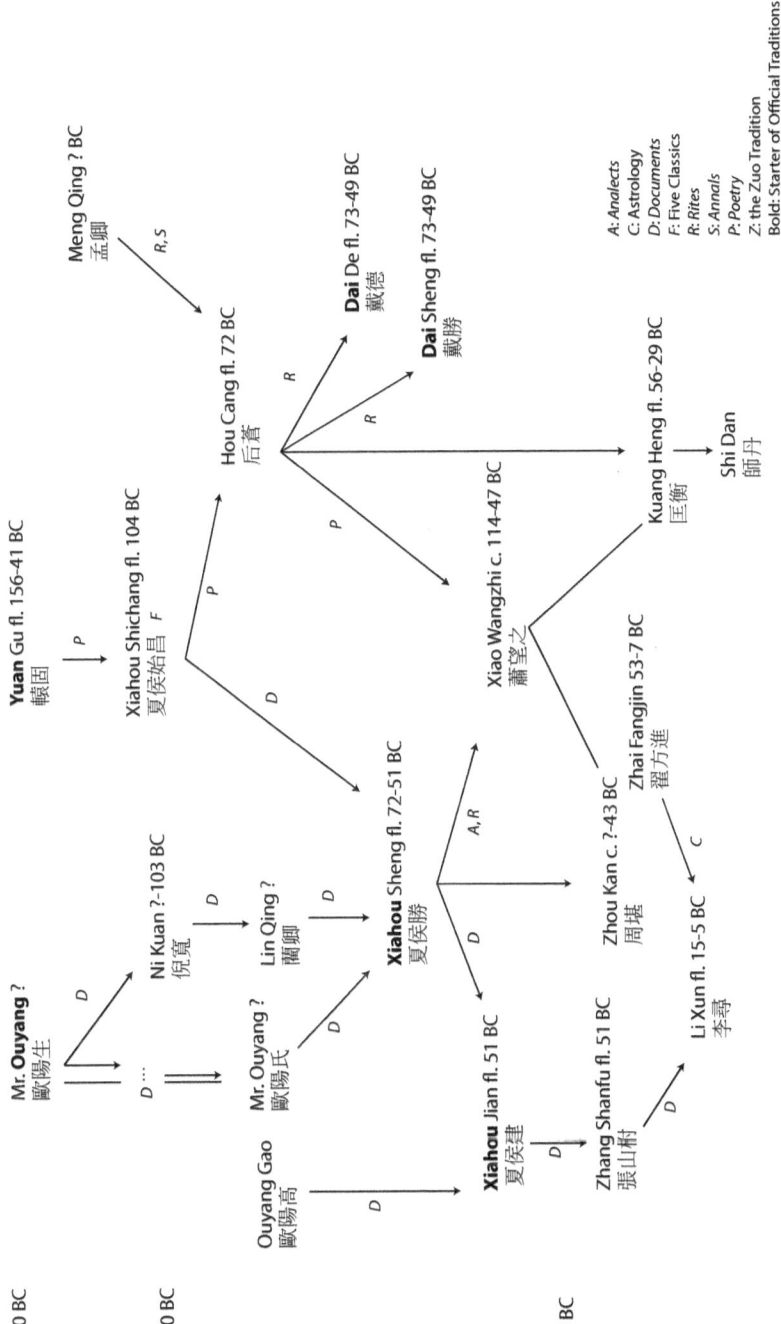

Chart 2. Hou Cang and His Disciples

The Six Classics: Complete and Fundamental

In the previous sections, we have seen that the anxiety about the heavenly mandate increased during Emperor Xuan and Emperor Yuan's times. Meanwhile, court literati, especially students of Xiahou Shichang and his affiliates (chart 2), intensified the anxiety. As the problem worsened, its solution grew more complex. An expeditious solution (such as appointing officials to regulate the cosmic order) was no longer enough. Instead, the ancient sage kings' rule became the exclusive remedy for the problem. Now it was the literati's responsibility to find the government of the sage kings. From this section on, focusing on virtually the same communities of Han scholars introduced earlier, we will see how the classics became the only window to the Golden Age and thus moved to the center of scholarly debates. The increasingly intense attention to this corpus of texts thus accelerated related innovations and brewed more dramatic actions among the literati, as we will see in the last section of this chapter.[67]

Xunzi, Lu Jia, and Hou Cang: From Humanity to Heaven

If the Kingly Way of antiquity was destroyed by the Qin, how were the people of the Han supposed to know what it was? According to Yang Xiong 揚雄 (53 BC–AD 18), an influential scholar in his time, the answer was in the sages' written words:

> 曰：聖人之言，天也。天妄乎？繼周者未欲太平也。如欲太平也，舍之而用他道，亦無由至矣。[68]
>
> I said, "The sages' words are Heaven. Is Heaven spurious? The successor of the Zhou did not desire the Great Peace. If one desires the Great Peace and he abandons the sages' words in favor of other Ways, there will be no way to achieve it."

Not all the written texts with accounts of the sage kings were of equal value; the classics were the sources most useful to literati. Of course this was not new, nor was the content of the "classics" arbitrarily decided during the Han dynasty. The *Book of Changes*, *Book of Poetry*, *Book of Documents*, *Rites*, and *Spring and Autumn Annals* had come together since the Warring States period. The earliest document in which the six texts' names are mentioned together is found in a fourth century BC text, excavated from a tomb in

Guodian 郭店, Hubei 湖北 Province, China.⁶⁹ From that time on, "the Five Classics" (or "the Six Classics" with the addition of the *Music*, putatively another text) meant this corpus of texts. They were a crucial inventory invested with much cultural capital, and not just to early Confucians. Many socio-intellectual groups, such as the Mohists, appreciated these well-known sources as well.⁷⁰ From Emperor Wu's time on, the promotion of the classics made them more important, especially politically. The Gongyang tradition of the *Annals* and the *Changes* enjoyed great privilege during Emperor Wu and Xuan's reigns, respectively.

Like other canons and scriptures, the classics were believed to include a comprehensive package of truth.⁷¹ However, by the third century BC, the literati focused on the aspects of moral cultivation in the corpus. In emphasizing learning, Xunzi remarked:

學惡乎始？惡乎終？曰：其數則始乎誦經，終乎讀禮；其義則始乎為士，終乎為聖人....《禮》之敬文也，《樂》之中和也，《詩》《書》之博也，《春秋》之微也，在天地之間者畢矣。⁷²

Where does learning start, and where does it end? I say: the regular course is to start with reciting the classics and end with reading about the *Rites*. The purpose of it is to start with becoming a gentleman and end with becoming a sage. . . . The reverence and refinement of the *Rites*, the precision and harmony of the *Music*, the breadth of the *Poetry* and the *Documents*, the subtlety of the *Annals*—with these, what exists in between Heaven and Earth is complete.

To Xunzi, the classics complete the whole process of learning, from being born and educated as a gentleman to becoming a sage. The classics are not merely one of many convenient repositories of knowledge; they contain all knowledge. Nevertheless, Xunzi does not include the *Changes* in his list, nor does he mention Heaven's will or its role in the human realm as his contemporaries do.⁷³ The learning process does not reach a climax when the student ascertains the secrets of the cosmos, but when the student approaches the "rites" as the most perfect development of morality. In Xunzi's philosophy, Heaven does show constancy like the rising of the sun or the changing of the four seasons. However, these phenomena are just part of Heaven and have no moral significance. Heaven's will is neither penetrable nor consequential for guiding the human world.⁷⁴ Therefore it is not a surprise that Xunzi excludes a text that connotes the mysterious power of Heaven.[75]

In the early part of the Western Han dynasty, Xunzi's successors, such as Lu Jia and Dong Zhongshu, began to link the classics to Heaven, but moral cultivation was still intimately associated with the classics. For Lu Jia, since the sages were capable of accord with Heaven, they could bring human society to completion.[76] After the decline of the ideal society of antiquity, the later sage Confucius established the Five Classics based on the former sages' government, which would guide people to harmonize with the heavenly pattern again.[77] Similarly, Dong Zhongshu highlighted the sages' pivotal role in following Heaven to establish the Way. The classics, especially the *Annals of Spring and Autumn*, thus provided guidance not only suitable for the heavenly order but also for human nature.[78] Although Lu Jia and Dong Zhongshu linked the classics with Heaven, moral virtues still played a core role in their understanding of the classics. Lu Jia even claimed that every passage of the corpus was filled with humanity (*ren* 仁) and righteousness (*yi* 義).[79]

In Emperor Xuan's court, Xunzi's attitude toward Heaven was no longer popular, and moral cultivation was downplayed. Instead, as we saw, the *Changes* received major attention. The anxiety about Heaven's will not only led to the promotion of the *Changes* as a way to understand Heaven's will and the cosmic order, it also affected people's readings of other classics. Hou Cang, who received teachings on the *Rites* and *Annals* from Meng Qing (chart 2),[80] revealed the cosmological order that he found in all of the Six Classics:

天地設位，懸日月，布星辰，分陰陽，定四時，列五行，以視聖人，名之曰道。聖人見道，然後知王治之象，故畫州土，建君臣，立律曆，陳成敗，以視賢者，名之曰經。賢者見經，然後知人道之務，則《詩》、《書》、《易》、《春秋》、《禮》、《樂》是也。《易》有陰陽，《詩》有五際，《春秋》有災異，皆列終始，推得失，考天心，以言王道之安危。[81]

Heaven and Earth set up positions. They hung the sun and moon [in the sky], distributed the stars and planets, divided *yin* and *yang*, determined the four seasons, and arranged the Five Phases. They (Heaven and Earth) revealed [all of] this to the sages, calling it the Way. When sages saw the Way, they understood the pattern of Kingly rule. Therefore, they divided up territories, established lords and subjects, set up astronomy and mathematical harmonics, and explicated [what leads to] success and failure. They (the sages) revealed [all of] this to the worthies, calling it the classics. When the worthies saw the classics, they knew the essentials of the human way, which are the *Poetry*, the *Documents*, the *Changes*, the *Annals*, the *Rites*, and the *Music*. The *Changes* includes *yin* and *yang*, the *Poetry* includes the Five Contacts, and the *Annals* includes omens. They set them out from beginning to end. They calculated gain and loss and examined the mind of Heaven in order to discuss the uncertainty of the Kingly Way.

Based on the natural order of Heaven and Earth, the sages designed the classics, which contain the patterns of kingly rule. The worthies learned what is important for the human realm from the Six Classics. The sages and worthies used the Six Classics to make connections from the realm of Heaven to the realm of humans.

Unlike that of Xunzi or Lu Jia, the core of Hou Cang's idea is in line with Wei Xiang: the cosmic order. He draws from three theories to indicate the function of the Six Classics, namely, the theory of *yin* and *yang*, the Five Contacts, and portents. The first one refers to trigram-*qi* correlation that was mentioned by Wei Xiang and other experts of the *Changes*. The Five Contacts is a theory not found anywhere in the plain text of the *Poetry*. Rather, it is a Han dynasty scholar's use of five particular poems, in conjunction with five of the Earthly Branches, to describe the timely changes of *yin* and *yang*.[82] And the portents refer to omens in the *Annals* as the will of Heaven, as we saw in Liu Xiang's speech. What is distinctive about Hou Cang's amalgamated theory is the absence of humanity or righteousness, which are central to Lu Jia's understanding of how to achieve the Great Peace.

Hou Cang points out that people need the classics to examine the cosmic order and thus understand the heart of Heaven before they can talk about the welfare of the Kingly Way, not to mention the Great Peace. Theories of moral cultivation were of little use in understanding Heaven, despite originating with Xunzi, who argued that people need to bring what Heaven gives them to perfection instead of wasting time on understanding Heaven,[83] or from Lu Jia, who argued that people need to cultivate morality, otherwise chaos prevails and the natural world becomes irregular.[84] For Hou Cang, penetrating Heaven's will is neither impossible nor useless. On the contrary, that is exactly what the classics can contribute to the Kingly

Way. By mastering the cosmological order, one can deal with the irregularity of nature and understand Heaven's will directly.

Like the group of masters of the *Changes* in Emperor Xuan's court, Hou Cang was not alone. He was a student of Xiahou Shichang 夏侯始昌 (fl. 104 BC), who received the Qi tradition of the *Book of Poetry* from Yuan Gu 轅固 (fl. 156–141 BC).[85] During Emperor Xuan's time, this intellectual group was already an important one (chart 2). Hou Cang, his aforementioned classmate Xiahou Sheng, and his disciple Xiao Wangzhi all took crucial official positions in the court. Xiao served as the Grand Tutor of the Heir Apparent (*taizi taifu* 太子太傅) until the heir apparent became the new emperor, Emperor Yuan.[86]

The Classics as All-Encompassing

During Emperor Yuan's time, Hou Cang's community carried on the search for the Kingly Way in order to harmonize Heaven and consolidate Han rule. But his intellectual successors were faced with a more intensified anxiety about Heaven, and a cosmological cure was not enough. Now they asked more from the classics. While sharing Hou's emphasis on the Six Classics, they envisioned the classics as more all-encompassing than Hou did. Many also brought human virtue back to bear on the interpretation of the classics.

Many of them believed that the Great Peace required more than cosmological regularity. For example, Hou Cang's student, Kuang Heng 匡衡 (fl. 56–29 BC), an official the new emperor had favored ever since he was heir apparent, asked for moral guidance:

> 陛下躬聖德，開太平之路，閔愚吏民觸法抵禁，比年大赦，使百姓得改行自新，天下幸甚。臣竊見大赦之後，姦邪不為衰止，今日大赦，明日犯法，相隨入獄，此殆導之未得其務也。[87]

> Your majesty practices sagely virtue and opens the road to the Great Peace. You sympathize with fool officials and commoners who break the law and violate the prohibitions. You issued amnesties year after year to make the populace able to correct their behavior and improve themselves. All-under-Heaven are so lucky. [However,] I have seen that after amnesties, the evil and deviant do not let up or stop. They receive an amnesty today, and

they break the law tomorrow. Following each other, they go back to jail. This is probably because they are not guided properly.

Kuang Heng appreciates the effort Emperor Yuan took to pursue the Great Peace. However, he thinks that the emperor has not gone far enough: amnesties and legal practices still bear too close a resemblance to Emperor Xuan's practices. He believes that the answer to good government lies in rites and virtue in the court.[88] Harsh punishments and strict laws will fail to change people's behavior because they do not work in accord with people's heavenly nature. In other words, for Kuang Heng, rites are a good way to eliminate bad behaviors because they work in harmony with people's nature.

On another occasion, Kuang expounds on his understanding of the importance of the classics to this project:

臣聞六經者，聖人所以統天地之心，著善惡之歸，明吉凶之分，通人道之正，使不悖於其本性者也。故審六藝之指，則人天之理可得而和，草木昆蟲可得而育，此永久不易之道也。[89]

I have heard that the Six Classics are that which the sages used to organize the heart of Heaven and Earth, to highlight the source of goodness and badness, to illuminate the division between auspiciousness and inauspiciousness, to comprehend the rectification of the human way, and to make people not disobey their nature. Therefore, if one has examined the main points of the Six Arts [the Six Classics], the principles of Heaven and of humans can be known and harmonized, and plants and animals can be nourished. This is the everlasting and unchangeable Way.

Kuang's viewpoint reincorporates an element of human agency into the views of his teacher, which emphasized that the Six Classics contain the cosmological order that the human realm needs to follow. On this occasion, echoing his previous speech to Emperor Yuan, Kuang contends that the model of rule that is found in the classics does not just accord with Heaven's will but also with human nature. Like Hou, Kuang insists that the ultimate truth of the Way can only be found in the Six Classics as a whole. He argues that although it is allotted by Heaven, human nature is unique. Accordingly, human society needs to be organized according to its own characteristics. Thus, in the previous passage the Six Classics are the ultimate guideline for the governance of the human realm in accordance with Heaven *and* human nature.

Indeed, from the time of Emperor Yuan on, scholars often understood the Five Classics as an integrated group of texts that encompassed the truth of the world. As Yang Xiong delicately put it:

天地之為萬物郭，五經之為眾說郭。[90]

Just as Heaven and Earth are the outer wall of the myriad things,
the Five Classics are the outer wall of the various sayings.

Just as nothing could be outside of Heaven and Earth, the Five Classics contain everything that can be found in other books. He does not negate the usefulness of others' sayings and works[91] but rather states that other works are not as comprehensive as the Five Classics. Moreover, for Yang, the Five Classics define the limits of all knowledge.[92] He writes succinctly:

舍五經而濟乎道者，末矣。[93]

It is the worst to traverse the Way but abandon the Five Classics.

He implies that although some works expediently illuminate the Way, such as *Dao de jing* 道德經,[94] the Five Classics are the most proper path to approaching the Way. While scholars like Hou Cang highlighted the classics as the essential road to the Kingly Way, Yang also excluded the other roads to it.

For people like Kuang Heng or Yang Xiong, one could no longer engage in one classic and ignore the rest as too long, less relevant, or repetitive. In the "Seven Summaries," composed by Liu Xiang and completed by his son Liu Xin,[95] the classics are not only all-encompassing like Yang Xiong mentioned; they are also internally complementary to each other. They explain how the classics are related to each other, and to human virtue:

六藝之文：《樂》以和神，仁之表也；《詩》以正言，義之用也；《禮》以明體，明者著見，故無訓也；《書》以廣聽，知之術也；《春秋》以斷事，信之符也。五者，蓋五常之道，相須而備，而《易》為之原。故曰"《易》不可見，則乾坤或幾乎息矣"，言與天地為終始也。至於五學，世有變改，猶五行之更用事焉。[96]

The writing of the Six Arts: With the *Music* the divine is harmonized, which is the appearance of humanity. [With] the *Book of*

Poetry speech is rectified, which is the application of righteousness. [With] the *Rites* deportment is illuminated. What is clear is obvious, so there is no explication on the *Rites*. [With] the *Book of Documents* one's hearing is broadened, which is the approach to intelligence. [With] the *Annals of Spring and Autumn* affairs are judged, which is the tally of trustworthiness. These five things are the way of the Five Constancies. They need each other to be complete, and the *Changes* is their source. Therefore it is said, "If the [meaning of] the *Changes* cannot be seen, then Qian and Kun probably would nearly be extinguished." This means that the *Changes* begins and ends in accord with Heaven and Earth. For the other five [kinds of] learning, the world changes as though each of the five phases is in charge, one after another.

For Liu Xiang, the Five Constancies (*wu chang* 五常) are virtues based on human nature and emotion.⁹⁷ Thus each of the five classics corresponds to them as a moral guideline that people need to follow. The passage does not take the cosmological order as a universal rule and apply it indiscriminately to the human realm. Instead, like Kuang Heng's theory, it considers the human realm to be somewhat autonomous, for human beings have a unique nature and distinctive characteristics.

In Kuang's understanding of the Six Classics, we have already seen this model of Heaven and the human realm: ancient sages passed down the classics not only in accord with Heaven but also human nature. The "Seven Summaries" elaborates on Kuang's ideas by assigning specific virtues to specific classics. It also singles out the *Changes* as the text that reflects Heaven and Earth's processes, an understanding of the *Changes* shared by many scholars in Emperor Xuan's time.⁹⁸ Without the *Changes*, people could not grasp the heavenly order; without the other five classics, people would lose the guidelines for the human realm. In different eras, different virtues of the Five Constancies are required; thus, each classic becomes more necessary than the others at a certain moment. Just like each of the Five Phases are necessary to form a complete cycle, the classics are each indispensable.⁹⁹ From virtues to cosmos, from human nature to the mandate of Heaven, scholars of the late first century BC unpacked competing understandings of the classics while forming a common ground: the classics were an indispensable unit for the revival of the Kingly Way.

If the classics were perfect and comprehensive, how was the Han still in a predicament? "Seven Summaries" ("Qi lüe" 七略) argued that they had been in jeopardy. According to them, the classics barely survived the Qin's outrage, and the surviving commentarial traditions of the classics had already deviated from their true meanings. Furthermore, Han scholars missed the big picture and had begun to focus on trivial issues of the classics. They could no longer master all of the classics but could barely hold on to one of the classics during their lifetime. Even worse, they dismissed anything outside their own narrow scope.[100] Similar to Hou and Kuang, the two authors were worried that people failed to appreciate the teaching in the Six Classics.[101] They were further concerned with the situation that scholars at that time were taking even less care to preserve the original classics.

From Emperor Yuan's time onward, when most scholars accepted the all-encompassing nature of the classics, the center of the debate shifted to textual preservation. Although few denied that the original classics recorded the Kingly Way as well as the means of realizing the Great Peace, many of them started to ask another question: Did they possess the original classics? There was yet a more challenging question: If they did not, what should they do?

This seemingly trivial issue set off one of the most heated and lasting debates in Chinese intellectual history, sometimes referred to as the "new script and old script controversy" (*jin gu wen zhi zheng* 今古文之爭).[102] In the last years of the Western Han, this debate incited dramatic clashes between scholars, and people died for their beliefs. In the rest of this chapter, we will see how the controversy was much greater than the different scripts of the classics, and how even retrospectively heterodox views could sprout from this controversy.

Restoring the Original Six Classics or Getting Rid of Them: Two Paths of Innovation

In the last years of the Western Han, literati had come to agree upon three assumptions: (1) the Han were about to lose the heavenly mandate, (2) the Great Peace could secure the heavenly mandate and save the dynasty, and (3) the original classics recorded the Kingly Way, which could lead to the Great Peace. The textual foundation of the classics thus became more than a philological question and crucial to reconstruct the Kingly Way. Following this trend, scholars started to ask how to reconstruct the Kingly Way based on the classics, and the validity of the classics in general. Among them, two scholars, Liu Xin and Li Xun 李尋, propagated two methods of intellectual innovation that had great influence on later generations. Both ideas received great attention, or more precisely, hostility from their contemporaries. Liu Xin favored methods of synthesis, which he applied to the classics. Li Xun, on the other hand, moved away from dependence on the classics and focused on understanding Heaven and the Great Peace through other, more direct means. As we will see from the rest of the book, their visions had long trajectories in the intellectual world of the first two centuries AD.

The Last Years of the Western Han Dynasty as Reflected in the Well-Field System

Step by step, the literati during the Western Han dynasty proceeded to restore the Kingly Way by developing particular policies that sought to bring the Great Peace to life. This movement culminated in the installation of the Well-Field (*jing tian* 井田) system, putatively an agricultural system of the Zhou dynasty, promoted most eagerly by Wang Mang 王莽 (45 BC–AD 23). He describes it as follows:

> 古者，設廬井八家，一夫一婦田百畝，什一而稅，則國給民富而頌聲作。此唐虞之道，三代所遵行也。[103]

> When the ancients established the cottages of eight families on the Well-Field system and one husband and one wife had a hundred *mu* of cultivated land and paid one-tenth in taxes, then the state had enough and the common people were affluent and composed songs of praise. The foregoing was the way of Tang [Yao] and of Yu [Shun], and that which the three dynasties practiced obediently.[104]

Shi Dan 師丹 (?–AD 3), a disciple of Kuang Heng, believed the Well-Field system to be the key way to achieve a peaceful state of society: "No ancient sage kings failed to set up the Well-Field System. Only then can the government reach the Peace."[105] This system followed the legendary model depicted in *Mencius* and the Guliang tradition of the *Annals*. The Well-Field system was a form of agricultural distribution, in which a given amount of land (usually 900 *mu* 畝 ≈ 42.885 acres) was divided into nine pieces resembling the shape of the Chinese character 井 *jing* (well). Eight units of peasants worked on the eight outer sections, or the Private Fields (*si tian* 私田). Meanwhile, they collaboratively cultivated the central piece, the Public Field (*gong tian* 公田), and handed in its harvest.[106]

The agricultural-economic situation of the late Western Han dynasty resulted in an appeal to this system, which at the time only survived in texts. Throughout the first half of the Han dynasty, an increase of population and immigration led to high population densities in certain areas such as the capital, Chang'an 長安. This in turn increased the price of the land in those areas, and the land became a good investment for dominant families. Peasants thus lost their land to these wealthy purchasers. If the peasants still wanted to continue their life on the same land, they had to submit to the dominance of those families and accept higher taxes. In the eyes of Wang Mang and many other literati, this situation greatly harmed the populace.[107]

Wang's policy reflected many scholars' assumption of the time: if the Han could practice the government of the Golden Age, it would permanently solve the social problems the empire was facing. Wang believed that there used to be a prosperous society based on the Well-Field system in the Three Dynasties, but it was ruined by the Qin dynasty. Could the Han ever revive the ruined practices of the ancient sage kings based on the classics? Liu Xin and Li Xun were prepared to answer this question in their respective ways.

Liu Xin's Approach to the Original Classics

During the reign of Emperor Ai (27–1 BC), Wang Mang started gaining power in the court based on his erudition in the classics, prudence, and, most often mentioned by historians, nepotism.[108] His favorite scholar, Liu Xin, led the project of editing texts in the imperial library. He proposed the installation of new Academician positions for the versions of the classics and the commentarial traditions that were not transmitted by Han classicists, namely, the Zuo tradition of the *Annals*, the Mao tradition of the *Poetry*, the excluded *Rites*, and the chapters of the *Documents* in scripts that were no longer commonly used at that time.[109] However, at that time the thirty standing Academicians and their supervisor, the Grand Minister of Ceremonies, showed very little interest in his proposal. Convinced that his proposal did not add unnecessary elements to the corpus but instead provided indispensable missing pieces to a dangerously incomplete package, Liu criticized them in an open letter:[110]

> 昔唐虞既衰，而三代迭興，聖帝明王，累起相襲，其道甚著。周室既微而禮樂不正，道之難全也如此。是故孔子憂道之不行，歷國應聘。自衛反魯，然後樂正，雅頌乃得其所；修《易》，序《書》，制作《春秋》，以紀帝王之道。及夫子沒而微言絕，七十子終而大義乖。重遭戰國，棄籩豆之

禮，理軍旅之陳，孔氏之道抑，而孫吳之術興。陵夷至于暴秦，燔經書，殺儒士，設挾書之法，行是古之罪，道術由是遂滅。[111]

Previously, after Tang [Yao] and Yu [Shun] declined, the three dynasties succeeded each other. Following each other, sage emperors and bright kings arose. Their Way was illuminating. When the Zhou house became weak, the rites and music were not rectified anymore. Preserving the Way was just as hard as this. Therefore, Confucius was worried that the Way would not be practiced, so he travelled around the states to take positions. After he came back from state of Wei to that of Lu, the music was rectified; Elegantiae and Hymns were put in the right place. He edited the *Changes*, arranged the *Documents*, and wrote the *Annals* to record the way of emperors and kings. After the master died, the subtle words became extinct. After the seventy masters [who were Confucius's disciples] passed away, the general meaning became deviant. Furthermore, the Warring States period came. The rites involving Bian and Dou dining vessels were abandoned, and the organization of troops was studied. The way of Confucius was suppressed, and the methods of Wu Qi and Sunzi became popular. The decline extended to the time of Qin. They burned the classics, killed the Ru, set up bans on private ownership of books, and practiced the persecution of [those who] praised antiquity. The method of the Way was thus destroyed then.

Liu first sets the stage, where the Kingly Way has been in jeopardy throughout history. Confucius once saved it by editing texts from antiquity and composing the *Annals*, but after his death, the transmission of those texts was tenuous, and the Kingly Way was again in jeopardy.

After introducing the crisis of the Kingly Way, Liu brings the Han dynasty to the spotlight:

漢興，去聖帝明王遐遠，仲尼之道又絕，法度無所因襲. . . . 至孝武皇帝，然後鄒、魯、梁、趙頗有《詩》、《禮》、《春秋》先師，皆起於建元之間。[112]

When the Han arose, it was already distant from the sage emperors and bright kings. The way of Confucius was also extinct. There were no principles to follow. . . . When it came to Emperor Wu's time, there were many masters of the *Poetry*, *Rites*, and *Annals* from the areas of Zou, Lu, Liang, and Zhao. They all arose around the time of Jianyuan (140–135 BC).

For Liu, the Han faced two difficulties: the distance from the sage kings and the isolation from Confucius's teachings. The former problem could only be solved by going back in time, so people could only count on solving the latter one. However, Qin destroyed the remnants of Confucius's teachings—thus the second problem posed the same difficulty as the first: Han had no model to follow. Liu did allude to a spark of light that might illuminate the gloomy reality: more and more classic texts and commentarial traditions gradually appeared.

However, the restoration of the Kingly Way still had long way to go:

當此之時，一人不能獨盡其經，或為雅，或為頌，相合而成。《泰誓》後得，博士集而讀之。. . . 時漢興已七八十年，離於全經，固已遠矣。[113]

At that time, an individual could not go over all the classics alone. Some of them did the Elegantia section of the *Poetry*, some of them did the Song section of it. They combined them together. "Tai shi" was obtained later, and the Academicians got together to read it. . . . At that time, it had already been seventy to eighty years since the Han had arisen. However, the Han was far away from [having] the complete classics.

In the previous section, Liu wrote that "it is difficult to preserve the complete Dao" (*Dao zhi nan quan* 道之難全). Here again, he mentions that the Han is far away from obtaining the "complete classics" (*quan jing* 全經). He depicts two crises of the Kingly Way through history. Confucius fixed the first one, and since then the Kingly Way has been preserved in textual form. The Han dynasty faces a second crisis, the loss of the texts that record the Kingly Way. To Liu, the completeness of the classics is crucial, for the Kingly Way can only be restored by a correct understanding of those classics.

Fortunately, texts excavated or hidden in the imperial library shed light on the reconstruction of the classics:

及魯恭王壞孔子宅，欲以為宮，而得古文於壞壁之中，逸《禮》有三十九，《書》十六篇。. . . 及《春秋》左氏丘明所修，皆古文舊書，多者二十餘通,藏於祕府,伏而未發。孝成皇帝閔學殘文缺,稍離其真。乃陳發祕臧,校理舊文,得此三事,以考學官所傳,經或脫簡,傳或間編。[114]

When King Gong of Lu demolished Confucius's house to make a palace, people found old texts in the broken wall. There were thirty-nine chapters that were not in the received *Rites*, and sixteen chapters from the *Documents*. . . . As for [the Zuo tradition of] the *Annals*, it was written by Zuo Qiuming. They were all old texts and ancient writings. There were more than twenty copies of it stored in private places. They were hidden without being publicized. Emperor Cheng lamented the incompleteness of learning and the departure of a text even slightly from its original form. He thus opened the stored collection. While editing the old texts, he obtained these three corpora of texts in order to collate what the Academicians had transmitted. Some strips of the classics were missing, and some commentaries were misarranged.

According to Liu, there are texts about three classics: chapters of the *Documents*, of the *Rites*, and the Zuo tradition of the *Annals*. The former two are excavated texts, and the latter is a received but neglected text. For him, they are very valuable sources with which to reconstruct the original Five Classics.

However, getting back to the conservative Academicians and their indifference, Liu Xin complains that even though they possessed these invaluable documents, contemporary classicists showed little interest in using them:

往者綴學之士不思廢絕之闕,苟因陋就寡,分文析字,煩言碎辭,學者罷老且不能究其一藝。信口說而背傳記,是末師而非往古。. . . 以《尚書》為備,謂《左氏》為不傳《春秋》,豈不哀哉![115]

Previous students have not thought about the abandoned and extinct missing parts. They have followed what is shallow and adopted what is scanty. They break down characters and make long-winded speeches and trivial sayings. The students even as they become old, could not even plumb the depths of a single Art [classic]. They believe in oral explanations but turn away written records. They consider the devolved [current] masters right but the past wrong. . . . They think that the [received] *Documents* is complete, and the Zuo tradition does not transmit the *Annals*. What a pity!

His criticism reflects two major concerns discussed earlier: (1) the completeness of the Six Classics and (2) the breakup of transmission lines. On the one hand, in scrutinizing trivial issues in the classics, classicists no longer try to master the whole package of the classics, so they fail to comprehensively grasp the Kingly Way. On the other hand, they prejudicially stick to transmission lines from after Confucius's time, which were already ruined by the Qin dynasty. For Liu these transmission lines are just the dregs of that superior and complete stock.

When it comes to specific classics, Liu Xin expresses the same concerns. He believes that the received *Documents* is not complete. He also brings up the *Annals*: his dissatisfaction does not lie with the content of the text per se, but with its commentarial tradition. He argues that Zuo Qiuming 左丘明, the author of the Zuo tradition, knew Confucius personally. Therefore, his tradition gives a much better interpretation than existing traditions.[116]

Facing the question "Did we possess the original classics?," Liu and his colleague Academicians gave different answers. He would answer no to the question, and his frustration in the open letter came from the assumption that the received versions were incomplete, which would not bring back the Great Peace. In contrast, his colleagues would say yes, because they did not share the assumption. And they had good reasons; for them, their transmission lines were protected by generations of scholars, many of whom could be traced back to Confucius's disciples. Why would they trust some unprovenanced texts without any authoritative transmission processes, especially in an age when texts were handwritten and passed down from person to person? No trustworthy people involved means no guarantee of quality and authenticity.

Liu challenged his colleagues in a fundamental way. He cast serious doubts on established transmission lines as the only source of the original classics. He argued that oral transmission deteriorates over time, and knowledge sometimes is better preserved in written texts, which might remain intact from deterioration. This view suggests a potential alternative to developing scholarship via oral transmission: people could actually read texts without a teacher's oral guidance. In the first century BC, when most of the scholars did not have the luxury of Liu Xin's access to a large number of texts in the imperial library, it was novel and dangerous to read a text without its teacher. But Liu Xin's view belonged to the future, when the circulation of texts was more common in the second century AD, as we will see in the last two chapters.

Ahead of many of his contemporaries, the incompletion of the corpus deeply troubled Liu Xin. Unlike them, he embraced as many materials as he could to complete the puzzle, no matter if they were omitted pieces of the ancient classics or contemporary works that were simply helpful to understand them. For example, in a letter to Yang Xiong, Liu asked for his *Regional Speech* (*Fang Yan* 方言), because its philological studies might be helpful to edit the classics.[117] Anything that could serve this aim would be of interest to Liu. Together with the goal of completing the classics, his inclusiveness was the precursor to literati's interest in philology and broad learning in the first two centuries AD. And ironically, it was precisely the pursuit of broad learning that eventually eclipsed classicism.

As heatedly debated, Liu did not deviate from his colleagues too far; he believed that they still had hope to obtain the original classics. For him, the breakup of the Kingly Way did interrupt the transmission of the classics, but it did not irreversibly damage the corpus. Therefore, they did not need to throw out the received classics but find missing pieces *in addition* to them. The choice of previously neglected texts, and the consequent proposition of corresponding Academician positions, served only two purposes: to complete the original classics and thereby bring back the Great Peace. But what if the classics were not the only source for the Great Peace?

An Abortive Path: Li Xun's Departure from the Classics

Until now, our focus has been on a generation of scholars who remained convinced that the classics held the key to good government. Although Liu Xin and his erudite colleagues had a hostile disagreement, they all insisted on using the classics to understand the Kingly Way. In contrast, Li Xun departed from the classics in promoting Xia Heliang's 夏賀良 group and the *Scripture of the Great Peace* (*Taiping jing* 太平經).

This is not to say that Li ignored his contemporaries' concerns. On the contrary, he maximally engaged in the two crucial foci of his time: Heaven's will and the destiny of the empire. To him, Heaven manifested its intentions in a univocal and anthropomorphic way:

《書》云："天聰明。"蓋言紫宮極樞，通位帝紀。太微四門，廣開大道。五經六緯，尊術顯士。翼張舒布，燭臨四海。少微處士，為比為輔。故次帝廷，女宮在後。聖人承天，賢賢易色，取法於此。[118]

The *Documents* says: "Heaven is keen in hearing and seeing." Perhaps it refers to the purple palace, the pole star, and its pivot, which connect to the emperor. Taiwei has four doors, opening to broad roads. The five warp planets and six weft stars respect the methods and promote gentlemen. Yi and Zhang open up, and they vigilantly approach the four seas. Assisting Taiwei, Shaowei takes care of gentlemen. The imperial court is accordingly arranged, and the palace harem is at the back. Sages adopt from Heaven. They value the worthies and decried beauty.[119] They take it [Heaven] as standard.

Li translates his specialized astrological knowledge into the Han bureaucratic system to make his point. In his description of the arrangements of stars in the sky, Heaven has an imperial palace (the purple palace) in the middle, a main office (Taiwei) and its assistant bureau (Shaowei) in front of the palace, and the celestial lodges Yi and Zhang reaching out even further forward.

Quoting from the *Documents*, Li emphasizes that Heaven is keen not because it has more ears and eyes than normal human beings. Many phrases such as "open up" and "broad roads" suggest openness to advice and talented people. Like a worldly ruler, Heaven's acuity depends on its willingness to listen to suggestions. Previously, we saw scholars discussing the observation of seasonal changes and natural movements so that human beings could adjust their activities accordingly. Li believes that Heaven's message is even more relevant to human beings. He does not just figuratively compare the human order to that of Heaven: he reminds his readers that the organization of Heaven is what sages imitated when they structured human society. This structure is so accessible and intelligible that it is right there when we gaze into the sky.

With his expertise in astrology, Li Xun took advantage of the Han emperors' anxiety over Heaven's mandate. While Emperor Ai was sick, Li Xun introduced Xia Heliang and others to the palace. In meeting with the emperor, they argued that the Han were losing the mandate of Heaven, an argument that we have seen repeated from Sui Hong to Liu Xiang. The emperor's sickness, natural disasters, and childlessness were warnings from Heaven. In order to regain the mandate, the emperor needed to change his title and reign name. Convinced by this proposal, in 5 BC, Emperor Ai changed his reign name from Jianping 建平 (Establishing Peace) to Taichu Yuan Jiang 太初元將 (The Great Beginning When Grandness Is in Charge).[120] He also changed his title to Chen Sheng Liu Taiping Huangdi 陳聖劉太平皇帝, or "The Great Peace Emperor Who Presents the Sagely Liu." The emperor's title shared the element "Great Peace" with the *Scripture of the Great Peace* (*Taiping jing* 太平經), the title of a text circulated among Li Xun and Xia Heliang's group.[121] By joining the surge of the Great Peace,

Li's proposals and the emperor's acceptance of them fit aptly to the political culture after 48 BC.

However, their group paid a price for their innovative approach to achieving the Great Peace: they were accused of deviating from the classics. Liu Xin did not approve the *Scripture of the Great Peace* because it did not agree with the Five Classics. Later on when Emperor Ai lost faith in Li Xun's group, he dismissed them, using similar reasons: "their proposal violated what is proper in the classics and deviated from the sagely design." As a result, Xia Heliang was executed, and Li Xun was exiled to Dunhuang 敦煌. In Emperor Ai's accusation, they were both depicted as "heterodox" (*zuo dao* 左道), who tried to sabotage the bureaucracy and overthrow the Han empire.[122]

Was Li Xun really "heterodox" as Emperor Ai accused? The answer is both yes and no. Li did not disparage the classics. However, his primary concern was more on Heaven and its will than on the classics. When Li was still an assistant of Zhai Fangjin 翟方進 (53–7 BC), he suggested that the Han court needed to recruit "gentlemen of Heaven," or *tian shi* 天士. After Emperor Ai's switch of reign name, his group of "gentlemen of Heaven" accused their opponents of "not knowing the mandate of Heaven." At that time, he also promoted the *Scripture of the Great Peace* as a revealed text from Heaven.[123] Using this text, Li's group opened the door to the idea that people could understand Heaven and achieve the Great Peace without the sages and their classics. For many others and especially Liu Xin, the Kingly Way was in the classics alone, and only by mastering them could one achieve the Kingly Way and the Great Peace. Liu Xin and his fellow classicists debated on how to approach to the classics, but they both believed that the classics contained the Kingly Way, and that the Way was, in fact, accessible.

In contrast, Li Xun argued that since Heaven was the source of human society, the classics, and its mandate, one could achieve the Kingly Way by turning directly to Heaven. His argument was seemingly against Liu Xin's, but they paradoxically followed the same line of logic. For Liu, the way to achieve the Great Peace lay in the texts of classics that remained outside the transmission lines.[124] Li took this direction one step further and pointed out that the way to achieve the Great Peace lay in texts outside the classics. Nevertheless, the deductions of the two arguments went opposite ways. Liu sought to include various classical texts in order to restore the original corpus; Li turned to the heavenly revealed text that overrode the classical corpus and transmission lines altogether.

Indeed, Li Xun's radical idea was deeply rooted in the world of classicism. His group and the classicists even employed a similar narrative structure in describing their transmission traditions. Both of them believed Heaven was the ultimate agent. In both theories, there was a middle agent to take messages from Heaven to the human realm, and the messages were also similarly preserved in written form (as the classics). Even the agents—the perfected men, or *zhenren* 真人, for Li Xun's group, and the sages of antiquity for classicists—were related.[125] In *Zhuangzi* 莊子, the term "perfected men" indicates people who grasp the Way and thus free themselves from physical attachments and hazards.[126] In line with *Zhuangzi*'s focus on self-preservation, the *Inner Canon of the Yellow Emperor* (*Huangdi neijing* 黃帝內經) ranks the perfected men above sages, because the perfected men liberate themselves from the burdens of the world and are in accordance with Heaven and Earth.[127] But "perfected men" and "sages" are not invariably different; the *Master Huainan* (*Huainanzi* 淮南子) often uses these two terms interchangeably.[128]

Li and his group developed this similar narrative to trump the classics. When they explained the appearance the *Scripture of the Great Peace*, they created a heavenly transmission: the perfected man Chijingzi 赤精子 (Master Red Essence), who is of the same origin, but better than the sages, brings a heavenly message to the world. In their description, the heavenly emperor sends the perfected man down to teach Li Xun and others.[129] Li referred to Heaven not as "Heaven," but as the "heavenly emperor." Heaven was not remote or abstract but personified and vigilant. For most literati of the time, sages never heard instructions directly from Heaven but learned them from observing heavenly phenomena. In contrast, Li's group claimed that Heaven transmitted the messages directly to the perfected man. They thus placed themselves in a relation closer to Heaven than the classicists. In their narrative, the *Scripture of the Great Peace* gained an advantage over the classics since its contents were more timely, direct, and relevant teachings from Heaven.

Liu Xiang, Liu Xin, and Li Xun's Careers

Beneath the hostility and radical disagreement, Li Xun, Liu Xin, and Liu Xiang shared common communities and similar career paths. Intellectual communities are not isolated units; they are open to contacts between individuals and the exchange of ideas. We can, for example, see many contacts between the *Changes* group and the Qi *Poetry* group represented by Hou

Cang and his disciples. Meng Xi's father, Meng Qing, let his son learn the *Changes*, and he passed down his own teaching of the *Rites* and *Annals* to Hou Cang. Hou's student Xiao Wangzhi appreciated Shi Chou's student Zhang Yu's 張禹 (?–AD 5) scholarship on the *Changes* and the *Analects*, and he recommended him to the court.[130] Contact and exchange are also essential for the dominance of an individual. An individual with more opportunities to gain access to contemporary conversations and resources is also more likely to gain power in his community. In order to convince others that his ideas are correct and important, the individual must use this advantage to respond to the concerns of the dominant figures in the group. Liu Xiang, Liu Xin, and Li Xun's career paths followed this pattern.

Liu Xiang, for example, always rode the tide of intellectual fashions. When Emperor Xuan was interested in spirits and immortals, Liu Xiang presented the *Secret Writing of the Garden of the Great Treasure in the Pillow* (*Zhen zhong hongbao yuan mishu* 枕中鴻寶苑秘書), a text about spirits and ghosts that originally belonged to Liu An 劉安 (179–122 BC), King of Huainan 淮南. Originally trained in the *Changes*,[131] Liu Xiang also became a student of the Guliang tradition of the *Annals* as part of a state-sponsored project.[132] Later on, when the debates between followers of the Gongyang and Guliang traditions were held in the imperial palace, Liu Xiang and his Guliang colleagues outperformed the Gongyang advocates. He not only formed a political alliance with Xiao Wangzhi and Xiahou Sheng's student Zhou Kan (see chart 4), but in the early years of the reign of Emperor Yuan, he also wrote a work called *Discussions of the Tradition of the Five Phases in the "Great Plan"* ("*Hong fan*" *wuxing zhuan lun* 洪範五行傳論), an elaboration of *Tradition of the Five Phases in the "Great Plan"* ("*Hong fan*" *wuxing zhuan* 洪範五行傳). The latter work was circulated among members of Xiahou Sheng's school (chart 3).[133] Emperor Cheng's 成 reign (33–7 BC) initiated a project to collect scattered books. In this project, Liu was in charge of editing the classics and their commentaries. As such, he gained access to the imperial library. As we can see from his career, he always kept on top of contemporary intellectual trends by focusing on the relevant texts and by cultivating relationships with a diverse group of people.

This generalization is also true for Liu Xin. Like his father, Liu Xin began his studies with the *Changes*. He then worked with his father to edit books in the imperial library. With Wang Mang's support, he took his father's position after he passed away. Liu Xin learned the Zuo tradition of commentary on the *Annals* from Yin Cheng 尹咸 and Zhai Fangjin. The father of the former, Yin Gengshi 尹更始, also attended the Gongyang versus

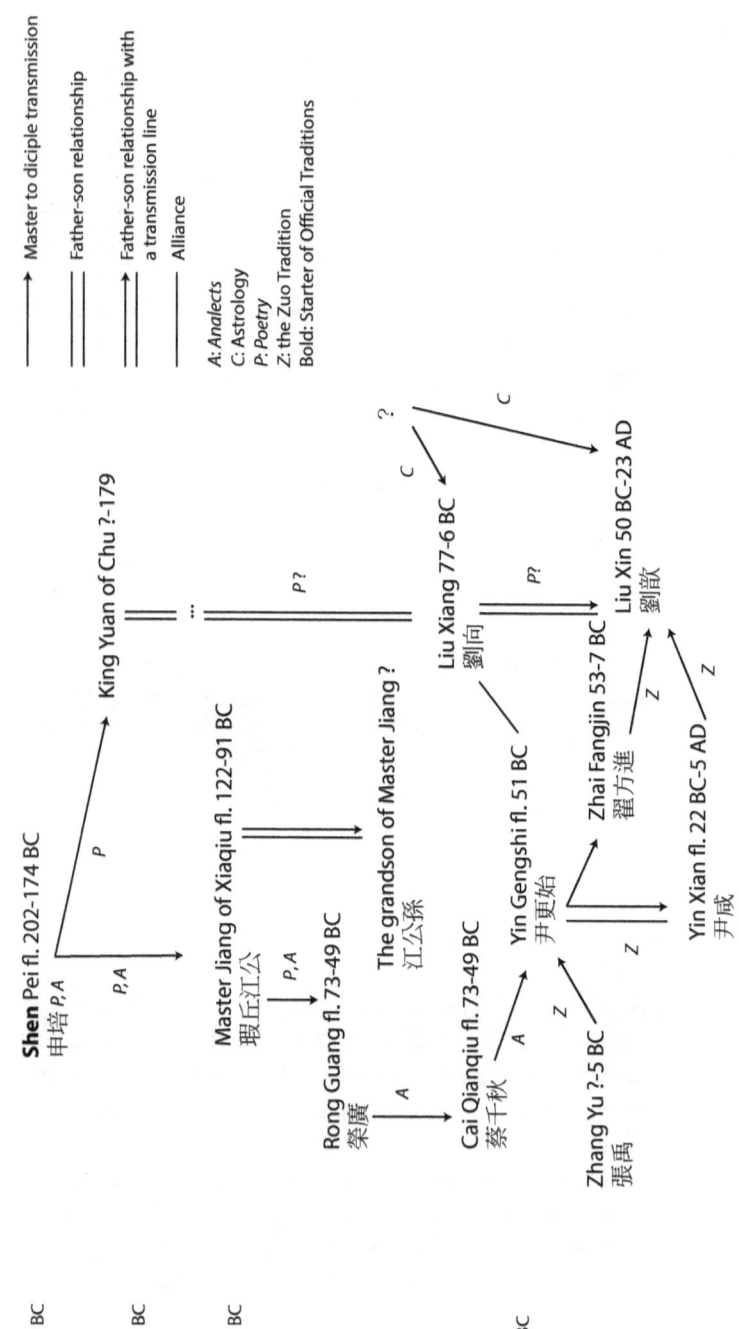

Chart 3. Liu Xiang and Liu Xin's Learning

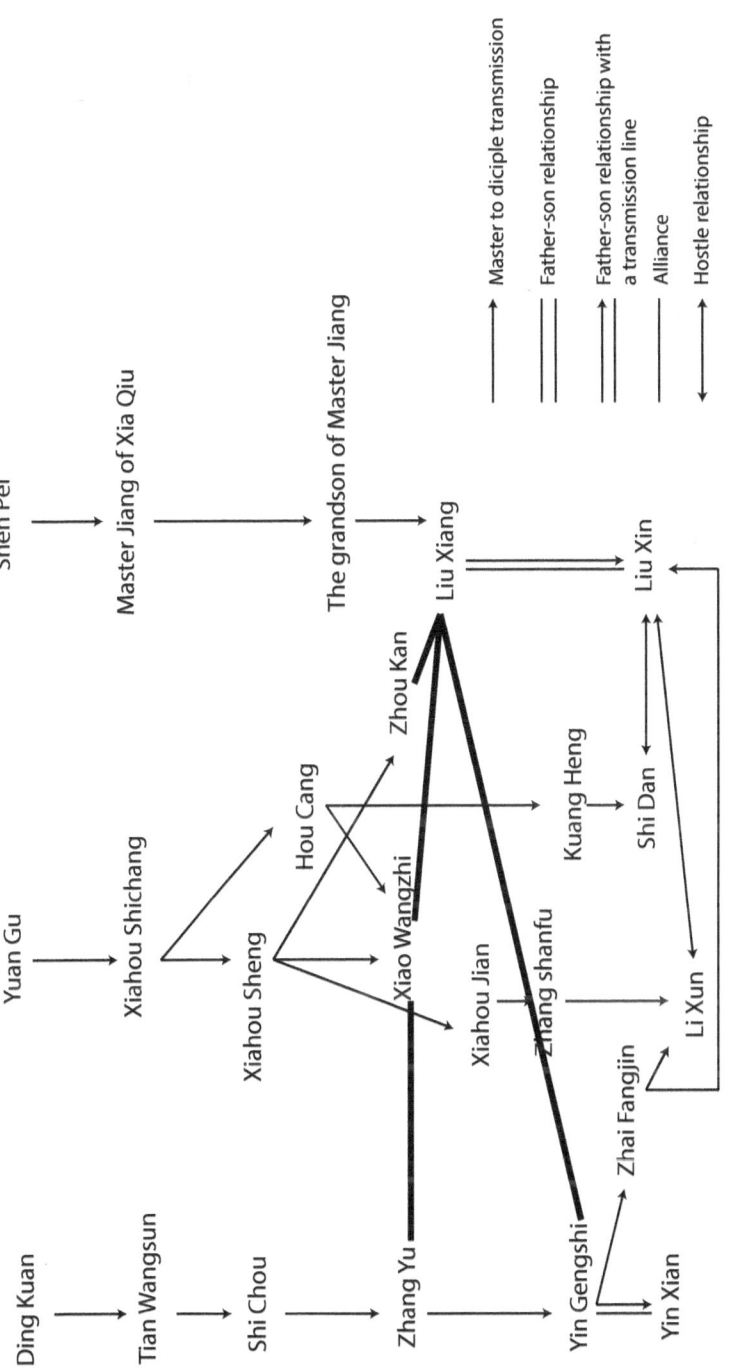

Chart 4. Liu Xiang and His Alliances (emphasis in bold)

Guliang debate as a Guliang proponent. Zhai Fangjin was a polymath who also studied the Guliang tradition. In the late Western Han, the Zuo tradition was hardly an obscure commentary among top-notch scholars. In addition to Yin and Zhai, Liu Xin's father's friend Xiao Wangzhi and Xiao's protégé Zhang Yu also preserved the Zuo tradition.[134] These scholars either studied *both* the Guliang and Zuo traditions or were closely associated with scholars of the Guliang tradition (chart 3). Like his father, Liu Xin's versatility was largely due to his sensitivity to his contemporaries' tastes and concerns and his frequent contact with diverse scholars. His experiences in the imperial library also cultivated his openness to texts without transmission lines.

Indeed, Liu Xin's choice of texts was not outlandish, but not all of his colleagues were willing to follow him far enough. Liu Xin could have just emphasized how useful his choice of texts was by how they would improve the understanding of the classics. Or he could have even promoted them as the classics by reasoning that more commentarial traditions were needed. Instead, he did so by reasoning that the official traditions were not reliable enough. It was this reasoning that sparked outrage. For example, Liu's aforementioned letter incited a very hostile reply from Shi Dan. The latter did not accuse the former of promoting nonsense but rather of disparaging the Academician tradition of the Han. In other words, what separated him from Liu Xin was the answer to the question: "Did they possess the original classics?" Shi still rooted for the trustworthiness of transmission lines. His view represented many of his contemporaries' stances, where a more reliable way of learning started with a text from a teacher.[135]

From this perspective, the so-called old script / new script controversy between Liu Xin and his contemporaries was more about whether the master-disciple transmission line alone was reliable enough to understand the classics than about defending one of the two contrasting transmission lines. Although they happened to defend the "old script" or "new script" texts, Liu Xin and Shi Dan were both Wang Mang's affiliates, and they also shared tightly knit scholarly connections (chart 5). The conflict was not so much about partisanship between discrete intellectual groups as a clash between innovators and conservatives in the same intellectual community.

Counterintuitively, Li Xun also belonged to the same circle as Liu Xiang and Liu Xin. He received learning of *Documents* from Zhang Shanfu 張山柎 (fl. 51 BC), a disciple of Xiahou Jian 夏侯建 (fl. 51 BC). Xiahou Jian was the founder of the "Younger Xiahou" (Xiao Xiahou 小夏侯) tradition of *Documents* (chart 6). He was not only related to but also received teachings from Xiahou Sheng,[136] who was the founder of the "Elder Xiahou" tradition

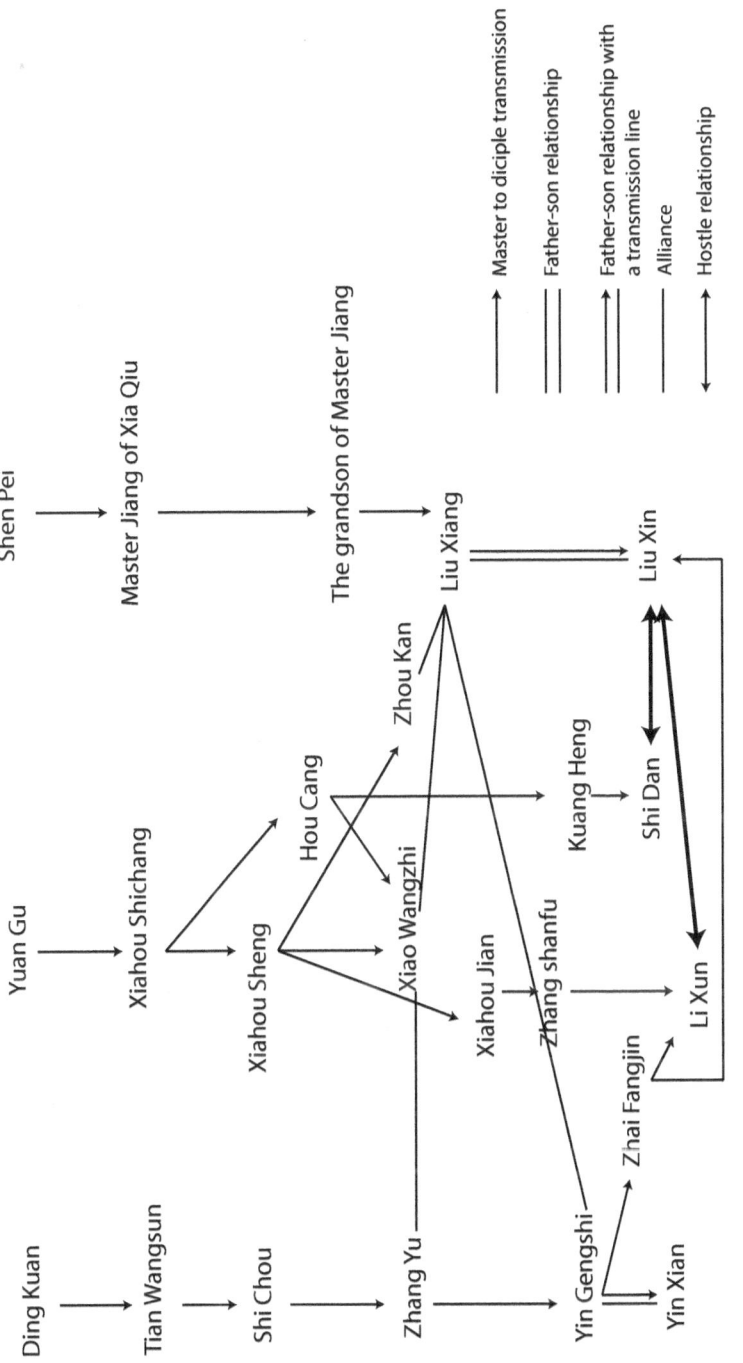

Chart 5. Liu Xin and His Enemies (emphasis in bold)

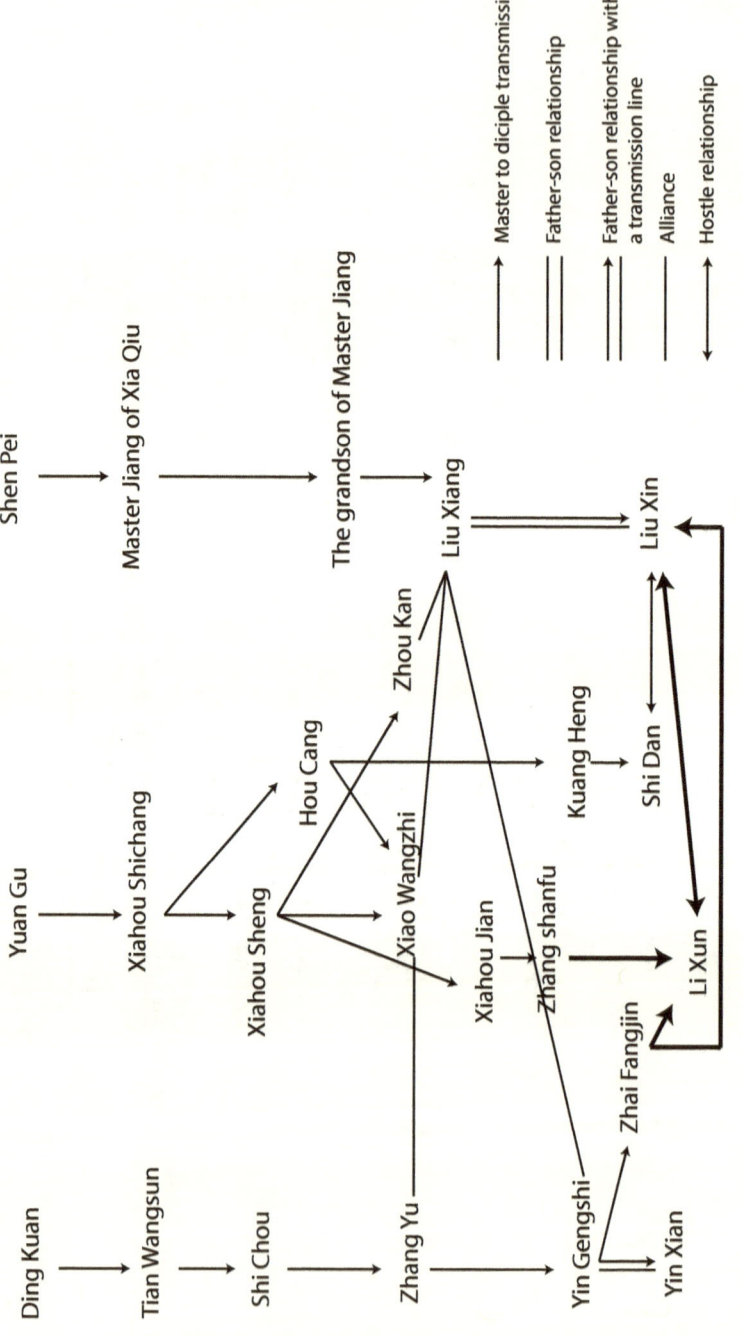

Chart 6. Liu Xin and Li Xun's Affiliates

of the *Documents* (Da Xiahou 大夏侯).[137] In Emperor Xuan's time, both of these traditions were institutionalized as official learning. From then on, they were two of the most dominant *Documents* traditions in the Western Han dynasty.[138]

Like Liu Xiang and Liu Xin, Li Xun outran his fellow classicists. He was not only devoted to transmitting his master's doctrines, he was also interested astrology, the theory of *yin-yang*, and almanacs.[139] His interest in the omenology of the "Great Plan" resembles Liu Xiang's. During Emperor Cheng's reign, Grand Chancellor Zhai Fangjin admired Li Xun's expertise in understanding the skies and recommended him as his assistant (*yi cao* 議曹).[140] During his time in Zhai's entourage, Li's astrological explanations of the decline of the Han house attracted attention from the chief advisor and uncle of Emperor Cheng, Wang Gen 王根 (?–6 BC), also an uncle of Wang Mang. In the beginning years of Emperor Ai's 哀 (r. 7–1 BC) reign, with Wang Gen's help, Li started working in the palace and was promoted to Attendant Gentlemen at the Yellow Gate (*huangmen shilang* 黃門侍郎).[141] Although Li made a radical departure from previous scholars on how to achieve the Great Peace, his education and relationships tell of a man deeply embedded in the classical scholarship and government of his time.

Regardless of their political triumph or failure, Liu Xin and Li Xun represented two paths of intellectual innovation deeply couched in the intellectual culture of the Western Han dynasty. Liu Xin's way reflects the multiplication of classical transmission lines and growing scholasticism beginning in Emperor Wu's time. His maneuver was to unite all the transmission lines and scattered texts about the classics to form a giant whole. In other words, his innovation was a type of combination. Li on the other hand, adopted and even reinforced the importance of Heaven that had been acknowledged since Emperor Xuan's time. His innovation was a departure: he skipped the tier of the classics in the Heaven-classics-sages model that was shared by many of his contemporaries.

Concluding Remarks

In this chapter, we have seen how a few central concerns led to innovation and affected the literati. To state our conclusions in a general way, we can see three intellectual transitions. First, in Emperor Xuan's time, the crisis of losing the mandate of Heaven crystallized. In this step, state policies turned to the regulation of the cosmos, and accordingly, the classics appeared as the means of understanding Heaven and its order. Second, from Emperor Yuan's time on, literati like Liu Xiang and Kuang Heng linked the ancient sages' ideal society with the remedy for the crisis. The classics thus became indispensable in realizing the sage kings' rule and the Great Peace. In this process, scholars focused on the integrity and all-encompassing nature of the classics. Third, at the end of the Western Han, the previous focus cast doubts about the received versions of the classics. Accordingly, more radical innovations appeared; Liu Xin and Li Xun pushed the realization of the Great Peace and followed Heaven's will to another level through the combination of and departure from classical traditions, respectively.

The love of antiquity sprouts from distress in the present. In the last fifty years of the Western Han dynasty, two issues dominated the court: Heaven's mandate and the Kingly Way of antiquity. They were not equal; the latter derived from the former. This model was not unheard of among early Confucian thinkers (for example, Xunzi). Nevertheless, for the literati of the late Western Han, Heaven became an increasingly active agent that could directly judge a government and decide its fate. In this period, leading scholars were the ones who managed to link these two issues with one of the most important cultural resources: expertise in the classics.

The intellectual trends of the mid-Western Han dynasty are not Confucian in the strict sense. The philosophies of Confucius, Mencius, and Xunzi are humanistic; the main theme is moral cultivation of individuals. Heaven plays only an indirect, if any, role in the human realm. Therefore, individuals turned to a system of humanist ethics instead of Heaven's will to understand how to organize the state.[142] This is not the case in the late Western Han. From Emperor Xuan's time, Heaven's will became a central issue in political discourse. In fact, for many literati, their reforms were based on the premise that Heaven did not approve of current Han policies. No matter whether it was Liu Xiang's "heavenly mandate" or the omens that appeared while Wang Mang practiced the Well-Field system, Heaven's permission became the crucial element in the determination of the Han dynasty's fate. Accordingly, sages became representatives of Heaven. They either penetrated Heaven's order or designed a human government in accord with Heaven's mandate.

Wang Mang's rule represented the extreme of these two tendencies, a fitting cap to the first century BC's intellectual innovation. On the one hand, he enforced the putative agricultural system of the Zhou dynasty, the Well-Field system, and reformed the bureaucratic system based on the classics, especially the *Rites of Zhou*, an obscure text Liu Xin promoted.

On the other hand, he employed many auspicious omens and revealed texts to show that Heaven had blessed his rule. His rule indeed embodied the political thought of generations of Han literati. However, his plan for the Great Peace only lasted fourteen years. In the next chapter, we will see how classicists adopted the style of heavenly revelations used by Li Xun and claimed that the classics were actually revealed by Heaven.

Chapter 2

The Conflation between Heaven and the Classics

The Rise of Apocrypha (*chenwei* 讖緯)

As radical as they were, Liu Xin and Li Xun's ideas had their own appeal at the time: Liu pursued a more comprehensive understanding of the classics; Li aimed for Heaven's direct guidance. Was there, then, an approach that could combine these two aims? Such an approach actually did appear and it became embodied in a corpus of texts. This corpus looks so alien to us nowadays that modern scholars call the collection "a mixture of theology and vulgar classicism" (*shenxue he yongsu jingxue de hunhe wu* 神學和庸俗經學的混合物),[1] "deviant and chimerical thoughts" (*yaowang de sixiang* 妖妄的思想),[2] or a "major collection of adulteration and forgery" (*zha wei chengji zhi da jieji* 詐偽成績之大結集).[3] This chapter tells the story of this specific approach and its embodiment into a corpus of texts, namely, apocrypha (*chenwei* 讖緯).[4] We will see how this corpus, damned by today's scholars, not only survived but, in fact, flourished in the first two centuries AD in China.

At the end of the first century BC, Han China experienced an increasing zeal for the classics and Heaven's mandate. The fate of the dynasty hinged upon Heaven's will as well as its officials' ability to bring the Great Peace to the Han, especially through the classics. In this context, Liu Xin and Li Xun created their own methods. Each vied for political and intellectual authority; they claimed that their method led to a correct understanding of Heaven. However, neither saved the Han dynasty. Wang Mang, a lover of the Golden Age, usurped the Han empire, seeking to bring the Kingly Way back to society.

Wang's grand undertaking led not to an ideal society in which the Great Peace prevailed but to social and political unrest.[5] After the collapse of his rule in AD 23, various political groups contended militarily and intellectually to establish a new dynasty. The tradition of apocryphal texts emerged in the context of this tumult. While the Han empire fell, the appeal to the classics and Heaven did not. This chapter will examine the apocryphal texts (*chenwei* 讖緯), a corpus that combines the interpretation of the classics with direct guidance from Heaven, from two perspectives. First, we will explore their contents to see how apocryphal texts claimed a stronger link to both Heaven and the classics than earlier commentarial traditions. Apocryphal texts pushed certain themes of late Western Han literati discourse to the extreme, such as the heavenly origin of the classics, their functions, and the notion of sages as intermediary agents between Heaven and the classics. Second, the latter half of this chapter will explore the formation and application of these texts. We will look at the sociopolitical context of these texts, especially how Liu Xiu 劉秀 (6 BC–AD 57), the later Emperor Guangwu, manipulated prophecies into a corpus of texts to legitimate his rule and the newly established Eastern Han dynasty (AD 25–220). This corpus of texts later came to be called "the apocrypha." Scholars with training in classics were the driving force behind this transformation.[6]

Discovering the Heavenly Nature of the Classics

Apocryphal texts were new to the first century AD, so that in many Eastern Han critics' eyes they did not have a long tradition, nor were they of authoritative origin. They dominated the intellectual world in the first century AD rather because they maximally exploited two sacred objects of the time: the classics and Heaven. Unlike Liu Xin or Li Xun, proponents of apocrypha did not claim that the texts were parts missing from the original classics or revealed scriptures from Heaven. Proponents had a better pitch; like a bridge, these texts stood in the middle: if one wanted to understand the message from Heaven in the classics, one needed to read apocryphal texts.

Their titles already make this apparent. For example, when an apocryphal text called the *Key to the Heavenly Pivot in the Book of Documents* (*Shangshu xuanji qian* 尚書琁機鈐) appeared in a debate in the imperial court in AD 100,[7] the title implied that its contents were in accord not only with the *Documents* but also with the "Heavenly Pivot" (天樞), a name for the four stars of the Big Dipper, one of several understandings of *xuanji* at the time.[8] Like its Western counterpart, the astronomy of early China saw the Big Dipper as a guidepost by which one could navigate using the sky.[9] This gives the Heavenly Pivot a special position in understanding astronomical movements—the movements of Heaven. Similarly, the title, the *Manipulation of the Pivot of the Big Dipper in the Annals of Spring and Autumn* (*Chunqiu yun doushu* 春秋運斗樞) resembles the structure of the *Key to the Xuanji*: name of classic plus name of heavenly phenomenon or principle.[10] Many apocryphal titles have such a structure that specifies a classic and a mantic activity (table 1). The titles suggest that their contents provide not just heavenly knowledge, but the specific kind that Heaven coded in the original classics.

The Five Classics: Reflections of Heaven

In the late Western Han, many literati such as Kuang Heng and Liu Xiang depicted the relationship between the classics and Heaven in this way: the sages penetrated Heaven with their understanding, and then they created the classics that were not only in accord with Heaven but also designed for human use. Apocryphal texts adopted this idea:

Table 1. A Literal Translation of Apocrypha Titles Quoted in Chapter 2

Chinese Name	English Translation
乾坤鑿度	*Cracking Open the Regularity of Qian and Kun*
河圖提劉予	*The Bestowal on the Promoted Liu of the River Chart*
尚書中候	*Documents' Match of Observations*
尚書帝命驗	*Documents' Verification of Emperors' Mandate*
禮稽命徵	*Rites' Examinations of the Omens of Mandate*
春秋演孔圖	*Annals' Diagrams Elaborating Confucius*
春秋說題辭	*Annals' Explications of Words in Titles*
春秋感精符	*Annals' Tallies Corresponding to the Essence*
春秋元命包	*Annals' Inclusion of the Primary Mandate*
春秋漢含孳	*Annals' Propagation included in the Han Dynasty*
春秋保乾圖	*Annals' Charts of Cherishing the Qian*
河圖錄運法	*Recorded Rule for the Movement of Mandate of the River Chart*
河圖括地象	*Inclusive Images of Earth of the River Chart*
河圖赤伏符	*The Red Hidden Tally of the River Chart*
河圖會昌符	*Tally for Meeting Prosperity of the River Chart*
孝經援神契	*Covenant for Assistance from Spirits of the Classic of Filial Piety*

> 《詩》者，天文之精，星辰之度。在事為詩，未發為謀。恬澹為心，思慮為志。故詩之所以為言志也。[11]

> The *Book of Poetry* is the essence of heavenly patterns and the principle of stars and planets. When it comes to [worldly] affairs, it becomes poetry. When it is latent, it is thought. Equilibrium is its heart; deliberation is its will. Therefore the *Poetry* is that by which one conveys the will.

The *Book of Poetry* transforms in accord with Heaven and human beings. By shifting from celestial patterns to states of the human mind, the *Poetry* does not just mimic Heaven, it also adapts itself to the peculiarities of the human psyche.

This is not unique to the *Poetry*; apocryphal texts understand the *Rites* in a similar way. For example, in the *Rites' Examinations of the Omens of the Mandate* (*Li ji mingzheng* 禮稽命徵), the following is written:

> 《禮》之動搖也，與天地同氣，四時合信。陰陽為符，日月為明。上下和洽，則物獸如其性命。[12]

> The movement of the *Rites* shares the *qi* of Heaven and Earth and matches the tally of the four seasons. They take *yin-yang* as their match, and the sun and moon as light. When the above and below are harmonious, the myriad things and animals all comply with their nature and the mandate.

Following cosmological order, the *Rites* harmonizes the cosmos ("above") with the human world ("below"). Practicing the *Rites* leads the myriad creatures to the right order based on their nature. *Ru qi xing ming* 如其性命 echoes Xunzi's view: the rites are not arbitrary but the sages' specific design and are based on human nature.[13] The passage argues that rites suit the nature of the myriad things on the earth.

Departing from Xunzi and the majority of early Han scholars, however, many apocryphal texts imply that Heaven took an active role in the formation of the classics:

> 伏羲氏有天下，龍馬負圖出于河，遂法之，畫八卦。[14]

> When Fuxi possessed the world, the dragon-horse emerged from the Yellow River carrying the Chart on its back. Fuxi then drew the eight trigrams based on it.

This scene combines two accounts from the "Attached Statements" (Xici 繫辭) commentary on the *Changes*. In one place in the text, the author says that while ruling the world, Fuxi made the eight trigrams based on his examination of the world: the sky's patterns, standards on earth, the patterns of the animal world, and things around him, including himself.[15] Based on this part, Heaven was only one of the objects that Fuxi examined; the trigrams are based on the sage Fuxi's understanding of the entirety of Heaven and the human realm. In the other part of the "Attached Statements," the author argues that the sage should take the "divine things" (*shenwu* 神物) produced by Heaven as a standard. These things include the Chart of Yellow River and the Writing of Luo River together with other revelations.[16] This account does not mention anything about the creation of the eight trigrams.

In the apocryphal passage, however, the "Chart of Yellow River" is taken out of its original place in the "Attached Statements" and is combined with the account of the creation of the eight trigrams. The apocryphal passage no longer mentions Fuxi's examination of the world, and the chart that emerges from the Yellow River on a dragon's back thus becomes the only subject that Fuxi used to create the eight trigrams. While in the "Attached Statements" the human sage Fuxi was the active agent who forged human society by observing the natural world, the apocryphal passage emphasizes Heaven's active role in the human world: the creation of the eight trigrams depended upon the chart from the Yellow River, which was presumably revealed by Heaven. Fuxi did invent the trigrams, but Heaven led the process.

According to many apocryphal texts, Heaven was even more involved in Confucius's composition of the *Annals* than in the creation of the trigrams:

昔孔子受端門之命，制春秋之義，使子夏等十四人求周史記。得百二十國寶書，九月經立。[17]

> In antiquity, Confucius received the mandate of the Duan gate, and he created the principles of the *Annals of Spring and Autumn*. He made fourteen people, including Zixia [an advanced disciple of Confucius], seek the historical records of Zhou. They obtained 120 states' precious writings. The classic [the *Annals*] was established after nine months.

Once again, apocryphal texts tailored existing narratives. Beginning with *Mencius*, many early Chinese accounts of the *Annals* attribute its authorship to Confucius. In these narratives, Confucius alone wrote the *Annals*. Some claim that Confucius did so because he intended to rectify the outrageous behavior of his contemporaries; others argue that the obstacles to political advancement that Confucius faced and his subsequent feelings of frustration inspired him to compose this work.[18] In none of these accounts does Heaven directly inspire Confucius's composition of the *Annals*. However, in this apocryphal passage, Confucius wrote the *Annals* precisely because he received a mandate from Heaven to teach the Way to subsequent dynastic founders.

The following allusion to the Duan gate presents Heaven's interference even more obviously:

得麟之後，天下血書魯端門曰：趨作法，孔聖沒，周姬亡。彗東出。秦政起，胡破術。書紀散，孔不絕。[19]

> After obtaining the *qilin* [an auspicious and ominous animal that normally only appears in a prosperous society], Heaven sent writing in blood on the Duan gate of the state of Lu, saying, "Set up the standard quickly! The sage Kong will die, and the Zhou dynasty's house of Ji will perish. A comet will appear in the east. [Ying] Zheng of Qin will arise. Hu Hai will break the arts. Books and records will scatter, but [the teaching of] Kong will not become extinct."

The passage contains many more allusions. "Obtaining the *qilin*" alludes to the last event in the *Annals*, as in the fourteenth year of Duke Ai 哀 of Lu (481 BC). In the Gongyang tradition, this event marks the end of an epoch and the completion of the *Annals*. It signifies the end of Confucius's way.[20] The riddle in the later part of the passage alludes to several historical events: the death of Confucius, the fall of the Zhou dynasty, the rise of the Qin dynasty, and the endangerment of the way of Confucius.[21] In the Gongyang tradition, Confucius does try to extrapolate Heaven's message from the capture of the *qilin*. Nevertheless, Heaven never explicitly expresses its will. In contrast, the apocryphal passage patches its own story about heavenly prophecy to the end of this event in order to create a new ending for the *Annals*. In this new story, Heaven not only presents its ideas via a "human" method (writing), it even speaks to command Confucius to set up the standard for later generations, or more specifically, composing the *Annals*.

Apocryphal Texts: Older than the Classics?

The reception of the prophecy from Heaven is not the end of the Duan gate story; in that apocryphal passage, the message in blood revealed itself to Zixia and turned into a text:

子夏明日往視之，血書飛為赤烏。化為白書。署曰演孔圖。中有作圖制法之狀。²²

> The next day, Zixia went there to check it [the blood writing]. The blood writing flew up and became a red crow. It then transformed into a white text, entitled: *Diagrams Elaborating Confucius*. It contains descriptions for making diagrams and setting up standards.

The title *Diagrams Elaborating Confucius* is actually the title of the apocryphal text from which this passage is taken. Thus, the passage implies that the apocryphal text in which it is written is of heavenly origin. What is more, it claims that the text contains instructions for setting up standards of good government, which allude to Heaven's command, "set up the standard quickly" (*qu zuo fa* 趨作法), in the prophecy.

If one considers this account with the one about Confucius composing the *Annals*, a larger agenda emerges. It implies that the *Annals* is derived from the apocryphal *Diagrams Elaborating Confucius*. The apocryphal text depicts a sequence of actions that led to its completion: Heaven first sent down a prophecy, asking Confucius to set up a standard. It then sent down the *Diagrams* for setting up the standard. After receiving this command, Confucius started composing the work and finished it in nine months. Apocryphal texts, because they inspired the classics, become earlier and more authoritative than the classics themselves.

In order to claim textual authority, the author of this text integrates the claims of apocryphal texts and well-known parts of the classical tradition. The whole scenario mentioned earlier is attached to the event of obtaining the *qilin*, which is a common narrative in the *Annals* and its commentarial traditions. As the continuation of the *Annals* story, the apocryphal passage further develops Heaven's message. Thus the apocryphal text appears to be part of the world of classics, filling a blank usually filled by commentarial traditions such as the Gongyang. It reveals the secrets about Heaven and the classics, which cannot be found anywhere else.

In order to demonstrate that they precede the classics, certain apocrypha also employ a textual genealogy. *Cracking Open the Regularity of Qian and Kun* (*Qian Kun zao du* 乾坤鑿度) lists an apocryphon with a very similar name, *Cracking Open the Regularity of Qian* (*Qian zao du* 乾鑿度), before the *Changes*, implying that it is its chronological predecessor:

庖氏著乾鑿度上下文。媧皇氏，地靈母經。炎帝皇帝，有易靈緯。公孫氏。周易孔子附。²³

Fuxi wrote the first and second half of *Cracking Open the Regularity of Qian*. For the Sovereign Wa, there was the *Classic of the Maternal Earthly Spirit*. For the Sovereign Yan, there was *Apocrypha of Spirits in Changes*. Gongsun.²⁴ Confucius attached [passages] to the *Changes of Zhou*.

Fuxi, Sovereign Wa, and Emperor Yan form the "Three Sovereigns" (*san huang* 三皇) group,²⁵ and Gongsun shi, or the Yellow Emperor, is the first emperor in the "Five Emperors" (*wu di* 五帝) group.²⁶ For most Han literati, these sage kings were the very first creators of human civilization, and they preceded the early dynasties Xia, Shang, and Zhou. In apocryphal texts, the span from the Xia to the Spring and Autumn period (720–476 BC) is divided into four successive periods. The first three, the "Three Sovereigns," the "Five Emperors," and the "Three Kings" periods, constitute the Golden Age of human civilization. The fourth, the "Five Hegemons" period, marks the end of that age. These four periods are marked by the gradual deterioration of the virtue of their rulers.²⁷ Thus the previous passage from *Cracking Open the Regularity of Qian* claims that the text is as old as the mythical sovereigns who created the human realm.²⁸

Based on this genealogy, the apocryphal passage quoted earlier puts *Cracking Open the Regularity of Qian* ahead of the *Changes*. In the first century AD, the received *Changes* were believed to be the work of King Wen of Zhou, who expanded the Eight Trigrams to the Sixty-Four Hexagrams, and Confucius, who wrote ten passages attached to them.²⁹ In contrast, apocryphal texts attribute *Cracking Open the Regularity of Qian* to Fuxi, the inventor of the Eight Trigrams and the first sage creator of human civilization. Fuxi obviously preceded King Wen and Confucius, and so did his text. In this narrative, *Cracking Open the Regularity of Qian* becomes the product of the Golden Age, and the received *Changes* was derivative from the chaotic period of the "Five Hegemons." This genealogy gives *Cracking Open the Regularity of Qian* a longer tradition and more authoritative origin than the classics and makes it better reflect the truth of the classics.

Apocryphal texts represent a new strategy of textual invention; they seek to solve the problems targeted by the innovations that preceded them, while avoiding the critiques Liu Xin and Li Xun suffered: Liu Xin wished to promote several texts as part of the classics, but his contemporaries could not accept unprovenanced texts as the classics, hence apocrypha do not appear as classics themselves; Liu complained about the loss of a comprehensive understanding of the classics, hence apocrypha claim to be revealed texts from Heaven that help to discover the essence of the classics; Li Xun proposed to directly follow Heaven's will, hence apocrypha appear to be of heavenly origin and reassure their readers that they contain information that Heaven wants them to know; promoting the Scripture of the Great Peace, Li was accused of deviating from the classics, hence apocrypha appear to be the commentaries of the classics. They might be outlandish to modern scholars, but they spoke right to the hearts of their readers in the first century AD.

The Function of Sages in Human Society

To possess knowledge is to possess power. In the previous chapter, we saw the sage and the perfected man become indispensable, given what corpora of texts were valued. When many literati promoted the classics, the followers of the sage or the classicists became important. When Li Xun advocated the *Scripture of the Great Peace*, the followers of the perfected man or the heavenly gentlemen became indispensable. Who stands on top of the apocryphal pyramid, and who is legitimated by the corpus? In this section, we will see how apocryphal texts perceive sages, ancient kings, and dynastic changes. And in the rest of the chapter, we will see the application of these ideas in action.

Since Heaven plays an active role in apocryphal texts, do sages then function merely as passive messengers, as the perfected man does in Li Xun's account of the *Scripture of the Great Peace*? Apocryphal texts' view of sages starts out more or less in line with the opinions of Xunzi, Dong Zhongshu, and others. In an example from *Cracking Open the Regularity of Qian and Kun*, Heaven starts the world and the sage completes it:

一大之物目天，一塊之物目地。一炁之霸名混沌。一氣分萬霜。是上聖鑿破虛無，斷氣為二，緣物為三，天地之道不濩。³⁰

A unitary bulk of things was categorized[31] as Heaven, and a unitary clot of things was categorized as Earth. A unitary fold of *qi* was called *hundun*. This unitary *qi* divided into myriad obscurities. Therefore, the primary sage chiseled the nebulous *qi* open. He broke the *qi* into two [*yin* and *yang*?] and followed the things to make them into three [Heaven, Earth, and the human realm?].[32] Therefore, the way of Heaven and Earth was not broken up.

Before the sage's undertaking, everything is clogged together. In that state, the cosmos is not static; *qi* splits. However, this split does not lead to the development of diversity, but more opacity. Eventually, the sage penetrates this nebulous *qi*. He is responsible for developing the world from its primordial state, but not by creating Heaven or Earth. He does so by following the way of Heaven and Earth.

Xunzi would only agree so far; apocryphal texts further show that after the sage clarifies the cosmos, Heaven does not leave the human realm alone:

鳳凰銜圖置帝前，黃帝再拜受。³³

A phoenix held the Diagram in its mouth and put it in front of the [Yellow] Emperor. Yellow Emperor bowed twice to accept it.

堯坐中舟，³⁴ 與太尉舜臨觀。鳳凰負圖授。³⁵

Yao sat in the boat and observed with his Grand Commandant, Shun. A phoenix carried the Diagram on its back and bestowed it on [them].

唐帝游河渚，赤龍負圖以出。³⁶

When the emperor of Tang [Yao], was traveling along the Yellow River, a red dragon carrying the Diagram on its back came out of the water.

Here we encounter the Diagram and, again, a repetitive theme: human sages receive messages of Heaven from auspicious creatures. Auspicious omens such as phoenixes revealing themselves were common in Western Han scholars' works, as in Liu Xiang's speeches.[37] However, the scenario depicted here provides a much closer relationship between Heaven and the human sages than what Liu imagines. Heaven does not just evaluate human governance and reveal its judgment through omens; it actually sends messages as guidance for human sages to follow. Xunzi explicitly argues against the idea of relying on Heaven's will, because it is impossible to know. Moreover, for Xunzi, the human realm is an autonomous region beyond the reach of Heaven's direct interference. Apocryphal texts, in sharp contrast, assert that Heaven shapes human society by communicating and guiding sage kings. The sage kings, while they accomplish great things, constantly follow Heaven's messages.

The Physical Features of Human Sages and Their Heavenly Origin

Not everyone could become a sage king; apocryphal texts draw a decisive line between the ordinary and the chosen. In addition to communication with Heaven, Xunzi would also object to the physiognomic features of the many human sages in apocryphal texts.[38] For example:

黃帝龍顏，得天庭陽。[39]

> The Yellow Emperor had a dragon face and [thus] had the [constellation] North of Heavenly Court.

North of Heavenly Court indicates the celestial constellation Taiwei 太微, or the Privy Council, which symbolizes the imperial house.[40] Because the Yellow Emperor's facial features resemble those of a dragon, a symbol of the emperor, they show his imperial nature. In many cases, features of the sages are linked to heavenly bodies in the sky:

孔子長十尺，大九圍。坐如蹲龍，立如牽牛。就之如昂，望之如斗。[41]

> Confucius was ten *chi* (2.31 m.) tall.[42] He was nine *wei* around.[43] He looked like a squatting dragon when he sat, and a harnessed ox when he stood. He looked like [the constellation] Mao when one approached him, and the Big Dipper when one looked at him from distance.

In this case, Confucius not only looks like divine or strong animals, he also looks like the constellation Mao and the Big Dipper.

We can see why Xunzi would disagree. He did not think there was a correspondence between one's appearance and his nature. If he were going to give a physiognomic reading of Confucius, it would not be positive. According to him, Confucius's face looked unappealing.[44] He argues that if we were to assume that Confucius's facial features reflected his intelligence and achievements, we would greatly underestimate him. Furthermore, many sage kings were short and ugly, while some tyrants were tall, strong, and handsome.[45] Xunzi's larger point is that the physical appearance of a person, whether desirable or not, has nothing to do with his mind or behavior.[46]

Indeed, the apocryphal world would seem alien or even repulsive to Xunzi, but it appears as such for good reasons. If, however, we reduce the passages about sage kings' unusual physiognomic features to only fortune-telling, we lose the larger point of these texts: sage kings were not randomly born; they were of extraordinary origin. For example, Yu was the "essence of the white emperor," or *baidi jing* 白帝精,[47] and King Wen was the "essence of the green emperor," or *cangdi jing* 蒼帝精.[48] Yao was the "essence of fire," or *huo jing* 火精,[49] and Confucius was the "essence of water," or *shui jing* 水精.[50]

The colors and elements signify heavenly nature. According to apocrypha, there are five emperors: the red emperor, Wenzu 文祖; the yellow emperor, Shendou 神斗; the white emperor, Xianji 顯紀; the black emperor, Xuanju 玄矩; and the green emperor, Lingfu 靈府, corresponding to fire, earth, metal, water, and wood, respectively. They are heavenly emperors who are located in the constellation Taiwei 太微. The human sage kings corresponded (*gan* 感) to their "essence," or *jing* 精.[51] The word "correspond" here does not imply an interaction on an equal basis, such as the human sage and the heavenly emperor communicating with and transferring spiritual power between each other. Instead, given the miraculous birth of the sage kings depicted in apocryphal texts,[52] they received essence from them passively and were subject to the heavenly emperors.

The miraculous birth of sage kings and their links to the heavenly emperors are derived from the theory of the Five Phases, a common understanding of the cosmos in the Han dynasty. From the late Warring States period to the Han dynasty, people understood dynastic change based on two sequences or types of the succession of the Five Phases: succession by conquest or 相勝 *xiang shèng*, and succession by generation or 相生 *xiang shēng*. The former type sequences earth, wood, metal, fire, and water, and in this way each phase is considered to be conquered by the one after it (table 2). This type perceives dynastic changes as military conquest of one over the other. The latter type sequences wood, fire, earth, metal, and water, in which case each generates the one after it (table 3). This type perceives continuity; the ending dynasty gives birth and passes down the mandate of Heaven to the succeeding one.[53]

The second theory came after the first and became dominant at the end of the Western Han dynasty. Officials in the court at the end of the first century BC such as Liu Xiang and Liu Xin began to prefer the theory of succession by generation. They thought that through this order the legitimacy of rule shifts from one phase to another based on the virtue of the person who received of the mandate of Heaven. And the person has to be the representative of the right phase at the moment.[55] This theory also implied that Qin was not a legitimate dynasty anymore, as "real" dynasties are founded by a moral ruler or in the right order of succession. The Zhou dynasty represented the phase of wood, and it could only give birth to a dynasty that represented the phase of fire. Qin, however, was a representative of water and could not possibly be the heavenly heir of Zhou (see table 3).

Tables 2 and 3. Two Theories of the Five Phases[54]

Table 2	Succession by Conquest 相勝	
	"Feng shan shu" of *Shiji*	
Earth	Yellow Emperor 黃帝	(Han 漢)
Wood	Yu 禹	
Metal	Tang 湯	
Fire	King Wen of Zhou 周文王	
Water	秦 Qin	

Table 3.	Succession by Generation 相生		
	"The Treatise of Music and Calendar" in *Han shu*		
Wood	Fu Xi 伏羲	Di Ku 帝嚳	King Wen of Zhou 周武王
(Water)	Gong Gong 共工		Qin 秦
Fire	Shen Nong 神農	Yao 堯	Liu Bang 劉邦
Earth	the Yellow Emperor	Shun 舜	
Metal	Shao Hao 少昊	Yu 禹	
Water	Zhuan Xu 顓頊	Tang 湯	

Together with the theory of succession by generation, what do apocryphal texts tell us about the sage kings and their relationship with Heaven? Most importantly, they construct a structured dynastic order of succession. In this order, one virtuous dynasty succeeds another. Heaven manipulates the process by producing human sages, the founders of each of the legitimate dynasties. That is to say, according to apocryphal texts, ordinary people, either through education or by unusual intelligence, might accomplish extraordinary achievements. Nevertheless, they can never rule the human realm, for they are not related to the heavenly emperors.

For early Confucians, especially Xunzi, a person's purported connection to Heaven was irrelevant to whether he became the ruler of a state. However, this had not been the case for most literati since the last fifty years of the Western Han dynasty. The opposite was true, especially in the apocryphal world:

天子至尊也。神精與天地通。血氣含五帝精。天愛之子之也。[56]

The son of Heaven is the venerable person. His spirit and essence are linked to Heaven and Earth. His blood and *qi* contain the essence of the Five Emperors.[57] Heaven loves him and takes him as its son.

The sons of Heaven, or emperors, are not mere human beings who are isolated in the human realm, but Heaven's beloved sons. Their unique status is more than nominal:

天子皆五帝精。寶各有題序。次運相據起，必有神靈符紀。諸神扶助，使開階立遂。王者常置圖籙坐旁以自正。[58]

All the sons of Heaven are the essence of the Five Emperors. Each of their seals expresses the succession of rulership. Their successive order follows each other. They always receive spiritually powerful tallies and marks. Spirits assist them to make steps and establish their way. The ruler always keeps the charts next to his throne to rectify himself.

For the founder of a legitimate dynasty, Heaven plays the primary role in their success. It bestows the essence of the heavenly emperor on them; it grants them unusual facial features that resemble Heaven itself; and on their way to establish a new dynasty, Heaven and other spirits assist them to defeat their ordinary human rivals. Ordinary leaders lack both the Five Phases inside them and the assistance of spirits.

Forming a Tradition: The Sociopolitical Background of the Emergence of the Apocryphal Texts

Indeed, the apocryphal world was built through the scaffolding of classicism. In this world, there is a wide gap between the recipients of the Mandate of Heaven and the rest of the people, and the throne only belonged to the special few. How do we understand this apocryphal world in the first decades of the first century AD? The most logic answer is, we understand it as a means of legitimizing the newly founded Eastern Han.[59] In this section, we will go further and ask why is this so.

Legitimization is an easily misunderstood process. It seems to assume a top-down process of persuasion, in which the ruling party imposes certain ideas on the rest of the population. However, the real situation was often that the ruling party attempted to adapt to the expectations of the population. The means of legitimization needed to be plausible to others, because after all, persuasion goes both ways. Apocrypha did serve to legitimize the Eastern Han. But we can still ask the question why the Eastern Han chose this method of persuasion instead of the others. From this perspective, the production and selection of apocryphal texts was not a self-sufficient monologue but a dialogue with the others that spoke to their beliefs and anxieties.

In the rest of the chapter, we will see how apocrypha grew from the soil of the intellectual world in the first fifty years AD. They took initial shape based on an appeal to the population's belief in heavenly messages. When the vacancy of the throne became competitive among several military groups, they adapted to the situation and transformed into the form of prophecies. After the Liu family retook China, apocrypha merged with classicism and turned into commentaries of the classics. If Liu Xin's innovation was the elephant in the intellectual room, apocrypha were the chameleons.

THE UNSTOPPABLE WHEEL OF FIVE PHASES

Reform movements and revolutions have happened throughout human history, and their initiators and leaders seem always to have had good reasons for them. In modern times the reasons include improving people's welfare, fighting for freedom, bringing democracy, and so on. Reformers in the last half of the first century BC were no exception, though they had their own ideas about what were good reasons for change. In the previous chapter, we saw that, for most of the dominant literati of the last fifty years of the Western Han court, restoring the Kingly Way, achieving the Great Peace, and following the blueprint in the classics were all plausible goals.[60] Behind these goals was their ultimate motivation: the desire to be in accord with Heaven's will.

The literati's goals were particularly motivated by a feeling of fin de siècle as the Western Han drew to a closure. From the time of Emperor Yuan's reign and Wang Mang's enthronement, scholars tried to pull the Han back from its impending doom by seeking harmony with Heaven. We have seen that in 78 BC, Sui Meng's divination alluded to the end of the Han's Heaven-granted right to rule. He suggested that the Han emperor ought to abdicate the empire to a virtuous person to whom the mandate of Heaven would pass. Later on, Liu Xiang warned Emperor Yuan that the increasing number of bad omens signified Heaven's rebuke of the dynasty, which would eventually lead to the reassignment of the mandate of Heaven. In 5 BC, Xia Heliang from Li Xun's group proposed to Emperor Ai that the mandate of the Han house to rule was exhausted, so it should try to receive a renewed mandate.[61]

This attitude of fin de siècle crystallized in the term *sanqi zhi e* 三七之阨, or "the Three-Seven Predicament." The "three-seven" here figuratively indicates 210, symbolizing 210 years of Han rule.[62] Lu Wenshu 路溫舒 (fl. 80–73 BC) predicted that the Han house would be endangered at the end of their 210-year reign.[63] In 12 BC, disasters took place frequently.[64] In responding to this, Gu Yong 谷永 (?–9 BC) mentioned that the Han house was heading toward the end of its 210 years of rule.[65] If we take 202 BC as the year when Liu Bang established the Western Han dynasty, then the end of the cycle would be in AD 8. Therefore, according to Lu, the emperor should be more careful about his behavior and governance.[66] As critical as the "Three-Seven Predicament" would be, Lu Wenshu and Gu Yong supported the Han imperial house as Liu Xiang and Li Xun's groups did and believed that the Han empire's better performance in government was essential in dealing with this crisis.

Wang Mang, on the other hand, used Lu Wenshu's prophecy to legitimate the establishment of his new dynasty. In AD 9, the year after the Han's 210-year cycle ended, Wang enthroned himself and enforced a series of reforms.⁶⁷ When abolishing the Han currency, Wang Mang gave a speech about the Three-Seven Predicament:

予前在大麓，至于攝假，深惟漢氏三七之阸，赤德氣盡，思索廣求，所以輔劉延期之述，靡所不用。. . . 赤世計盡，終不可強濟。皇天明威，黃德當興，隆顯大命，屬予以天下。今百姓咸言皇天革漢而立新，廢劉而興王。⁶⁸

When I previously was in [the position of] the chief director of the administration, and became Regent and Acting [Emperor], I pondered deeply the Three-seven Predicament of the Han dynasty, that the emanation of virtue from the Red was exhausted. I thought and sought, searching widely for means whereby I might support the Liu [house] and lengthen its period [on the throne]. There was nothing that I failed to do. . . . Since the calculated [number of years allotted] for the age of the Red was exhausted, I could not eventually have had the power to save [that dynasty]. August Heaven made plain its majesty, so that the virtue of the Yellow [Lord] was due to arise and to make [Heaven's] great mandate abundantly apparent, entrusting me with the empire. Now the people all say that August Heaven has dethroned the Han [dynasty] and set up the Xin [dynasty], that he has dismissed the Liu [clan from the throne] and caused the Wang [clan] to rise.⁶⁹

Wang Mang explicitly points out that the Three-Seven Predicament indicates the end of the ruling cycle for the Red, or the Liu house.⁷⁰ Following Liu Xiang and Liu Xin's proposal of the succession order of the Five Phases by generation, Wang Mang claims that the Yellow, a metonym for the phase of earth, rose and thus he ruled (see tables 2 and 3).⁷¹

In his speech, Wang Mang presents himself in dual roles. On the one hand, he used to be a subject of the Liu house. As a diligent official and enthusiastic supporter of the imperial house, he tried his best to prolong their mandate. However, this is the prelude to what he really wants to say: the cycle of Five Phases is unstoppable, and he, representing the Yellow, will replace the Liu family in ruling China. Therefore, he is the new emperor of a new era, equal to that of the Liu house.

For Wang Mang, the progression of the Five Phases was so powerful that he was obliged to abolish the current imperial house and take the crown.

Could the Han emperor cultivate his morality more, bring more benefit to the populace, and try to connect to Heaven more closely to prolong his rule? For Wang Mang, the answer would be no. His strong insistence on dynastic change defined the political culture of the first century AD. When new generations of warlords competed over the throne, they carried on Wang's understanding of dynastic changes.

Which Phase, Whose Rule?

Wang Mang's frequent but ineffective reforms upset his fledgling regime, and his implacable opponents eventually overthrew him. However, they faced a question: Who was qualified to found the next dynasty? There were two easy options. The first one follows the proceedings of the Five Phases. After Wang Mang's rule, the next receiver of the mandate would be a representative of the phase of metal, after the phase of earth. The second one simply treats Wang's regime as an interruption of the normal succession, like the Qin dynasty; it states that the wheel of the Five Phases still rests at the Liu family.

Both theories and the rationales behind them circulated widely in China in the first century AD. Three major military groups, that of Gongsun Shu 公孫述 (AD?–36), that of the Red Eyebrow (Chimei 赤眉),[72] and that of Liu Xiu 劉秀 (6 BC–AD 57), advocated one of the two theories to claim the mandate to rule. Gongsun Shu, a warlord occupying the Shu 蜀 area (approximately modern Sichuan Province), claimed that he represented the phase of metal, and he would follow Wang Mang's reign to become the new emperor.[73] The leaders of the Red Eyebrow and Liu Xiu, on the other hand, believed that the Liu family would come back and rule.[74]

The three groups competed for military dominance as much as political legitimacy. For example, they all named an emperor in AD 25. In their claims, they employed vocabulary that was familiar to literati in the first century BC and common to apocryphal texts. It was in this context that apocryphal texts took shape from a few sentences of prophecy to a corpus of books attached to the classics.

Gongsun Shu's Revealed Message

Based on the *History of the Later Han*, a revealed dream triggered Gongsun Shu's decision to enthrone himself. One night, he dreamed of a person saying to him: "*Basi zixi*, take twelve as the expected time" (八厶子系，十二為期). Not befuddled by this apparently confusing sentence, he woke up and asked his wife whether the throne was worth pursuing, since according to the dream, he would not possess it very long. She replied by paraphrasing a saying from the *Analects*: "If one hears the Way in the morning, it will even be fine for him to die in the afternoon, not to mention twelve!"[75] Even more bizarre, a dragon appeared shining in the hall of their house while they were having this conversation. Fully convinced by these omens, Gongsun Shu had the phrase "Emperor Gongsun" (Gongsun Di 公孫帝) tattooed on his palm. In the fourth month of AD 25, he claimed the crown and chose white—corresponding to metal—as the color of the dynasty and the reign name "Rising Dragon" (Longxing 龍興).[76]

As outlandish as this anecdote might sound, it contains several elements and motives familiar to Wang Mang and many literati then. First, *basi zixi* 八厶子系 is an easily recognized way to refer to Gongsun 公孫, by juxtaposing the components of the two characters. Second, in the story, we find a message to Gongsun Shu that advises him to accept the mandate. This kind of omen with an unambiguous message is plentiful in Wang Mang's reign, such as a white stone with the inscription announcing Wang Mang as the new emperor, and a bronze tally commanding Wang Mang to take the mandate. In fact, Wang Mang used up to twelve omens to weave a delicate narrative of how the Liu family lost their mandate, and how he was named the rightful successor.[77] Third, Gongsun Shu adopted white as his dynastic color. According to the theory of the Five Phases, white symbolizes the phase of metal. Therefore, he claimed that his dynasty followed Wang Mang's reign in the order of Succession by Generation.

Liu Xiu and His Enthronement

The later founder of the Eastern Han, Liu Xiu went through a similar process to claim the throne, in which prophecies played a very important role. He also claimed to have had a dream, in which a red dragon rose into the sky. After telling his followers, as Gongsun Shu did, he received a positive response that he should claim the throne: the dream manifested the mandate of Heaven.[78] When Liu Xiu and his group arrived in the place called Gao 鄗, Qiang Hua 彊華, Liu Xiu's old classmate when he was in Chang'an studying the *Documents*,[79] came from Guanzhong 關中 with a prophecy called the *Red Hidden Tally* (*Chifu fu* 赤伏符). The prophecy reads this way:

劉秀發兵捕不道，四夷雲集龍鬥野，四七之際火為主。⁸⁰

> Liu Xiu will send out the troops to capture those who deviate from the Way. The barbarians of the four directions will gather like clouds, and the dragon will fight [them] in the wild. At the time of Four-Seven, the Fire will become the master.

Taking advantage of this event, Liu Xiu's followers, after several unsuccessful attempts, convinced him to enthrone himself:

受命之符，人應為大，萬里合信，不議同情，周之白魚，曷足比焉？今上無天子，海內淆亂，符瑞之應，昭然著聞，宜答天神，以塞群望。⁸¹

> As for the tallies of receiving the mandate, the people's response is the most significant. Having matched the tally from over ten thousand *li* away, the situation identical [everywhere] without having consulted, how can [even] the white fish of Zhou compare with this? Now there is no son of Heaven above, and within the four seas all is chaotic. The correspondence of tallies and omens is clearly obvious. It will be proper to respond to the heavenly spirits, and to satisfy the crowd's hope.

This time, they succeeded. On August 5, AD 25, a few months after Gongsun Shu's declaration, Liu Xiu made a sacrifice to Heaven and claimed the throne. His followers all believed that this "matched the heart of Heaven and Earth."⁸²

In the *Red Hidden Tally* as well as the pleas of Liu Xiu's followers, all the allusions and circumlocutions point to a central message: Liu is the legitimate recipient of the heavenly mandate, representing the phase of fire. In the former text, "Four-Seven" means "twenty-eight," referring to the 228 years since the establishment of the Western Han dynasty (202 BC) to AD 25. The sentence thus means at the time of 228 years, the phase of fire will still be dominant.

As if the message were not clear enough, the prophecy specifically mentions the name Liu Xiu. And this is not the first time prophecies mentioned the name Liu Xiu. The *History of the Later Han* records that when Liu Xiu was still a nobody, a prophecy predicted that a man of his name would be the next son of Heaven. Liu Xin, the hero of our last chapter, even changed his name to "Liu Xiu" in order to fulfill the prophecy.⁸³ Therefore, for Liu Xiu and his followers, the appearance of the *Red Hidden Tally* confirmed the previous prophecy and hence their belief that Liu Xiu was to be the next son of Heaven.

The speech of Liu Xiu's followers alludes to the world of omens. It first points out that the "people's response," or Qiang Hua's arrival from Guanzhong, is the most significant omen. Then it alludes to the event of white fish, a story from the *Documents* transmitted in the Western Han dynasty. When King Wu of Zhou was traveling by water to overthrow the evil Shang king Zhou 紂, a white fish jumped into his boat—an auspicious omen.[84]

Surrounded by rivals' omens, Liu Xiu's followers were aware of the competition over omens. They claimed that the omen Liu Xiu just received, namely, Qiang Hua's handing in the *Red Hidden Tally*, was the supreme one. By using comparison, their speech enters the competition over legitimate omens. Even the omen for King Wu, the one stressing the legitimacy of the great Zhou's Golden Age, could not compare to it.

Competing Authority between Liu Xiu and Gongsun Shu

In AD 27, Gongsun had been claiming that the phase of fire had already expired, and that he, representing the phase of metal, should be the next son of Heaven.[85] Most interesting is not what he wanted but the way he promoted this idea. Following Wang Mang, Gongsun Shu alluded to the *Annals*. Based on the number of dukes in the *Annals* (twelve), he argued that the Han should have had twelve emperors as well. Since at the time there had already been twelve rulers,[86] the Han had used up its allotment. Once again, Gongsun Shu appropriated the link between the Han house and the *Annals* in order to sabotage rather than consolidate the Han's, and therefore his rival Liu Xiu's, legitimacy.

Besides referring to the classics, Gongsun Shu alluded to passages from three texts:

《錄運法》曰：廢昌帝，立公孫。

The *Recorded Rule for the Conveyance of the Mandate* says: "Abolish Emperor Chang, and establish Gongsun."

《括地象》曰：帝軒轅受命，公孫氏握。

The *Inclusive Images of Earth*[87] says: Emperor Xuanyuan [Yellow Emperor] received the mandate, and Gongsun grasps it.

《援神契》曰：西太守，乙卯金。⁸⁸

The *Tally for Assistance from Spirits* says: The western Grand Minister crushed *maojin* (Liu).⁸⁹

The titles of these texts were later included in the apocryphal corpus,⁹⁰ and the *Tally for Assistance from Spirits* was frequently mentioned in Emperor Ming's 明 reign (AD 57–75).⁹¹ The three quotations all identify someone named Gongsun as the new receiver of the mandate and the exterminator of the Liu family.

Agitated by this, Liu Xiu wrote Gongsun Shu a letter. Interestingly, he did not invalidate the texts Gongsun Shu used. For example, he did not say that the *Recorded Rule for the Movement of the Mandate* was a forgery. Instead, he questioned Gongsun Shu's understanding of it. As to the name "Gongsun," Liu Xiu claimed that it did not refer to Gongsun Shu but to Emperor Xuan of Han. In chapter 1, we have already seen Sui Meng predict the end of the Han dynasty based on the prophecy: "*Gongsun bingyi* will be established" (*gongsun bingyi li* 公孫病已立).⁹² Liu Xiu took this prophecy out of context and identified the *gongsun* part as reference to Emperor Xuan, since Emperor Xuan's original name was Bingyi 病已.⁹³ The term *gongsun* thus means "the grandson of the lord," instead of a surname. In this way, Liu Xiu turned Gongsun Shu's prophecies around to support the Liu house.

Neither Liu nor Gongsun invented his arguments out of nothing. The competition for legitimacy between them highlighted existing propaganda tools, especially classics and ways of interpreting omens. These seemingly befuddling prophecies are carefully designed to win their audience's support. The twelve dukes of the *Annals*, the story of the white fish, the content of the *Red Hidden Tally*, and even the paraphrasing of the *Analects* by Gongsun Shu's wife are allusions to the classics and to well-known incidents with definite meanings to intellectual communities in the first century AD. The debate between them was thus an occasion for each of them to challenge his opponents and impress potential supporters through shared knowledge. This political conflict is the context in which the corpus of apocryphal texts took its initial shape. The campaigns of both sides were no more irrational, keeping in mind their audiences, than those of the most recent US presidential election.

Classicists and the Great Families

Who was the intended audience of Liu Xiu and Gongsun Shu's performances? "The classicists" seems to be the answer. Based on the prophecies and on accounts of Liu Xiu and Gongsun Shu's self-enthronement, the intended audience consisted of those familiar with the *Annals* and the *Documents*, and who had a basic understanding of the Five Phases as well as a decent acquaintance with Han political history. They might also be well informed about prophecies and revealed texts that are no longer extant.[94] Undoubtedly, the polymaths who had lived through the last fifty years of the Western Han dynasty would find these speeches easy to follow, and some of them would even find them convincing. The minor ones who went to the capital to learn the classics during Wang Mang's time were probably also able to penetrate these riddles, given Wang Mang's high-profile propaganda.[95]

Why, then, did Liu Xiu and Gongsun Shu strive to gain support from classicists? In the first century AD, most people trained in the classics were from well-off families who owned local lands and controlled local social connections. Since the mid–Western Han, they had accumulated great wealth and social power through landownership.[96] By investing in classical training, they turned themselves into officials and literati. These families would provide logistical as well as military support to warlords like Gongsun Shu and Liu Xiu. Behind Liu Xiu's glorious image as the chosen son of Heaven, these families paved the road to the throne.[97] According to Kimura Masao 木村正雄, competing military groups such as those of Gongsun Shu and Kui Xiao 隗囂 (?–AD 33) relied heavily on local gentry in the Tianshui 天水 and Shu 蜀 areas.[98]

The local gentries had started to study the classics since Emperor Wu's reign because such expertise led to official positions and even the emperor's favor.[99] After several generations, in Emperor Yuan's reign (49–33 BC), the majority of high governmental officials had training in the classics, and some of them were leading scholars in the court.[100] Until Wang Mang's time, the classics had become indispensable for structuring the government, and classicists like Liu Xin took some of the highest positions. The classics had become a sacred object among the literati in intellectual and political spheres.

Consequently, the classics became central in maintaining solidarity and forming alliances. The leaders of those groups, such as Liu Xiu and Kui Xiao, were trained in the classics. In Wang Mang's interregnum, Liu Xin even recommended Kui for the prestigious appointment as a Gentleman (Shi 士), an assistant to the *shanggong* 上公, or the Upper Ducal Minister (*shanggong* 上公), a position designed specifically for Liu Xin himself.[101] Group leaders without training in the classics tended to seek people with that training. For instance, Fan Chong 樊崇, the leader of the Red Eyebrow, nominated Xu Xuan 徐宣 as their Grand Chancellor because of the latter's expertise in the *Changes*.[102] The warlord leaders were also eager to make alliances with the local gentry in the places that they occupied. Occupying Sichuan, Gongsun Shu had a list of people there to pursue: scholars like Qiao Xuan 譙玄 with expertise in the *Changes* and the *Annals*, Li Ye 李業 with training in the Lu tradition of the *Poetry*, and Ren Yong 任永 and Feng Xin 馮信 with "affection for learning."[103]

The Classicists and Prophets from Liu Xiu's Group

So far we have seen how, after Wang Mang's interregnum, knowledge of the classics became crucial in the sociopolitical realm through the period of war. The literati continued to exploit and appropriate this knowledge together with contemporary intellectual issues, which had developed in the last fifty years of the first century BC. With classicism in mind, we might have a better chance in answering these questions: If the prophecies were not from Heaven, then who made them up? What was their intellectual background?

Because these prophecies do not directly reveal their human authorship, a handy way to examine this issue is to search for people who first mentioned these prophecies or were in charge of dealing with them. Following this rule of thumb, we have a few candidates in Liu Xiu's group, whom the *History of the Later Han* describes as specialists in apocrypha and prophecies. This attribution is based on hindsight, because the apocrypha of the classics probably did not grow into a corpus of texts until AD 50.[104] In the twenties and before, there were only short, scattered prophecies without obvious links to the classics.[105]

We can find people who brought prophecies to Liu Xiu, such as his old classmate Qiang Hua or Cai Shaogong 蔡少公.[106] Nevertheless, the most important person who inspired Liu Xiu to use prophecies and who later compiled apocrypha is Li Tong 李通 (?–AD 42). The background of Li Tong matched every criterion of a good alliance for warlords like Liu Xiu. He came from a great family of Nanyang and studied the classics with Liu Xin. During Wang Mang's time, he was the Teacher of the Imperial House (*zong qingshi* 宗卿師).[107]

Liu Xiu first went to meet Li Tong during the last years of Wang Mang's rule because he considered Li a "gentleman" (*shi junzi* 士君子). The latter did not waste this compliment. He brought up a prophecy from his father Li Shou 李守: the Liu lineage will rise again, and the Li lineage will assist them (*Liu shi fuxing, Li shi wei fu* 劉氏復興，李氏為輔). After hearing Li Tong's plans, Liu Xiu made an alliance with him and determined a time for their revolt.[108] Later on, while Liu Xiu was on military campaigns, Li Tong was in charge of maintaining morale in the capital and restoring the National Academy—that is, he was in charge of propaganda.[109] Because he decided what to teach people in the capital and in the academy, Li did not just restore the academy but renewed the routine curriculum with more current issues as well as knowledge concerning the ideological debates of the time.

Having the opportunity to implant their agenda with the rest of the literati, Liu Xin and Li Tong faced another issue: how to naturally do so without shaking the existing curriculum. With certain prophecies in hand, they could follow the way conventional since the mid-second century BC: promote the texts as the classics. As convenient as it might sound, a lesson we learned from Liu Xin and Li Xun's debate is that the classicists then were repulsed by unprovenanced "classics" (*jing* 經). Thus Liu Xiu was cautious in raising any of those prophecies to the position of the classics; he was unwilling to promote any text to even compete with the classics. For example, Su Jing 蘇竟 (fl. 40 BC–AD 30), a scholar of the *Changes* and a colleague of Liu Xin editing texts in Wang Mang's time, quoted the *Secret Classic of Confucius*, or *Kong Qiu mijing* 孔丘秘經 to persuade Liu Xin's nephew Liu Gong 劉龔 to surrender to Liu Xiu. Although Su Jing succeeded in persuading Liu Gong, Liu Xiu did not recognize any legitimacy in the *Secret Classic of Confucius*.

Instead, Liu Xiu and his followers integrated the prophecies with the classics; he made them the commentaries instead of the body of the classical canon. He further refined and transformed the prophecies by employing classicists to edit them and link them with the classics. Beginning very early in his reign, he employed the classicists to edit these prophecies. For example, he ordered Xue Han 薛漢 (fl. AD 25–72), an Academician of the Hán 韓 tradition of the *Poetry*, to edit these prophecies (or *tuchen* 圖讖, as the *History of the Later Han* renders them). He also asked Yin Min 尹敏 (fl. AD 26–68) to do the same thing, precisely because the latter was a great classicist with training in the Ouyang and old text traditions of the *Documents*, the Mao tradition of the *Poetry*, and the Guliang and Zuo traditions of the *Annals*.[110] In AD 50, when Zhang Chun 張純 (?–AD 56) suggested that Liu Xiu follow classical traditions and build an imperial ceremonial hall and school called Biyong 辟雍, "prophecies" (*chen* 讖) did not appear just as prophecies in the list of texts alone, but were preceded by "seven classics" (*qi jing* 七經), namely, the Six Classics with the *Classic of Filial Piety* (*Xiaojing* 孝經).[111] Zhang explicitly linked this corpus of prophecies to the classics.

Seen as contamination of the original corpus, this innovative strategy of combining prophecies with the classics met stiff but failed resistance from some classicists. Yin Min, for example, argued that the prophecies were not written by the sages, implying that they therefore should not be included among the sages' writings.[112] Huan Tan 桓譚 (23 BC–AD 50), who had academic interactions with Yang Xiong and Liu Xin, disparaged the prophecies, disclaiming their links to the classics.[113] However, none of these arguments stopped the process of integration. In AD 56, Liu Xiu announced the apocryphal texts to the world.[114] After years of use in supporting of Liu Xiu's legitimacy, prophecies became apocryphal texts and eventually gained official recognition as part of the commentarial traditions of the classics.

In the first decades of the first century AD, the competition over the throne led to intellectual innovation. Heaven's will was still the largest concern among the literati. But in contrast with the last years of the Western Han, it did not necessarily go to the Liu family; people explored various possibilities and theorized them. Classicism was not obliterated by this political orientation but adapted to it. If we just saw Liu Xiu as a schemer who contaminated existing transmission lines, and apocrypha as political hokum, we would miss the innovativeness: apocryphal texts were designed as much to gain the literati's support as to be less provocative than Liu Xin and Li Xun. Their themes about Heaven and the classics were aimed to blend into the intellectual conversations of the time; their mentioning of the Five Phases and omens were aimed to communicate with fellow literati; their cloak of commentary was aimed to avoid disapproval. Liu Xiu did not have Liu Xin's luxury of protection from Wang Mang and various leading scholars of the time; in the literally cutthroat competition, his plans for apocrypha were an example of innovation for survival.

A Case Study: Liu Xiu's *Feng* and *Shan* Sacrifices

Legitimacy always haunts a founder of a new dynasty. In the previous sections, we have already seen the competition among Liu Xiu and his contemporaries for political legitimacy. After Liu defeated his rivals, the problem of legitimating his rule was not yet resolved. He needed to prove that he was more than just another ruthless conqueror. As the chosen one, he was expected to deliver the ideal state of society: the Great Peace. Now the question was how to make the establishment of the Great Peace clear. In AD 56, Liu Xiu made a journey to perform ceremonies for this purpose. As we will see, apocryphal texts played an important role.

The ceremonies were the *feng* 封 and *shan* 禪 sacrifices.¹¹⁵ The basic principle of the former is to build an altar at the top of Mount Tai 泰山 to sacrifice to Heaven. In the latter ceremony, one clears an area of ground at a minor mountain near Mount Tai and sacrifices to Earth.¹¹⁶ In the Han people's eyes, the *feng* and *shan* sacrifices were a response to Heaven's mandate and to inform Heaven of an emperor's achievement.¹¹⁷ According to many Eastern Han scholars, emperors should do the *feng* sacrifice only after they achieved the Great Peace.¹¹⁸ In Liu Xiu's time, the two most recent precedents were the sacrifice made by the First Emperor (r. 259–210 BC) and Emperor Wu.¹¹⁹ For Han historians like Sima Qian 司馬遷 (ca. 145–ca. 87 BC) and Ban Gu, the First Emperor's sacrifice failed, since Heaven sent down storms to show its disapproval.¹²⁰

Therefore, when Zhao Xi 趙憙 (4 BC–AD 80) brought up the sacrifices in AD 54, Liu Xiu was very cautious about them. Zhao proposed that Liu's sagely virtue (*sheng de* 聖德) had led to clear peace (*qing ping* 清平) so he should do the *feng* sacrifice in order to "follow the heart of Heaven" (*cheng tian xin* 承天心).¹²¹ Liu immediately declined: "I have ruled for thirty years, but resentful *qi* fills the populace's bellies. Whom am I going to deceive, Heaven?"¹²² Given the poor situation of the people, he seemed unwilling to make this controversial claim.

The final decision of practicing the *feng* and *shan* sacrifices was, not surprisingly, inspired by an apocryphal text. One night in the first month of AD 56, the emperor was reading the River Chart's *Tally of Meeting with Prosperity* (*Hetu huichang fu* 河圖會昌符), and he encountered this passage:

赤劉之九，會命岱宗。不慎克用，何益於承。誠善用之，姦偽不萌。¹²³

> The ninth generation of the red Liu will encounter the mandate at Daizong [Mount Tai]. If you do not carefully employ it, what is the benefit of receiving it? If you indeed use it well, the evil and fraudulent will not germinate.

The ninth generation of the red Liu indicates Liu Xiu, since he was the ninth generation since the founder of the Western Han. The word *cheng* corresponds to the same word in Zhao Xi's "follow the heart of Heaven." As puzzling as the passage is, the central message is clear: Liu Xiu needed to go to Mount Tai, so that he would not waste his mandate. Following this instruction, Liu ordered people to prepare the *feng* and *shan* sacrifices based on relevant apocryphal texts that were named after the River Charts and Luo Writing.[124]

On the second day of the second month in AD 56, Liu Xiu with his entourage performed the *feng* sacrifice at Mount Tai. The general idea of the ceremony was to send a message inscribed on a jade plate to Heaven. The main procedure involves putting a 1.2-x-0.7-x-1.2-meter jade plate with an inscription on it below two 1.2-x-1.2-x-0.2-meter stones at the altar and sealing them with stone bars and the imperial stamp.[125] The ceremony ended by erecting a stele at the altar, which was prepared before the ceremony. On the twenty-fifth day, the imperial party held the *shan* sacrifice at the northern part of Liangfu 梁甫, a minor mountain near the foot of Mount Tai. The ceremony was to sacrifice to Earth, though unlike the *feng* sacrifice, it did not include a message sent to Earth, nor was a stele erected.[126]

The inscription on the stele is informative; from it we can understand what was in Liu Xiu's mind in communicating with Heaven. The inscription starts by introducing the attendants of the ceremony, why the event was held, Liu's achievement, and the schedule of the ceremonies. In the inscription, apocryphal texts play a very important role in justifying this occasion and establishing Liu's achievement. It quotes from several apocryphal texts in the following order:

《河圖赤伏符》曰："劉秀發兵捕不道，四夷雲集龍鬥野，四七之際火為主。"[127]

> The *Red Hidden Tally of the River Chart* says: Liu Xiu will send out the troops to capture those who deviate from the Way. The barbarians of the four directions will gather like clouds, and the dragon will fight in the wild. At the time of Four-Seven the Fire will become the master.

This passage is the one that around AD 25 Liu's classmate Qiang Hua brought to him. In AD 56, this prophecy no longer stood alone; its title included the modifier *River Chart*, the text from which, according to the apocryphal texts, the eight trigrams were derived. Among the quotations, this is the only one that is not directly relevant to the *feng* and *shan* sacrifices. It was aimed to show that Liu Xiu was the legitimate recipient of the heavenly mandate.

The next quotation is an elaborate version of what Liu Xiu had earlier read from the *River Chart's Tally of Meeting Prosperity*:

The Conflation between Heaven and the Classics

《河圖會昌符》曰:"赤帝九世,巡省得中,治平則封,誠合帝道孔矩,則天文靈出,地祇瑞興。帝劉之九,會命岱宗,誠善用之,姦偽不萌。赤漢德興,九世會昌,巡岱皆當。"128

The *River Chart's Tally of Meeting Prosperity* says: "The ninth generation of the red emperor does traveling inspections. When he achieves orderly peace, he carries out the *feng* sacrifice. When it corresponds to the Way of [sage] emperors and the standard of Confucius, heavenly patterns marvelously come out, and earthly deities auspiciously arise. The ninth generation of the red Liu is destined to receive the mandate at Daizong [Mount Tai]. If you indeed use it carefully, the evil and fraudulent will not germinate. The virtue of the red Han has been rising, and it meets with prosperity in the ninth generation. Traveling to Mount Tai is quite suitable."

According to this passage, the emperor should do the *feng* sacrifice after he achieves the orderly peace, which should be based on the way of the sage kings and Confucius. In order to achieve that state, the emperor still needs to work on implementing the way. The word *hui* 會 indicates that it was the right time for Liu to rise. This passage does not emphasize his personal qualities, but it claims that it was his destiny to achieve a peaceful state.

The following quotation turns to Liu Xiu's characteristics to a greater degree:

《河圖提劉予》曰:"九世之帝,方明聖,持衡拒,九州平,天下予。"129

The *Bestowal to the Promoted Liu of the River Chart* says: "The emperor of the ninth generation is bright and sagely. He holds the yard-arm scale and carpenter's square, and the Nine Provinces are peaceful. Then All-under-Heaven are bestowed [to him]."

The yard-arm scale and carpenter's square are metaphors for standards and principles. This passage admits Liu Xiu's distinctive characteristics as a sage king. Given these traits, the world is peaceful. Together with the two previous quotations, these apocryphal texts convey a message: Liu Xiu was the destined emperor who was sagely and able to bring a peaceful state to the world.

The *feng* and *shan* sacrifices reveal a repetitive motif in Chinese political history: the announcement of one's superior rulership through political propaganda. Many elements in this incident were familiar: Heaven's mandate, the sagely king, and the "orderly peace." The crux that links them together is rather new: apocryphal texts. Through them, Liu claimed to be the sage king who was destined to bring the Great Peace to the world. No matter whether there was someone who was more virtuous than Liu Xiu, Heaven as the ultimate agent had already decided everything. It is hard to say how many people really believed Liu Xiu's claims. However, this question became a moot point when he died two years after the sacrifices. All-under-Heaven, then, needed a new ruler to lead them to the Great Peace, and he too would be responsible for proving that he was the chosen one.

Concluding Remarks

In this chapter, we have seen the formation of apocryphal texts. As intellectual innovations, they were the continuation of late Western Han debate: Should one understand Heaven's will through the classics or directly through Heaven? They joined this debate by offering their stance: they claim to be the divinely revealed commentaries on the classics. They decode the hidden messages in the classics so that one can understand Heaven's will. The sociopolitical context generates needs, which innovations are designed to fulfill. Specifically in the first decades of first century AD, when warlords competed over the legitimacy of their rule, they manipulated prophecies, a popular strategy then, to convey Heaven's preference for them. Taking this a step further, Liu Xiu and his group started the process of integrating the classics with these prophecies. Through this process, scattered prophecies grew together as keys to the classical traditions of the period. In turn, Liu Xiu used apocryphal texts to perform the *feng* and *shan* sacrifices to legitimate his rule.

Apocryphal texts did not cease to exist after Emperor Guangwu. With the sponsorship of the imperial house and many scholars' favor, they lived on as a means of understanding the classics in the Eastern Han dynasty. In the next chapter, we will see how Liu Xiu's son Liu Zhuang 劉莊 (AD 28–75), or Emperor Ming 明 (r. AD 58–75), the other emperor who still had firm control of his dynasty,[130] used apocrypha along with other texts for his own purposes, and how he appropriated the image of Confucius to legitimate himself as a sage king who was able to achieve the Great Peace.

Chapter 3

Apocrypha, Confucius, and Monarchy in Emperor Ming's Reign (AD 58–75)

In the previous chapter, we saw some main characteristics of apocryphal texts, and how they were of interest in political struggles in the first half of the first century AD. Liu Xiu and his followers were not the only group that sought to manipulate prophecies and the classics, but they were certainly the most successful. His group integrated prophecies with commentarial traditions of the classics. Apocrypha—revealed commentaries that could decode the classics—were the product of this integration. If one opens the compilation of apocryphal texts by Yasui Kōzan 安居香山 and Nakamura Shōhachi 中村璋八, one can easily find fragments that celebrate the legitimacy and superiority of the Liu family.[1] Heaven's approval and support undoubtedly played a crucial role in singling Liu Xiu out from his competitors and convincing others that he was the one to rule.

His son, Liu Zhuang 劉莊 (AD 28–75), or Emperor Ming 明帝, faced a different situation: he needed to convince others that among his brothers, or any other Lius, he was the right person to rule. As the fourth son of Liu Xiu, he did not become the heir apparent until AD 43.[2] In comparison with his elder brother Liu Qiang 劉彊 (AD 25–58), who became the heir apparent at age one, Liu Zhuang was less well recognized.[3] He might have been anxious about his credentials as heir apparent, particularly because his appointment resulted from his mother Yin Lihua's 陰麗華 (AD 4–64) victory in harem politics and her promotion to the position of empress in AD 41.[4] These issues were more than just psychological complexes in Emperor Ming's mind; they could be used by his opponents to sabotage his rule.

Therefore, Emperor Ming needed to appear as a qualified ruler, more qualified than any of his brothers—he needed to be the sage ruler who could bring the Great Peace to the Han empire. This chapter tells the story of Emperor Ming's sage king dream. In this process, Emperor Ming took certain elements from existing classical traditions and rearranged them. We will see that emperors, especially those in positions similar to Emperor Ming, were not isolated from contemporary intellectual changes. On the contrary, they eagerly and anxiously engaged in and responded to them.

Emperor Ming had a plan to appear as a sage king: he represented himself as a latter-day Confucius. Confucius has been a compelling figure to people of all walks of life over time. However, the image of Confucius has not been stable, and people of different periods imagined this philosopher in very different ways. From the last century BC to the second century AD, scholars of the Han dynasty thought of Confucius not as a great, human philosopher but as a semi-divine being. In these scholars' writings, they view Confucius as *xuan sheng* 玄聖, the dark sage, and *su wang* 素王, the uncrowned king.[5] This is particularly true in apocrypha. In this chapter, we will see how Emperor Ming tried to fit into this particular image of Confucius.

We will start with Confucius's divine origin in apocrypha, and how with divine power as the uncrowned king, he was able to confer the mandate of Heaven upon the legitimate successor of the Zhou dynasty, namely, the Han, and to convey the ultimate political principles and moral teachings to its emperor. Apocryphal texts depicted Confucius as a sage king who used the *Annals* to convey information and the mandate of Heaven to the new Han emperors. Correspondingly, in apocrypha, his major disciples became his subjects in an "ideal kingdom," defined by a set of ideal relationships between Confucius (the king) and his disciples (servants). The parallelism between the lord-minister relationship and the master-disciple relationship drawn in a conversation between Emperor Ming and one of his officials compares the Han dynasty with Confucius's "kingdom." Emperor Ming thus claimed that he was a sage king, defending himself against contemporaries' dissatisfaction with Han rule, but accepting their principle that only sages could bring the Great Peace (*taiping* 太平) to the world.

Xuan sheng: The Dark Sage

In apocryphal texts, Confucius often bears the names *xuan sheng* 玄聖 and *su wang* 素王. The two terms come from one of the outer chapters of *Zhuangzi*; they describe the relationship between the way of Heaven, the way of the emperor, and the way of the sage:[6]

夫虛靜恬淡，寂寞無為者，萬物之本也。明此以南鄉，堯之為君也；明此以北面，舜之為臣也。以此處上，帝王天子之德也；以此處下，玄聖素王之道也。⁷

Emptiness, stillness, placidity, mildness, quietude, indifference, nonaction—these are the root of the myriad things. Understanding this as the south-facing ruler, Yao was lord; understanding this as the north-facing minister, Shun was his subject. Occupying a superior position with this understanding is the virtue of emperors, kings, and the son of heaven; occupying an inferior position with this understanding is the way of dark sages and plain kings [uncrowned kings].⁸

The passage focuses on what human beings will become after they achieve "emptiness, stillness, placidity, mildness, quietude, indifference, nonaction," or Zhuangzi's characteristics of the Way. The practitioners of the Way surely will become supreme persons.⁹ However, since their supremacy based on the Way does not affect distinctions in the social realm, they may occupy unequal social positions, as shown in the case of the mythic dynastic founders Yao 堯 and Shun 舜. The passage does not complain that people are treated differently in society even when they possess equal virtues; it rather says that with a grasp of the Way, no matter what position a person is in, he will become a supreme person.¹⁰ Even if he is just a commoner, his understanding of the Way will still make him a sage, perhaps a sage king, but he will not ever hold an official position. In this context, the "plain king" can actually refer to the plain color of the person's dress, indicating low rank. "Dark" in "dark sage" can mean "obscure," implying that his position is a low one: he is a sage whom no one knows.¹¹

Based on this context, *xuan sheng* and *su wang* carried several connotations in Han times. First, they indicated people who had achieved spiritual power. Later on in the Han, spiritual power was not only linked to the Way as it was in the *Zhuangzi*, but it could also include moral authority and ultimate political principles. Second, this spiritual power was unaccompanied by political authority. Third, since Shun in the example became a king after having been a vassal, a "dark sage" or "uncrowned king" had virtues that made a person a candidate for kingship. When writers of this time described Confucius with these names, they did so with extended meanings that resolved the following contradiction: If Shun became a king, why not Confucius?

Let us survey how the use of these two terms in Han apocryphal texts resolved that contradiction. In *Chunqiu yan Kong tu* 春秋演孔圖 (The Diagrams of the *Annals of Spring and Autumn* Deduced by Confucius),[12] Confucius is called *xuan sheng* 玄聖, or the "dark sage":

孔子母徵在，夢感黑帝而生，故曰玄聖。[13]

Confucius's mother Zhengzai ["The Omen Is Present"] dreamed of being stimulated by the Black Emperor, and then gave birth to [Confucius]. Therefore he is called the "dark sage."

In view of the obvious fabrication of Confucius's mother's name, Zhengzai, the passage was intended to be prophetic. It explains why Confucius is *xuan sheng* by claiming that his mother conceived him by dreaming of being moved, or stimulated, by the Black Emperor. Therefore, following the logic of the passage, Confucius represents the color black and correspondently "water" in terms of the Five Phases. The passage depicts Confucius as half-human, half-deity; it assigns him a place in the cycle of the Five Phases. In the system of succession of dynasties, as found in apocryphal texts, founders of dynasties such as Yao, Shun, Tang, King Wen, and King Wu share two characteristics: they are conceived through a supernatural process in which a human father is not involved, and they belong to one of the Five Phases.[14] By fulfilling these criteria, this prophetic passage tries to depict Confucius as a potential emperor.

If Confucius was qualified, why did he not become an emperor? Apocryphal texts use the cycle of the Five Phases to in fact rule him out. They claimed that the reason for this was not because a former king did not recommend him;[15] it is because as a representative of the phase of water, he was not in the right sequence. As mentioned in chapter 2 (tables 2 and 3), by then, the literati perceived the dynastic changes based on how each phase generated the one next to it, or the generative succession (*xiang sheng* 相生). In this theory, the Zhou dynasty represented the phase of wood, and its successor should rightly be a representative of fire.

What is interesting as well, is the occasional contingency in the succession theory. Although it indicates how dynasties *ought* to succeed one another, a perfect succession was not always the case in reality.[16] The theory allows for the existence of dynasties that did not follow the right sequence, or that lacked virtue. In the *History of the Han* (written in the first century AD), for example, both the Qin dynasty and Gong Gong 共工, representatives of water (tables 2 and 3), are considered deviations from the "correct sequence" (非其序). But the theory does not explain why succession sometimes fails. Since the *History of the Han*'s explanation is based on generative succession, it is hard to see why a theory so fundamental would sometimes fail to explain what actually had occurred in history. However, one of the main aims of the discussion was to legitimize the Han dynasty. That is to say, despite how we tend to think of such things in modern times, the theory's proponents were not so much forming a philosophically or metaphysically rigorous theory, as identifying the Han dynasty as the legitimate successor of the Zhou dynasty.

At the same time, the notion of legitimate succession creates leeway that reconciles the problem of why Confucius, a great sage, did not actually become a king. As a sage of divine origin, he ought to have been quite capable of establishing a new dynasty. However, as a Shang descendant he represented the water force (since that dynasty was correlated to water). Because of the succession order, Confucius could not gain the throne, but he did have a unique function in it that was peculiar to the much later Han dynasty, and which can be seen in the apocryphal texts, where he is called "the lord of standard making" (制法之主):

邱為制法之主，黑綠不代蒼黃。[17]

Confucius was the lord of standard making. Black-green did not replace green-brown.

聖人不空生，必有所制，以顯天心。邱為木鐸，制法天下。[18]

The sage was not born in vain. He had to institute something to show the heart of Heaven. Confucius was the wooden tongue. He made standards for all under Heaven.

黑龍生為赤，必告示象，使知命。[19]

The black dragon was born for the red. It had to show the portents and make [people] know the mandate.

In the first quotation, Confucius, represented by the color black-green, could not replace the color of green-brown, the Zhou dynasty. However, he was responsible for forming standards, or *fa* 法, which were the templates and guides for later generations to use in correcting laws, rituals, and governing procedures. The second quotation conveys the notion that the birth of Confucius was not an accident but a necessity. He existed to show the intentions of Heaven via the standards he would make. A metaphor from the *Analects*, "wooden tongue," also emphasizes Confucius's role as the agent of Heaven who admonishes people.[20] The third quotation further indicates Confucius's specific mission: he came to the world to reveal the real successor of the Zhou dynasty, namely, the Liu 劉 family of the Han dynasty. Therefore, Confucius had two functions determined by the sequence of the Five Phases: to make standards and to reveal the true successor of the Zhou. These two functions have a corollary because Confucius was responsible for making human standards that showed Heaven's mandate, thus the successor of the Zhou dynasty he selected would not only possess but also keep the standards.

In what way did Confucius receive this message from Heaven and pass it on? As we saw in the previous chapter, according to apocrypha, sage kings constantly received guidance from Heaven. It is the same case for Confucius in apocrypha:

邱攬史記。援引古圖。推集天變。為漢帝制法，陳敘圖錄。[21]

Confucius perused historical records and cited old diagrams. He deduced and compiled the changes of Heaven. He made principles for the Han emperor, and set in order the diagrams and records.

孔子論經，有鳥化為書。孔子奉以告天。赤爵集書上，化為玉。刻曰：孔提命，作應法，為赤制。[22]

When Confucius talked about classics, there was a bird transforming into a book. Confucius took it to announce Heaven; red sparrows collected on the book and transformed into a piece of jade. The inscription on it said, "Kong, take up the mandate; make the corresponding principles for the red."

麟出周亡。故立《春秋》，制素王授當興也。[23]

The *qilin* appeared and the Zhou died out. Therefore, [Confucius] established the uncrowned king's *Annals of Spring and Autumn* to give it to whoever would arise.

In the first quotation, Confucius uses ancient material and the apparent changes in the heavens (e.g., celestial changes, changes of season, etc.) to make standards for the Han emperor. His citations of ancient texts and his astronomical calculations point to the Han dynasty as the successor of Zhou. Confucius is seen as the sage who possesses the correct guides and is able to understand the movements of Heaven. In other words, the first quotation emphasizes the crucial role Confucius plays in revealing Heaven's mandate. In the second quotation, through a series of preternatural transformations, the will of Heaven responds to Confucius and announces itself. In this context, Confucius is the messenger of Heaven. This quotation emphasizes the idea that the emergence of the Han dynasty, represented by the color red, follows the mandate of Heaven, which appears at the moment when Confucius is discussing the classics. This implies a connection between the classics and the will of Heaven. Later on we will see more examples of the mandate of Heaven, Confucius, and the classics as a triad that guarantees the legitimacy of Han rule.

The third quotation is another example of how the triad works. The untimely appearance of the mysterious *qilin* (an ancient mythic animal whose appearance was often considered auspicious) indicates that Heaven no longer favored the Zhou. Receiving this heavenly sign, Confucius composed the *Annals* in order to reveal to the future that the Han are the real successors of the Zhou. The author strings Heaven, Confucius, and the *Annals* together to show the legitimacy of Han rule. In order to understand the function of the *Annals of Spring and Autumn* and Confucius's role in this context, we now take up the references to Confucius as author of the *Annals* and as "uncrowned king."

Su Wang, the "Uncrowned King"

As *Zhuangzi* states, the "uncrowned king" refers to a person who possesses virtues equal to a sage king but has no official position. In the case of Confucius, his status as an "uncrowned king" was based on his purported authorship of the *Annals of Spring and Autumn*. During roughly the third century BC, people began attributing the authorship of the *Annals* to Confucius. This remained a dominant opinion throughout imperial China up to the early twentieth century,[24] particularly as it had been adapted by Mencius 孟子 in a famous statement, as follows:[25]

[孟子曰]世衰道微,邪說暴行有作,臣弒其君者有之,子弒其父者有之。孔子懼,作《春秋》。《春秋》,天子之事也。是故孔子曰:'知我者其惟《春秋》乎!罪我者其惟《春秋》乎!'[26]

[Mencius said] Again the world fell into decay, and principles faded away. Perverse speakings and oppressive deeds waxed rife again. There were instances of ministers who murdered their sovereigns, and of sons who murdered their fathers. Confucius was afraid, and made the *Annals of Spring and Autumn*. What the *Spring and Autumn* contains are matters proper to the sovereign. On this account Confucius said, "Yes! It is the *Spring and Autumn* which will make men know me, and it is the *Spring and Autumn* which will make men condemn me."[27]

In this passage, the motivation for Confucius to compose the *Annals of Spring and Autumn* was to criticize the wrongdoings of contemporaries. In the *Grand Historian's Records* (*Shiji* 史記), Sima Qian 司馬遷 (146–86 BC) elaborates the so-called praise-and-blame theory and claims that Confucius aimed to "make the affairs of the true king comprehensible 以達王事."[28] The scholars who studied and transmitted the *Gongyang* commentary on the *Annals* followed this reading, tending to find subtle praise and blame in every entry.[29] As Yuri Pines points out, they shared the idea that Confucius was a supreme sage and associated him with the *Gongyang* commentary.[30]

When it came to the first century CE, apocryphal texts held that the *Annals* reflect the moral authority and ultimate political principles formed by Confucius.[31] Confucius's composition of the *Annals* indicates his conception of an ideal kingdom ruled by virtue. Since he was born in a chaotic time, Heaven did not grant him the opportunity to practice his ideas. This theory also implies that every ruler must turn to Confucius's hidden teachings in the *Annals* to achieve an ideal state.[32] The image of Confucius as the uncrowned king was well received throughout the Han dynasty,[33] as Liu Xiang aptly wrote in his *The Garden of Persuasion* (*Shuiyuan* 說苑):

[孔子]卒不遇,故睹麟而泣,哀道不行,德澤不洽,於是退作春秋,明素王之道,以示後人。[34]

[Confucius] was not being appreciated at his end, so he wept when he saw the *qilin*. He lamented the Way not being practiced, and that virtue was not harmonized. Therefore he retreated to compose the *Annals* and illuminate the way of the uncrowned king in order to show it to later generations.

However, does the appellation "uncrowned king"[35] merely indicate Confucius's fulfillment of his political ideas through the composition of the *Annals*? The answer is no. In *Huainanzi*, the term "uncrowned king" has several connotations that are worth discussing:

孔子之通，智過於萇弘，勇服于孟賁，足蹠效菟，力招城關，能亦多矣。然而勇力不聞，伎巧不知，專行教道，以成素王，事亦鮮矣。《春秋》二百四十二年，亡國五十二，弒君三十六，采善鉏醜，以成王道，論亦博矣。[36]

The capacity of Confucius was such that his intelligence surpassed that of Chang Hong, his courage exceeded that of Meng Ben, his feet were faster than a nimble rabbit, his strength was such that he could hold up a portcullis. His abilities were indeed numerous. But he is not known to the world for his courage or his dexterity. Solely through practicing the way of teaching[37] he became an uncrowned king. This would indicate that his affairs were indeed few. The 242 years of the Spring and Autumn period saw fifty-two states destroyed and thirty-six cases of regicide. By singling out the good and condemning the bad, he established the Kingly Way. This would indicate that his discussion was indeed broad.[38]

The phrase "he established the Kingly Way" (*yi cheng wang dao* 以成王道) echoes the grammar of the aforementioned phrase, "make the affairs of the true king comprehensible" (*yi da wang shi* 以達王事), which Sima Qian used to reveal Confucius's goals. But teaching, or *jiao* 教, is the main theme. Confucius, as versatile as he was, focused on transmitting his teachings and in the process became an uncrowned king. The parallelism between *shi yi xian yi* 事亦鮮矣 (his affairs were indeed few) and *lun yi bo yi* 論亦博矣 (his discussions were indeed broad) links Confucius's teachings to the *Annals*. While teaching is not usually considered a grand undertaking, in this case, it was Confucius's greatest achievement. Confucius refers to various historical events, pointing out the good ones and bad ones in order to clarify the Kingly Way. Since the word *jiao* has the connotation of teaching and the cultivation of a large audience, it implies the spread of Confucius's doctrines, hidden in the *Annals*, throughout the human realm.

Up to now in our discussion, we have learned that in the apocryphal texts and in Western Han texts generally, when Confucius is described with the epithets "uncrowned king" and "dark sage," he has several characteristics: (1) he is chosen by Heaven as a potential candidate to replace the Zhou dynasty, and is of divine origin; (2) based on the Five Phases generative succession, his life did not come at the right point of Five Phases cycling in order to succeed the Zhou; (3) instead, he is in charge of forming standards for the Zhou's actual successor; (4) he hides the message in the *Annals*; (5) through teaching and spreading the *Annals*, he completes the way of the uncrowned king.

In line with these characteristics, in apocryphal texts the title "king" as in "uncrowned king" is not merely moral or rhetorical; there are occasions when Confucius forms a lord-minister relationship:

仲尼為素王，顏淵為司徒，子路為司空。[39]

Confucius was the uncrowned king; Yan Yuan was the Minister of the Masses, and Zilu was the Minister of Works.

左丘明為素臣。[40]

Zuo Qiuming was the untitled minister.

In the first quotation, when Confucius takes the title of the uncrowned king, his disciples become his subjects. The master-disciple relationship turns into a lord-minister relationship. In the second quote, Zuo Qiuming (ca. 556–451 BC), the supposed author of the Zuo commentarial tradition on the *Annals*, becomes a rank-and-file minister. While his relationship to Confucius is historically unclear, he is linked to Confucius because of his commentary on the *Annals*. Presumably, his explication of the text contributes to completing the undertaking of the uncrowned king, so that in the domain of the text as well as the ideal kingdom he is the minister of Confucius. In other words, this lord-minister relationship is not exclusive to Confucius and the disciples he taught directly. It extends to others later along the transmission lineages of Confucius's work.

Wang Chong 王充 (AD 27–ca. 97) expresses this lord-minister relationship in transmission more explicitly:

孔子作《春秋》以示王意,然則孔子之《春秋》,素王之業也;諸子之傳書,素相之事也。觀《春秋》以見王意,讀諸子以睹相指。[41]

Confucius composed the *Annals* to illustrate the intention of the kings. However, Confucius's the *Annals* is the undertaking of the uncrowned king; the masters' transmission of the text is the undertaking of untitled ministers. [Therefore,] one observes the *Annals of Spring and Autumn* to see the intention of the king; one reads [the work of] those masters to see the point of ministers.

The undertaking of the uncrowned king is to explicate the project of the sage king. Correspondingly, the transmission of his work is the undertaking of the rank-and-file ministers. It is clear that outside the embodied social relationships between Confucius and his disciples, a lord-minister relationship emerges in the domain of writing between Confucius and transmitters of his teachings. Here, Confucius is a true king with a kingdom of texts, and his ministers are those who perpetuate it. Notice that although he lived in the early Eastern Han and was a skeptic of many contemporary literati beliefs, Wang does not doubt that the lord-minister relationship became formed in the transmission process. From this, we may infer that the theory that the social master-disciple relationship corresponded to the textual lord-minister relationship was popular during the reigns of Emperor Ming and the subsequent Emperor Zhang's 章帝 reign (r. AD 75–88).

If we accept these inferences, we might ask what the blending of officialdom and the master-disciple relationship implies. Han apocryphal texts in particular have been interpreted as possessing a strong political orientation.[42] More specifically, which political concerns were the reasons for the blending of these two relationships? In supporting the legitimacy of Han rule, the apocrypha seek to spread their agenda while avoiding blunt assertions, such as "the Han is successor to the Zhou dynasty." In the next section, I will analyze their indirect approach by studying how Emperor Ming proposed a certain type of political image of Confucius and Zixia 子夏, one of Confucius's major disciples.

Zixia and Confucius: A Political Analogy

Who is Zixia? Based on *Shiji*, his surname was Bu 卜, his first name Shang 商, with the style name Zixia 子夏. He was forty-four years younger than

Confucius (551–479 BC), and therefore was born in 507. After Confucius's death, Zixia went to Xihe 西河 to teach and became a mentor of Marquis Wen of Wei 魏文侯.[43] Since Sima Qian thought highly of Confucius and his disciples, his *Shiji* no doubt contains both believable facts about the historical Zixia as well as some biased reflections on Sima's part. More certain is Zixia's name and his status as Confucius's disciple, because there is corroboration in the *Analects* and elsewhere, before the composition of *Shiji*. For our purposes, however, historical facts are less important than how people during the Han perceived Zixia and the bases on which they regarded him as a paragon of Confucian disciples.

Another crucial record in the *Analects* shaped the Han dynasty image of Zixia. In the *Analects*, Confucius sees the "study of culture" (*wenxue* 文學) as Zixia's specialty.[44] What the "study of culture" denoted in Confucius's time is not clear, but many Han literati considered it to be knowledge of documents and classics that stemmed from the ancient sage kings.[45] To these literati, Zixia was a competent transmitter of the classics, making him unique among Confucius's disciples. For instance, as opposed to Zigong 子貢, who was characterized as "good at political affairs,"[46] Zixia was the transmitter of the canon. As opposed to Zisi 子思, who led a school of early Confucianism,[47] Zixia's transmission lineage was distinguished by the faithful teaching and transmission of the classics.

A typical anecdote emphasizing Zixia's ability to preserve the original meaning of the classics can be found in *Lüshi chunqiu* 呂氏春秋, compiled during the Qin dynasty (221–207 BC):

子夏之晉，過衛，有讀史記者曰："晉師三豕涉河。"子夏曰："非也，是己亥也。夫'己'與'三'相近，'豕'與'亥'相似。"至於晉而問之，則曰"晉師己亥涉河"也。[48]

Zixia went to Jin. When he passed through Wei, there was a person reading the records of history in this way: "three swine of the Jin troops crossed the Yangtze River." Zixia said, "This is wrong. It should be the *ji hai* day. The character *ji* 己 looks like *san* 三; the character *shi* 豕 and *hai* 亥 are similar." When he arrived in Jin and asked about it, people there said, "on a *ji hai* day, the troops of Jin crossed the Yangtze River."

This anecdote shows why people should critically examine what is written in texts. The narrator does not depict Zixia as an outstanding transmitter of the classics. Rather, the latter part of the story, in which the Jin people's version of the historical record agrees with Zixia's reading, does provide an example of Zixia's competence in editing corrupt ancient texts. However, the later Han version of the story in *Kongzi jiayu* 孔子家語, compiled by Wang Su 王肅 (195–256 AD), considers Zixia's talent in reading ancient texts even more valuable: "From then on, [the people of] Wei considered Zixia a sage" (於是衛以子夏為聖).[49] Here the comment shifts the focus from praising prudence in the editing of texts to lauding Zixia as a sagely transmitter of them.

Xu Fang 徐防, who served as the Minister of Works (*sikong* 司空) during Emperor He's 和帝 reign (r. AD 89–105), even considered Zixia the initiator of the study of *zhang ju*, or "chapter and verse." In a memorial to Emperor He, Xu Fang wrote:

臣聞詩書禮樂，定自孔子；發明章句，始於子夏。其後諸家分析，各有異說。[50]

I have heard that the *Book of Odes*, the *Book of Documents*, *Rites*, and *Music* were given definitive form by Confucius. The explanation and clarification of chapter and verse was started by Zixia. Then the various traditions split and have maintained different explanations.

In this memorial, by identifying Zixia as the person who invented the study of chapter and verse—a great scholarly fashion of the Eastern Han—Xu Fang implies, first of all, that Zixia initiated a certain technique to explain the classics that Confucius had selected, and that later scholars adopted the tools of Zixia in devising their own numerous interpretations. Xu Fang was inclined to preserve the study of chapter and verse passed down from Zixia in order to retain the direct lineage of transmission from Confucius. He makes Zixia crucial in linking Confucius's teaching to Han scholarship. By transmitting the classics and inventing a technique for reading them that Han scholars widely accepted, Zixia was given a unique historical role among Confucius's disciples.

After discussing who Zixia was, it is helpful to briefly examine who he was not. We need a sense of the limitations of Zixia's role and image to fully understand the roles and functions that he represented in the Han dynasty. Most importantly, Zixia was not Confucius, or more specifically, Zixia's image was different from that of Confucius. This deceptively simple point produces a crucial inference: Zixia was not considered the successor of Confucius philosophically and socially, especially in the context of the Han dynasty. We can find evidence of this as early as Mencius (third century BC):

"昔者竊聞之: 子夏、子游、子張皆有聖人之一體, 冉牛、閔子、顏淵則具體而微. 敢問所安." 曰: "姑舍是."[51]

[Gongsun Chou said,] "Previously I have heard that Zixia, Ziyou, and Zizhang each had a facet of the sage. Ran Niu, Minzi, and Yan Yuan had all the facets but in a small way. I venture to ask where you are at." [Mencius] said, "Let's skip this for now."

Although Mencius did not answer his disciple Gongsun Chou's 公孫丑 (ca. fourth century BC) question, the question nevertheless provides an interesting understanding of Zixia. He depicts Zixia with certain, but not all, attributes of the sage, in contrast with Yan Yuan, who had all the qualities of Confucius, but all were underdeveloped. This language suggests that there was a barrier for Zixia to become a full and completely new version of Confucius. In the apocryphal texts, Confucius's miraculous birth creates another sort of barrier between him and Zixia, and finally, unlike Yan Yuan, who is said to represent the force of water, Zixia is not paired with any of the Five Phases.[52]

During the Han, to deny that Zixia could achieve the sagehood of Confucius was to exclude the possibility of his becoming an "uncrowned king." By emulating Zixia, one might achieve an excellent understanding of the classics and thus of Confucius's philosophy, but one could never become an "uncrowned king."

This image of Zixia and Confucius became relevant in a conversation between Huan Yu 桓郁 and Emperor Ming:

其冬, 上親於辟雍自講所制五行章句已, 復令郁說一篇. 上謂郁曰: "我為孔子, 卿為子夏, 起予者商也."[53]

In the winter,[54] after lecturing on his own *Chapter and Verse of the Five Phases* in the Biyong Hall, the Emperor [Ming] asked Huan Yu to explain one chapter. Emperor [Ming] said to Huan Yu, "I am Confucius, and you are Zixia. The person who raises me up is Zixia."

In the conversation, by quoting an anecdote from the *Analects*,⁵⁵ the emperor compares himself to Confucius and Huan Yu to one of Confucius's most famous disciples, Zixia. The emperor uses the master-disciple relationship of Confucius, in the position of master, and Zixia his supporter and student, as a historical analogy to the present. As Hsing I-tien 邢義田 mentions, comparisons to Confucius were a common locution and device among classicists throughout the Han era.⁵⁶ But we must take the device further: we need to ask why, as emperor, did Emperor Ming conform to the practice of classicist scholars, and how such rhetoric in practice could benefit him.

Michael Loewe provides three major ideas that bolstered the supremacy and legitimacy of a Han emperor, and by extension the whole monarchical system: (1) the emperor's divine origin granted by spiritual powers, (2) his status as a moral authority and paragon, and (3) his image as the preserver of the value system. In the Han dynasty, the theory of the Five Phases, as already discussed, was used to construct the divine origin of the Han rulers. As for the status of moral authority, the perception was that if the emperor lived up to this role, auspicious omens would appear accordingly; otherwise, calamities and inauspicious omens would come instead.⁵⁷ Also, embodying moral values and preserving ancient traditions were obligations for the Han emperors.⁵⁸ The conversation between Emperor Ming and Huan Yu forms a parallelism between Confucius and the emperor, which allows Emperor Ming to claim legitimacy for his reign. However, did Emperor Ming fit Loewe's generalization of the three major ways to claim legitimacy for a monarchy, and did the emperor consciously use apocryphal texts to achieve this political purpose?

In modern scholarship, Emperor Ming, Liu Yang 劉陽 (AD 28–75, the fourth son of the founder of the Eastern Han, Liu Xiu 劉秀), has been characterized as "narrow-minded with a penchant for revealing confidential information."⁵⁹ Several records show that he was highly aware of the need to affirm the legitimacy of Han rule, and was as enthusiastic about apocryphal writings as his father was.⁶⁰ In the eighth month of AD 60, Emperor Ming changed the official title "Grand Musician," or Tai Yue 大樂, to "Grand Yu Musician," or Tai Yu Yue 大予樂, because in an apocryphal text *Shangshu xuan ji qian* 尚書旋機鈐 (The Big Dipper Key to the *Book of Documents*), "a Han emperor composed music named Yu 予, with harmonious virtues."⁶¹ Emperor Ming thus could fulfill a prophecy to become that "virtuous ruler."

Moreover, in the tenth month of AD 65, Emperor Ming issued an edict concerning a solar eclipse. In it, based on one of the apocryphal texts of the *Annals of Spring and Autumn*, *Chunqiu tu chen* 春秋圖讖 (The Diagrams and Prophecies of the *Annals of Spring and Autumn*), he considered the eclipse a huge calamity and linked it to his lack of moral authority.[62] Aside from this inauspicious omen, many auspicious omens appeared during Emperor Ming's reign, such as those signaling sweet dew, divine fungus, and divine birds.[63] Wang Chong also reported that more auspicious omens appeared during Emperor Ming's reign than during most other reigns.[64] If we assume that observing, categorizing, and reporting auspicious omens formed a tendentious process, and may have been a type of propaganda, then we might conclude that anxiety over the legitimacy of his rule caused both the emperor and his subjects to seek such signs.

But why was Emperor Ming anxious about his own legitimacy? Why did he make the political gestures I have mentioned? To answer this question, it is worth exploring, first, whether there were any competing political camps during Emperor Ming's time, and, second, whether there existed then any notions about political legitimacy that did not subscribe to the same criteria.

Emperor Ming had good reasons to worry about his throne. He had become the heir apparent in AD 43, and in contrast to his elder brother Liu Qiang 劉彊 (AD 25–58), who became the heir apparent at the young age of one, Emperor Ming was recognized as being on a lower tier for succession. He might have been anxious about his credentials, particularly because his appointment as heir resulted from his mother Yin Lihua's 陰麗華 (AD 4–64) victory in harem politics and her promotion to the position of empress in AD 41.[65] These issues were more than just irrational fears in Emperor Ming's mind; his opponents could use them sabotage his rule.

His brothers had coveted the throne ever since the disinheritance of Liu Qiang. In the capital, they cajoled the literati cliques. In AD 44 the resultant public competitions over the type of theorizing we have examined and the politics of succession caused an uprising; as a result, the brothers were sent to their own fiefs and were supervised by the imperial government. After Emperor Ming's accession, he frequently met them to closely monitor their actions. This did not, however, stop their plotting. For example, right after Emperor Guangwu's death in AD 57, Emperor Ming's full brother Liu Jing 劉荊 (?–67 AD) wrote to Liu Qiang to conspire to take over the throne by military force. Even after their conspiracy failed, Jing kept seeking the means to overthrow the emperor, such as performing cursing rituals, which eventually cost him his life in AD 67.[66]

As a type of intellectual foundation for claims of legitimacy for the Eastern Han, the apocrypha became a focus of this political competition. In

AD 70, Emperor Ming's half-brother Liu Ying 劉英 was accused of plotting rebellion. One of the points of the accusation was that his partisans forged diagrams and prophecies 圖讖 (*tuchen*). In AD 73, another half-brother, Liu Yan 劉延 (AD?–89), was accused of forging *tu chen* as well, and also of having made a cursing ritual and of seeking to form a retinue. In yet another incident, one involving the case of the half-brother Liu Kang 劉康 (AD?–97) and his clique, their referring to apocrypha was considered a crime.[67] Emperor Ming was thus apparently aware of the multiple ways to claim political legitimacy, including references to apocrypha. The actions of Ying, Yan, and Kang were considered subversive because they could be construed as attempting to claim legitimacy for themselves, especially when they forged apocrypha and formed cliques.

In the third month of AD 72, the emperor turned to other links with the notion of Confucius and his disciples in order to promote his legitimacy. He was highly involved with the dissemination and transmission of the classics, and thus went to Confucius's residence to make sacrifices to the Sage and his seventy-two disciples. Upon returning, he made the princes give explanations of the classics, and in AD 66 he created positions for tutors to teach the minor nobles. By making connections to Confucius and Zixia in the passage discussed earlier, he had already presented Confucius and the disciples in a particularly high position.[68]

In light of the *Huainanzi* passage and apocryphal texts, Emperor Ming's promoting the transmission of the classics proves that he aimed to fulfill the "way of teaching" (*jiao dao* 教道) mentioned in *Huainanzi*. This qualified him to be an "uncrowned king" and to comprehend true kingship. Unlike Confucius, however, he was a real emperor. By comparing himself to Confucius, he claimed that he ruled in two domains. As a moral authority, and transmitter of the Kingly Way in the world, he was a ruler in the sense that Confucius was—a ruler of a moral domain. However, unlike Confucius, he was also able to apply those teachings to a physical kingdom.

The implication of the title "uncrowned king" is that Confucius had the virtues of a king, but never held that position. Virtues in this context are not apolitical: they legitimize the ruler's right to rule. Moreover, having already drawn the parallel between the Confucius-Zixia relationship and relationships with his own ministers, Emperor Ming established the right to rule. In comparing Huan Yu with Zixia, Emperor Ming also imagined an ideal classicist—one who can transmit the lord's words and sometimes enlighten the lord. At the same time, his conception of Zixia's role, the preserver of Confucius's words and undertakings, presented an image of Zixia that was seen in apocryphal texts. Emperor Ming's words created a parallelism by which the emperor, or lord, not only dominated in the lord-minister relationship but also took the position of master in the master-disciple relationship.

Emperor Ming's ultimate goal was to reach the Great Peace. In the previous two chapters, we have seen in various occasions this ideal society under the rule of the sage king.[69] *Chunqiu fanlu*, in explaining the significance of the *Annals of Spring and Autumn*, says:

孔子明得失,差貴賤,反王道之本。譏天王以致太平。[70]

> Confucius clarified gain and loss, differentiated the noble from the petty, and returned to the root of the way of the sage king. He criticized the kings of Heaven in order to attain the Great Peace.

Confucius, thus, had encoded into the text of the *Annals* the way of the sage king and the means to achieve the Great Peace. Here, *Chunqiu fanlu* does not say how to achieve the state of the Great Peace. Nevertheless, it does imply that the *Annals* contains a means for it.

Compared to *Chunqiu fanlu*, Yang Xiong's 揚雄 (53 BC–AD 18) ideas about the Great Peace are more explicit:

聖人之言,天也,天妄乎?繼周者未欲太平也。如欲太平也,舍之而用它道,亦無由至矣。[71]

> The word of sages is [from] Heaven. Is Heaven reckless? The dynasties that succeeded the Zhou dynasty do not want to achieve the Great Peace yet. If they do want to achieve the Great Peace, and [yet] abandon [the words of the sage] and employ some other way, there is no method that will achieve it.

Although Yang does not specifically mention the *Annals*, the words of the sages include all the ancient sage kings and Confucius's teaching. His statement implies two things: it is possible for someone to bring the Great Peace to the world as long as he is willing to follow the words of the sages. The dynasties after the Zhou dynasty, meaning the Qin and the Western Han, did not do so and thus did not achieve the Great Peace.

This dissatisfaction with the Han's failure to realize the latter continued during the Eastern Han dynasty. Wang Chong described certain ideas in his time this way:

儒者稱五帝、三王致天下太平。漢興以來，未有太平。彼稱五帝、三王致天下太平；漢興以來，未有太平者，見五帝、三王聖人也。聖人之德，能致太平。謂漢不太平者，漢無聖帝也。賢者之化，不能太平。[72]

[Some] Confucians argued that the Five Emperors and Three Kings brought the Great Peace to all under Heaven. Since Han arose, there has been no Great Peace. [The reason why] they argue that the Five Emperors and Three Kings brought the Great Peace to all under Heaven, and that since Han rose, there has been no Great Peace, is [because] they see that the Five Emperors and Three Kings are sages. The virtue of the sage can bring the Great Peace. [The reason why] they argued that Han is not in the state of the Great Peace is [because] Han has no sage emperor. The cultivation of the [merely] worthy [by itself] cannot enable the Great Peace.

Wang Chong has represented certain attitudes toward Han rule and understandings of how to achieve the Great Peace. He claims that people asserted a natural, definite distinction between the worthy and the sage: worthies are not able to bring about the Great Peace. Such a notion would seem to us to be more rigid than Yang Xiong's idea of following the words of sages. Therefore, they argue that the Han dynasty has never achieved the Great Peace and will never achieve it unless a sage, as opposed to a worthy, appears on the throne.

In Emperor Ming's responses to a certain dissatisfaction behind this trend of thought, it was no longer sufficient merely to enforce good policies or transmit the words of sages, or more specifically, the classics. In this case, it was necessary for the emperor to claim to be a sage, or more precisely, the successor of Confucius. Because Confucius as a sage encoded the way to achieve the Great Peace in the *Annals* and predicted the emergence of the Han dynasty, being a successor to him granted Emperor Ming the capability to achieve the Great Peace and thus the legitimacy to rule.

Concluding Remarks

Emperor Ming had his own way to achieve the Great Peace. Unlike his father, he did not practice the well-known *feng* and *shan* sacrifices. Instead, he attempted to conform to the image of Confucius. While his father was faced with doubts about the Liu family, Emperor Ming was faced with a different doubt: Why should he be the chosen one among his brothers? In addition, a belief had also gained credence among the literati: most of the Han emperors were not sages, so that they could not bring the Great Peace to the world. Drawing from apocryphal texts and old traditions such as *Zhuangzi*, Emperor Ming showed that he was the emperor who was as sagely as Confucius. In this way, he was not only better than his brothers, but *the* one who could lead the Han empire to a better place.

But why Confucius? Why not the Yellow Emperor, Yao, Shun, and other sage kings who were actually rulers? In Emperor Ming's speech, the master-disciple relationship between Confucius and Zixia is an analogy to the ruler-subject relationship he was eager to establish and properly maintain. Furthermore, he also went to the Biyong Hall to give an academic lecture. He wanted to not only be the ruler of his subjects but also the grandmaster of all the classicists. Why is that the case? As we have already seen in this chapter, Emperor Ming's moves were responses to his contemporaries. In the next chapter, we will switch our focus to the sociology of the audience in Emperor Ming's many political movements, the Eastern Han literati, to explore the importance of the master-disciple relationship, its sociopolitical background, and its impact on the study of the classics and intellectual trends in general.

Chapter 4

Finding Teachers versus Making Friends

The Gradual Departure from Classicism in the First Two Centuries AD

In chapter 1, we witnessed the abortive intellectual movement of the *Scripture of the Great Peace*.[1] In AD 166, Xiang Kai 襄楷 brought a scripture with the same name to Emperor Huan 桓 (r. AD 147–167),[2] and later the movement became massive, aiming to achieve the Great Peace.[3] In the previous chapter, we saw that Emperor Ming was devoted to Confucius and his mission. Emperor Huan, by contrast, sacrificed to Laozi 老子 in AD 165.[4] In AD 178, his successor, Emperor Ling 靈 (r. AD 168–189), established the Hongdu Gate school (*Hongdu men xue* 鴻都門學), which emphasized literature, calligraphy, and miscellaneous minor skills.[5] What happened during this hundred years? What happened to the restoration of the Kingly Way and the attempt to achieve the Great Peace? Were people still primarily interested in Confucius's project, or did they expand their interests beyond the classics? If their interests expanded, why?[6]

If these hundred years did host these intellectual changes, the next question is what led to these changes. Can we attribute these changes to the emperor or other dominant individuals? Normatively, Chinese emperors had autocratic power, but this does not mean that they could fully exert it, especially in the decentralized Eastern Han political environment.[7] Can we explain this shift by the rise of certain socio-intellectual groups, such as the religious movement led by the sect of the Great Peace (Taiping Dao 太平道)? This explanation might sound intriguing, but the chronology of these movements tells us that the new popularity of the *Scripture* was actually a result of these changes rather than the cause of them. Before examining the popularity of the Great Peace movement, we need to explore why Eastern Han literati started to consider the movement's scripture useful, even more so than the classics. In other words, we need to find out what created leeway inside the system of dominant ideas for important new ones to arise.

Despite his enthusiasm and commitment toward Confucius and the classics, Emperor Ming was just one side of the story. In the Eastern Han dynasty, great families also played a significant role.[8] They extended their power from local society to central government by learning the classics, making alliances in the court, and marrying into the imperial house.[9] They hosted significant scholars, sponsored local schools, influenced students at the National Academy, and even taught future emperors. The imperial house provided important patronage for contemporary scholars.[10] Nevertheless, half of the Eastern Han emperors were significantly young or died prematurely (table 4). All were part of the intellectual environment instead of the sole manufacturers of thought. Therefore, looking into the lives of scholars from the great families will help us to understand this shift.

Table 4. Ages and Reign Years of the Eastern Han Emperors[11]

Emperor	Age Deceased	Reign Years	Crowned Age	Dominant Parties in Control
Guangwu 光武	62	33	30	
Ming 明	48	18	30	
Zhang 章	33	13	19	
He 和	27	17	10	Empress Dowager Dou and Dou Xian (b)
Shang 殤	2	1	Hundred days	Empress Dowager Deng and Deng Zhi (b)
An 安	32	19	13	Empress Dowager Deng and Deng Zhi (b)
Shun 順	30	19	11	Empress Liang, Liang Shang (f), and Liang Ji (b)
Chong 沖	3	1	2	Empress Liang, Liang Shang (f), and Liang Ji (b)
Zhi 質	9	1	8	Empress Dou and Dou Wu (f)
Huan 桓	36	21	15	
Ling 靈	34	22	12	Empress He and He Jin (b)
Xian 獻	54	31	9	Dong Zhuo, then Cao Cao

This chapter will explore life in the scholarly communities of the Eastern Han dynasty to trace the social basis for the aforementioned intellectual transitions. First, we will inquire into how one could make an official career through learning the classics in the first two centuries AD. In this section, we will see how classicism became a driving force for the traveling culture of literati, a fashion that involved students leaving home to seek training in the classics, and the circulation of knowledge. After that we will focus on a specific group of literati including Ma Rong 馬融 (AD 79–166) and Zhang Heng 張衡 (78–139 AD), who were active in the first half of the second century, in order to show how traveling culture encouraged horizontal social connections among literati and the consolidation of their culture.

My observation here is both social and intellectual: I argue that traveling culture, initially with an exclusive emphasis on classicism, led to increasing contact among Eastern Han literati and thus set the stage for the intellectual trend of broad learning. This trend encouraged the scholars to engage more and more classical texts and commentaries, such as apocrypha and the so-called "old script" texts. It also provided impetus and space for literati to consider and practice other forms of learning as a path to the Great Peace. Ironically, this broad learning and search for the Great Peace outside the classics gradually eclipsed classicism.

How to Succeed in the Han: Sketching the Han Official Recruitment System

Imagine that you are the scion of a well-off family from the Eastern Han, and you are about to start a career as a Han official.[12] One of the first things you need to know is where to find vacancies. The most advertised openings were the so-called Capable and Good (*xianliang* 賢良) or Sincere and Upright (*fangzheng* 方正) positions, which guaranteed official positions later.[13] However, these positions were only intermittently available by the authority of the emperor. And when they were available, they seemed only open to intellectual celebrities of the society. Therefore, as a beginner, your chances would be less than slim. Besides, these rare positions, regular vacancies in the imperial government were also prestigious. Although the ruler's position is never open, there were positions just below it: the Three Ducal Officials (*san gong* 三公), namely, Grand Commandant, Minister over the Masses, and Minister of Works. Obviously, these positions are similar to the senior partner positions in a large company; they were directly appointed by the leader and were granted to seasoned veterans. Nevertheless, it was realistic to hope to work for the Three Ducal Officials at their offices (*fu* 府). These offices were further divided into departments: one could be a Department Head (*yuan* 掾), leading the department, or a Subordinate Clerk (*shu* 屬), assisting the head.[14] Similar to working at the White House or a top-twenty university, competition could still be stiff to the extent that you, as a beginner, might not stand a chance for the moment.

Your chances would further increase at the level of local governments. Although the heads of commanderies (*jun* 郡) and principalities (*guo* 國), the two largest administrative units, were reserved for the emperor's appointees, the heads of lower units, such as Prefects (*ling* 令) or Chiefs (*zhang* 長) of Prefectures (Xian 縣) and especially functionaries for their offices would be realistic goals. Because of the large territory of the empire, the need for functionaries in local government was also much higher than that of the central government.[15] In fact, local government was open to more novices, and later on the central government promoted these junior officials to higher positions. Here could be the place where you start.

The next issue you would need to know is the criteria for hiring. Similar to our society, one needed connections and credentials to be selected to the Han government, and the connections served as the verification of the credentials, often through recommendations.[16] In local hiring, officials essentially recruited people based on how local societies saw them, and they did so by consulting influential households, and, in the case of the Eastern Han dynasty, the great families (who also participated in local government). If one was already a local official, his supervisors were responsible for recommending him to higher positions. Therefore, good connections to officials and great families would be greatly advantageous at the start of your official career.

How would you make connections? You might want to do so while gaining your credentials, which, for the better part of the Han dynasty, meant mastering classicism. Like most bureaucratic systems, that of the Han relied on paperwork, which required literacy and expertise in regulations and laws. During Emperor Wu's time, expertise in the classics became a qualification as well. From Emperor Xuan's time on, the need to understand Heaven became stronger, and the classics as means of revealing Heaven's will thus became increasingly valuable in officialdom. Following this need, people who wanted to engage in Han officialdom embraced the learning of the classics.[17] As we saw in chapter 1, the classics were transmitted through the master-disciple relationship. Novices in government work thus formed this relationship with their potential recommenders in order to gain their credentials as well as connections. As a result, classism, together with the master-disciple relationship among officials, permeated every level of Han official life from one's career planning to training programs, and then to real positions in the bureaucracy.

How One Learned Classical Knowledge in the Han: Schools and Curricula

Given the circumstances just described, you decide to be a disciple, but where could you find your teacher? The several choices available to you would have included the central government's National Academy (Taixue 太學), the local official schools, such as commandery schools (*jun xue* 郡 學) and private schools. In the capital, the National Academy periodically recruited students mainly for training in the classics. In the late Western Han, and especially during Wang Mang's reign, the number of official schools at the level of commanderies and counties rapidly increased. However, the opening of these local official schools mainly depended on local officials' decisions instead of empire-wide mandatory rules. These schools provided training in basic clerical skills, including drafting administrative documents and processing legal cases.[18] Besides these official schools, there were more and more private schools in the Eastern Han dynasty, which became the backbone of literati communication and eventually shaped literati culture.

In this section, we will examine how these schools, especially the National Academy and private schools, trained the literati and gradually transformed the literati culture of early imperial China. We will explore how these schools were responsible for institutionalizing the social networking of the literati via the transmission of the classics. I argue that a process of searching for classical training led to a peripatetic culture: young students left their hometown to seek teachers for classical knowledge as well as opportunities to socialize with local officials for the sake of eliciting recommendations. Through oral as well as written circulation of knowledge, a student of the classics encountered a much larger repertoire of texts than his Western Han predecessors. In order to better understand the classics, scholars turned to various classics and commentaries, including the so-called "old script texts," "new script texts," and apocrypha. Following this polymathic tendency toward classicism, a trend of broad learning gradually emerged. In the following pages, contrary to what scholars have previously shown, we will see that the so-called "old script texts," "new script texts," and apocrypha did not separate scholars into three segregated schools that were hostile to each other.[19] Instead, they all appealed to the majority of Eastern Han scholars in the context of this new intellectual trend. We will also examine the classical traditions and social connections under the misnomers of "new script" and "old script."

The Rise and Fall of the National Academy, or Taixue 太學

Assume you were about to choose a school to start your life as a disciple. The first choice that might come to your mind might well be the National Academy. As the most powerful and best-known educational organization, the National Academy had a long tradition of classicism in the Han dynasty. Beginning in 141 BC, certain Academicians (*boshi* 博士) at the Academy took charge of teaching the classics.[20] These Academician positions originally numbered five for each of the Five Classics, making a total of twenty-five. By AD 4, the number grew to thirty, five for each of the classics plus another five under the category of music. From 124 BC to the end of first century BC, the enrollment of students gradually increased from fifty to more than a thousand. The rapid growth of the student population made Emperor Cheng restrict the number of enrollees to one thousand in 7 BC.[21]

The popularity of the National Academy was largely due to its close connection to the central government and the court. As mentioned earlier, in the Han dynasty, the primary way to achieve a civil official position was through the recommendation of officials. Students of the Academy not only obtained a better chance to be appointed to minor official positions after a certain period of study,[22] but they also received more opportunities to socialize with the Academicians, who later on often achieved higher official positions.[23] Academicians might recommend, or even directly appoint, some of the students to official positions. A student with the support of his teacher and classmates was more likely to survive the environment and thrive later in his career. The study of the classics thus was a ticket to upward social mobility and cultural prestige among great families.[24]

However, on second thought, the Academy might not be your first choice because of the competition. Just like finding an official position in the capital, you would face cutthroat competition to gain Academicians' and other officials' attention. For this reason, many Eastern Han literati went to local schools before attending the Academy. Besides, local schools also led to local hiring, which was a much larger pool than positions in the capital. If the students of great families went to areas that were in their families' reach, their family connections would significantly accelerate their careers.²⁵ Young starters would be better prepared to move up to a higher level of work after accumulating enough political stock from these schools and local officialdom.²⁶ This situation led to the blossoming of local schools and encouraged travel to numerous locations.²⁷ At the same time, after the reestablishment of the National Academy in Luoyang 洛陽 in AD 29, local schools gradually eclipsed the popularity of the Academy in the first two centuries AD.²⁸

This does not mean that in the Eastern Han the National Academy was completely dismissed. Although the Academy as a bureaucratic institution was indeed deteriorating, its prestige and the scholars attached to it kept it viable as a means to network and circulate knowledge about the classics,²⁹ especially when in the Eastern Han dynasty the Academy was open to auditors without registration.³⁰ People could use this opportunity to make connections with scholars who worked elsewhere in the capital, such as in the imperial libraries. There was also a book market in the capital that placed students in advantageous positions for the circulation of knowledge.³¹ All of these aspects made visits to the Academy attractive. In other words, the Academy would be an important stop for your learning career.

CURRICULA INSIDE AND OUTSIDE THE NATIONAL ACADEMY

What could you learn from the Academy? In the Eastern Han, the National Academy had a fixed official curriculum for classical training.³² Based on this curriculum, Academicians would teach one of the fourteen commentarial traditions: the Shi 施, Meng 孟, Liang 梁, and Jing 京 traditions of the *Changes*; the Ouyang 歐陽, Elder Xiahou 大夏侯, and Younger Xiahou 小夏侯 traditions of the *Documents*; the Qi 齊, Lu 魯, and Han 韓 traditions of the *Poetry*; the Elder Dai 大戴 and Younger Dai 小戴 traditions of the *Rites*; and the Yan 嚴 and Yan 顏 traditions, two branches of the Gongyang tradition of the *Annals*. All of these traditions were well known and had already become part of the Academy curriculum in the 50s BC (hereafter, I will refer to these traditions as "Western Han traditions" for the sake of convenience).³³ These fourteen traditions formed the skeleton of the Academy's curriculum in the Eastern Han.

The Academy's curriculum was a contested space. Several traditions were close to entering the curriculum due to their popularity, but never did. The most famous ones were the Zuo tradition of the *Annals*, the Mao

毛 tradition of the *Poetry*, the *Rites of Zhou*, and the old script *Documents*, four traditions often mislabeled as "old script texts." However, they were less "old script" versions of the classics than classical texts and commentaries that were different from the Western Han traditions. Thus I heuristically refer to them as the old text traditions to convey that this is not merely a matter of paleography. As we will see in this section, because of Liu Xin's promotion, these four traditions were lumped together from time to time.[34] Besides the old text traditions, the Guliang tradition of the *Annals* was well known in the Eastern Han court as well as among the literati, but it never became an official curriculum as in the Western Han. In the *History of the Later Han*, the Guliang tradition was often mentioned with the titles of the old text traditions as the worthy traditions outside the Academy's curriculum.[35]

The National Academy became particularly important for the transmission of apocryphal texts. In the early years of the Eastern Han dynasty, the compilers of the apocryphal corpus were also Academicians. For example, one of the editors, Xue Han 薛漢 (fl. AD 25–68), came from a family that transmitted the Han tradition of the *Poetry* for generations.[36] Later, people like Xu Zhi 徐穉 (AD 97–168), Li Xia 李郃 (fl. 88–125 AD), and Wei Lang 魏朗 (?–AD 169) also gained knowledge about apocryphal texts from the Academy. Wei Lang was also famous among the partisans (*dang ren* 黨人) in the massive protest at the Academy in AD 166.[37] Fan Ying 樊英 (fl. AD 106–144), who was the teacher of one of the most famous partisans, Chen Shi 陳寔 (AD 104–187), was an Academician who specialized in apocrypha from Emperor An's reign (r. AD 106–125) onward (see chart 11).[38]

Family Transmission

Local schools seem to be the best first stop before you enter the competition of the capital. But even before that, your family could provide you with initial classical training. In fact, in Han China family traditions were the most common and stable way to transmit knowledge of the classics or any kind of expertise.[39] This is not only because valuable expertise should go to the family first; sons usually received a much higher level of attention from their fathers than students received from their teachers. Immersed in the family tradition, one often connected to the tradition better and had a better chance to continue in study.

Because of that strong connection, family tradition could run for generations and it rewarded the family greatly. The most observable family tradition of the classics through the whole of the Western Han was the Kong 孔 family of Qufu 曲阜, Lu Principality 魯國, who were putatively the descendants of Confucius. In the Eastern Han dynasty, they continued to flourish in transmitting the Yan 嚴 tradition of the Gongyang *Annals*.[40] In addition to them, the Huan 桓 family from Longkang 龍亢, Pei Commandery 沛郡, also transmitted the Ouyang tradition of the *Documents* within their family in the first hundred years of the Eastern Han. The Huan family succeeded greatly in teaching the imperial family the classics. Huan Rong 桓榮 (ca. 20 BC–ca. AD 59) was the teacher of Emperor Ming. His son Huan Yu 桓郁 (?–AD 93) taught Emperor Zhang, and his grandson Huan Yan 桓焉 (?–AD 143) taught Emperor An and Emperor Shun.[41] The Yuan 袁 family from Ruyang 汝陽, Runan 汝南 Commandery, was another formidable family. Many of their members occupied positions of the Three Ducal Ministers. They passed down the Meng tradition of the *Changes* through their family for four generations (see chart 7).[42]

These families became even more formidable when they promoted and patronized other great families' traditions. For example, Yang Zhen 楊震 (AD 59–124) of Huayin 華陰, Hongnong 弘農 Commandery, received the Ouyang tradition of the *Documents* from Huan Yu. This was the starting point of the Yang family's four generations of transmission from Yang Zhen to his son Yang Bing 楊秉 (AD 92–165), grandson Yang Ci 楊賜 (?–185 AD), and great-grandson Yang Biao 楊彪 (AD 142–225), whose highest positions were Grand Minister of Ceremonies (*taichang* 太常), in charge of recruiting Academicians; Master of Writing, the imperial secretary position as powerful as the Three Ducal Ministers; and Mayor of the Capital (*jingzhao yin* 京兆尹), respectively.[43] The relationship between the Huan and the Yang families was not just limited to a one-time master-disciple connection. Huan Yan was also the teacher of Yang Ci. There was also intermarriage between the two families.[44]

Family traditions existed not only in these extraordinary families; they permeated literati families in general. For example, Xue Han's family transmitted the Han tradition of the *Poetry* for five generations. Fu Gong 伏恭 (5 BC–AD 84) and his two uncles, Fu An 伏黯 (fl. AD 9–23) and Fu Zhan 伏湛 (?–AD 37), were descendants of Fu Sheng 伏生 (fl. 246–140 BC), an expert in the *Documents*. At the end of the first century BC, the Fu family transmitted the Qi tradition of the *Poetry*. Fu Zhan even tutored Emperor Cheng.[45] Xu Fang 徐防, an advocate of conforming commentarial lines, came from a family of the *Changes*. His grandfather Xu Xuan 徐宣 taught Wang Mang the *Changes*.[46] (See chart 8.)[47]

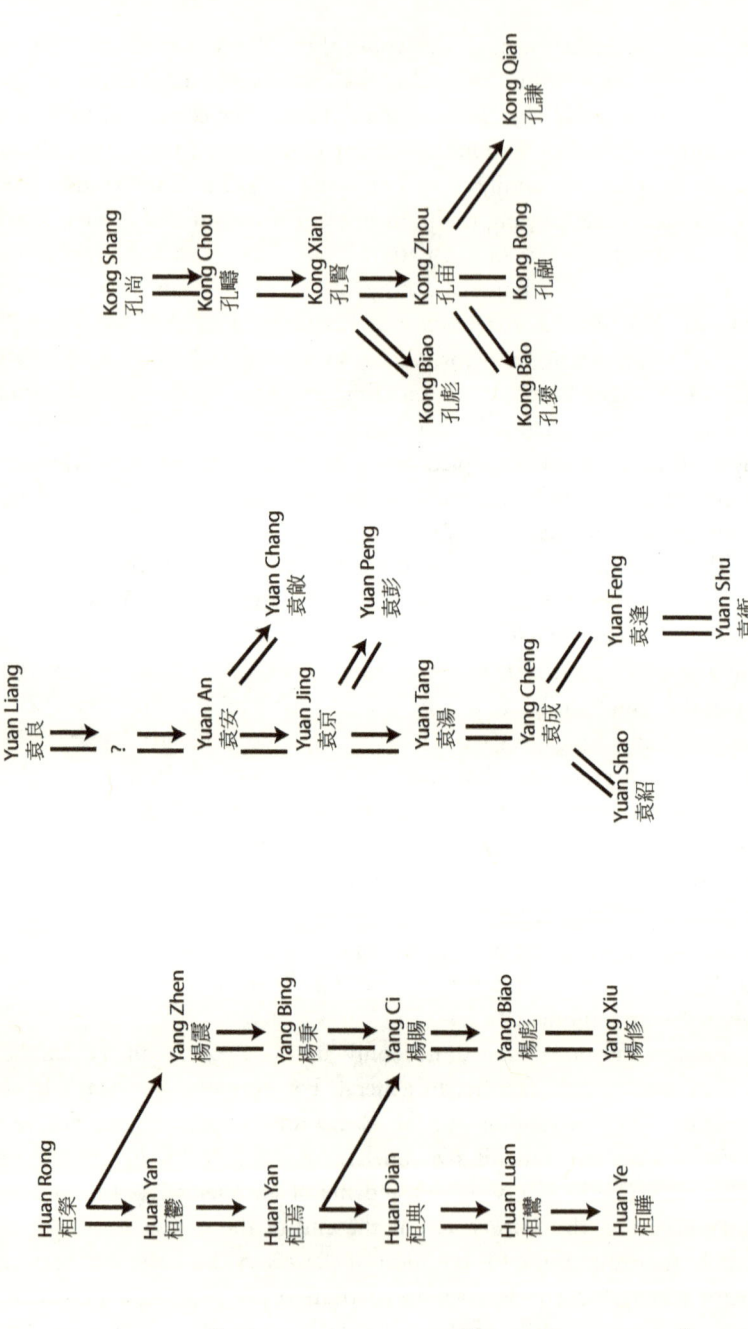

Chart 7. Family Transmission Lines 1

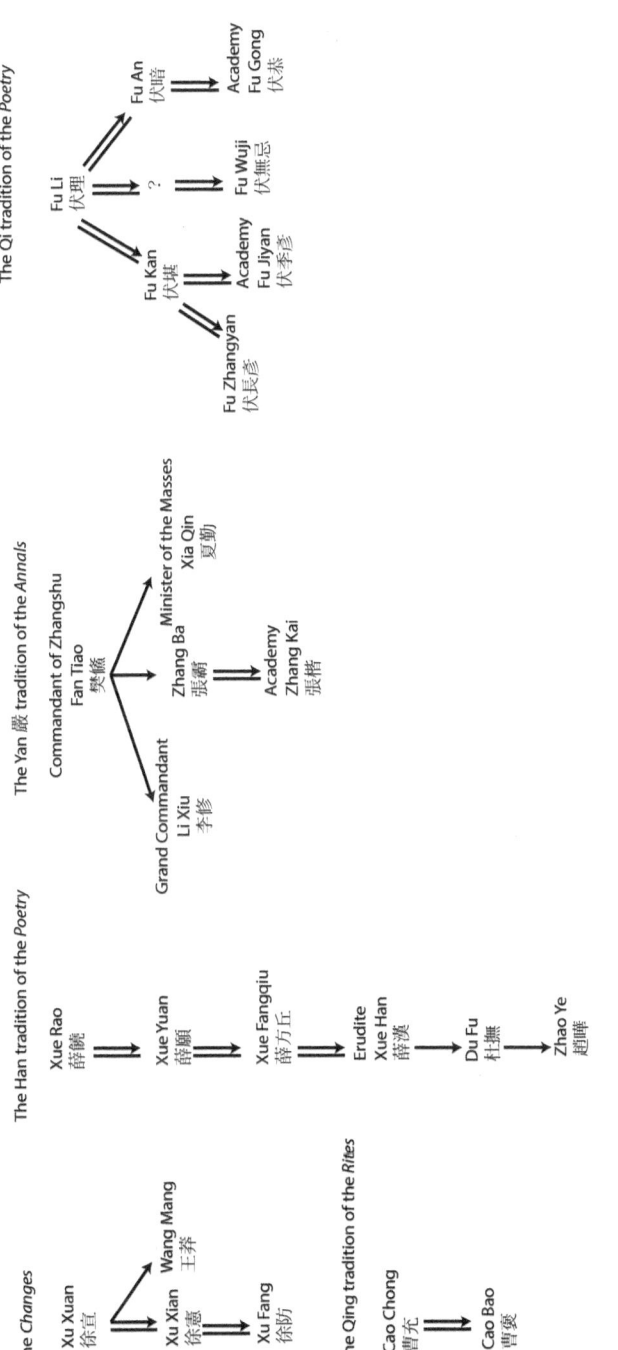

Chart 8. Family Transmission Lines 2

All the aforementioned family traditions were Western Han classical traditions. In contrast, the old text traditions that Liu Xin promoted never gained much popularity through family transmission. Single transmission from father to son are the longest lines we can find in the sources. This kind of transmission tended to happen in the first fifty years of the Eastern Han, when the first generation had a chance to receive teachings from either Liu Xin or his followers. For example, Jia Kui 賈逵 (AD 30–101) was the most eager advocate of the Zuo tradition during Emperor Zhang's reign (AD 76–88). His knowledge about the Zuo tradition and the *Rites of Zhou* came from his father Jia Hui 賈徽 (fl. 6 BC), a disciple of Liu Xin. Similarly, Zheng Zhong 鄭眾 (?–AD 114) received the Zuo tradition from his father, Zheng Xing 鄭興 (fl. AD 14–33), who learned the Zuo tradition and the *Rites of Zhou* from Liu Xin, among other classical traditions (chart 9).[48]

These fathers and sons were all versed to various extents in other Western Han traditions as well. Kong Fen's great-grandfather Kong Ba 孔霸 (fl. 48–43 BC) also received the *Documents* directly from Xiahou Sheng and thereafter passed down the Xiahou tradition.[49] Before becoming a disciple of Liu Xin, Zheng Xing was a student of the Gongyang tradition. In addition to the Zuo tradition, his son Zheng Zhong was also an expert on the *Poetry* and *Changes*.[50] Jia Kui, who received the teachings on the old text traditions from his father, was a teacher of the Elder Xiahou tradition at the National Academy. He was also familiar with explications of the Guliang tradition.

That is to say, the old text traditions rarely stood alone in family transmission; they were part of the broader learning of many literati. All the families introduced earlier were involved in one or more Western Han commentarial traditions, but no family specialized in only old text traditions. The asymmetrical situation meant that certain families had knowledge of the old text tradition in addition to the Western Han traditions rather than being solely devoted to either the "Old Script School" or the "New Script School." This is because Liu Xin and his cohorts taught the old text classics to people with classical training, which could only be the well-established Western Han traditions. In addition, they did so only at the end of the Western Han instead of doing so over a long period of time. The old text traditions thus had both a shorter history inside families and were less widespread among them than the Western Han traditions. The first generation of recipients passed down to their sons the old text knowledge together with their own classical knowledge. Both sets of knowledge eventually became family-owned.

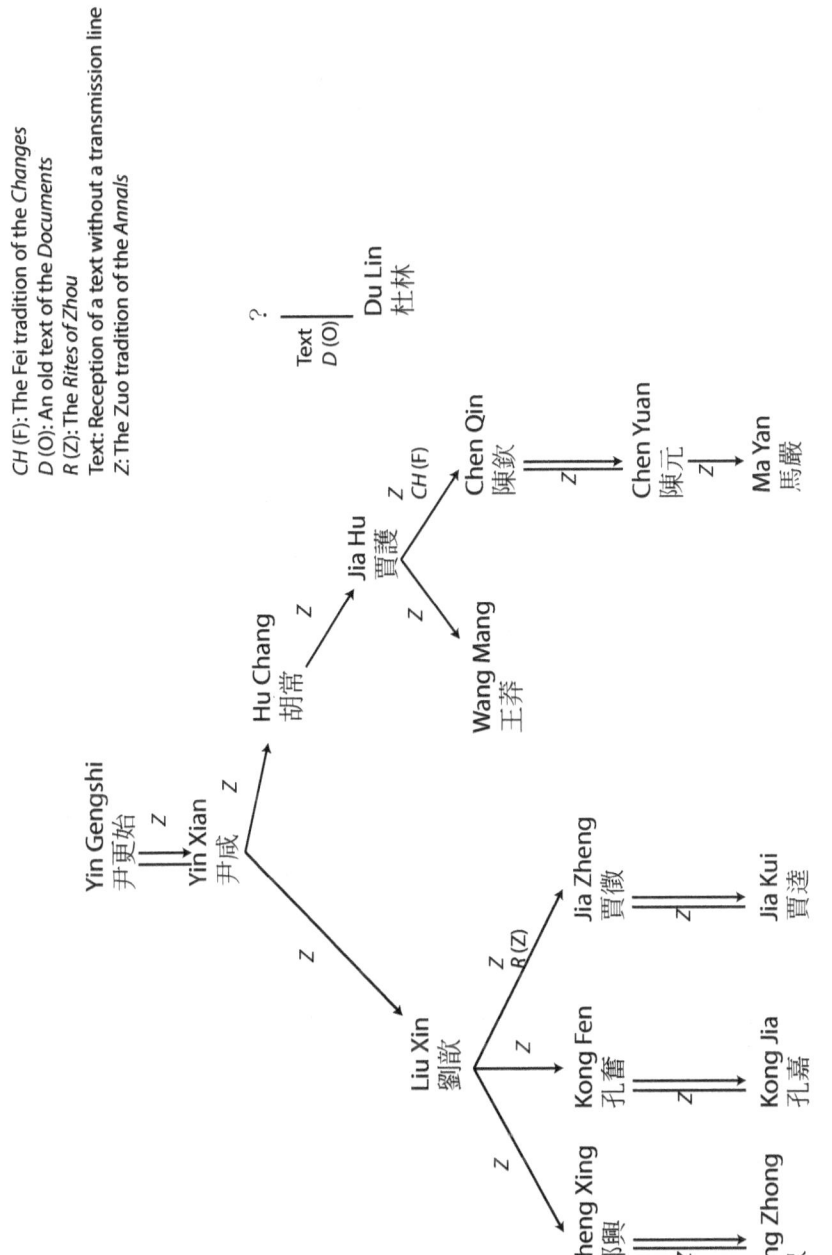

Chart 9. Transmission Lines of Old Text Traditions

The transmission of apocryphal texts within families was even less observable than that of old texts. Part of the reason was that the primary sources did not always specify the transmission of apocrypha. For example, Cao Chong 曹充 and his son Cao Bao 曹襃 were a pair of ritual experts in the early Eastern Han. The *History of the Later Han* only mentions that Cao Bao was able to "pass his father's undertaking down" (*chuan fu ye* 傳父業), but father and son were also largely involved in study of the apocrypha. Cao Chong quoted from apocrypha to convince Emperor Ming to change the name of the official of music from Grand Musician to Grand Yu Musician.[51] Cao Bao tried to design a ritual manual based on apocryphal commentaries on the Five Classics.[52] That is to say, apocryphal texts were part of his family undertaking, but primary sources seldom specified which ones.

This lack of specification in many cases is due to the mingling of apocryphal texts and Western Han commentaries on the classics. The two corpora resembled each other in form and tenor. Primary sources often do not label apocryphal texts in biographies of scholars who transmitted Western Han traditions. For example, in their biographies, Chen Yuan and Fan Sheng appear respectively to be solely transmitters of the old text traditions and of the Liang tradition of the *Changes*.[53] In another account, however, Li Yu 李育 (fl. AD 79) disagrees with Chen Yuan and Fan Sheng precisely because both of them relied too much on the apocrypha.[54] This textual issue makes it difficult for us to identify the transmission of apocryphal texts, suggesting an integration between apocrypha and other commentarial traditions.

A family tradition could prepare you well in classical training and even officialdom. But your teacher is only one person, your father. Your peers were your siblings, at best your cousins. If you wanted to increase your chances of finding a position, connecting with other teachers and peers would have been essential. In the next section, we will examine the flourishing of private schools, a characteristic of the Eastern Han dynasty. Each school was smaller in scale than the Academy, but they formed a much larger, empire-wide unified network. Combined with the situation of official recruitment, these private learning programs formed a literati culture that was peculiar to the Eastern Han.

Without exception, these great families transmitted commentarial traditions that were well established since the Western Han dynasty. Some of them had fairly long family traditions of scholarship. Huan Rong started the tradition around the time of the establishment of the Eastern Han.[55] The Yuan family's tradition was initiated by Yuan Liang 袁良 (fl. AD 1–25) in the last days of the Western Han. We can even trace the Kong family's study of the *Documents* back to Kong Ba 孔霸 of Emperor Cheng's reign

(33–7 BC).⁵⁶ Compared to the old text traditions and imperially sponsored apocryphal texts, the dominance of the existing traditions is due more to their early establishment and wide distribution than to their supporters' suppression of the old text traditions.

INDIVIDUAL DISCIPLESHIP AND TRAVELING

Because the master-disciple relationship permeated the Eastern Han bureaucracy, ideally you could become a disciple of an official. In this way, you would receive his recommendation for junior positions or even appointment as his clerk. While others are fighting for registration at the National Academy or cramming for its examinations, you might have already secured a position that your master reserved for you.⁵⁷ Even if your master were not an official, you would still move forward through his local connections.

The aforementioned Huan family perfectly exemplifies the dynamic of students, their teachers, and their careers in the Eastern Han. Their students benefited from their connections in the court in Luoyang, and many of them found success in teaching. For example, Zhang Pu 張酺 (?–AD 104) of Xiyang 細陽, Runan 汝南 Commandery (in modern Henan 河南 Province), who had already received a tradition of the *Documents* from his father, became a student of Huan Rong, the current Grand Minister of Ceremonies. Later on in AD 66, he became a tutor of the *Documents* for the major imperial harem families.⁵⁸ After a while, he was appointed to tutor the heir apparent.⁵⁹ Hu Xian 胡憲 (fl. AD 51) of Jiujiang 九江 Commandery (in modern Jiangxi 江西 Province) was recommended by his teacher Huan Rong to take over his position of teaching the heir apparent. And Hu became the tutor of the future Emperor Ming.⁶⁰

Many of the Huan family's disciples also became high officials in the court. Zhu Chong 朱寵 (fl. AD 126) of Jingzhao 京兆, one of the Three Adjunct areas (Sanfu 三輔) in modern Shaanxi, and Yang Zhen (AD 54–124) were two students of Huan Yu, then Grand Minister of Ceremonies. Later on, they were appointed to be Grand Commandant (Taiwei 太尉) in AD 126 and Grand Minister of Ceremonies in AD 117, respectively.⁶¹ The family of Yang Zhen became dominant after that appointment. Huan Yan's student Huang Qiong 黃瓊 (AD 86–164) of Anlu 安陸, Jiangxia 江夏 Commandery (in modern Hubei 湖北 Province), was another case. His father Huang Xiang 黃香 (AD 18–106) was the Grand Administrator (*taishou* 太守) of Wei 魏 County and had also worked at the imperial library Dongguan 東觀. After studying under Huan Yan in the capital, Huang Qiong became the Grand Minister of Ceremonies around AD 150 (chart 10). Behind these

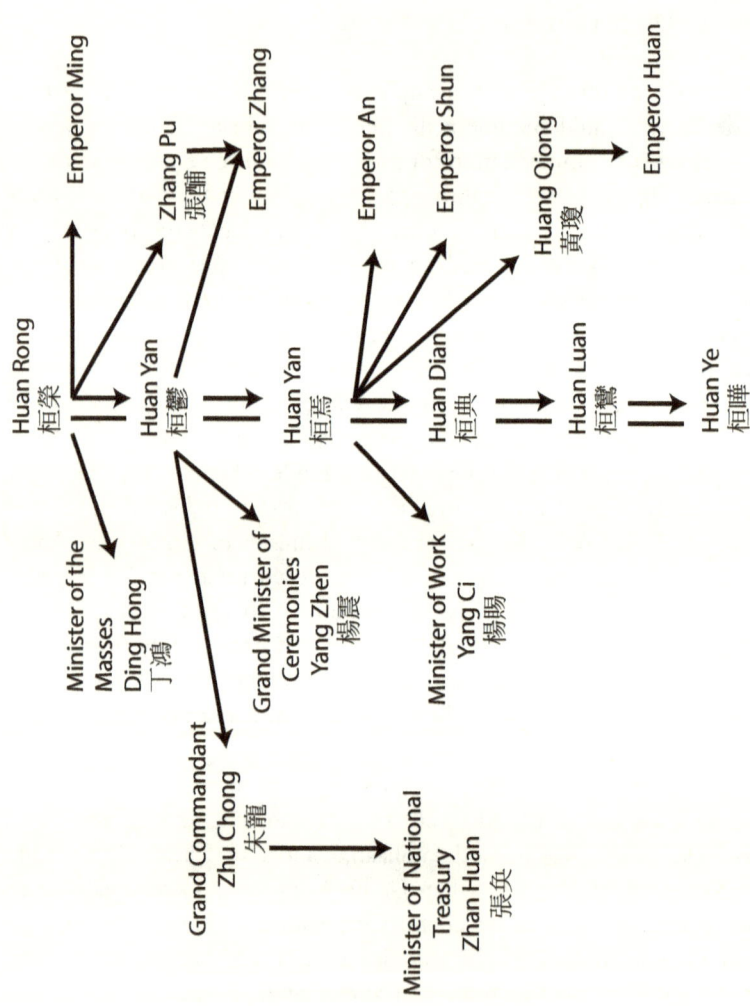

Chart 10. The Huan Family and Their Disciples

successful cases, we see a pattern in literati careers: a young learner, often from a literati family, traveled around to meet his teachers for certain kinds of knowledge and received a position afterward based on the expertise and social connections gained from his learning experience.

In the Eastern Han dynasty, this type of career path was so prevalent that even martial officials engaged in it. A good example is Zhang Huan 張奐 (AD 104–81), a general who fought against the Southern Xiongnu in the 160s and secured the Eastern Han's northwest frontier (chart 10). Although he was born in the far west of the empire, Jiuquan 酒泉, Dunhuang 敦煌 Commandery (in modern Gansu 甘肅 Province), he gradually moved to the heart of the empire: he first traveled to the Three Adjunct areas to study and then became a student of Grand Commandant Zhu Chong in the capital, Luoyang, in order to learn the Ouyang tradition of the *Documents*. Afterward, the Grand General (Da Jiangjun 大將軍) Liang Ji 梁冀 (?–AD 159), a powerful figure from the most dominant imperial harem family since the 130s, appointed him to his entourage. Zhang took this opportunity to present his improved version of the Ouyang tradition to Emperor Huan 桓 (r. AD 147–167), who then promoted him to work at the Dongguan library. It was only through these civil positions that he received a military position and battled against Xiongnu.[62]

Indeed, Eastern Han scholars were part of a peripatetic culture. Their academic career might constitute multiple learning experiences in different regions. As the number of students increased, teachers needed to find ways to organize them. Local academies thus emerged from this context. The local academies probably started from assemblies of students around famous individuals, often with local official titles or previous Academician experience in the National Academy.[63] For example, during his career as Aide for Chencang County (*Chencang xian cheng* 陳倉縣丞), Zhang Xuan 張玄 (fl. AD 25–55) had more than a thousand registered students (*zhulu* 著錄), who came for his versatile knowledge of the classics. In another case, the fame of Li Yu 李育 (fl. AD 79) at the National Academy attracted not only hundreds of students but also noblemen from the capital.[64]

In the first two centuries AD, running local academies and teaching was a rather sophisticated business. Registration suggests that the size and fluidity of the student body was large to the extent that they had to be recorded in writing.[65] Facing this number of students, some academies divided them into groups and managed them differently. For example, Ma Rong's academy had three hundred to four hundred students at a time, but only about fifty of them ever met Ma Rong face to face. The rest were divided according to seniority and were taught by those more senior.⁶⁶ This was also the case at Zheng Xuan's 鄭玄 (AD 127–200) school. Furthermore, at Zheng's school, question-and-answer sessions were one of the major pedagogical techniques between the teacher, Zheng Xuan, and students, or seniors and juniors. In order to make the teaching easy to understand, illustrations and allegories to the Han legal and administrative system were all used to explain ancient customs and administration in the classics.⁶⁷ All these administrative and pedagogical measures show a sensitivity to a large student body with differing levels of achievement and ability.

The need for classical learning was so substantial that opening a local academy was a viable career option for scholars. After studying with Ma Rong, two of his famous students, Zheng Xuan and Lu Zhi 盧植 (AD 139–192), chose to go back home to teach.⁶⁸ In this way, private teaching became an alternative to officialdom.

These private schools supported themselves in various ways. Teachers with official positions, such as Song Hong 宋弘 (fl. AD 26), might use their salary to support the school.⁶⁹ The financial support of Zheng Xuan's school came from agricultural work and the sponsorship of high official Kong Rong 孔融 (AD 158–203) (chart 11).⁷⁰ Students' tuition was also a main source, because many of the students came from well-off families. For example, in order to live close to their teacher, some of Zhang Ba's 張霸 students bought property around his house. It seems unlikely that ordinary people could afford real estate solely for the purpose of study unless they were from great families. In fact, some people invested in real estate around the academies to make money from the traveling students.⁷¹ Economic activities on a considerable scale surrounded these academies.

Therefore, if you decide to attend a private school, you need to pay for your education. But how much? One example illustrates the amount of money a student brought into this private school economy. When Wang Fu 王阜 (fl. AD 77–91) of Shu Commandery 蜀郡 (modern Sichuan Province) wanted to go to the neighboring Qianwei 犍為 Commandery (modern Sichuan Province),⁷² he took two thousand bronze coins and thirteen meters of cloth.⁷³ In the second half of the first century AD, two thousand coins equated to 120 kilograms of wheat.⁷⁴ If a young adult male consumed 0.25 kilograms of wheat per day, two thousand coins would feed him grain for 480 days. If we assume the cloth from Wang Fu was linen, common among Han families, it was worth two hundred coins, another forty-eight days of wheat.⁷⁵ Additionally, taking transportation and accommodation into account, this amount would pay for no more than fifteen months without outside help. This amount, nevertheless, would be affordable for even minor official families. Even if a person took a minor position in local government, he might still earn six hundred kilograms or more of wheat in salary per year. The cost of education outlined here is not too bad compared to the average tuition at Ivy League schools in the United States (an average of $46,632 in 2014 to 2015, vs. $166,200 annual income of the top 5 percent of the middle class).

Even students from ordinary or poor families had a chance to engage in these schools. In the previous case, it was unclear how Wang Fu eventually filled his financial gap, but many students could labor to pay for their expenses. For example, while studying under the Academician Zhu Pu 朱普 (fl. 20 BC–AD 8), Huan Rong had to work as a hired laborer (*keyong* 客傭) to support himself.[76] Wei Sa 衛颯 (fl. AD 8–23), another eager learner from a poor family, often worked as a laborer when he ran out of grain.[77] In the late Eastern Han, Yu Cheng 庾乘 (mid-second century AD), a future capital patrician, became the Academy students' servant in order to study there.[78]

Comparable to graduate scholarship, support from teachers was not uncommon either. We have already seen the case of Song Hong, who used his own salary to support his students. Others such as Cao Shen 曹參 (ca. second century AD) used their family fortunes. There were yet other means for those who were neither high officials nor from wealthy families. For example, Li Xun 李恂 (ca. first century AD) wove straw mats with his students to help them sustain themselves. Ren An's 任安 (AD 124–202) mother provided accommodations for her son's students, which made Ren's school very popular in Guanghan 廣漢 Commandery (modern Sichuan Province).[79]

Thus, in the Eastern Han dynasty, students came from a wide spectrum of socioeconomic backgrounds. On one side of the spectrum, students were of wealthy and powerful origin. Their families could afford even more than the tuition and travel fees. They probably contributed considerably to the local schools' finance. On the other side, students from poor families also had a chance to get involved in this culture with financial support from other sources. They either received funding from the local school or did certain kinds of work to subsidize the expense. As a result, many poor students were tied not only educationally but also financially to their private academies.

It might seem puzzling to many modern readers why a teacher would want to lose money to maintain a local private school. Unlike in the modern world, money came from privilege, rather than vice versa. Fame in local society could help a teacher achieve higher social status and thus pave the road to officialdom. Successful teacher families like the Huan, Yang, and

Yuan preserved their family privileges and had great influence at the court precisely because they produced many students who later became officials at the local or central government.

The privileges lay in students' lifelong duties. Teachers had greater authority in the ancient world than in twenty-first-century universities, and their interactions with their students extended into daily life. Besides social etiquette and miscellaneous daily tasks for the teacher,[80] the teacher's death also called for the involvement of students. Normally, former students and former subordinates, if the teacher had any, would contribute to the erection of his funerary stele. In more dramatic situations, such as executions, students behaved more dramatically. For example, when Dou Xian 竇憲 (?–AD 92)[81] forced his political rival Yue Hui 樂恢 (fl. AD 89) to commit suicide, hundreds of the latter's students went into mourning, donning hemp cloth as family members did.[82] The master-disciple relationship was to a large extent analogous to blood relationships, so the obligations of a disciple compared to that of a family member.[83]

In some people's eyes, in the late second century AD the core of such relationships was obedience. A remark of the tactician Zhang Hong 張紘 (AD 151–211) about a descendant of the Yuan family revealed this tendency: "His [Yuan Shu's] negligence of temperance in following the Way and emphasis on the desire for aggression is like saying 'all people in the world are either [his] family servants or students, so who would not obey me?'"[84] Zhang Hong grouped students with family servants, and obedience was the characteristic they shared. His words revealed two sides of a symbiotic relationship between students and their teachers: while teachers provided knowledge and social connections to help their students in their careers, students reciprocated with obedience. Through this relationship, the possession of knowledge and a teaching position transformed into social privilege and political power.

The Spread of Apocryphal Texts

In chapter 2, we looked at the editors of apocryphal texts in the early Eastern Han.[85] Now let us examine how apocryphal texts spread in the Eastern Han.[86]

Since the apocryphal corpus initially took shape under the hand of the compiler group in the capital, it had a one-way direction from the capital to local regions. One example from the early Eastern Han is Du Fu 杜撫 (fl. AD 56–83), who learned apocrypha from Xue Han 薛漢 (fl. AD 25–72), an editor of apocrypha as well as an Academician of the

Han 韓 tradition of the *Poetry*. Afterward, Du took the teachings home to Qianwei 犍為 Commandery and started his own teaching career there. His school attracted more than a thousand disciples, including the author of the *Springs and Autumns of Wu and Yue* (*Wu Yue Chunqiu* 吳越春秋), Zhao Ye 趙曄 (fl. AD 56–83) from Guiji 會稽 (located in modern Suzhou 蘇州, Jiangsu Province). (See chart 8.)[87]

Another example shows the interaction between the Han court and localities in the transmission of apocrypha. Yang Tong 楊統 (fl. AD 58), a native of Xindu 新都 (in modern Chengdu 成都, Sichuan Province), studied the *River Chart*, *Luo Writing*, and various astrological techniques with Zheng Boshan 鄭伯山 (before AD 25), who was also from nearby. Around AD 25, Yang was summoned to the court to answer questions about omens and was eventually promoted to the Imperial Court Grandee. He wrote an explication on the esoteric prophecies (*neichen* 內讖) and taught his son Yang Hou 楊厚 (AD 72–153) apocryphal texts.[88] Hou continued his father's role as an omen consultant until the empress dowager was dissatisfied with his interpretation of apocryphal texts. He was sacked and returned to his hometown Xindu to establish an academy.[89] His school attracted local people, such as Ren An and Dong Fu 董扶 (ca. AD 108–189), both of whom had studied at the National Academy earlier. After finishing his studies of apocrypha, Dong went home and opened his own academy.[90]

It is noteworthy that the two examples are both from the area around Qianwei (southwest of modern Sichuan Province), a commandery that did not become part of the Han empire until Emperor Wu's time.[91] Qianwei was not the only example; another was Zangke 牂柯 Commandery, approximately two hundred miles southeast of Qianwei. This was where the Yelang 夜郎 kingdom (ca. fourth century–27 BC) was located. It was a rainy place, unsuitable for animal husbandry and the silk industry, and thus a poor place to live. The local people also had different religious practices from the majority of the Han empire. However, in the mid-second century AD, a native of Zangke, Yin Zhen 尹珍 (AD 79–162), traveled to Runan 汝南, a commandery approximately 168 miles from the capital, to learn the classics and apocryphal texts. His teachers included Xu Shen 許慎 (ca. AD 58–147), a student of Ma Rong and an expert in old text traditions, and the historian Ying Feng 應奉 (fl. AD 144). He then returned home to teach.[92] Compared to the Henan 河南 area, where the capital was located, or the Three Adjunct areas, Qianwei and Zangke were isolated areas. However, in the second century, individual academies flourished in the periphery as well. For that reason, apocryphal texts were transmitted to such previously isolated areas.

Beginning in the second century, the transmission of apocryphal texts was no longer a one-way street. Thanks to the prosperity of the local schools, many scholars were already well trained in apocrypha even before they went to the capital and the National Academy. For example, Li Gu 李固 (AD 94–147), a scholar who engaged in political conflict with Liang Ji after witnessing the latter's murder of Emperor Zhi 質 (r. AD 146), had spent more than ten years in the Three Adjunct areas learning the Five Classics, apocryphal texts, and divination. His experience of travel and dedication to learning made him famous in the capital. He thus received recommendations as a member of the Filial and Uncorrupted and for appointment as Clerk in the Ministry of Works (Sikong Yuan 司空掾).[93]

Fan Ying 樊英 (fl. AD 107–143), one of the scholars whom Li Gu recommended to Emperor Shun (r. AD 126–144), had a similar experience. He went to the Three Adjunct area to study and mastered the Jing tradition of the *Changes* and apocryphal texts, as well as several kinds of divination.[94] Afterward, he traveled to Mount Hu 壺, a place close to his hometown, Luyang 魯陽 of Nanyang 南陽 Commandery (present-day Nanyang, Henan Province), to teach apocrypha. His school became popular and attracted attention from local and central officials. At the beginning of Emperor An's reign (AD 107–125), Fan Ying was appointed as an Academician.[95] His students included Chen Shi 陳寔 (AD 104–187), a leader of the early partisan movement, and Fan Ran 范冉 (AD 112–185), who later became a student of Ma Rong, an "old text tradition" scholar (chart 11).[96]

The Spread of Old Text Traditions

What if you were not satisfied with the common curriculum and desired to learn the old text traditions or even other texts? Besides the small circle Liu Xin created, there were few choices in the first decades of the first century AD. For example, Du Lin 杜林 (?–AD 47) came from a family with an abundance of books.[97] He began to teach the old script version of the *Documents* after he had obtained one chapter of this text in Hexi 河西 area (present-day western Gansu Province).[98] Chen Yuan 陳元 (fl. AD 25) received the Zuo tradition of the *Annals* from his father Chen Qin 陳欽 (ca. 34 BC–AD 15), who had taught Wang Mang the Zuo tradition.[99] Chen Yuan then taught the Zuo tradition to Ma Rong's father, Ma Yan 馬嚴. This transmission line can be traced back to Yin Gengshi 尹更始 (fl. 50 BC), from whose son, Yin Xian 尹咸 (fl. 25 BC–AD 5), Liu Xin learned the Zuo tradition (chart 11).[100]

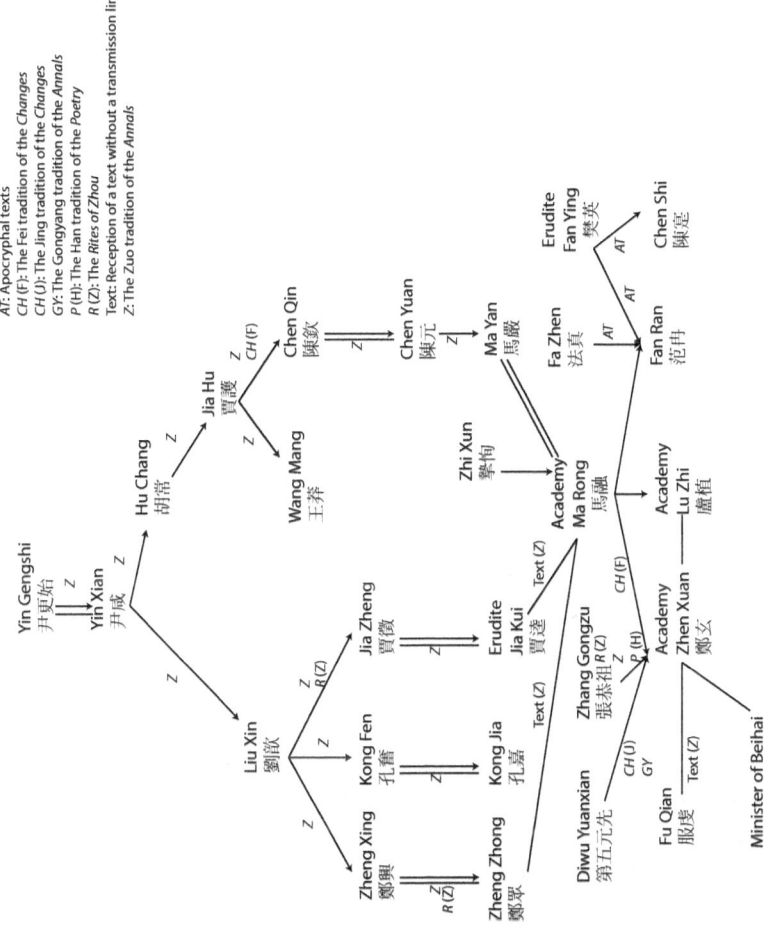

Chart 11. Transmission of Knowledge in Ma Rong and Zheng Xuan's Time

Modern scholars as well as Qing classicists have warned us about the hostility between the followers of the "old script texts" and of the "new script texts." But one's choice of course of study is far from equivalent to choosing a political side. Taking Chen Yuan again for an example, while he was famous for being a radical advocate of the Zuo tradition, he was recommended by two experts on the Western Han commentaries, Li Tong 李通 (?–AD 42) and Ouyang Xi 歐陽歙 (?–AD 39). The two recommenders were the current Minister of Works and an expert on apocryphal texts,[101] and current Minister of the Masses (situ 司徒) and expert on the Ouyang tradition of the *Documents*, respectively.[102] In the Eastern Han bureaucracy, where social connections were directly linked to political positions, it is hard to see in this case political partisanship based on the choice of old script texts.

The old text traditions were obviously a part of the Eastern Han intellectual culture, but less often transmitted independently than the Western Han traditions. We do have a few examples suggesting independent transmission, such as Zhou Fang 周防 (fl. AD 25) receiving the teaching of the old text *Documents* from Gai Yu 蓋豫 (fl. AD 60), the Inspector of Xu Province (*Xuzhou cishi* 徐州刺史), and Yang Lun 楊倫 (fl. AD 92–135), who had received the old text *Documents* from then–Minister of the Masses Ding Hong 丁鴻 (?–AD 92).[103] Nevertheless, Ding Hong was mainly a transmitter of the Ouyang tradition of the *Documents*.[104] In other words, the old text traditions were transmitted along with the Western Han traditions.

It was also rare to exclusively see old text traditions in local academies. In the Eastern Han, Ma Rong's academy was one of the most famous places associated with the old text traditions. However, they were just part of the curriculum; Ma's list of books also included *Laozi* 老子,[105] the *Biographies of Significant Women* (*Lie nü zhuan* 列女傳), *Master Huainan* (*Huainanzi* 淮南子), and Qu Yuan's 屈原 "Encountering Sorrow" ("Li sao" 離騷).[106]

Eastern Han funerary inscriptions document similar phenomena. According to a stele in commemoration of Wu Rong 武榮 (ca. ?–AD 167), Wu mastered (*zhi* 治) the Lu tradition of the *Poetry* and "transmitted and lectured on" (*chuan jiang* 傳講) the Zuo tradition, *Analects*, the *Classic of Filial Piety*, the *History of the Han*, the *Grand Historian's Records* (*Shiji* 史記), and the *Speeches from the States* (*Guoyu* 國語).[107] In this respect, the Zuo tradition was simply one of the texts in Wu Rong's repertoire.

Since many texts from the old text traditions were discovered in written form and still stored as written documents, they were free from the control of a teacher, more so than the Western Han traditions. The capital, especially, possessed resources such as book markets and libraries that minor cities or towns lacked.¹⁰⁸ Literati who worked in the imperial library could gain access to documents and commentarial traditions that were otherwise unobtainable. This is part of the reason why in the Western Han the old texts were not well known among most literati. In contrast, in the Eastern Han, increasing travel to places like Luoyang and the Three Adjuncts area gave scholars more chances to be exposed to written documents and thus helped these texts to spread.

Manuscripts of commentaries became an indispensable element in many anecdotes about scholars of the old text traditions, especially the stories that concern written texts. In the previous section, we examined three father-son pairs of transmitters of the old texts. Among them, Jia Kui and Zheng Zhong passed on their study of the Zuo tradition and other old texts in written form. When Ma Rong had a chance to work at the imperial library, he managed to read Jia and Zheng's studies of these texts. According to the *History of the Later Han*, Ma had written a commentary on the Zuo tradition, but after reading Jia and Zheng's study of it, he signed: "While Mr. Jia's work is refined but not comprehensive, Mr. Zheng's work is comprehensive but not refined. [However, taken together] they are refined and comprehensive. What can I add to their work?"¹⁰⁹ Rather than a commentary, he then wrote the *Explications of the Similarity and Difference between the Three Traditions* (*San zhuan yitong shuo* 三傳異同說) (chart 11).¹¹⁰

Admiration of others' works was not peculiar to Ma Rong, nor did it happen only at the imperial library. His equally celebrated student Zheng Xuan once wanted to write a commentary on the *Annals*. However, during a trip, after overhearing Fu Qian 服虔 (fl. AD 189)¹¹¹ discussing his own commentary, Zheng Xuan said: "I have desired to make a commentary but have not finished it yet. I heard what you have just said, which is similar to my commentary. Now I should give all of my commentary to you." Fu Qian then took it and finished his own work on the Zuo commentary of the *Annals* (chart 11).¹¹²

These anecdotes reflect an increasing involvement in written transmission that is parallel to the oral transmission. One could receive certain knowledge through writing without the guidance of a teacher. In contrast, oral transmission was not as free from supervision. The teacher might scold a student for misinterpretation or simply not understanding a text in the way the teacher did. Working with solely textual material thus allowed one to absorb certain knowledge without joining any transmission line. Certainly, written transmission was hardly new in Han China, but it became increasingly common. For instance, Liu Xiang was only free from higher scholarly authority to supervise and correct his readings when he was an imperial official in charge of editing. Seventy years later, when Wang Chong was able to wander around the book market in Luoyang reading texts however he wished, he was merely a commoner.[113]

The increasing reliance on written forms changed not only the old text traditions but classicism in general. The Han empire was built upon written documents; the entire bureaucratic system was heavily based on the transmission of words on bamboo, and, less often, silk and paper.[114] Therefore, everyone was more or less involved in this writing culture at various levels.[115]

This reliance on writing further interacted with peripatetic culture and led to the adoption of new writing materials. For example, during frequent and constant traveling, the weight of bamboo and wooden slips would become a fatal burden and lighter material was needed. Xing Yitian estimates that a 23.13-x-1.18-x-0.34-centimeter slip's average weight was either 7.335, 3.875, 3.538, or 4.21 grams, if the material is, respectively, branchy tamarisk, pine, diversifolius poplar, or Taiwanese bamboo. Based on excavated examples in Wang Mang's reign, such slips could fit thirty-five to thirty-eight characters on one side. That is to say, if one wanted to use these kinds of slips to carry the entire *Grand Historian's Records*, which contains around 526,500 characters, one would need 13,855 slips, weighing about 48.1 to 55.9 kilograms, depending on the material. These slips would occupy 0.28 cubic meters of space if they are perfectly arranged, but they would certainly take up much more space in reality, since they were bound as scrolls in the Eastern Han. That is to say, while this number of characters could be carried by a modern paper book 15 x 21 x 4 centimeters (0.0013 cubic meter) from Zhonghua Press 中華書局 in China, the version on wooden slips takes at least 225 times more space. The weight and volume of the Zhonghua version of the *Records* is already costly to transport nowadays when traveling. How much more so if written on slips two millennia ago?

Furthermore, in the Eastern Han dynasty, traveling created social connections over long distances. In order to maintain them, one needed to invest in writing letters.[116] The need for lighter writing materials for travel and communication thus accelerated the use of paper, which in turn greatly affected contemporary scholarship.[117] Also, skills in writing communicative genres and calligraphy became increasingly valued, and knowledge traveled through their written forms more and more frequently.[118]

Travel marked Eastern Han scholars' social life, and thus had fundamentally changed their intellectual perspectives. You might start out pursuing an official career. But what if, after studying with your father, you travel to another place and encounter something completely different from what you had learned previously? What if this situation happened constantly during one's career? Suppose one was a true learner who took knowledge seriously. Would you then insist on the family tradition, or would you reconsider what you had learned? After reading works such as the *Grand Historian's Records*, would you finally realize that the classics were not the sum of knowledge? Would you thus reflect that achieving the Great Peace required more than just the classics? In the following sections, we will see a growing tendency toward an exploration of a larger textual universe, and a scholarly inclination to explore texts beyond the corpus of the classics. At the same time, applying the abstract essentials of the classics to the Han dynasty, rather than imposing the specific details of the ancient Kingly Way, increasingly became a topic.

Ma Rong and His Friends: A Case Study of Horizontal Relationships

Classicism enjoyed its heyday for more than a hundred years, but it was gradually clouded by political instability. The first half of the second century AD was marked with the lack of working emperors. From Emperor Zhang's successor Emperor He 和 (r. AD 89–106) to the last emperor, Xian 獻 (r. AD 190–220), no emperor was enthroned at an age above fifteen. Dominant imperial harem families, eunuchs, and warlords competed to fill the power vacuum; through political conflicts, power shifted frequently from one imperial harem family to another and from one eunuch group to another (see table 4). When a certain group was in power, it tended to further strengthen its power by appointing its own partisans to official posts and getting rid of enemies' supporters.[119] The frequent occurrence of this situation not only compromised the emperor's authority, but more importantly it interrupted normal recruitment and frustrated people who planned to take regular career paths through learning and traveling.[120] Eventually, the literati's discontent erupted in a massive protest in the National Academy in AD 166, which later developed into bloody political conflicts and ended with a two-decade proscription of many literati.[121]

In this section, we will examine a group of literati who lived through this gradual decline to instability, namely, Ma Rong and his allies, who grew up in the environment where classical training could often lead to an official position, and they witnessed how this path narrowed. They were immersed in the flourishing classical culture, but they were also the forerunners who departed from classicism. Their lives are particularly telling for the intellectual trends of the peripatetic and writing culture.

Besides Ma Rong, their intellectual community included Dou Zhang 竇章 (ca. ?–AD 144) from the imperial harem family, Cui Yuan 崔瑗 (AD 77–142) from a family of historians, Zhang Heng from a great family of Nanyang 南陽,[122] and Wang Fu 王符 (ca. AD 85–163),[123] a concubine's son who was socially marginal in his hometown, Linjing 臨涇 of Anding 安定 (Zhenyuan 鎮原, Gansu Province).[124] They probably met each other during their travel to Luoyang and some of their editorial jobs at the Dongguan 東觀 library,[125] the institute for compiling the national history (chart 12).[126]

Written words were essential to this group. As mentioned earlier, letters were an indispensable method for communication across distances in the Eastern Han.[128] For this group, sending letters was not a chore, but a respected mode of social contact occasionally parallel to personal encounters. For example, after receiving Dou Zhang's letter, Ma Rong wrote back:

孟陵奴來，賜書。見手跡，歡喜何量，見於面也。

> Mengling's[129] servant came and bestowed your letter. When I saw your handwriting, my pleasure, beyond measurement, showed on my face.[130]

Ma Rong's letter responded to Dou Zhang's earlier letter, which contained eight lines of seven characters on two pieces of paper.[131] Since it was Dou Zhang's servant who delivered this letter, Dou Zhang and Ma Rong seemed to live within a distance that allowed personal encounters. Whether Dou Zhang's letter contained fine verses, beautiful calligraphy, or important messages, he did not seem to think that the letter or the message should be orally delivered by himself. Ma Rong, similarly, did not consider receiving the letter or sending a message back to Dou Zhang inappropriate. On the contrary, "meeting" Dou's handwriting was good enough for Ma Rong to be happy. In other words, for both of them, letters were normal forms of contact.

As a group of literati, one of Ma Rong and his friends' major activities was to discuss knowledge, scholarship, and in many cases, books. This community also carried out such discussions via letters.[132] For example, in a letter to Cui Yuan, Zhang Heng suggested that Cui should make a copy of Yang Xiong's work:

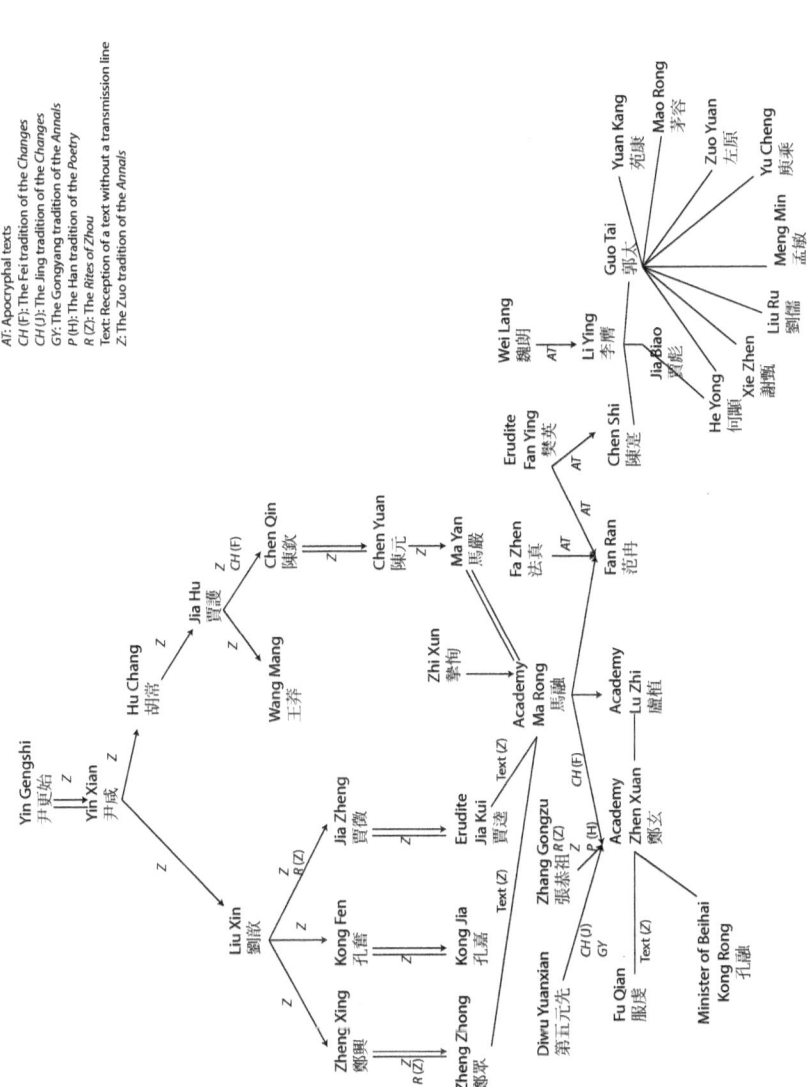

Chart 12. Partisans and Their Affiliates[127]

乃者以朝駕明¹³³日披讀《太玄經》。知子雲特極陰陽之數也。以其滿汎故，故時人不務此....《玄》四百歲其興乎。竭已精思。以揆其義。更使人難論陰陽之事。足下累世窮道極微。子孫必命世不絕。且幅寫一通藏之。以俟能者。¹³⁴

Previously during my morning carriage trip every day, I perused the *Classic of Supreme Mystery*. I realized that Yang Xiong [knew] *yin-yang* exhaustively. Because [this book] is so high-flown, people nowadays do not devote themselves to it. . . . Will the *Supreme Mystery* not become popular in four hundred years? [I] exhausted my mind to penetrate its meaning. [Because of its subtlety,] it increases people's difficulty in discussing matters of *yin-yang*. Your family has comprehensively known the Way and its subtlety for generations. Your descendants will command the world without end. [You might] write a copy of it and store it to wait for one who is able [to fully understand it].

As an enthusiastic recommendation for Yang Xiong's *Classic of Supreme Mystery*,¹³⁵ Zhang Heng's letter tells us something about Eastern Han literati life: during travel, one read a famous scholar's work and found certain parts of the work related to his interest and focus.¹³⁶ Impressed by the work, he wrote a letter to recommend it to a friend and suggested the latter should have a copy made for his permanent collection too. All of this sounds similar to modern scholars' lives, although in the Han it involved vastly more trouble.

If gift-giving is ubiquitous in building and maintaining social relationships in any society,¹³⁷ then the contents of the gifts suggest what is valued in a relationship. In a letter to socialize¹³⁸ with Ge Gong 葛龔 (fl. AD 89–113), an appreciated memorial writer,¹³⁹ Cui Yuan noted his gift:

今遣奉書錢千為贄。并送《許子》十卷。貧不及素。但以紙耳。¹⁴⁰

Now I send one thousand coins for books as a gift. I also send you *Xuzi* in ten scrolls. I am poor so that cannot afford silk [for the *Xuzi*], but only paper.

Behind the "paperback" *Xuzi*, we see not only a book market but a market specific to various writing materials.¹⁴¹ We might infer that the choice of bamboo, wood, paper, or silk reflected social status. And by then, paper as a new writing material was fairly approachable among the literati. Texts, both their material form and content, became one of the major sacred objects that bonded and defined Eastern Han literati, and Ma Rong's intellectual community in particular.

Ma Rong and His Family: A Versatile Tradition

Ma Rong 馬融 (AD 79–166) came from a great family in Fufeng 扶風, one of the Three Adjunct areas (Sanfu 三輔) in modern Shaanxi.[142] His grandfather's younger brother Ma Yuan 馬援 (14 BC–AD 49) was an accomplished general and Emperor Ming's father-in-law. Ma Rong's father, Ma Yan 馬嚴 (17–98 AD), was the Grand Court Architect (*jiangzuo dajiang* 將作大匠).[143] Ma Yan learned the Zuo tradition under Chen Yuan 陳元 (fl. AD 25),[144] and he was also well informed about miscellaneous writings (*baijia qunyan* 百家群言) under Yang Taibo's 楊太伯 (ca. first century AD) instruction (chart 12).[145] Later on, with one of the authors of the *History of the Han*, Ban Gu, Ma Yan edited a historical document about Emperor Guangwu's reign, *Comments on Records of the Jianwu Reign* (*Jianwu zhuji* 建武注記).[146] Ma Rong's brother Ma Xu 馬續 (AD 70–141) was also a versatile scholar[147] who mastered the *Poetry*, *Documents*, and *Nine Chapters on the Arithmetic Art* (*Jiu zhang suanshu* 九章算術).[148]

Ma Rong's educational background reflected his family's broad taste. He studied with the famous recluse Zhi Xun 摯恂 and was well versed in various texts.[149] His perspective was further broadened when, around AD 107, Empress Dowager Deng 鄧太后 (AD 81–121) sent him to the Dongguan library to edit the classics, commentarial traditions, and other texts.[150] His wide-ranging commentarial works also reflect his broad interests. Earlier in this chapter, we noted that Ma Rong undertook the substantial project of writing a commentary on the Zuo tradition. In addition to this, he also wrote commentaries on all of the other classics, namely, the Mao tradition of the *Poetry*, the Fei tradition of the *Changes*, the *Documents*, the *Records of Rites*, *Rites and Etiquettes*, the *Rites of Zhou*, *Analects*, and the *Classic of Filial Piety*.[151] It seems that Ma Rong intended to cover the whole corpus of the classics.[152] However, as we have seen (chart 12), his textual world was wider still. It is unclear whether Ma Rong thought such texts as *Laozi*, *Huainanzi*, or "Li sao" as significant as the classics, but he certainly considered their contents deserving explication just like the classics.[153] While scholars at the end of the Western Han such as Yang Xiong narrowed their perspective to the Five Classics in search of the ancient sage kings' legacy,

Ma Rong and his contemporaries expanded their scope to explore a wide range of texts beyond the classics.

Cui Yuan and His Family Tradition: From Transmitter to Author

Cui Yuan was also from a great family in Anping, Zhuo Commandery 涿郡 (present-day Zhuozhou, Hebei Province).[154] His great-grandfather Cui Zhuan 崔篆 (fl. AD 9–55), Governor of Jianxin (Jianxin *dayin* 建新大尹) under Wang Mang's interregnum, was an expert in the *Changes*.[155] Yuan's father, Cui Yin 崔駰 (?–AD 92), was well versed in the *Changes*, *Poetry*, *Annals*, philological works, and various kinds of thought.[156] Instead of devoting his life to transmitting the classics, Cui Yin made a career in the capital with his literary talent.[157] His panegyric "Hymn of Four Journeys" ("Si xun song" 四巡頌), a work praising the greatness of the Han,[158] greatly impressed Emperor Zhang, and thus earned him an official title.[159] Cui Yin left no commentaries, only literary works, including poetry, hymns, rhapsodies, and inscriptions.[160]

Like his father, Cui Yuan was also trained in classicism but involved more in literary writing. As for classical training, he not only received all of his father's teachings, he also became one of Jia Kui's favorite students when he went to Luoyang at eighteen years of age (AD 94). In Luoyang, he also learned mathematical astronomy, astrology, and the Jing tradition of the *Changes*. His eagerness to learn never flagged; even in jail, he learned the *Rites* from a janitor.[161]

Like those of his father, Cui Yuan's works concentrated more on discovering the contemporary world than on classical commentary. For example, as a celebrated calligrapher using cursive "draft script" (*cao shu* 草書), Cui Yuan wrote the "Shaping of Draft Script" ("Caoshu shi" 草書執[162]), promoting this rising fashion as part of Eastern Han literati culture:[163]

> 書契之興，始自頡皇。寫彼鳥跡，以定文章。爰暨末葉，典籍彌繁；時之多僻，政之多權。官事荒蕪，剿其墨翰。惟多佐隸，舊字是刪。草書之法，蓋又簡略。應時諭指，用於卒迫。兼功並用，愛日省力；純儉之變，豈必古式。[164]

The rise of writing started with Sovereign Jie [Cang Jie 倉頡]. He drew traces of birds to decide the pattern of words. Later, texts became more and more intricate. The era was rich in wrongdoing, and governance was full of cunning. Official affairs were neglected, and [thus] ink and brushes were disused. [Then] clerical style became common, and old characters fell out of use. Draft script was perhaps a further simplification. It suits the times and conveys the gist [of what people write], and it is useful in urgency. It concentrates and saves effort. It saves time and energy. Since the trend is toward simplicity, why does the standard have to be the ancient?

In this passage, the evolution of calligraphy was in line with that of classics as mentioned by Liu Xin: a sage king's invention, its deterioration and loss, and then attempts in the present to revive it. Nevertheless, Cui Yuan does not lament the loss of the ancient tradition, nor does he condemn anybody responsible for the deterioration. He does not want to resume the ancient way. On the contrary, he celebrates this change, and moves on to the draft script, as a contemporary style.

Cui Yuan was good at writing admonitions (*zhen* 箴), a genre devoted to rectifying the Han bureaucratic system.[165] From Commandery Grand Administrator (*jun taishou* 郡太守) to Colonel-Director of Retainers (*sili Xiaowei* 司隸校尉), and from Master of Writing to Captain of the Northern Army at the Capital (*beijun zhonghou* 北軍中候), he wrote down what these positions ought to be, and how they evolved from the ancient sage kings' time. However, he was more interested in how officials could learn from history, especially from the outrageous Qin, than in overthrowing the current system and installing one from the Golden Age.[166] For him, the Han should have picked up where the Qin left off rather than reviving the relics of the sage kings that Qin ended.

Indeed, Cui wrote for his contemporaries, privately and publicly. In addition to his renown as a writer of admonitions, he was also famed for writing inscriptions (*ming* 銘),[167] a literary genre that was not only written down but also inscribed on objects for exhibition and exchange. These inscriptions contained mottos, praise, admonitions, and best wishes. Cui wrote inscriptions for canes, hairpins, pillows, and other people's vessels and lockets.[168] Most importantly, together with his calligraphy, Cui interacted with other literati through his written words. If a master-disciple relationship requires an intimate and private transmission of knowledge from the top down, then writing inscriptions created a more horizontal, instant, and open kind of social networking among the author, owner, and audience. Michael Nylan mentions how the Han government invested in the display culture to consolidate its rule.¹⁶⁹ Here Cui Yuan turned this culture around to bring the literati together.

Zhang Heng: "I Am Ashamed of Not Knowing Even a Single Thing"

Zhang Heng was even more versatile than Cui Yuan. He was a productive writer, famous poet, and an enthusiastic panegyrist of the Han dynasty.¹⁷⁰ More than that, his scholarship represented a broad spectrum from book learning to designing a seismoscope to predict earthquakes and armillary spheres.¹⁷¹ Like many of his contemporaries, Zhang traveled to the Three Adjunct areas and then continued his studies in Luoyang, where he studied at the National Academy. He was not only well informed in the Five Classics, but he was particularly good at mathematical astronomy, astrology, and cosmology.¹⁷² Because of his expertise, Emperor An appointed him as a Gentleman of the Palace. Later he was promoted to Grand Historian (*taishi ling* 太史令), a position Sima Qian and Ban Gu both once occupied.

Zhang Heng then followed the career path of a Grand Historian. From about AD 107, the Empress Dowager Deng summoned Supervisor of the Receptionists (*yezhe puye* 謁者僕射)¹⁷³ Liu Zhen 劉珍 (?–AD 126), Editor (*jiaoshu lang* 校書郎) Liu Taotu 劉騊駼 (?–126 AD), Ma Rong, and many other Academicians to edit the classics, commentarial traditions, and various kinds of thought at the Dongguan library.¹⁷⁴ In AD 120, she asked Liu Zhen and Liu Taotu to lead the project of writing the *Records of the Han* as well as drafting Han ceremonies and etiquette.¹⁷⁵ In AD 126, Zhang was about to join Liu Zhen and Liu Taotu's project, but this did not happen because the latter two soon died. Around AD 132, Zhang Heng asked for appointment to the Dongguan library to continue his editorial work on the library's abundant collections.¹⁷⁶ He then compiled a list of discrepancies between Sima Qian and Ban Gu's historical works and other texts, and suggested corrections.¹⁷⁷

Behind these diverse accomplishments was Zhang Heng's general perspective about knowledge and its relationship with the classics, as represented in his "Response to Critiques" ("Ying jian" 應閒):

公旦道行，故制典禮以尹天下，懼教誨之不從，有人不理。仲尼不遇，故論六經以俟來辟，恥一物之不知，有事之無範。¹⁷⁸

The Duke of Zhou's way was practiced, so that he designed rites and protocols to govern All-under-Heaven. He was afraid that his teachings would not be followed, and people would fail to be cultivated. Confucius was not recognized, so he explicated the Six Classics to later generations. He was ashamed if there was even a single thing he did not know, and if there were affairs without standards.

Zhang points out that the former sages made great efforts to elucidate the way by using the rites or the classics. In the project of the Six Classics in particular, he believes that Confucius was pursuing two things: the completeness of knowledge and the various kinds of standards in the world. By using the words *shi* 事 (affairs) and *wu* 物 (things), he refers to everything in the world through history. In other words, for him, Confucius's project of the Six Classics was to understand everything that took place in the world and set up standards for them in words. Unlike Liu Xin, in his mind, Confucius was not just a transmitter; as the author of the *Annals*, he was also a writer who sought to regulate the world. And it was this dual role that Zhang intended to emulate.

As for the relationship between an author and a transmitter of the classics, Zhang Heng expressed his view in a letter to Cui Yuan, which discussed Yang Xiong's *Supreme Mystery*:

非特傳記之屬，心實與五經擬。漢家得[天下]二百歲[之書也。復二百歲，殆將]卒乎？所以作興者之數，其道必顯一代。常然之符也。《玄》四百歲其興乎！[179]

[The *Supreme Mystery*] does not particularly belong to the genre of commentary [on the classics]; its heart actually resembles [that of] the Five Classics. [The *Mystery*] is a text of the Han, the dynasty that has held All-under-Heaven for two hundred years. Is it going to end in another two hundred years? As for the regular pattern of authors,[180] their way will be manifest for an era. This is always the case. Isn't the *Supreme Mystery* going to rise in the four hundredth year [of the Han dynasty]?

In this rather twisted comment, Zhang Heng divides the Han dynasty into two two-hundred-year periods, with the beginning of the Western Han dynasty to Yang Xiong's composition of the work as the first two hundred years. He predicts the fall of the Eastern Han dynasty after a span of two hundred years and believes that only then will Yang Xiong's intentions receive widespread recognition, just as it took three hundred years for Confucius's

Annals to be celebrated by most people.[181] In addition to reconstructing the Five Classics to illuminate the Kingly Way, Zhang pointed out another way for the literati to transmit the Way: composing their own works that could carry the spirit of the classics and become prominent in later generations. In other words, the continuation of ancient sages' projects did not necessarily lie in the preservation of the classics; new writings could carry them too.[182]

More explicitly than many of his contemporaries, Zhang Heng emphasized the "heart," or the essence in the classical corpus. A text can become a classic at the right moment, as long as it contains the essence of the classics. In this respect, he created a certain abstraction in his understanding of the classics. How do we explain this phenomenon? As Durkheim mentioned, the development of abstraction is due to an appeal to maintain unification across diverseness.[183] Randall Collins further elaborates: "The mind of a 'sophisticated' intellectual, heir to a historically complex network of oppositions and changes in level, internalizes an invisible community of diverse viewpoints, unified by looking on them from a yet more encompassing standpoint."[184] In the Eastern Han, peripatetic culture led to the increased circulation of texts. Scholars were thus more frequently faced with expanding, often contradictory knowledge. In addition to constant debates, another path to the resolution of contradictions was to raise the level of abstraction to unify diverse opinions. Emerging from this context, Zhang Heng sought to bring the old (the classics) and the new (literary writing) together.

Concluding Remarks

Embodied in Zhang Heng's failed attempt to continue the *Book of Changes*, classicism did not make peace with literary writing. From Emperor Ming's enthronement in AD 58 to the establishment of the Hongdu Gate school in AD 178, gradual intellectual changes among the literati became more and more observable. At the beginning of the time span, Emperor Ming thought of himself in the image of Confucius as a transmitter of the classics. For him, the literati were his disciples, meant to carry out this project of transmission. Emperor Ling, at its end, engaged in literary works, calligraphy, and other arts. In the middle of the period, peripatetic culture brought the literati closer and closer together. This culture spread the classics and other writings and hence led to a broader perspective. Closer bonds increased the need for communication, which made people increasingly value literary works. More often than before, scholars addressed a known or unknown audience who were not their students but people who understood them. They wrote not to teach but to tell.

This change in turn affected the study of the classics. Among the Huan, Yang, Yuan, and Kong families, which transmitted the classics for generations, fewer and fewer descendants still chose to transmit the classics as their major occupation. After AD 150, people like Huan Bin 桓彬 (AD 133–78), Yang Xiu 楊修 (AD 175–219), and Kong Rong 孔融 (AD 153–208) became great writers instead.[185] Yuan Shao 袁紹 (?–202 AD) and Yuan Shu—whether they were classically trained is unknown—planned to use the former subordinates and students whom their family had accumulated for generations in their rebellion (chart 7). Leaders in the proscription of partisans such as Li Ying 李膺, Guo Tai 郭太, and Chen Shi 陳寔 enjoyed great popularity in the National Academy, not so much because of extraordinary expertise in the classics as due to their skill in making alliances (chart 12). The majority of their followers appeared as "friends" (*xiang you shan* 相友善) rather than their students.[186] The quality they valued when making friends was skill in discussion (*tanlun* 談論).[187] Some Academy students probably no longer considered knowledge about the classics fashionable.[188]

Given this change, were there still advocates of the classics? If so, how would they deal with such changes? Was the Great Peace that generations of literati sought to be found in the classics, or was it somewhere else entirely? In the next chapter, we will see how Zheng Xuan, He Xiu, and the *Scripture of the Great Peace* dealt with the decline of the classics and perpetuated the search for the Great Peace.

Chapter 5

The Radical and the Conservative

Zheng Xuan, He Xiu, the *Scripture of the Great Peace*, and Their Stances on the Classics

As we saw in the previous chapter, classicism encouraged a traveling culture, which brought the literati to a broader world of knowledge. In this new world, the classics could no longer cover the literati's need. This trend of erudition accompanied the departure of the classics. In chapter 1, we witnessed the abortive intellectual movement of the *Scripture of the Great Peace* at the end of the first century BC.[1] However, in AD 166, Xiang Kai 襄楷 brought the scripture to the attention of Emperor Huan 桓 (r. AD 147–167),[2] and later the movement became a massive one aiming to achieve the Great Peace.[3] In chapter 3, we witnessed that in late first century AD Emperor Ming was devoted to Confucius and his undertaking. Emperor Huan, by contrast, sacrificed to Laozi 老子 in AD 165.[4] In AD 178, his successor, Emperor Ling 靈 (r. AD 168–189), established the Hongdu Gate school, or *Hongdu menxue* 鴻都門學, which emphasized literature, calligraphy, and miscellaneous minor skills.[5] How would the classicists posit themselves in these new developments?

Previous Western scholarship on the intellectual history of the Eastern Han dynasty usually focuses on how ideas from texts like *Han Feizi* or *Zhuangzi* became popular again and began to overshadow the study of the classics.[6] Given the tendency toward broad learning that we saw in the previous chapter, this is not a surprising finding. In this chapter, we will examine how the other end of the intellectual spectrum, classicism, was related to this increased interest in texts other than the Five Classics. We will investigate two very different scholars, each renowned for his classical erudition, Zheng Xuan 鄭玄 (AD 127–200) and He Xiu 何休 (AD 129–182), and one text, the *Scripture of the Great Peace* (*Taiping jing* 太平經), which at first might seem completely unrelated to the classics.

Zheng and He made contributions to classical studies that their contemporaries found lively and engaging, because their aim was to establish the Great Peace (*taiping* 太平). The *Scripture of the Great Peace* seems irrelevant to classicism, or even opposed to it. It has primarily been treated as one of the earliest medieval Daoist scriptures, and thus representative of an intellectual rupture.[7] However, in intellectual transitions, departures and oppositions from existing knowledge are common means of intellectual innovation. Instead of treating the *Scripture of the Great Peace* as the beginning of medieval Daoism, I will put it in the context of Han classicism and demonstrate how both the *Scripture* and Han classicism are products of the intellectual world of the second century AD.

In what follows, we will examine what was unique about the scholarship of Zheng and He and compare these characteristics with specific sections of the *Scripture*. We will also see what common ground they shared in the broad learning that was a basic trend in the late Eastern Han. First, we will explore Zheng Xuan's scholarship. Following his teacher Ma Rong, Zheng made commentaries on four of the Five Classics, which he saw as a unitary corpus derived from heavenly revelations. More than just recapitulating the words of the ancient sages, Zheng, basing himself on the classics, sought a set of principles particular to the situation of his own time. Second, we will see how He Xiu focused on the Gongyang tradition of the *Annals*. Unlike Zheng, He was devoted to uncovering the hidden message in the *Annals* transmitted by Han Gongyang scholars, which he felt was more important than the other classics. Third, we will discuss how the *Scripture of the Great Peace* claimed to be superior to the classics. Zheng, He, and the unknown authors of the *Scripture of the Great Peace* understood differently what made the classics important. Their works reflect many issues that were heatedly debated among their contemporaries, such as how to achieve the Great Peace, the need for broad learning or comprehensive knowledge, and what determined the transmission patterns of texts in the first two centuries AD.

Historical Background

On many occasions, people's discontent with politics arises from the comparison between a normative ideal and hard, cold reality. This is particularly obvious in the second half of the second century AD.[8] Beginning in 159, the Han dynasty's political situation deteriorated sharply. Emperor Huan, who should have enjoyed unlimited power, now needed his eunuchs to outweigh the dominant figure in the court, Liang Ji 梁冀 (?–AD 159), who came from the Liang consort family. After a coup that year during which Liang was imprisoned, eunuchs such as Tang Heng 唐衡, Dan Chao 單超, Zuo Guan 左悺, and Xu Huang 徐璜 obtained great power as a reward for their service and loyalty.[9] Using their status as imperial favorites, they cut themselves a slice of what the great families enjoyed: they sent their affiliates to Han officialdom, occupied lands, and dominated their local society.[10] This was one of the several such instances since AD 89.[11]

When eunuchs inserted their allies into the already crowded bureaucracy, this source of great families' status shrank. The alternatives were making alliances with eunuchs or with harem families. Neither of these approaches was new,[12] but frequent power shifts now made such alliances risky. The dominant figure today might become a prisoner tomorrow, and his family and their allies would be executed. While the bloody power struggle at court repelled many literati, others sought to solve this problem. The literati culture of the second century embodied their discontent and their will to implement reform not only in the capital but in local society.

From AD 163 to 166, leading literati like Yang Bing 楊秉 (92–165) and Li Ying 李膺 (AD 110–69) carried out anti-eunuch initiatives. In AD 167, however, Li and others were arrested. This conflict paused midyear. This is partially because Dou Wu 竇武 (?–AD 168), the father of the empress, managed to save Li. In addition due to the complex nature of relationships at court (described earlier), the conflict halted because many of Li's followers were affiliated with eunuchs. In order to preserve their own positions and their affiliates, the eunuchs agreed to an amnesty. When Li, Dou, and others came back to their official positions, it seemed to many literati that the right people were finally in the court, and the Han had a chance to achieve the Great Peace.[13] However, the conflict resumed when Dou Wu and his fellows hatched a radical plan to massacre the eunuchs, who, of course, were greatly displeased. On October 25, AD 168, eunuchs brought the frontier general Zhang Huan's 張奐 (AD 104–181) troops to face Chen Fan, Dou Wu, and their followers. Eventually Chen Fan died fighting, and Dou Wu committed suicide. The eunuchs banished Chen and Dou's followers and even the followers' affiliates. This exile, known as the Great Proscription, lasted fifteen years until AD 184, when the group Yellow Turbans (Huangjin 黃巾) rebelled. After this, when leaders of some of the great families came back to the capital, they no longer competed to be the emperor's favorites but rather attempted to control the throne directly.[14]

Many Han literati fully retreated from this political turmoil to become recluses, while others enthusiastically engaged in political affairs. Some strove to support the Han dynasty; some began to contemplate what should replace it. However, the majority of them suffered from this turmoil. At this moment, the intellectual diversity of these scholars became more apparent.

Zheng Xuan and His Scholarship

Zheng Xuan is no stranger to students of the classics through Chinese history.[15] If one opens any official version of the *Thirteen Classics* from the past millennium, one will find that Zheng Xuan's commentaries take a considerable amount of space: sub-commentary on the Mao commentary of the *Poetry* and commentary on three rites classics, the *Records of Rites*, the *Rites and Etiquette*, and the *Rites of Zhou*. Zheng's dominant position as a scholar was a fact during his lifetime. In this section, we will explore his life and his scholarship from two interrelated perspectives: how his career fit into the common pattern of scholars' social lives in his time and in what way his contemporaries considered his scholarship outstanding.

Zheng's Experience of Travel

Zheng was a native of Gaomi 高密 County, Beihai 北海 commandery (modern Shandong Province). He came from a family powerful enough to make him a Village Bailiff (*xiang qiangfu* 鄉嗇夫) in his hometown when he was young.[16] However, Zheng was more interested in learning than becoming an official. At a young age, he gave up his official career and went to the National Academy to study. Like many of his contemporaries, he studied with multiple teachers. Diwu Yuanxian 第五元先 (fl. AD 150) taught Zheng Xuan the Jing tradition of the *Changes*, the Gongyang tradition of the *Annals*, the *Triple Concordance Calendar* (*Santong li* 三統曆), and *Nine Chapters on the Arithmetic Art*. Zhang Gongzu 張恭祖 (fl. AD 150) taught him the *Rites of Zhou*, the *Records of Rites*, the Zuo tradition of the *Annals*, the Han tradition of the *Poetry*, and the old text *Documents*.[17] This reading list contains most of the Five Classics, and the commentarial traditions include both the Western Han ones (those on the Gongyang tradition) and the relatively newly developed ones (those on the Zuo tradition and the old text tradition of the *Documents*). After studying with these two teachers, Zheng went west to Fufeng (modern Baoji, Shaanxi Province) to study with Ma Rong, for he thought that nobody in the east could teach him anymore.[18] Zheng was not only ambitious, but his taste was eclectic and he sought broad learning, not specialization.

Like his teacher Ma Rong, Zheng touched on most of the classics and made commentaries on the *Changes*, the *Documents*, the Mao tradition of the *Poetry*, the three rites classics, *Analects*, and the *Classic of Filial Piety*. This list includes most of what his contemporaries considered the classic corpus.[19] The only classic he omitted was the *Annals*. As mentioned in the previous chapter, Zheng Xuan thought his commentary of the Zuo tradition was similar to Fu Qian's, so he gave his notes away to Fu. In seeking to understand the whole corpus of the classics, Zheng Xuan did not deviate from his teacher's path.

After studying with Ma, Zheng moved to Donglai 東萊 commandery (around modern Yantai 煙台 and Weihai 威海 area, Shandong Province) to teach, while farming to support himself. Thereafter, Zheng Xuan experienced two major disturbances in his life that drove him further away from Han officialdom: the Great Proscription of 168 and the rebellion of the Yellow Turbans.[20] Included in the proscription, Zheng Xuan was forced to live a retired life until 184. His encounter with the Yellow Turbans in AD 196 made him more pessimistic about the future.[21] In a letter to his son, he asserted that he was not suited to be an official and would rather focus on the words of the sage kings.[22] Although high officials such as Kong Rong or warlords such as Yuan Shao recognized him as a great scholar, Zheng always avoided official obligations. In AD 200, Yuan Shao forced Zheng Xuan to come to Guandu 官渡 (modern Zhongmou 中牟, Hebei Province) to prepare for a battle with Cao Cao 曹操 (155–220). This time Zheng Xuan could not decline; he died on his way.[23] Zheng Xuan's experience was not odd for people who lived in the second half of the second century AD. Facing political turmoil, retreating from struggles was the choice of many scholars who nevertheless got embroiled in complicated political battles.

In the previous chapter, we have seen that polymathic scholarship became fashionable after the second century AD. In this respect, Zheng's scholarship went along with this trend. But he became a predominant scholar and won esteem from his contemporaries in ways particular to his time. Then one occasion for a scholar to be recognized was during a banquet held by local political leaders:

紹客多豪俊，並有才說，見玄儒者，未以通人許之，競設異端，百家互起。玄依方辯對，咸出問表，皆得所未聞，莫不嗟服。[24]

> Among Yuan's guests, there were many other talented people who were excellent speakers. They saw Zheng as a [typical] *ru* and did not yet acknowledge him as a polymath. They vied to suggest topics and initiated [ideas] of the Hundred Families (*baijia*) [in order to test Zheng]. Zheng replied and argued accordingly. [His answers] all went beyond the purport of the questions, and [his questioners] learned things they had not heard before. None failed to admit his superiority.

Several issues are involved in the other guests' recognition of Zheng Xuan's scholarship. First is the *ru/tongren* dichotomy. If we accept a remark by Wang Chong in *Doctrines Evaluated*, or *Lun heng* 論衡, approximately a hundred years earlier, *ru* had the negative connotation of a narrow focus on the Five Classics.[25] As we have seen in the previous chapter, what started to come into fashion in Wang's time, AD 100, was a broad range of knowledge that included many ancient texts that were excluded from the state's classics. The word *baijia* (literally, "hundred households") does not indicate discrete philosophical schools—as many modern scholars redefine *jia*—but transmitted texts that had in common attribution to a single ancient author. In other words, at the banquet, the guests challenged him with texts beyond the Five Classics. As a result, they "learned things they had not heard before," and Zheng went beyond the questions they put to him: he was even more erudite than they. He was not only a scholar of the classics but a paragon of second-century polymathy.

Second, the occasion was essential. A local warlord, Yuan Shao, a member of the prominent Yuan family, held a banquet during a military campaign. It thus provided an occasion to exhibit literati prestige. This gave Zheng a chance to show his ability in front of Yuan's circle of scholars. Such literati circles built around warlords were not unusual. The patronage of Yuan, the Cao family, and Liu Bei 劉備 (AD 161–223) of Shu was a major means of support for literati, especially as the Han dynasty fell apart. In this way, the circulation of ideas and thoughts took place in the courts of these local warlords, some of whom were members of the greatest families in the Eastern Han.

The other context of Zheng's popularity was the well-developed epistolary and writing culture. During the Great Proscription, the debate between Zheng Xuan and He Xiu 何休 (AD 129–182), a scholar of the Gongyang tradition, put both of them on the intellectual map. He Xiu wrote "*Gongyang* Protected [Its Doctrine] Like Mozi Protecting [Forts]" ("Gongyang moshou"

公羊墨守), "The Mortal Sickness of Zuo Tradition" ("Zuo shi Gaohuang" 左氏膏肓), and "*Guliang* as a Cripple" ("Guliang feiji" 穀梁廢疾) to assert the superiority of the Gongyang tradition. In response, Zheng Xuan wrote "Unclenching Mo's Protection" ("Fa Mo shou" 發墨守), "Curing the 'Mortal Illness' with Acupuncture" ("Zhen Gaohuang" 鍼膏肓), and "Helping 'the Cripple' Walk" ("Qi feiji" 起廢疾). Although at the end He was convinced, their debates made their scholarship extremely prominent especially at the capital and earned both of them great fame:[26]

及鄭康成鋒起而攻之，求學者不遠千里，嬴糧而至，如細流之赴巨海。京師謂康成為經神，何休為學海。[27]

> When Zheng Xuan raised his lance and attacked them (He Xiu's assertions), people who wanted to become their students ignored distance and [carried] stored food, traveling to meet them like small streams flowing toward the sea. [People in] the capital called Zheng the "spirit of the classics" and He "the sea of learning."

The debates that won them this adulation did not take place during physical encounters, but in written form. However the texts were transmitted between them, they did not keep their writings to themselves but opened their debate to the public. The impact of their exchanges actually created a form for decentralized scholarly competition. Compared to the Western Han dynasty, when debates primarily took place in the court,[28] late Eastern Han literati more often exchanged their ideas in writing, whether agreeing or disagreeing with each other.

As the sociologist Randall Collins has mentioned, the most dominant scholars are members of chains of known teachers and students, in a circle of "significant contemporary intellectuals."[29] Zheng Xuan's life accords with this generalization. His teachers either taught at the National Academy or were well-known scholars such as Ma Rong. His friends and patrons included Kong Rong, an eminent scholar and descendant of Confucius, and the warlord Yuan Shao, both of whom had considerable political influence. While historical documents such as the *History of the Later Han* describe Zheng Xuan as a hermit who strove to avoid political struggles, his scholarly activities, such as debates with He Xiu, being Yuan Shao's guest, or his encounter with Fu Qian, all show his active engagement in intellectual circles of his time.

Zheng Xuan's Construction of the Great Peace

Indeed, the people around Zheng Xuan gave him many opportunities to become a significant scholar. In a scholarly community, the importance of one's scholarship also depends on how it engages with topics and issues that members consider crucial. In Zheng's case, were his studies of the classics unique or original enough to distinguish him from his many contemporaries? In the last section, we have seen how his broad learning made him stand out among classicists. In this section, we will discuss the classical scholarship that his contemporaries prized. In order to extract his general understanding of the classics from his inevitably miscellaneous commentaries, we will first examine his "Discussion of the Six Arts," or "Liuyi lun" 六藝論, where he generalized the origin and functions of the classics. Then we will turn to his construction of the rites to see its relationship with the Great Peace. In his understanding of the Great Peace, we will explore his attempt to capture the essence of the classics.

Responding to doubts about the classics, Zheng emphasized the essential role they played in human society. In his "Discussion of the Six Arts," Zheng states:[30]

> 六藝者，《圖》所生也。[31]

> The Six Arts are from what the *Chart* bore.

The *tu* here is short for *Hetu* 河圖, or the *Chart of the Yellow River* mentioned in the *Changes*. What is the *Chart*? He continues:

> 《河圖》、《洛書》，皆天神言語，所以教告王者也。[32]

> The *Chart of the Yellow River* and the *Writing of the Luo River* are the words of the heavenly spirits, by which to teach and tell the one who is ruling.

We have already seen in chapter 2 that, according to apocryphal texts, the *Chart* and *Writing* are messages from Heaven. Zheng agrees, and goes on to assert that the classics are derived from them. In Zheng Xuan's opinion, this teaching was not meant for ordinary people, but for their rulers. Zheng Xuan proceeds to discuss when the heavenly teaching appeared in the human world:

太平嘉瑞,《圖》、《書》之出,必龜龍銜負焉。黃帝、堯、舜、周公,是其正也。[33]

> As for the auspicious omens of the Great Peace, the appearance of the *Chart* and *Writing*, they were always offered by a turtle in its mouth or a dragon on its back. They appeared in their regular forms to the Yellow Emperor, Yao, Shun, and the Duke of Zhou.

Zheng identifies the *Chart* and the *Writing* as messages from Heaven, but also as signs that the Great Peace had been attained during the rule of the ancient sage kings. The classics as derivations of the *Chart* and *Writing* are also linked to the Great Peace.

Zheng Xuan was not arguing that Heaven told the ancient sages how to achieve the Great Peace. Rather, because the sages' good rule accorded with Heaven, they brought the Great Peace as well as the *Chart* and *Writing*. The revelations appeared more than once in history; the sage kings received them whenever they achieved perfect governance. In other words, Zheng saw an initial separation of the human world from Heaven. Heaven started to interact with the human world after the sagely undertakings of the ancient kings. Heaven's supervision was constant, for it revealed its teachings every time the sage kings' governance was beneficent enough to bring the Great Peace. As we have seen in chapter 2, the heavenly nature of the classics was not a new idea; Zheng Xuan adopted the apocryphal texts' idea that the classics contain hidden messages from Heaven.

However, human sages went beyond mere scribes or compilers of heavenly messages; Zheng believed that they created the classics. For example, in talking about the Hymn section of the *Poetry*, he mentions:

周公致太平,制禮作樂,而有頌聲興焉。[34]

> The Duke of Zhou brought the Great Peace [to the world], established the rites, and composed music, and then the sound of Hymns rose from them.

The duke's design became the classic the *Rites of Zhou*. Zheng also believed that Confucius compiled the *Documents* based on ancient texts and wrote the *Annals* for future rulers.[35] From the heavenly revelation to human elaboration in writing, in the "Discussion of the Six Arts," Zheng Xuan describes ideal rule, which is marked by the Great Peace and by a constant connection between Heaven and human rulers. With Heaven and human rulers in touch, the classics transmitted the heavenly teachings.

Since Heaven constantly reveals its messages, Zheng was not as vexed as Liu Xin about the loss of the Kingly Way through the breakdown in the transmission of the classics. During his time, that was no longer the main concern of the literati. For him, the direct and active role Heaven took in revealing its teaching made the loss less of a problem. If the motivation for preserving a complete version of the classics no longer existed, why did he still seek to preserve the commentarial traditions and different versions of the classics? He was facing the challenge from the tide of broad learning, in which many literati departed from the classics. Like the guests at Yuan Shao's banquet, they stigmatized classicism as ossified and classicists myopic.[36] In reacting to this context, Zheng Xuan defended the classics and brought the legacy of Liu Xin to another level.

Rites and the Undertakings of the Ancient Sage Kings

So far Zheng Xuan's arguments are similar to those in apocryphal texts. Indeed, apocryphal texts played an important role in Zheng's scholarship.[37] Nevertheless, he did not believe that revelations and prophecies were the most important part in the classics or they could solve all the problems that concerned literati:

左氏善於禮，公羊善於讖，穀梁善於經。[38]

> The Zuo tradition is best for rites, the Gongyang tradition is best for prophecies, and the Guliang tradition is best for [explicating] the classics.

By "rites," Zheng Xuan means the rites of the Zhou dynasty. In this passage, Zheng assigns different characteristics to the three traditions of the *Annals*, and he claims that the Gongyang tradition is best for prophecies. However, in the debate with He Xiu, Zheng supported the Zuo tradition. In this respect, he chose the "rites" over "prophecies." Then, what significance did the rites of Zhou have in his mind? In his preface to the *Rites of Zhou*, Zheng argues that King Wen and King Wu used the rites to rule the Zhou kingdom after the Duke of Zhou organized them, and that eventually made the omens of peace appear. For him, the contents of the *Rites of Zhou* are the means by which the Duke of Zhou achieved the Great Peace.³⁹ In other words, while Heaven's message might be significant, it needs to be transformed into a form that is suitable for human societies.

To many people in early China, the rites of Zhou were exactly this suitable form. In chapter 1, we saw cases in which the literati tried to apply the putatively Zhou rites or administrative systems such as the Well-Field system to restore the Kingly Way and bring the Great Peace to the Han dynasty. Zheng Xuan too considered the Zhou rites essential. He also explained in detail the rites in the *Records of Rites*, *Rites and Etiquette*, and the *Rites of Zhou*.

But Zheng Xuan went further to a different path; in contrast with his Western Han predecessors, his agenda is not to reconstruct the whole package of the Zhou rites in order to apply them to the Han dynasty but to make them a reference point for the contemporary world to find rites of its own. In the chapter "Ritual as Vessels," or "Li qi" 禮器, from the *Records of Rites*, Zheng Xuan expresses his understanding of the making of rites in history. In commenting on the sentence "The Rites of the Three Dynasties are the same. People all follow them. Sometimes there is plain [used in rites] and sometimes there is dark [used in rites]. [This is because] the Xia dynasty created the rites that Yin [i.e., Shang] followed" 三代之禮，一也，民共由之。或素或青。夏造殷因,⁴⁰ he wrote:

言所尚雖異,禮則相因耳。孔子曰："殷因於夏禮，所損益可知也。周因於殷禮，所損益可知也。"⁴¹

It means that while what people value is different [from dynasty to dynasty], rites [of various times] are based on each other. Confucius said: "Yin was based on the rites of Xia. What was added and deleted is knowable. Zhou was based on the rites of Yin. What was added and deleted is knowable."

The sentences from "Ritual as Vessels" do not say clearly whether the rites of Xia and Shang were identical. By quoting from the *Analects*,⁴² Zheng understands the rites of each dynasty as not identical. This is why Zheng Xuan did not take "same" to mean "the same set of rites" but "same rationales" or "same essence."

For Zheng Xuan, additions and deletions in the adaptation of rites are not arbitrary. In fact, when ancient kings created or adopted rites, righteousness and accordance with Heaven were the essential criteria.⁴³ Only by following them can the ruler bring the Great Peace to the world.⁴⁴ In this respect, ancient and contemporary rites were not very different. In commenting on the sentence: "Therefore, there are three hundred Zhou rites, and three thousand contemporary rites. Their aim is the same" 故經禮三百、曲禮三千。其致一也, he remarks:

> 致之言至也。一謂誠也。經禮，謂周禮也。《周禮》六篇。其官有三百六十。曲，猶事也。事禮，謂今禮也。⁴⁵
>
> *Zhi* is a way to say "arrival." Another explanation [for *zhi*] is "completion."⁴⁶ *Jing li* means the Zhou rites. The *Rites of Zhou* contains six chapters, and there are 360 official positions. *Qu* is similar to "affairs (*shi*)." *Shi li* means today's rites.

Although *zhi* 致 in the body text as well as in many other classical Chinese texts means "to bring about," Zheng Xuan understands it differently. Between his two explanations for the word *zhi*, the former one, "aim," or more literally, "arrival," emphasizes the results rites can bring. The latter one "completion," or the classical Chinese word *cheng* specifically denotes the full realization of something's innate nature, which emphasizes the intrinsic characteristics of the rites. For the first reading, he claims that the Zhou rites and contemporary rites have the same effect. The gloss for his second reading, "completion," indicates that contemporary and ancient rites are of the same nature and substance in their fully realized form. He does not prefer one over the other but sees the ancient and contemporary rites as equal in certain respects.

If the ancient and contemporary rites are virtually the same, one might ask why people cannot just use the former without adjustments. Zheng Xuan argues that a change in the mandate of Heaven leads to a change of institutions and standards (*shou ming gai zhi du* 受命改制度).⁴⁷ Each ruler of a new dynasty is obligated to have his own rites. Every dynasty could use the ancient *Rites* to design its own. This is not an unprecedented idea for Han scholars. For example, in the conference on the imperially approved understanding of the classics held in the White Tiger Pavilion (Baihu Guan 白虎觀) in the palace in AD 79, scholars reached a consensus that new rulers should revise the calendar and dress color based on those of the prior dynasty.⁴⁸ Zheng went further, intending that the rites be more significantly revised.

On the other hand, without the ancient rites, the contemporary ones would appear arbitrary. Dealing with potentially arbitrary design, Zheng Xuan further elaborated that the rulers needed to follow the "fundamental" and the "ancient." In the "Rites as Vessel," it says:

是故先王之制禮也必有主也。故可述而多學也。⁴⁹

Therefore, when the ancient kings set up rites, they had to have what is primary. That makes it possible to transmit and learn them abundantly.

Zheng Xuan explains the vague word "primary":

主謂本與古也 . . . 以本與古求之而已。⁵⁰

"Primary" means the "fundamental" and "ancient." . . . [By saying "one can explicate and learn it abundantly," it means] simply that one can seek it through the fundamental and ancient.

By saying "the fundamental," Zheng Xuan refers to the innate characteristics of human beings. Zheng Xuan further unpacks this point by giving an example: one mourns because the mourning comes from inside him (*zhong* 中), not from others.⁵¹ In other words, he emphasizes that the proper rites should be in accordance with human nature. "The ancient" indicates the traces of the ancient kings, including the *Rites of Zhou* and the classics in general.

Zheng Xuan's argument might seem to resemble Xunzi's earlier philosophy: the proper rites should go along with human nature, and people should follow the ancient kings' rites, for their rites are properly designed for human nature. However, for Zheng, the motivation for the change of rites was not to make them fit better with human nature or human society. Rather, the mandate of Heaven triggered dynastic changes, which led to such changes. Moreover, Heaven's teachings imbue the classics, and Heaven's interaction with the human world via texts is constant. In contrast, Xunzi did not believe that people could penetrate the will of Heaven. In general, as people believed of apocryphal texts, in Zheng's scholarship, Heaven played a primary role in the formation and continuation of human civilization. Going beyond the apocrypha, Zheng often mentioned the reform of rites to support the legitimacy of a new dynasty.

More importantly, the intellectual and political context of Zheng Xuan's time was very different from that of Xunzi. While during Xunzi's time, no empire existed or was clearly imagined, Zheng clearly understood the ideal one: a kingdom of the Great Peace approved by Heaven. Xunzi focused on how moral cultivation was crucial for the ruler, and Zheng emphasized the reception of the mandate of Heaven for a dynasty. Since the Warring States period, the classics had become well-accepted texts, and Xunzi was particularly eager to recommend them as a guide to becoming a true gentleman. In the later Western Han dynasty, the prosperity of the classics reached an unprecedented climax as the Han empire adopted five of them to bring the Great Peace to the world. In the second century AD, as the Han house declined, scholars stopped taking the classics literally. Some of them valued more the spirit that they convey rather than the details of the ancient rules.

Putting these pieces of Zheng Xuan's comments together gives us a whole picture of his understanding of the classics: of heavenly origin, they were the go-to reference for understanding Heaven and ruling the world. There is a significant difference between Liu Xin, or whoever sought to use the classics as the blueprint to bring the Great Peace, and Zheng. Liu Xin was anxious about the loss of the full, original classics for reviving the Kingly Way. This was less a concern for Zheng Xuan. In his opinion, a new recipient of the mandate of Heaven needed to have his own set of rites to be in accordance with Heaven. Although he refers to the available classics to design his own, he does not copy them. While the rediscovery of the original corpus of the classics was enough for Liu Xin, Zheng Xuan asked for more than just a complete copy of them.

What Zheng Xuan looked forward to was an author who captured the essence of the classics. Such an author's intention would be based on the classics, not imitating their words but embodying their spirit. When Wang Yi 王逸 (ca. AD 89–158) talked about the significance of "Encountering Sorrow" ("Li sao" 離騷), a lyric written in late fourth century BC, he stated the reason: "As for 'Encountering Sorrow,' it establishes its meaning based on the Five Classics" 夫《離騷》之文，依托五經以立義焉.[52] When Zhang Heng referred to Yang Xiong's *Supreme Mystery* in the mid-second century AD, he saw the essence of the classics in it and believed it as a future classic. This was the kind of authorship Zheng expected.

Zheng's understanding of rites reflects this intellectual transition. On the one hand, he greatly highlights the function of the classics for understanding Heaven and human history. On the other hand, solely imitating what the classics record is not enough for the contemporary ruler. Only after comprehending the spirit of the classics and applying it to the current rule can one truly bring the Great Peace to the world. His interest in seizing the essence of the classics represents a long-term intellectual development in the middle and late Eastern Han, a time of rapidly expanding intellectual communities with the trend toward abstraction. In Cui Yuan and Zhang Heng's writing in chapter 4, we saw a sense emerging that contemporary writing could embody the classics, a dichotomy of old and new, and a search for a form to fit the Han empire. Zheng's meticulous commentaries reflected these issues. He employed his erudition in the classics to argue that it was still necessary to abide by the classics in this new era. For him, an author could bridge the gap between old and new, just as Confucius once did in composing his *Annals*, by capturing the constant spirit of the classics.

He Xiu and His Return to the Gongyang Tradition

He Xiu's Family Background and Career

He Xiu,[53] a native of Fan 樊, Rencheng 任城 commandery (modern Shandong Province), came from a high official family.[54] His father He Bao 何豹 used to be the Chamberlain for the Palace Revenues (*shaofu* 少府). His father's rank entitled him to the position of Gentleman of the Interior (*lang zhong* 郎中), a stepping-stone to a responsible post. Like Zheng, he was not fond of taking official positions and resigned using the excuse of illness. This does not mean that He Xiu was isolated from his official contemporaries. Later on, he joined Grand Mentor (*taifu* 太傅) Chen Fan 陈蕃, a leader of the partisan group, and was banned because of his relationship with Chen during the Great Proscription. After the proscription, He was promoted to Minister of Education (*situ* 司徒). He became Court Gentleman for Consultation (*yilang* 議郎) and Grand Master of Remonstrance (*jianyi dafu* 諫議大夫), because he was willing to give constructive criticism.

He Xiu was also a broad learner. Although we do not know much about his teachers except for Yang Bi 羊弼, an Academician with a strong preference for the Gongyang tradition, He was clearly well educated in the Six Classics, apocryphal texts, and various forms of divination.[55] In addition to the Gongyang tradition, he wrote commentaries on the *Classic of Filial*

Piety and the *Analects*. The debates between him and Zheng also won him fame as a scholar of remarkably broad learning. Based on what we have already seen in the cases of Zheng and others, this ambition is not a surprise in the second half of the second century. His speech impediment is also noteworthy in the context of the second century. It must have been hard for him to be impressive in the court of Emperor Wu or at the banquets of the warlords, for eloquence was demanded on these occasions.[56] However, the flourishing epistolary culture covered for He Xiu's speech impediment and spread his fame as a broad scholar.

The intellectual fashion in the last fifty years of the dynasty encouraged broad learning and more comprehensive knowledge than before.[57] More and more students of the classics immersed themselves in commentarial traditions that were not limited to those of the Western Han. The old text classics increasingly became an indispensable part of classicism. Zheng's scholarship reflects this tendency. As mentioned in the second chapter, a scholar's eminence largely depended on how his works engaged his contemporary scholars' foci and paradigms. From this point of view, Zheng's dominance was not a surprise.

Can we say the same thing for He? Indeed, the breadth of his learning was impressive. Nevertheless, how could he convince his contemporaries that his scholarship was more crucial and truer than that of others? Intellectual innovations tend to take place through rearrangement of existing knowledge. If Zheng's strategy was to synthesize the existing commentarial traditions, He's was mainly to depart from the tendencies toward synthesis and increasing emphasis on old text traditions. Unlike Zheng, He primarily focused on one classic, the *Spring and Autumn Annals*, and one of its commentaries, the Gongyang tradition.

The Significance of the Annals

He Xiu emphasized the *Annals* in the preface to his commentary of the Gongyang tradition:

> 昔者孔子有云：" 吾志在《春秋》，行在《孝經》。" 此二學者，聖人之極致，治世之要務也。[58]

> Previously, Confucius said: "My will is in the *Annals*, and my deeds are in the *Classic of Filial Piety*." The study of these two is the ultimate achievement of the sage and the essential imperative for governing the world.

He singled out the *Annals* from the rest of the Six Classics corpus as a guide to rulership. Based on Confucius's words cited from an apocryphal text,[59] what makes the *Annals* so essential is the will, or *zhi* 志, that the sage Confucius embodied in it. Unlike Zheng, who discussed the combined legacy of the ancient sage kings, He promoted and concentrated on the classics by Confucius. In chapter 3, we have seen the significance of Confucius and his *Annals* for the legitimacy of the Han dynasty in the first thirty years of the Eastern Han. He Xiu's understanding of the *Annals* confirmed this belief.

Although holding erudite knowledge, He Xiu preferred to appear as a specialist in order to react to the trend of broad learning. In contrast with people like Ma Rong and Zheng Xuan, who commented on most of the Five Classics corpus, He Xiu focused exclusively on the Gongyang tradition of the *Annals*. At the end of his commentary, he remarked that the *Annals* was "that upon which Confucius based his making of the Five Classics" 據以定作五經.[60] He specifically contended that the *Annals* was the source of the other classics. His understanding of the Five Classics and his commentarial practices appeared odd to his contemporaries, who tended to combine more and more versions of them and commentarial traditions on them. Instead, He resembled many classicists in the late Western Han, for they specialized in one of the classics by carefully following their teachers' transmission. But by his time, the tendency toward erudition in all the classics significantly replaced this fashion.

He was not isolated from the new trend, but his thought was based in it. In fact, He Xiu built up his understanding of the *Annals* through combining Liu Xin's words with the changed relationship among the Five Classics mentioned in the "Seven Summaries." In the "Seven Summaries," the Five Classics and the *Classic of Music* (later lost) are dependent on each other, while the *Changes* is the origin of the other classics because of its close correlation with Heaven and Earth.[61] For Liu Xin, Confucius preserved the ancient Kingly Way by composing the *Annals* and then tailored the rest of the classics to accord with it.[62] He Xiu replaced the *Changes* with the *Annals* as the center of the classics. In this way, he announced to his contemporaries that the *Annals* was key to mastering classical erudition.

Building a Commentarial World toward the Great Peace

He Xiu went further than his predecessors to elaborate on how specifically Confucius coded his vision of rulership in the *Annals*. Although claiming to follow Hu Wusheng 胡毋生 (fl. 157–141 BC), he created a commentarial world unprecedented in the transmission of the Gongyang tradition. He argued that in writing the history of the state of Lu, Confucius divided the chronicle into three periods based on their remoteness: "the transmitted era" (*suo chuanwen zhi shi* 所傳聞之世) from the rule of Duke Yin 隱公 (722–712 BC) to Duke Xi 僖公 (659–627 BC), "the heard era" (*suo wen zhi shi* 所聞之世) from the rule of Duke Wen 文公 (626–609 BC) to Duke Xiang 襄公 (572–542 BC), and "the seen era" (*suo jian zhi shi* 所見之世) from the rule of Duke Zhao 昭公 (r. 541–510 BC) to Duke Ai 哀公 (r. 494–468 BC).[63] Accordingly, the words Confucius putatively chose in the *Annals* to judge these events differed by period. The three periods were marked by the successive deterioration of Zhou rule.

Unlike his predecessors, He believed that beneath the apparent deterioration from one period to the next, Confucius encoded three periods, progressively moving toward the Great Peace. Confucius's first era was actually a period of chaos, whence order was to emerge:

於所傳聞之世，見治起於衰亂之中。用心尚麄觕，故內其國而外諸夏，先詳內而後治外，錄大略小。內小惡書，外小惡不書。大國有大夫，小國略稱人。內離會書，外離會不書是也。[64]

From the transmitted era, Confucius saw that government emerged from chaos. He used his mind in a still unrefined way. Therefore, he included his own state and excluded the other Zhou states. He made detailed records about the inside first, and only then dealt with the outside. He recorded significant [incidents] and omitted minor ones. He wrote down minor evil [deeds] inside [Lu], but not minor evil [deeds] outside. He mentioned [people by their] titles for big states but [by] abbreviated names for small states. He wrote down departures and meetings inside [his own state] but not outside.

於所聞之世，見治升平，內諸夏而外夷狄，書外離會。[65]

From the heard era, he saw the government of the rising peace. He included all the Zhou states and excluded the barbarians. He wrote down the departures and meetings outside [his own state].

至所見之世，著治大平。夷狄進至於爵，天下遠近小大若一，用心尤深而詳，故崇仁義。[66]

From the seen era, he recognized the government of the Great Peace. Barbarians came to court and attained noble ranks. All-under-Heaven, no matter how far or close, he treated as one. He used his mind deeply and elaborately. Therefore he promoted humanity and righteousness.

For He, Confucius's comments on certain events in the *Annals* chronicle implied his assumption of a progressively better and more united world. He argued that Confucius's focus, in the part from Duke Yin to Duke Xi in the chronicle, was on his mother state, Lu. Confucius's range of focus increased as the world progressed. When progress eventuated in the Great Peace, the whole world was within Confucius's perspective. He used an inside/outside (*nei* 內/*wai* 外) dichotomy to generalize Confucius's writing in the chronicle. Through the progression of periods, previous "outsiders" became "insiders" until the world was united.

He's appropriation of the *Annals* merges historical records and interpretation of the canon. The *Annals* as a historical record of the state of Lu inevitably has less detailed information about the remote past than the near past. As Henderson mentions, the interpreters of canons and scriptures tend to see them with deeper meaning and coherence than others do.[67] He Xiu, like many of his predecessors, turned the chronicle, a fragmentary and vague compilation, into a coherent and profound scripture. The author of this scripture, he asserts, is Confucius, and its main point is to record the realization of the Great Peace.

He Xiu's hermeneutical strategy was to map two opposite narratives on each other: the chronicle and the Gongyang commentary mainly record the chaotic wars, bad behavior of the warlords, their disrespect to the Zhou kings, and the decline of the moral ethos of Zhou society. Many of He's predecessors saw the work as a critique of the degeneration of the Spring and Autumn period, implying that Confucius hid a larger blueprint behind his critiques. He took a further step and fleshed out that blueprint. Confucius meant it, He believed, to guide society from chaos to the rising peace,[68] then to the Great Peace. Here beneath the seemingly deteriorating past world seals a rising future world.

The *Annals*' guidance was not for just anyone, but for the destined inheritor of the Zhou kings. Along with his predecessors, He believed that Confucius wrote the *Annals* specifically for the Han imperial house. He inserted his understanding of the *Annals* as well as the history from the death of Confucius to the rise of Han into the episode of the capture of the mystical animal *qilin* 麒麟 that ends the *Annals*. The text of the *Annals* only briefly records the capture:

十有四年,春,西狩獲麟。⁶⁹

In the Spring of the fourteenth year [of Duke Ai] (481 BC), [a man of Lu] captured a *qilin* during a hunt in the west.

The Gongyang tradition explicates the significance of this incident:

何以書?記異也。何異爾?非中國之獸也。然則孰狩之?薪采者也。薪采者則微者也,曷為以狩言之?大之也。曷為大之?為獲麟大之也。曷為獲麟大之?麟者仁獸也。有王者則至,無王者則不至。有以告者曰:"有麇而角者。"孔子曰:"孰為來哉!孰為來哉!"反袂拭面,涕沾袍...西狩獲麟,孔子曰:"吾道窮矣!"⁷⁰

Why is this written down? It is to record its bizarreness. What kind of bizarreness is this? [A *qilin*] is not a beast from the central states. Then who hunted it? A firewood gatherer did. Why did [the *Annals*] use [the word] "hunt" (*shou* 狩) to mention it? It is to amplify it. Why amplify it? It is to amplify it for the sake of the capture of the *qilin*. Why? *Qilin* are humane beasts. If there is a kingly ruler, they will come; otherwise they will not. There was someone who reported it [to the Duke of Ai], "there is a river deer with horns." Confucius said, "For whom did it come? For whom did it come?" He turned his sleeve to mop his face. His tears wet his robe. . . . As for the capture of the *qilin* during a hunt in the west, Confucius said, "My way has reached its end!"

In the Gongyang tradition's elaboration, the *qilin* is known for its humane and auspicious nature, as well as its link to the kingly ruler. However, the Gongyang tradition does not believe that its appearance was a good sign, because at the time the area once ruled by Zhou lacked a kingly ruler. Instead, it attributes the sign of *qilin* to Confucius, who was not mentioned in the original text of *Annals*. In the Gongyang story, the sign symbolizes the end of Confucius's way.⁷¹

He Xiu further points out that the *qilin* is not only related to the death of Confucius but also to the rise of the Han dynasty:

夫子素案圖錄，知庶姓劉季當代周。見薪采者獲麟，知為其出，何者？麟者，木精。薪采者，庶人燃火之意。此赤帝將代周居其位，故麟為薪采者所執。西狩獲之者，從東方王於西也。東卯西金象也。言獲者，兵戈文也。言漢姓卯金刀，以兵得天下。[72]

Confucius had often referred to the charts and knew that the Liu family would replace Zhou. By seeing the firewood gatherer capturing the *qilin*, how did he know for whom the *qilin* came? *Qilin* is the essence of wood. The "firewood gatherer" means commoners lighting a fire. This means that the red emperor will replace Zhou[73] and take its position. That is why the *qilin* was captured by the firewood gatherer. The reason it was captured during a hunt in the west is that the kingship moved from the east to the west. It symbolizes *mao* 卯 of the east and *jin* 金 (metal) of the west. "Capture" [means] a word about weaponry. This refers to Liu 劉, the surname of the Han [imperial house], made up of *mao* 卯, *jin* 金, and *dao* 刀, and the fact that they obtained All-under-Heaven by weaponry.

He Xiu's explanation of the incident involves wordplay and cosmology common at the time. First, we spot the theory of the Five Phases. As we have already seen in chapter 2, the Zhou dynasty represented wood and the Han dynasty fire. In this incident, the *qilin* represents the wood and the firewood gatherer the fire. According to this interpretation, the incident then symbolizes replacement of the phase of Wood by that of Fire.

In addition to applying the Five Phases, He Xiu further appropriates this incident as a prophecy about the Liu 劉 family as the next ruling family. In chapter 2, we have already seen that people played with the three components, 卯 *mao*, 金 *jin*, and 刀 *dao* of the character 劉 at the end of the Western Han.[74] Following this wordplay, He first points out that certain elements in the incident symbolize these three components. Based on the correspondence between directions and the twelve earthly branches, he associates the branch *mao* 卯 with the direction east, which is based on the characters for wood (wood as one of the Five Phases corresponds to the east) and of *qilin*. Second, he points out the link between "metal" (*jin* 金) and the location of the capture, west, for the direction west corresponds to metal in the Five Phases. Third, he interprets the word "capture" (*huo* 獲) in the chronicle as a piece of military vocabulary, linking it to "sword" (*dao* 刀),[75] another item of military vocabulary. Therefore, from the chronicle, to the Gongyang tradition, then to He Xiu's commentary, a bare mention grows into an unambiguous prophecy about the rise of the Liu family.

He Xiu's arguments and innovations are deeply rooted in Han dynasty commentarial traditions and intellectual discourse. For example, He defends the early Western Han Gongyang scholar, Hu Wusheng, thereby identifying himself as a reviver of the Gongyang tradition.[76] He was reacting to his contemporaries' promotion of the Zuo commentarial tradition, which had been rising since the late Western Han. Zheng Xuan's commentarial world was not specific to the Han dynasty, but He believed in Han rule as the intended recipient of the mandate of Heaven, even when he was banned from the court.[77] His faith in the Han sharply contrasted with many literati's suspicion that a new dynasty would soon replace the Han.[78] Therefore, He Xiu's scholarship largely opposed that of his contemporaries.[79]

He Xiu was not simply copying his predecessors' scholarship. He used innovative strategies to engage with the issues his contemporaries cared about most. Concepts like the rising peace and the Great Peace were well accepted in Eastern Han political discourses.[80] He systemized these concepts, using time terminology from the Gongyang tradition (such as "the transmitted era," "the heard era," and "the seen era") to create a coherent historiography. In this optimistic historiography, the world, after a period of turmoil, is heading toward peace. Through the wordplay that was common in prophecies and apocryphal texts, He Xiu identified the Liu family as the savior of humanity.[81]

He tacitly answered the question mentioned in chapter 3: did the Han emperor need to be a sage to achieve the Great Peace? Based on He's theory, there was no need, for Confucius already packed the essential teaching in the *Annals*. The Han rulers needed only to follow it, as revealed in the right commentarial tradition of the *Annals*, to accomplish their goal.

What was innovative about He Xiu was often not so much what he believed as how he proved those beliefs. Like his many predecessors and contemporaries, he believed that the Liu family was now the recipient of the mandate of Heaven. Although apocryphal texts claim the legitimacy of the Liu family, they do not engage with the texts of the classics. In other words, while claiming to transmit the esoteric teachings in the classics, the apocrypha avoid getting involved in their details. In explaining the capture of the *qilin*, He Xiu used various means common in prophecies and apocryphal texts in order to prove that the *Annals* predicted that the Liu family would receive the mandate of Heaven.[82] To put it in another way, the Eastern Han compilers of prophecies invented apocryphal texts as a middle ground where they could place certain concerns and claims in order to associate them with the classics. He used his hermeneutic skills to take the next step, proving that these concerns and claims actually existed in the classics.

HE XIU AND ZHENG XUAN: MORE SIMILAR THAN DIFFERENT

Seen against the intellectual background of the Eastern Han dynasty, Zheng Xuan and He Xiu were more similar than different. First, although their preferences for certain classics and commentarial traditions were sharply dissimilar, both pictured the classics as a coherent system and believed that they contained the most significant teachings for human society. Second, despite the differing ranges of their commentarial works, both dove into the trend of broad learning, ranging from classical studies to astronomy and divination. Despite this erudition, they still similarly appeared as classicists in front of their contemporaries. Third, although their attitudes toward the Han imperial house differed, they had the same understanding of the ideal empire: the ultimate goal for the legitimate recipient of the mandate of Heaven was to achieve the Great Peace. The ancient sage kings had achieved it, and their legacy lay in the classics to await upcoming rulers.

Their career paths, social lives, and scholarship all suggest that Zheng Xuan and He Xiu were products of Eastern Han literati culture. Their innovations were deeply rooted in Han classicism and commentarial traditions. As we have already seen in chapter 4, Eastern Han scholars had gradually moved away from their sole devotion to the classics in the second century AD. In this respect, can we now find further departures from classicism? In the next section, we will move to Xiang Kai's 襄楷 presentation of the *Scripture of the Great Peace* to Emperor Huan to explore another side of the intellectual world.

The (Re)emergence of the *Scripture of the Great Peace*

THE POSSESSORS OF THE SCRIPTURE

During the late Eastern Han, a scripture with the "Great Peace" appeared again, but this time, it survived criticism and became popular.[83] In AD 166, Xiang Kai 襄楷 sent a memorial to Emperor Huan about the eunuchs' outrageous deeds, the lack of an imperial successor, and several inauspicious omens. In order to solve these problems, he recommended the teachings of the *Writing of the Great Peace with Blue-Green Headings* (*Taiping qingling shu* 太平清領書), often known as the *Scripture of the Great Peace*. Before Xiang Kai, Gong Chong 宮崇 from Langye 琅琊 (modern Qingdao 青島, Shandong Province) had presented the same *Scripture* to Emperor Shun (r. AD 125–144), which he claimed he received from his teacher Gan Ji 干吉.[84]

Their rivals immediately criticized them severely but could not eliminate them. Some officials charged that Gong Chong presented a "deviant text" (*yaowang bujing* 妖妄不經), and they confiscated it. After inspecting Xiang Kai's memorial, the Master of Writing announced a series of accusations including "disobeying the purport of the classics" (*weibei jingyi* 違背經藝) and suggested that the emperor punish him severely.[85] However, Emperor Huan thought that Xiang's astrological readings were too good to execute him. If this treatment were not different from what Li Xun's group had encountered 150 years ago, what happened was. When Emperor Ling (r. AD 168–189) succeeded to the throne, he not only accepted Xiang's text but also appointed him as an Academician along with Zheng Xuan and Xun Shuang 荀爽 (AD 128–190), another famous classicist.[86] In other words, the court eventually recognized the legitimacy of the *Scripture*.[87]

The *Writing of the Great Peace with Blue-Green Headings* also seemed to be once in the hands of Zhang Jue 張角 (?–AD 184), who led the Yellow Turban (Huangjin 黃巾) rebellion.[88] Nevertheless, the agenda in the emperors' version of the *Scripture of the Great Peace* and that of the Yellow Turbans did not match.[89] In fact, other than Li Shan's 李善 (AD 630–689) commentary on relevant passages in the *History of the Later Han*, no primary source from the time states that the lost *Book of Great Peace* and the *Scripture of the Great Peace* later included in the Ming dynasty Daoist Canon (*Daozang* 道藏) were identical.[90] How these two texts are related to Li Xun's *Scripture of the Great Peace* is not mentioned either.[91]

DIFFICULTIES IN DATING AND A TENTATIVE APPROACH

Unlike the well-preserved classics, the *Scripture of the Great Peace* had a harder time surviving through the years. The majority of modern scholars do not believe that the received version of the *Scripture of the Great Peace* is identical to any of the Han "Great Peace" texts. Many scholars suspect that the *Book* might be related to the *Scripture of the Great Peace* that Li Xun presented at the end of the Western Han. And it gradually developed into the received version of the *Scripture of the Great Peace* in a time span of six hundred years, from the second to the eighth centuries. Now only this heterogeneous version is extant in the Daoist Canon.[92] According to Kristofer Schipper's hypothesis and Barbara Hendrischke's elaboration of it, the received version contains materials from various sources from the end of the Eastern Han to the late Six Dynasties (AD 220–589).[93] Max Kaltenmark argues that the received version does contain a considerable number of themes from the Eastern Han version *Scripture*, but neither he nor anyone else can specify which they are.[94]

In practice, it is better for us to treat the many "Great Peace" texts in the Han dynasty as separate ones instead of constituents of a single text, given the fact that the agendas of the interested groups, the times of composition, and even the titles of these texts were different. I especially do not intend to impose any kind of coherent traditions or ideas among the Great Peace texts. Instead, our question here is how to understand them as intellectual innovations of the time in reaction to classcism.[95]

Since essentially only the received *Scripture* is accessible for us, we need to at least consider how to obtain from it useful information that is not anachronistic. Relevant to classicism, I will discuss two themes that are datable. The first theme is the *Scripture*'s references to the classics and apocryphal texts. I consider the passages that mention the classics, especially those that compare the classics with the *Scripture*, to be from the Eastern Han. This premise is based on the fact that in Celestial Masters' scriptures from the Six Dynasties, to the extent that the Ming Daoist Canon reflects those texts, references to and comparisons with the classics are largely absent. This is rather different from the situation of the *Scripture*, in which the classics are regarded as valuable, although less essential than the *Scripture* itself. I think in the Eastern Han dynasty the classics were prestigious enough that claiming the superiority of a text over the classics was a viable strategy to promote that text. However, during the Six Dynasties, the classics no longer enjoyed their paramount prestige, and Daoist sects were already well established. Such comparison was no longer necessary.

When we turn to other Six Dynasties texts like the *Master Who Embraces Simplicity* (*Baopuzi* 抱樸子) (ca. AD 307) or the *Yan Family Instructions* (*Yan shi jiaxun* 顏氏家訓) (ca. AD 589), we find that they accept the classics as one, but not the only, important corpus. The author of the former text, Ge Hong 葛洪 (AD 284–363), an enthusiast of immortality, believed that both the classics and immortality scriptures had their merits, which differed.[96] Yan Zhitui 顏之推 (ca. AD 531–591), the author of the latter book, emphasized the importance of reading for literati families. For Yan, the classics as well as books of various ancient masters all belonged on their reading lists, and literati should dive into all of them to open their minds and broaden their perspectives.[97] Since the classics were not the only worthwhile canon, one could promote the authority of a text by claiming its superiority to the classics, but one need not deny the value of the classics to do so. Similarly, in competitions over authority among various Daoist traditions of the Six Dynasties, one group of followers tended to superpose their own scriptures above rival ones instead of trying to eliminate them.[98] Nevertheless, the *Scripture*'s merciless attack on the classics, as we will see in the next section, hardly fits into this context.

The second theme is mentioning the "perfected man" (*zhenren*) versus the "sage" (*shengren*). As we have already seen in chapter 1, Li Xun and his group promoted the perfect man over the sage, while most Han literati celebrated the sage. In the received *Scripture*, there are fairly frequent references to the perfected man and the sage together, with the perfected man consistently ranked higher than the sage. I consider these passages to have Eastern Han roots, because the comparisons suggest an ongoing competition between the "sage" and "perfected man." On the one hand, the term "sage" was popular in Eastern Han political discourse. On the other hand, at the end of the Eastern Han, the Cao family, who eventually established the Wei dynasty, sought to install the "perfected man" in their political propaganda.[99] This reflects the popularity of the "perfected man" at the end of the Eastern Han. Therefore, it is reasonable to imagine that the author of the *Scripture* needed to emphasize the superiority of the "perfected man" over the "sage." Although I am aware that these criteria for identifying Eastern Han passages do not fully exclude later passages, they provide a helpful place to begin.

To Be Better than the Classics: Comprehensive and Essential

While previous scholarship is silent on the relationship between the classics and the *Scriptures*, many scholars have substantially contributed to the understanding of the connections between apocryphal texts and the *Scripture*. Anna Seidel, for example, studied how apocryphal texts and Daoist texts share many topics, such as the emphasis on tallies (*fu* 符) and other revelations like the *River Chart*, and discussions about the teacher of the emperor and the mediator between the human world and Heaven.[100] Some scholars take similar approaches too far when speculating about the relationship between the texts.[101] Although the same topics can be found in the two corpora, they are not exclusive to these two corpora. In fact, they were shared by

Eastern Han scholars. Therefore, it is hard to differentiate "Taoism's roots in apocrypha"[102] from "Taoism's roots in the Eastern Han intellectual world."

I will take a different approach to the topic. Instead of identifying floating topics as evidence for a relationship between texts, I will trace direct references to the classics and apocryphal texts in the received *Scripture*. This method will give us a clear picture of how the *Scripture* understands the classics and apocrypha.

As we have seen from the previous chapters, many scholars were convinced that the Han dynasty was facing crises that would eventually lead to the collapse of the dynasty. This is also the case in the *Scripture*. The text describes the current world as full of problems, and it is aimed to help the current emperor to save humanity and achieve the Great Peace.[103] It attributes the chaos in the human realm to people's failure to understand the "heart of Heaven" (*tian zhi xin* 天之心) as well as their excessive and contradictory words:

> 故治亂者由太多端，不得天之心，當還反其本根。夫人言太多而不見是者，當還反其本要也，迺其言事可立也。故一言而成者，其本文也；再轉言而止者，迺成章句也；故三言而止，反成解難也，將遺真，故有解難也；四言而止，反成文辭也；五言而止，反成偽也；六言而止，反成欺也；七言而止，反成破也；八言而止，反成離散遺道，遺復遺也；九言而止，反成大亂也；十言而止，反成滅毀也。故經至十而改，更相傳而敗毀也。[104]

Therefore, by [drawing on] too many means to impose order on disorder, the government does not obtain Heaven's heart. Instead, we should return to the root of things. When men speak so much that they lose sight of this, they should instead return to what is essential. If they do that, they can sustain their words and deeds. Therefore, the original text is completed in a single layer of words. With its transmission comes the creation of chapter and verse commentaries. At the next level is an analysis of difficult passages. Difficult passages must be explained in order to prevent men from moving away from truth. The fourth level of words consists of adaptations [of the original text]. At the fifth level, fake texts are produced, and at the sixth level [these fake products] are meant to deceive men. At the seventh level lies the distortion of the original text. At the eighth level, the distance from what has originally been taught becomes bigger and bigger. At the ninth level, the text is in great disorder; at the tenth, it is completely corrupted. Therefore, the classics that have reached this tenth stage are altered; their transmissions are supplanted and will end in extinction.[105]

The passage points out that the true meaning of texts deteriorates through transmission. It mentions the phrase "chapter and verse," or *zhangju* 章句, which is peculiar to the deep but myopic commentarial traditions of Han classicism. In this context, "chapter and verse" is thought to follow the original meaning of the texts,[106] but it is also the beginning of textual corruption. It further mentions that after ten bouts of transmission, the classics are bound to deviate seriously from their original form.

If the preceding asserts dissatisfaction with classicism, the following is an open attack on the Han commentarial traditions:

夫學之大害也，合於外章句者，日浮淺而致文而妄語也，入內文合於圖讖者，實不能深得其結要意，反誤言也。[107]

As for the great harm of these studies, the ones that accord with the external, "chapter and verse" [commentaries] lead day by day to a lack of reality, to ornamentality and ranting; the ones that enter via esoteric [interpretations of] words that accord with apocrypha actually cannot preserve the essentials; instead they become erroneous.

In chapter 2, we have already gone through certain themes of apocryphal texts. Although we can use the word "commentary" to characterize both apocryphal texts and passages of "chapter and verse," the latter are more pertinent to most of the classics than the former. Based on the surviving fragments, apocrypha primarily contain prophecies and legends to reveal the classics' heavenly nature and the state of the mandate of Heaven. Accordingly, this passage criticizes these two kinds of commentaries according to their natures. Like the critique of "chapter and verse" from the "Seven Summaries,"[108] it assails the style's empty wordiness. As for apocryphal texts, which appear to be a key of heavenly origin to understanding the classics, the passage accuses them of being so narrow that they fail to grasp the essential principles. The *Scripture* thus claims to possess a truer understanding of Heaven.

The *Scripture* further evaluates the relationship among disasters, previous sages, and the texts they wrote:

> 古今天文聖書賢人辭已備足，但愁其集居，各長於一事耳。今案用一家法也，不能悉除天地之災變，故使流災不絕，更相承負後生者，日得災病增劇。故天怜德君，復承負之。天和為後生者，不能獨生，比積災諸咎也。實過在先生賢聖，各長於一，而俱有不達，俱有所失。天知其不具足，故時出河雒文圖及他神書，亦復不同辭也。夫大賢聖異世而出，各作一事，亦復不同辭，是故各有不及，各有短長也。是也明其俱不能盡悉知究洞極之意，故使天地之間，常有餘災，前後訖不絕，但有劇與不耳。[109]

Old and new heavenly texts, sagely books, and words by the worthy are quite sufficient, but when put together the trouble is that each excels in only one topic. If you rely on the model [set up by] one school [only], you will not be able to abolish all the disasters that happen in Heaven and on earth, and they will continue to be received and transmitted without end. Later generations suffer from calamity and illness that increase every day. For this reason Heaven pities the virtuous lord and his ongoing reception and transmission [of evil]. It knows that, because of these calamities, later generations are unable to survive on their own. The mistake lies really with the worthy and sage men of former generations. They all excelled in one thing, but there was also much that they misunderstood or neglected. Since Heaven knew that something was missing, it occasionally issued the *River* and Luo texts and charts and other spirit writings. These again differed from each other in what they said. The great worthies and sages of different generations each dealt with one specific matter. They again differed from each other in what they said. On some issues, they were not good. Each had their weak and their strong points. Thus it is clear that all of them were unable to fully understand what "all-pervading" means. Thus between Heaven and earth calamities never ceased to occur. They were never brought to a halt, not in former times or in later times, but sometimes they were increasing and sometimes they were not.[110]

According to this passage, the accumulation of disasters is due to former sages' and worthies' narrow expertise. Although the words from the ancient to contemporary world, from Heaven to the human realm are enough, the narrow focus of scholarly lineages block them from seeing the "principle of comprehensiveness and ultimacy" (*dongji zhi yi* 洞極之意). The passage mentions revelations such as the *River Chart* and the *Writing of the Luo River*, which many Eastern Han scholars considered the origin of the classics and of human sages' textual inventions. However, this passage claims that scholars' narrow foci make it impossible for them to solve the world's problems.

In this regard, based on Heaven's will, human society needs a scripture that is comprehensive enough to save the world. The passage continues:

是故天上算計之，今為文書，上下極畢備足，迺復生聖人，無可復作，無可復益，無可復容言，無可復益於天地大德之君。[111]

Therefore, Heaven above calculated it, and now there is a text that from beginning to end is completely adequate. Were another sage to be born, there is nothing further he would be able to write, to add, or to formulate to benefit Heaven, earth, and lords with great virtue [beyond this scripture].[112]

The passage makes explicit that Heaven has revealed a comprehensive text that is so sweeping that there is no need for supplements. This ultimately comprehensive text makes even future sages' words obsolete.

The *Scripture*'s claim of syncretism in order to govern the world was certainly not unprecedented.[113] Back as early as the early Western Han, the king of Huainan, Liu An 劉安 (179–122 BC) and his consultants compiled the *Master Huainan* (*Huainanzi* 淮南子) as an attempt to syncretize various kinds of thought "in order to unify the world, bring order to the myriad things, respond to alternations and transformations, and to comprehend all distinctions and categories" 以統天下，理萬物，應變化，通殊類。[114] They proudly stated that their text was the result of observing the phenomena of Heaven and Earth as well as comprehending ancient and contemporary affairs.[115] Their text was neither specialist nor a product of narrow-mindedness: "it does not just follow the path of a single footprint, or adhere to instructions of one corner, or allow itself to be entrapped or fettered by things so that it does not advance with the world" 非循一跡之路，守一隅之指，拘系牽連之物，而不與世推移也。[116] Like the *Master Huainan*, the *Scripture* does not stick to just one corner of knowledge and provides the most comprehensive knowledge to help the world.

This similarity between the claims from the two texts lies within the intellectual context of the Eastern Han. We can even find that Eastern Han literati's increasing interest in the *Master Huainan* coincided with this trend of broad learning. From Xu Shen 許慎 (ca. AD 58–147), a knowledgeable scholar of the Five Classics[117] and an expert in paleography, to Ma Rong, from Ma Rong's disciple Lu Zhi to Lu's student Gao You 高誘 (fl. AD 205–212), generations of literati wrote commentaries on this book.[118] As Gao You wrote in his preface to his commentary, this was because "of previous worthies, scholars of broad learning, and authors [that] none failed to refer to it in order to verify the classics and their commentaries" 是以先賢通儒述作之士，莫不援采以驗經傳.[119]

How was the *Master Huainan* helpful to verify the classics? Gao You further explained: "Its meaning is marked; its words are rich. Of the various kinds of things and affairs, none is missing, but the general idea follows the Way" 其義也著，其文也富，物事之類無所不載，然其大較歸之於道.[120] In other words, for Gao You, the appeal of *Master Huainan* not only lies in its comprehensiveness but also its preservation of the Way. Here the Way, or "Dao," is not the Kingly Way mentioned in the late Western Han. Rather, it is the mystical being whence the cosmos generated. It was the ultimate origin as well as the ultimately underlying order of the world. As Gao You understood the *Master Huainan*, the *Scripture* presents itself similarly: it is both comprehensive and able to capture the essential, the heart of Heaven.

Unlike the intention of Liu An, who proposed to unpack his ideas for the future sage ruler, or that of the Eastern Han commentators, who aimed to clarify the written legacy of the ancient sages, in the *Scripture*, the human sages are no longer necessary:

> 若天復生聖人，其言會復長於一業，猶且復有餘流災毒常不盡，與先聖賢無異也。是故天使吾深告敕真人，付文道德之君，以示諸賢明，都并拘校，合天下之文人口訣辭，以上下相足，去其復重，置其要言要文訣事，記之以為經書。[121]

If Heaven gave birth to another sage, his words might excel in one particular field, but, even so, the growth of natural disasters would never come to an end, just as was the case for the sages and worthies of previous ages. For this reason Heaven has sent me to strictly command you to give texts to a virtuous lord so that he can show them to all the worthy and enlightened men around him. They must collect and revise these writings together with all the world's texts and the instructions and expressions men have given voice to, which from beginning to end support each other. They must cut out duplicates, put forth a digest of instructions, and record it as a classic.[122]

The person speaking in this passage is a celestial master (*tianshi* 天師), and he is talking to a perfected man. The celestial master predicts that even if there were more sages in the future, their narrow expertise would not be helpful for saving the world. Again, following the intellectual trend of the second century, the passage rejects specialization and celebrates comprehensiveness. Earlier in this chapter, we saw how the rest of the guests scorned Zheng Xuan at a banquet because they thought Zheng was a *ru*, a classicist. They eventually respected him because they found out he was a man with comprehensive knowledge (*tongren* 通人), a term that emphasizes broad erudition. In this passage, the sages, as the inventors of the classics, become narrow in perspective, and the perfected man is needed to rescue the world.

How could perfected men replace the sages to save the world? They play an essential role in the project that the celestial master commands. This project resonates with the literary world of the first two centuries. According to the passage, the project is about the transmission of texts, in which the perfected men are collators of texts. Their job description resembles that of Liu Xiang, Liu Xin, Ma Rong, and many others in the imperial library. The texts they need to collate are not limited to certain corpora, but all of literature. Men of letters are needed to join this project. The outcome of this undertaking is also a *jing*, the word for "classic," which in religious traditions soon came to mean "scripture." Unlike the classics, the new *jing* is sufficient to heal the world's chaos. Possessing the new *jing*, the perfected man becomes the new *tongren*, the "man with comprehensive knowledge."

This idealistic description depicts a community producing texts like those who explicated the classics in the Eastern Han dynasty. This text-centered community has a celestial master, resembling the classicists' ancient sages who understood Heaven (see the case of Zixia in chapter 3). Better than the sages, the workings of his mind match those of Heaven (*yu tian he yi* 與天合意), so that he knows what Heaven wants for the contemporary world. The perfected men's project is not just to preserve and clarify a number of texts but all the texts of the world. In other words, while the classicists, or worthies, tend to be exclusive in preserving their texts, perfected men are eclectic. Their goal is to attract the literati and even the imperial house into the transmission project described in the *Scripture*. In accordance with the peripatetic and epistolary culture of the time, this undertaking would be an open one that brought scholars together. Behind the critiques lies a relationship between certain sections of the *Scripture* and Han classicism: based on the world of the latter, the former creates a similar but superior one and wields authority in it.

Concluding Remarks

When classicism was dominant in the first half of the Eastern Han, new trends were also sprouting. Similarly, when the Han dynasty was going through political crises and scholars departed from classicism, it did not simply die out, for it was based on men and institutions. From He Xiu to Zheng Xuan, classicists adapted themselves to the changing realities and shifting concerns of their time. From Emperor Ming's sage-worthy transmission line to the *Scripture*'s celestial master / perfected men project, Han classicism remained a primary source of innovations.

In this chapter, I have positioned Zheng Xuan, He Xiu, and the *Scripture* in their own contemporary world instead of a specialized history of the classics or of Daoism. This means locating them on a continuum of positions adopted by Eastern Han scholars vis-à-vis the classics. In their world, a broader perspective of knowledge started to dominate intellectual communities, and interest in the classics was fading away. From this perspective, Zheng Xuan was neither a partisan nor scourge of the old text traditions; He Xiu did not belong to the new script cult; the *Scripture of the Great Peace* did not belong to any imagined transmission line of "Daoism" from *Zhuangzi* or the *Dao De Jing*. Instead, Zheng Xuan brought synthesis to a higher level: not only did he combine previous commentarial traditions, he also argued for a higher abstraction level in the classics. He Xiu departed from the tendency of broad learning by concentrating on the Gongyang tradition of the *Annals* in order to preserve the pure transmission line of Confucius. The authors of the *Scripture of the Great Peace*, more radically, replaced classicism with its own revelation and scriptures. These people were all preoccupied by the general concern of Han literati: the fate of the dynasty as the mandate of Heaven seemed threatened. They engaged in the pursuit of the Great Peace in their own ways. Whether they adhered to or departed from them, the classics were the center of their attention, for it was on the common ground of scholars that they strove to carry out their ideas. They critically learned from and innovatively responded to Eastern Han trends of literati culture. Focused on Heaven's will and comprehensiveness, they searched for the Great Peace in their own innovative way through synthesis, fractionation, or departures from previous models.

Conclusion

In this book, I have traced the people and texts in the Han dynasty that scholars often label as "Confucian," "Daoist," "Old Script," "New Script," and so forth, and I have tried to understand who they were, what they did, and why they did so. What insights and general patterns can we gain from the literati world of this roughly three hundred years of imperial China? In the following, I will zoom out from the specific pictures and look at the panorama. I will start with how the Han literati connected with each other and sustained their communities. Then I turn to the intellectual discourses among the communities, particularly concerning the Great Peace and Heaven, in order to see the patterns of intellectual innovations in Han China. Finally, I will examine the long-term impact and legacy of Han classicism.

Han Intellectual Communities and Their Features

The most commonly shared feature of Han intellectual communities was their experience in the study of the classics. However, this experience varied from person to person. In Emperor Wu's reign, dominant officials like Gongsun Hong and Zhufu Yan changed their focus from legal issues to a classic, the *Annals*. In Emperor Xuan's court, Wei Xiang and Bing Ji took the *Changes* as an expedient means of testing Heaven's will. People like Kuang Heng, Liu Xiang, and Liu Xin concentrated on the full package of the classics to revive the Kingly Way. Unlike these great visionary scholars, ordinary teachers and students of the classics were mainly focused on specialist textual studies. Furthermore, Li Xun, whose scholarship as well as academic connections were deeply rooted in classicism, tried to move away from the classics.

At the beginning of the Eastern Han, apocryphal texts were involved in literati's classical repository, and their interest in the texts became increasingly broad and no longer exclusive to the classics. Although defenders of the classics such as He Xiu and Zheng Xuan were still active in the intellectual communities of their time, literati's zeal for the classics was crucially declining. Through the Han dynasty, scholars did not share a single, unitary agenda for why they were engaged in classicism, nor did they consider themselves a tight, unified group. Squabbles were constant among them. On one hand, a similar knowledge base did provide them common ground; on the other hand, that common ground led to constant ruptures.

These communities also shared a similar experience in learning the classics. Most of the time, they went through the process of finding teachers, committing to them, staying to learn with them for a rather long period of time, and then becoming a teacher for someone else. Again, we witnessed in the Eastern Han a more massive traveling experience and easier access to teachers and books than in the Western Han. In this process, certain manners, etiquette, values, and virtues became commonsense to them. Although it seems that they did not know every single other literatus, Han literati nevertheless had this social common ground to form large communities as well as intimate circles.

However, there is a complete lack of detailed sets of rules from these academies that parallel either Daoist community principles and liturgy or Paul's pastoral Epistles about how to organize local churches.[1] This is likely due to the scarcity of received texts, but it might also imply that these local academies as social organizations were comparatively rather loose and less unified. They did not feel the need to form a unified "Confucian" school outside the National Academy in any institutional sense, nor did they consider the National Academy their headquarters. Social solidarity was established between students and their teachers, and students thus did not attach themselves to any certain institution but rather to their teachers. On the contrary, the Han court's maneuvers to monopolize authority over the students such as National Academy recruitment were not as successful. In this respect, it is not a surprise that while Yuan Shao could form his troops by recruiting students of his family, students even at the National Academy were disobedient to the Han court.[2]

By further asking what kinds of values and virtues they believed in, we saw a more or less similar sentiment: the emperor needed the literati's help to be in accordance with Heaven's mandate and to achieve the Great Peace. In Han literati's works, we do not see a complex discussion of morality as in the *Analects*, *Mencius*, and *Xunzi*. In fact, with the exception of a few scholars such as Lu Jia, Dong Zhongshu, and Wang Ji, morality did not take any decisive role in their philosophies. Heaven instead took the essential role. This was partially due to a long-term intellectual development from the mid–Warring States period, when a series of texts such as *Laozi* and certain chapters of *Zhuangzi* engaged in cosmology and cosmogony. Han literati's discussion thus emerged from these discourses. More importantly, from the Zhou to the Han dynasty, Heaven's mandate had been directly linked to the legitimacy of a dynasty.[3] At the same time, Han literati were faced with an empire that had an unprecedented degree of centralization. While the Warring States rulers sought various means to compete with each other, Han emperors were concerned with consolidating their rule. This more compressed political order left scholars with less liberty and choices than their Warring States predecessors. This political and intellectual environment thus perpetuated literati's continuous focus on Heaven's will.

The position of the lord was one of the essential themes in political philosophies of early China. We can find the appeal for worthy rulers and the imitation of ancient sage kings in the words of Confucius, Mozi, Mencius, and Xunzi. We can also find mystical suggestions for rulers in the *Laozi*, as well as Han Feizi's tips for the mediocre lords of the Warring States.[4] Although there were various expectations for rulers, almost no one suggested a permanent abandonment of the ruler. In fact, scholars of the Warring States period spent most of their careers persuading rulers to practice their philosophy. In the Han empire, an emperor with more concentrated power and resources replaced the previously diverse political authorities with a high degree of autonomous power, such as kings and dukes. This political situation encouraged discussions about the emperor and kept him as the center of the empire.

By defining the position of the ruler, literati also defined themselves in this political hierarchy. Although seldom explicitly expressed in Han literati's writings, they tended to think that they possessed special knowledge to assist the emperor, although this was seldom explicitly expressed in their writings. The knowledge they possessed separated them from the rest of the bureaucratic servants. The hierarchical distinction between the emperor and Han literati lay in the mandate of Heaven. As mentioned in the discussion about Confucius in the apocryphal texts, it was not that Confucius was not worthy or intelligent enough to become a ruler. It was rather Heaven's will that Confucius would not become a ruler. Based on apocrypha, Heaven instead wished Confucius to be the possessor of superb knowledge with which to help future rulers to realize the Kingly Way. In many Han literati's eyes, Confucius codified his teaching for the later rulers in the Five Classics. For them, he not only wrote the *Annals* but also edited the rest of classics, which were the legacy of the ancient sage kings. Han classicists, as the transmitters of Confucius's undertakings, thus engaged his legacy to assist the heavenly ordinated new rulers, the Liu family, or any potential recipients of Heaven's mandate.

The Matter of the Great Peace

I might have disappointed those in the audience who are waiting for a clear-cut definition of what the Great Peace was in the Han dynasty, but the Han literati usually did not give a clear definition, and for those who did, they did not provide a unitary definition. This, however, does not prevent the term from becoming a center of attention in intellectual and political discourses. Most Han literati believed that by following the classics, the emperor would bring the Great Peace to the world.

The term was largely an invention of the Han intellectual world. Although we occasionally see "peace" or "peaceful" (*ping* 平) used to describe a temporary political state, the term crystalized in Han political discourse to denote an ideal society. It is noteworthy that in the *Records of Rites*, there was a description of the ideal world, Great Equality (*datong* 大同),[5] in which people not only love their children but also other people's children. This passage implies a world where the fundamental social relationships, such as the father-son relationship, were replaced by a more impartial love. Even though the Great Equality takes a whole chapter in the classics, it was absent in Han literati's conversations. On the contrary, the Great Peace (*taiping* 太平), a term that can rarely be found in the body of the classical corpus, was abundant.[6]

The preference for the Great Peace over the Great Equality reflects how Han literati and emperors imagined Han rule. They did not conceive of an empire where people had an extremely convenient life by means of highly advanced technology. Nor did they imagine it as a radical utopia where social distinctions were abandoned. Instead, they depicted their ideal world as a peaceful state where social distinctions were well carried out and carefully maintained, and the populace celebrated such order. In other words, the state of the Great Peace was one with all the social distinctions but without the social conflicts. This conception of the ideal society did not die out after the collapse of the Han empire but was preserved in the movements and scriptures of Celestial Masters. The term *taiping* has reoccurred in Chinese history again and again since the Han dynasty. We can find it even in the name of the rebellious regime during the late Qing 清 dynasty (AD 1636–1911): the Heavenly Kingdom of the Great Peace (Taiping Tianguo 太平天國) (AD 1850–1864).

The Production of Innovation and Its Driving Force

Han scholars gave various constructions of the Great Peace and Heaven that did not necessarily match imperial propaganda. This suggests that political dominance was only one side of the story in perpetuating certain ideas. Intellectual communities were responsible for producing, accepting, adapting, or departing from these ideas. As we have seen through this book, scholarly squabbles were constant among intellectual communities. From Emperor Wu to Emperor Yuan's reign, advocates of the classics constantly argued for the unique importance of the classics, and the commentarial traditions multiplied with an increasing tendency toward scholasticism.[7] At the end of the Western Han, a two-way innovation took place: via Liu Xin with a great synthesis and Li Xun with a grand departure. Explicitly or inexplicitly, they reacted to the scholastic fashion in the study of the classics, and their driving concern was securing the mandate of Heaven. Following such discourse, in the beginning of the Eastern Han, apocryphal texts appeared as revealed commentaries to accommodate the literati's preference for the classics and the legitimacy of the newly established empire. In many of these cases, the emperor and the empire needed to adjust to these intellectual moves in various ways, such as adopting a new reign title (as in Li Xun's case) and creating new erudite positions (as in Liu Xin's case), among others.

From the late Western Han, the classics started to gain cultural prestige in the court due to emperors' insecurity regarding the mandate of Heaven, and the local gentry and elites tried to catch up with this trend. Because recommendation was an important means of official recruitment in the local and imperial government, social networking was essential in maintaining a family's status. The classics thus served as a medium by which people could socialize with well-established officials and scholars in the framework of "studying the classics." This situation served as the social basis for the spread of the classics and the initiation of the peripatetic literati culture of the Eastern Han and early medieval China.

During the first hundred years of the Eastern Han, literati's career patterns resulted in an increasing degree of access to knowledge. Erudition became a fashion among scholars, and the classics were faced with two challenges. On the one hand, in terms of comprehensiveness, they do not provide detailed information about cosmogony, the genealogy of ancient kings, or precedents of Han legal and administrative systems that *Huainanzi*, the *Grand Historian's Records*, the *History of the Han*, and many others do. Therefore, some scholars turned to these texts to find answers for those issues. On the other hand, an increasing level of abstraction drove many scholars to extract the essence from the classics instead of putting their technical details into practice. This opened a door to the question of whether only the classics contained the essence of the Way and whether one needed to master the classics to obtain the essential knowledge they offered. In Zhang Heng's letter about Yang Xiong's *Supreme Mystery*, it is clear that he already believes Yang's work is in accordance with the classics and that it will become popular among later generations. It is not clear whether Zhang Heng believed that the *Supreme Mystery* would become one of the new classics, but it is certain that he thought that Yang's work would be just as helpful as guidance for later generations as the classics were for the contemporary dynasty.

This compromise of the authority of the classics led to a three-way innovation. On one side of the spectrum, He Xiu advocated a return to the "pure" form of the fundamental classic. Since Confucius left his teaching in the *Annals*, which had been transmitted for generations to the Western Han dynasty, He argued that one should stick to Confucius's words preserved in the uncorrupted Gongyang tradition to revive classicism and the Han empire. His approach appeared not only as a response to the contemporary fashion of broad learning but also as a reminiscence of Western Han transmission lines.

The *Scripture of the Great Peace* stands on the other side of the spectrum, where one should completely depart from the classics. For the *Scripture*, the essence the classics contain is neither permanent nor comprehensive enough for people to follow anymore. The sages and worthies do not even possess the most important message from Heaven. According to the *Scripture*, the celestial master and perfected men hold the true and everlasting teachings of Heaven. The *Scripture* advocates a new relationship, celestial master–perfected man, over the existing one in Han classicism: sage-worthy or master-disciple.

Zheng Xuan stood in the middle; he embraced broad learning with an emphasis on classicism. He synthesized commentarial traditions that were established in various times in the Han dynasty: the Western Han commentarial traditions, the old text traditions promoted by Liu Xin and Wang Mang, and apocryphal texts from the beginning of the Eastern Han. Yet he did not encourage people to imitate every single detail in his enormous commentarial world; he argued for practicing the essence of the classics. Therefore, his commentarial world served as guidance for the extraction of this essence as well as a reference for the latter-day sage.

The Impact and Legacy of Classicism

The study of the classics brought the Han empire crucial social changes, many of which were linked to the frequent travel of literati. Like any other civilizations, early Chinese traveled for various reasons.[8] However, for the first time in Chinese history, studying, especially the classics, became one of the major reasons to travel. One long-term impact was the establishment and consolidation of social connections. People traveled from their hometown to the capital Luoyang, the Three Adjunct areas, and wherever the private academies were located. They socialized in those locations as well as on the road. Han China, like the Roman empire, invested vastly in the transportation of information and knowledge. Individuals, in contrast, did not have as much means of mobilizing information other than depending on servants as messengers or people who happened to go to the same direction as the letter went. Massive traveling contributed greatly to the private mobilization of knowledge and information. Ostensibly, a student of the classics carried texts with his master's teachings from one place to another. He carried not only letters for his acquaintances but also news and hearsay gathered on his way. Such travel of information constituted a rival method for the official transportation of information. Certainly such transportation was not as efficient and centralized as the postal system of the empire. Nevertheless, it constituted a rival narrative of the empire where the voice of the literati instead of the bureaucracy dominated.

Accordingly, that voice was embodied in various literary forms. Literati used letters not only to send their most essential messages but also to hold intellectual discussions and debates. They wrote prefaces to texts not for the emperor's convenience but as guidance for fellow literati. They inscribed inscriptions on steles and tombstones, in which they celebrated their friends, former teachers, or former lords' virtues or conveyed their condolences. These inscriptions served as a window to confirm to their fellow literati as well as to show potential traveling students what this imagined literati community was supposed to be. Famous writers provided mottos inscribed on daily objects to remind them of the proper behavior for a gentleman.[9] Through this literary world built on the traveling culture, a sense of literati community crystallized, as a poem drastically proclaimed: "Bonding relies on mutual understanding; why do blood relatives have to be intimate?" (結交在相知, 骨肉何必親？).[10]

This traveling culture also accelerated the use of paper. Although the earliest sample of paper is from Emperor Jing's reign (157–141 BC),[11] bamboo and wooden strips constituted the main body of Western Han writing material. With official roads, inns, and messengers, the Han empire could certainly afford to move voluminous chunks of wood from one place to another. However, this was not the case for individual travelers in the Eastern Han, who needed to carry some classical texts from one location to another. These texts were much longer than most administrative documents and letters. The weak points of wooden strips became increasingly observable. This situation coincided with Cai Lun's 蔡倫 (AD 63–121) improvement of papermaking technology, the motivation for which was his dissatisfaction with heavy wooden strips and expensive silk pieces.[12] The materials required for his method were scraps of daily commodities, namely, tree bark, hemp scraps, old cloth, and fish net. In AD 105, he presented his method to Emperor He and it became very popular afterward.[13] The ready acceptance of his method implied a great need for a lighter and cheaper writing material. This need was precisely derived from the traveling culture of training in the classics.

Did the classics leave any impact or did they disappear after the collapse of the Han dynasty? As scholars have elaborately shown, during the second and third century AD, many literati engaged in the so-called "study of mystery" (Xuanxue 玄學), which examines metaphysical features of certain concepts such as "nothingness" (*wu* 無), "existence" (*you* 有), "language" (*yan* 言), and "meaning" (*yi* 意) from texts like the *Changes* and *Laozi*.[14] On many occasions, literati carried out these discussions during banquets or personal conversations. People then called this kind of dialog "pure discussions" (*qingtan* 清談).[15] Apparently, they moved to a higher level of abstraction and departed from the elaborate commentarial traditions of Han classicism.

However, the classics did not die out. Despite the fact that they no longer enjoyed the prestige of imperial patronage until the Tang 唐 dynasty (AD 618–907), literati of the Six Dynasties still valued them as one of the most important corpora of literati lives. In fact, we can always find defenders of the classics. For example, Li Quan 李權 (?–AD 188), a member of a great family in Sichuan, wanted to borrow the *Strategies of the Warring States* (*Zhanguo ce* 戰國策) from a classicist Qin Mi 秦宓 (?–AD 226) because "the vastness of the sea lays in convergent tributaries, and the greatness of a gentleman lays in erudite knowledge" (故海以合流為大，君子以博識為弘). The latter disagreed: "Although gentlemen should be with erudite knowledge, they would not look at anything [that does] not [accord with] rites. Now [the text is about] the sabotage of the warring states and the methods of Zhang Yi and Su Qin, by which one killed and eliminated others to survive. This is what the classics criticize" (君子博識，非禮不視。今戰國反覆儀、秦之術，殺人自生，亡人自存，經之所疾).[16]

Buddhism took advantage of the collapse of the Eastern Han as well as the tide of the broad learning in order to flourish in China. However, Buddhist monks also needed to find a way to explain the essentiality of their scriptures in the context of the classics. For example, in doubting what Buddhism could offer, Sun Hao 孫皓 (AD 242–284), the fourth Wu kingdom (AD 229–280) ruler, said: "If so, then the Duke of Zhou and Confucius already illuminated it. Why the teachings of Buddha?" (若然, 則周孔已明，何用佛教). Kang Senghui 康僧會 (?–AD 280), a Buddhist monk erudite in the classics and apocrypha answered: "What the Duke of Zhou and Confucius said sketchily points out recent traces, but the teachings of Buddha fully and comprehensively reach to subtlety and nuance" (周孔所言略示近迹; 至於釋教則備極幽微).[17] Indeed, the classics could no longer satisfy literati's much broader curiosity about the world. However, as Ge Hong and Yan Zhitui state, they still took a central position in understanding the human world.[18] The transmission of the classics never died but rather waited for a newcomer to reopen the gate to the Great Peace.

Appendix 1

The Chinese Classics

This appendix introduces the inventory of the classics (*jing* 經) that is conventionally accepted today. In modern-day academia, the oft-referred version is *Thirteen Classics with Commentaries and Sub-Commentaries* (*Shisan jing zhushu* 十三經注疏), which is an AD 1816 reprint based on a Southern Song dynasty version. The general editor of this version was Ruan Yuan 阮元 (AD 1764–1849).[1] In this edition, the classics are a corpus of the following texts:

The *Changes of Zhou* (*Zhou yi* 周易, usually referred to as *Yijing* 易經, or the *Classic of Changes*)[2]
The *Book of Documents* (*Shangshu* 尚書)[3]
The Mao tradition of the *Book of Poetry* (Mao *Shi* 毛詩, initiated by Mao Heng 毛亨 of the early Western Han, in which Mao refers to a commentary tradition of the *Book of Poetry*, or the *Classic of Poetry*, *Shijing* 詩經)[4]
The *Rites of Zhou* (*Zhouli* 周禮)
The *Ceremonies and Rites* (*Yili* 儀禮)
The *Records of Rites* (*Liji* 禮記)[5]
The Zuo tradition of the *Spring and Autumn Annals* (*Chunqiu* Zuo zhuan 春秋左傳)
The Gongyang tradition of the *Spring and Autumn Annals* (*Chunqiu* Gongyang zhuan 春秋公羊傳)
The Guliang tradition of the *Spring and Autumn Annals* (*Chunqiu* Guliang zhuan 春秋穀梁傳)[6]
The *Analects* (*Lunyu* 論語)
The *Classic of Filial Piety* (*Xiaojing* 孝經)
Approaching What Is Refined (*Er ya* 爾雅)
Mencius (*Mengzi* 孟子)

In the list, the "Thirteen Classics" are not on the same level. For example, the text of the *Spring and Autumn Annals* appears three times with three different commentarial traditions. Therefore, what is counted three times here actually are the three commentarial traditions instead of the plain text of the *Annals*.

The corpus of Thirteen Classics contains sets of texts that were advocated at one time or another as the subject of "the study of classics," now referred to as *jing xue* 經學, which aimed at illuminating the classics written by the ancient sages.[7] Because people from different periods had different ideas of what the classics are and how they ought to be understood, there have been various lists of the classics and different theorizations of them.[8] This 1816 version is thus the one accepted by the imperial government of the Qing dynasty and many Qing scholars. It is more a reflection of and compromise of the previous traditions than a pure invention by Qing scholars.

The "Thirteen Classics" as a group of texts can be loosely divided into distinct layers based upon how people in Chinese history related them to each other. For example, if we turn to the *Annotated Catalog of the Complete Library of the Four Treasures* (*Siku quanshu zongmu tiyao* 四庫全書總目提要) completed in the forty-seventh year of Qianlong 乾隆 (AD 1782), we would find several layers in the "Thirteen Classics" corpus. The first layer is the "Five Classics" (Wujing 五經) section, including the *Classic of the Changes*, *Book of Documents*, *Classics of Poetry*, the three *Rites* corpus, and *Spring and Autumn Annals*. This layer is most relevant to the context of Han classicism. This list of texts has existed since Liu Xiang 劉向 (ca. 77–6 BC) and his son Liu Xin's 劉歆 (50 BC–AD 23) bibliography, "Seven Summaries" ("Qi lüe" 七略), later included in Ban Gu's 班固 (AD 32–92) *History of the Han* (*Han shu* 漢書). In the "Seven Summaries," the section that contains the Five Classics is called "Six Arts" ("Liuyi" 六藝), in which texts about the *Music* are also included. However, the author already mentions that the learning of *Music* became "more and more obscure,"[9] which suggests that *Music* did not exist as a text then.

In addition, in the "Seven Summaries," the *Classic of Filial Piety* is attached to this category as well. The "Seven Summaries" explains the significance of the *Classic of Filial Piety* by pointing out the special role of filial piety among Heaven and Earth. Han dynasty scholars also considered Confucius the author of the text.[10] In the *Annotated Catalog*, the author of that section no longer believes Confucius is the author, and the *Classic of Filial Piety* was no longer part of the civil examination inventory in the

Qing dynasty.[11] Nevertheless, it is still one of the classics preserved in Ruan Yuan's reprint of the Thirteen Classics.

The second layer is the "Four Books" ("Si Shu" 四書) section. It includes the *Analects*, the other text attached to the section of Six Arts in the "Seven Summaries"; *Mencius*; and two chapters from the *Records of Rites*: "The Doctrine of Mean" ("Zhongyong" 中庸) and "The Great Learning" ("Daxue" 大學). Zhu Xi 朱熹 (AD 1130–1200) from the Southern Song dynasty (AD 1127–1270) strongly advocated this curriculum along with his commentaries on these four texts. Later the Mongols adopted his curriculum and the philosophy represented by his lineage into the civil examination system.[12] Despite growing dissatisfaction with Zhu Xi's philosophy and his approach to them, the Four Books with Zhu Xi's commentary became part of the civil examination system for most of the period from the Yuan dynasty (AD 1271–1368) to the last civil examination in AD 1905.[13]

The third layer visible in the *Annotated Catalog* is *Er ya*, a glossary text compiled under the section of "Elementary Learning" ("Xiao Xue" 小學) in the *Annotated Catalog*. According to the editor of this section, the "Elementary Learning" is supposed to be about texts for learning the writing system and vocabularies. This theory agrees with the definition of the same section in "Seven Summaries." However, counterintuitively, in the "Seven Summaries," *Er ya* is not listed under the section of the "Elementary Learning," which concerns texts for learning script and vocabularies, like later bibliographies do,[14] but as the "Classic of Filial Piety." It is unclear why this is the case. However, judging from the other titles in this section, this section also includes texts that cannot be categorized into other sections.[15]

Appendix 2

The Origin of the Old Script / New Script Controversy

Because Qing scholars were directly responsible for coining the so-called "New Script" and "Old Script" controversy in modern scholarship,[1] a brief survey on the origin of this framework in the Qing dynasty would be helpful for us to better understand the sequent modern Chinese scholarship on classicism.

Intellectual Transitions of the Qing Dynasty

Qing scholars' interest in Han classicism resulted from a "philological turn." In the late Ming dynasty, Wang Yangming's 王陽明 (AD 1472–1529) philosophy became popular among the literati. Wang's intellectual descendants extended his philosophy to the extreme, denying the value of ancient classics, and the distinction between good and evil. Dissatisfied with these polemic arguments, some literati criticized such tendencies and sought means of correcting it.[2] Huang Zongxi 黃宗羲 (AD 1610–1695), for example, pointed out that Wang Yangming's pondering on the human mind is based on scrutinizing the classics.[3] Huang thus encouraged scholars to go back to the classics and histories.[4] With the same concern, Gu Yanwu 顧炎武 (AD 1613–1682) argued that scrutinizing the classics was the prerequisite for understanding the Dao 道, or the Way.[5] More specifically, the method for doing so was to determine the ancient pronunciations of the words and then scrutinize texts.[6] The works of Han classicists, especially Zheng Xuan's 鄭玄 (AD 127–200) commentaries, became a crucial base of Gu's understanding of the classics.[7] Gu further incorporated Dao learning into his methodological framework with his famous slogan: "The learning of Dao is indeed the learning of classics."[8]

Gu and Huang's proposals led to a reevaluation of many Song and Ming scholars, especially Zhu Xi's philosophy and philological approach to the classics. In the mid-Qing period, scholars labeled Zhu Xi and his Northern Song predecessors' approach as the "learning of Song." The critics of this approach disparaged it as deviant from the commentarial traditions of the Han dynasty; they accused it of being full of adulterating sayings.[9] They accordingly called the methodology they preferred the "learning of Han," implying their commitment to the Han commentarial traditions and philological methodologies.[10] It is noteworthy that the philological methods under criticism were only putatively characteristic of Song scholarship. Moreover, not all of the Qing scholars accepted Han commentaries indiscriminately, nor did they necessarily have a clear-cut preference among the Han commentaries.[11]

With renewed methodology and broadening perspectives, scholars in the eighteenth century became dissatisfied with the label "learning of Han." Some of them thought that this label could no longer accurately summarize their approach. Some of them thus substituted "learning of Han" with "Evidential Research" (Kao Ju 考據).[12] They saw philology as both a means and ends.[13] This strong philological orientation was not satisfactory to some of the scholars. For instance, Jiao Xun 焦循 (AD 1763–1820) argued that "evidential research" cannot help us to understand why the sages wrote their words.[14] The concern embedded in Jiao Xun's criticism is that their approach should not be merely about method; it ought to illuminate the intentions of the sages as well.

The Changzhou School and the New Script versus Old Script Controversy

The reorientation toward the sages' message in the classics brought the Changzhou 常州 school,[15] previously a marginal school in the intellectual atmosphere of the Qianlong and Jiaqing periods, into the center of academia during the Daoguang (AD 1821–1850) reign.[16] As Benjamin Elman mentions, the Changzhou school was the designation of a Qing-dynasty intellectual school located in the modern city Changzhou 常州, Jiangsu 江蘇 Province.[17] It mainly indicates the branch of classical scholarship of the Zhuang 莊 family and their affiliates.[18] In this school, the Gongyang commentary was the most crucial source for seeking the intention of the sage Confucius.[19]

Members of the Changzhou school in the Qianlong period such as Zhuang Cunyu 莊存與 (AD 1719–1788) were faced with a rising trend of doubting the authenticity of the classics.[20] Certain parts of the classics were under intense appraisal by their contemporary and predecessors. Yan Ruoqu 閻若璩 (AD 1638–1704), in his *Sub-Commentary and Evidence on the Old Script* [sections of the] *"Book of Documents"* (*Guwen "Shangshu" shuzheng* 古文尚書疏證), and Hui Dong 惠棟 (AD 1697–1758), in his *An Examination of the Old Script* [sections of the] *"Book of Documents"* (*Guwen "Shangshu" kao* 古文尚書考), forcefully demonstrates that the twenty-one chapters once identified in old script in the *Documents* are forgeries.[21] Wang Su 王肅 (AD 195–256) became the scapegoat in this case of forgery.[22] The doubt extended to other classics that were associated with the term "old script," including the Zuo tradition of the *Spring and Autumn Annals* and the *Rites of Zhou*. The forger of these texts became Liu Xin, who supposedly played a major role in Wang Mang's usurpation.

Reacting to this doubt, the Zhuangs from the Changzhou school, especially Zhuang Cunyu and Zhuang Youke 莊有可, were cautious about completely abandoning the old script classics. Instead, they believed these texts had contained original information, but later on some scholars added, deleted, or rearranged certain parts of them to suit their own purposes.[23] In other words, they saw the old script classics as "contaminated." They thus turned to the "pure" portion of the classics and its commentarial traditions.

Liu Fenglu 劉逢祿 (AD 1776–1829), a grandson of Zhuang Cunyu, adopted his grandfather's scholarship on the Gongyang tradition.[24] He expressed his preference for the Gongyang tradition and He Xiu's 何休 (AD 129–182) commentary on it with well-accepted philological methodologies and premises.[25] Carrying on his predecessors' search for the "pure" part of the classical tradition, Liu Fenglu systematically argued that the Western Han transmission of the Five Classics was pure and trustworthy. He also argued that He Xiu preserved the authenticity of the original teachings. He referred to this transmission line of the Five Classics in the Western Han as the New Script school. Old script classics like the Zuo tradition and the *Rites of Zhou* thus became the tradition of the Old Script school, mainly forged by Liu Xin with the support of many Eastern Han scholars, especially Zheng Xuan.

Three beliefs of Liu Fenglu greatly influenced later generations of scholars in understanding Han classicism: (1) Western Han scholars transmitted the Five Classics in an exclusive, clear-cut manner that preserved the authenticity of the commentarial tradition of earlier generations;[26] (2) Liu Xin was the "master of forgery," responsible for ruining the authenticity of the transmission line through the manipulation of the old script classics;[27] and (3) since there was a debate between Zheng Xuan, who had a preference for the Zuo tradition, and He Xiu, there has always been a hostile relationship between the Han New Script scholars and Old Script scholars.

Appendix 3

The Contrast-Debate Model and Its Critique

Carrying on their predecessors' legacy, Chinese scholars from the late nineteenth to the twentieth century had fully developed the two sides of the controversy into two contrasting social and political parties. This appendix will introduce this framework, which I call the "contrast-debate" model, and some scholars', especially Michael Nylan's, critique of it.

Pi Xirui and Ma Zonghuo: The Twentieth-Century Legacy of the Changzhou and Yangzhou Schools

In his *A History of the Learning of Classics* (*Jingxue lishi* 經學歷史) first published in 1907, Pi Xirui 皮錫瑞 (AD 1850–1908) adopted many of Liu Fenglu's assumptions.[1] He believed that during Emperor Wu of Han's time (r. 140–87 BC) the learning of classics was the "purest" (*zui chun zheng* 最純正).[2] In transmitting the classics, Han scholars followed their masters' teaching strictly.[3] The dichotomy of the Old Script and New Script schools grew initially from the difference in script,[4] but after Liu Xin's advocacy of the old script classics, in the Eastern Han dynasty, the commentarial traditions pertaining to them also differed.[5] Although he does not consider Liu Xin a villain for forging classics like Liu Fenglu did, Pi Xirui does think that Liu Xin managed to decode the old script and invented explanations of it (*chuang tong guwen* 創通古文).[6] The Old Script and New Script schools were still sharply divided until the appearance of Zheng Xuan's commentary. For Pi Xirui, Zheng mixed the old script tradition with the new script one, making these traditions indistinguishable.[7] He thus accuses Zheng Xuan of undermining Han classicism.[8] Following the Changzhou school's tradition, Pi Xirui also believes that Confucius wrote and compiled the Six Classics to transmit the ultimate principles to later generations. He thus dismisses the theories that weight the Duke of Zhou or the mysterious sage king Fu Xi 伏羲 over Confucius.⁹

Not everyone agreed with the Changzhou school's perspective. Beginning in the eighteenth century, the Yangzhou school, for example, favored the old script classics. The Liu family of the Yangzhou school from Liu Wenqi 劉文淇 (AD 1789–1854) to his great grandson, Liu Shipei 劉師培 (AD 1884–1919), among others such as Yu Yue 俞樾 (AD 1821–1907), are useful examples. They did not take as dismissive a tone toward the new script tradition as the Changzhou school adopted toward the old script tradition,¹⁰ and they often reacted strongly against such stridently formulated attacks on the old script tradition.

For example, from the last years of the nineteenth century to the early twentieth century, Wei Yuan 魏源 (AD 1794–1857), Liao Ping 廖平 (AD 1852–1932),¹¹ and Kang Youwei 康有為 (AD 1858–1927) adopted Liu Fenglu's understanding: Liu Xin forged the Zuo tradition together with other old script classics, and hence the transmission of the old script classics was impure. This culminated in Kang Youwei's *An Examination of the Forged Classics of the Xin Learning* (*Xin xue wei jing kao* 新學偽經考), in which Kang Youwei reduces the value of the old script classics to nil. Reacting to Kang's polemic view, Liu Shipei of the Yangzhou school made a more moderate argument; he argued that the old script classics had transmission lineages in the Western Han dynasty too,¹² but the Han government did not put old script lineages' teachings in the official curriculum.¹³ Although Liu maintained that there was a division between an old script and a new script tradition, he explicitly argued that there was no division between those traditions before the Han dynasty.¹⁴ The difference between the two traditions lay only in the writing system.¹⁵ Therefore, he argued, there was no tension or factionalism peculiar to these two traditions in the beginning of the Western Han dynasty.¹⁶ Liu found that during that time, scholars usually learned and transmitted the old script classics no matter what commentarial traditions they followed.¹⁷ He also argued against Wei Yuan's theory that the Old Script schools dominated in the Eastern Han and caused the Western Han lineage to perish.¹⁸

Liu Shipei did have a preference for what he saw as two separate traditions; he preferred the old script tradition, for the new script tradition was largely associated with teachings outside the Confucian tradition, such as Zou Yan's 鄒衍 (fl. fourth century BC) association of the Five Phases with Confucius and other sage kings. For Liu Shipei, Zou Yan's bizarre theory was not part of the classics' transmission tradition but a notion that some

Western Han scholars adopted to cater to the Han emperors.[19] Accordingly, Liu Shipei turned around the accusation of impurity and insinuated that the new script classics' transmission was not pure.

Upholding a similar stance to that of Liu Shipei, Ma Zonghuo 馬宗霍 (AD 1897–1976) wrote another "history" of the learning of classics. In his *A History of the Learning of Chinese Classics* (*Zhongguo jingxue shi* 中國經學史, 1936), Ma Zonghuo relates Liu Shipei's theory of the old script classics' transmission line to the dichotomy of official learning and private learning (*guan xue / si xue* 官學/私學). He argues that the Han literati did transmit old script classics beginning in the early Western Han dynasty, but the Han government never institutionalized these schools of learning.[20] Accordingly, Liu Xin did not invent the old script traditions but simply tried to include them as official, institutionalized schools of thought.[21] Following Liu Shipei, Ma Zonghuo believed that the Western Han followers of the new script classics were also well informed regarding the old script tradition. Their hostile attitude toward each other began in the Eastern Han dynasty.[22] Ma Zonghuo follows Pi Xirui's assumption that Han scholars strictly followed their masters' teaching.[23] He further agrees with Pi Xirui that Zheng Xuan integrated the old script tradition with the new script tradition. However, instead of lamenting the confusion of the clear-cut lineages, Ma Zonghuo celebrates Zheng Xuan and his predecessors' eclecticism.[24]

It is clear that Pi Xirui favors the new script tradition, and Ma Zonghuo the old script tradition. Their works, however, hold many assumptions in common. First, both believe that in the Han dynasty the old script and new script traditions were the only two camps of classical scholars. The various commentarial traditions belonged to either the former or the latter. Second, despite contact between the two traditions, carriers of each tradition transmitted their master's teaching exclusively and faithfully. Third, during the Eastern Han dynasty, supporters of the new script tradition and of the old script tradition vigorously competed with each other. Fourth, after Zheng Xuan integrated the two traditions, the boundary of the two camps became blurry and eventually disappeared. Fifth, both attribute the collapse of Han classicism to its scholasticism and its trivial, but longwinded commentarial style.[25]

Modern scholars adopt many of the aforementioned assumptions, especially the sharp contrast between the old script and new script traditions. Zhou Yutong 周予同 (AD 1898–1981), in his "Jing jin, guwen xue" 經今古文學 ("The Learning of Old Script and New Script Classics"),[26] focuses on the difference between the two traditions. Accepting Pi Xirui's framework, he delivers the characteristics of the two traditions by contrasting each of them and listing the debates of the two traditions.[27] In his "The Foundation of the History of Chinese Classics" ("Zhongguo jingxue shi de jichu" 中國經學史的基礎), Xu Fuguan 徐復觀 (AD 1904–1982) depicts the transmission line of all the received commentarial traditions in the Western Han dynasty in great detail.[28] His thick textual study of the transmission lines is an elaboration of Pi/Ma's model of the lineage of Han classicists. This contrast-debate model based on the presumption of seamless lineages became a standard theory of Han classicism.[29] For example, in Renmin Press's newly reprinted *A History of Chinese Learning of Classics* (*Zhongguo jingxue shi* 中國經學史) in 2010, the section on Han classicism still focuses on the differences and conflicts between the Old Script and New Script schools.[30]

The First Critiques of the Contrast-Debate Model: Qian Mu's Criticism of Kang Youwei

In 1930, Qian Mu 錢穆 (AD 1895–1990) published his "The Chronicle of Liu Xiang and His Son Liu Xin" ("Liu Xiang Xin fuzi nianpu" 劉向歆父子年譜), a systematic refutation of Kang Youwei's theory that Liu Xin forged all the old script classics.[31] The format of this article is annalistic: Qian first lists the year; then he lists events concerning relevant people, especially Liu Xiang or Liu Xin; then he quotes from the *History of the Han* or other sources to explain those events; he gives his comments on the quotation; and then if necessary, he quotes passages from Kang Youwei's *An Examination of the Forged Classics of the Xin Learning* and disputes him.

Nevertheless, Qian Mu's ambition is greater than simply criticizing Kang Youwei. By focusing on the difference between the beliefs of Liu Xiang 劉向 (77–6 BC), a follower of the Guliang tradition, and his son Liu Xin, a follower of the Zuo tradition, Qian Mu examines diachronic intellectual transitions through debates or conflicts at the end of the Western Han dynasty. Qian Mu differs from Pi Xirui and Ma Zonghuo in that he does not adhere to the assumption that the old script tradition and new script tradition were exclusive or static transmission lineages. He believes that the classicists did not stick to a single commentarial tradition, and the so-called "old script tradition" is merely a combination of several commentarial traditions shared by contemporary scholars.[32] The dichotomy of the old script and new script traditions is an invention of Qing New Script school scholars such as Liao Ping.[33] At this point, Qian Mu's argument seems to be little more than an extension of Liu Shipei and Ma Zonghuo's theory that there was no division of the two traditions in the early Western Han dynasty; he argues that this is true through the end of the Western Han period. And he goes even further. In "The Chronicle of Liu Xiang and His Son Liu Xin," Qian Mu attempts to explicate *why* Liu Xin advocated the use of old script texts and why Wang Mang adopted Liu Xin's ideas. Qian Mu's theory is that the emergence of the old script tradition was an outgrowth of intellectual developments since Emperor Wu's time (r. 140–87 BC) rather than part of Wang Mang's scheme of usurpation.[34]

Gu Jiegang's Study of Han Classicism and His Emphasis on the Political Factor

Qian Mu states that the aims of his study are to override the old and new script dichotomy and to discover historical facts about Han classicism.[35] The article was never intended to be a comprehensive study of Han classicism.[36] With the same goal, Gu Jiegang, a pioneer of the "doubting antiquity" movement,[37] extended his research on Han classicism to span 250 years, from Emperor Wu's reign (r. 140–87 BC) to the end of the Eastern Han dynasty (AD 220).[38] He was not content with discovering how Qing scholars misinterpreted Han-dynasty usage of old script and new script texts; more radical than Qian Mu, Gu examined who invented the commentarial traditions of the Han dynasty, and how they did so.[39] In his *The Masters of Methods and the Confucian Scholars in the Qin and Han Dynasty* (*Qin Han de fangshi yu rushing* 秦漢的方士與儒生),[40] Gu Jiegang maintains a division between new script and old script traditions but argues that both were corrupted in the service of political power. He argues that the new script tradition in the Western Han dynasty deviated from Confucius's original teaching, because Confucian scholars adopted practices and thought from the masters of methods (*fangshi* 方士). The latter group originated in the states of Qi and Yan during the Warring States period (475–221 BC). They pursued practices for obtaining immortality and further included Zou Yan's theory of correlation between the cosmos and humans in their teachings. In the Western Han, especially during the reign of Emperor Wu, Confucian scholars started to adopt the practices and theories of masters of methods in order to suit the emperor's preference. This virtually made the former group indistinguishable from the latter one. Since the emperor liked what he heard from these scholars, he appointed more and more of them to official positions, resulting in the institutionalization of a corrupt "new script" tradition. As for the old script texts, Gu further argues that at the end of the Western Han dynasty, while working at the imperial library, Liu Xin had the chance to manipulate texts in old script to forge the Zuo tradition in support of Wang Mang's usurpation. Gu argues that the founder of the Eastern Han dynasty then had to use apocrypha, "something that is deviant and preposterous" (*yaowang guaidan de dongxi* 妖妄怪誕的東西), to claim legitimacy superior to that of Wang Mang. The conspiracy between the emperors and some literati made apocryphal texts dominant in the Eastern Han dynasty. However, Gu writes, these texts were too preposterous, so some scholars turned to the philological study of the old script texts to achieve a certain degree of objectivity (*keguan xing* 客觀性).[41]

By and large, Gu Jiegang's ambition was to reevaluate ancient Chinese history.[42] We can see that Gu Jiegang combined scholars' criticism of both the new and old script traditions. In his arguments, we find Liu Shipei's statement that the new script tradition adopted Zou Yan's theory. We also find the theory that Liu Xin was the forger of the Zuo tradition, advocated by Kang Youwei and others. In explaining the dynamics of Han-dynasty intellectual transitions, he not only added a political dimension but further pointed out that the political factor was actually the driving force behind "Chinese history."[43] In his theory, there was a conspiracy between the emperor and the literati, in which the former became the ultimate beneficiary of enforcing intellectual schemes.[44]

Gu Jiegang did not concentrate on depicting lineage lines, but neither did he deny the existence of a new script tradition lineage.[45] However, both of these supposed traditions were low in his esteem, which distinguished him from Pi Xirui and Ma Zonghuo. In his theory, the literati and their thought were merely tools of the "ruling class," and their thought mere political slogans.[46] In some respects, Gu's study takes Pi Xirui and Ma Zonghuo's work one step further, for it explains the motivation for the evolution of Han classicism. This emphasis on the interaction between Han classicism and the political climate opened a new research trend.

Following this trend, Xu Fuguan states that the learning of the classics was the "face" (*mianmao* 面貌) of Han politics.[47] This theory implies that Han politics shaped Han classicism, and that classicism was thus of primary importance in the intellectual realm. The Renmin Press version of *A History of Chinese Learning of Classics* holds a similar view in explaining intellectual transitions in the Han. For example, in explaining the emergence of the old script classics, it says: "At the end of the Western Han, social crises increased, and the new script tradition could no longer provide any effective medicine to cure them. However, in the newly discovered old script classics [Han people] seemed to be able to find the institution, regulations, and model of reforms that could solve the crises."[48] Social factors incontestably affect intellectual developments.

Nevertheless, why certain plans "seemed to be" better than others has yet to be explained. As in this example, why would Wang Mang, Liu Xin, or whoever was of a similar mind think that using old script classics was a better idea than any other? Gu Jiegang's theory of political interaction between the emperor and the literati does not demonstrate why any given ideology would have been considered convincing to scholars of various sophisticated schools of thought.

Gu Jiegang's negative attitude toward apocryphal texts is also apparent, since he calls them "deviant and preposterous." He attributes the popularity of these texts to the preferences of the founder of the Eastern Han, Liu Xiu 劉秀 (6 BC–AD 57), who found them politically useful.[49] Nevertheless, this does not explain why adopting apocryphal texts could help the founder gain political power in the first place. Also, since the Eastern Han dynasty was a period of decentralization,[50] the emperor could not publicly support apocrypha without taking his officials' preferences into account. Even if we were to accept that the emperor could do so, we still could not explain why "mastering apocrypha" has positive connotations in epigraphs on memorial steles.[51] This throws doubt on Gu Jiegang's theory that scholars were merely a tool for the ruling class. If we reduce apocryphal texts to political nonsense empowered by imperial authority as Gu Jiegang does,[52] we will obscure the role these texts played among Han literati and the intellectual traditions they adopted, transmitted, and appropriated. In summary, we must entertain other approaches that seek a more comprehensive causal analysis of Han classicism. Michael Nylan and Chen Suzhen are two scholars that have employed unique approaches to the topic.

In her "The *chin wen/ku wen* Controversy in Han Times," Michael Nylan convincingly refutes the idea that there was an old script and new script controversy in the Han dynasty.[53] She surveys, and challenges, the main assumptions about the controversy that most modern scholars accept. The article begins by explaining modern scholars' understanding of the term *guwen* 古文 and points out that however differently many modern scholars use it, the term reflects the Old Script and New Script controversy in the Qing dynasty instead of the Han.[54] *Guwen* does not mean "a cohesive interpretive 'school' " as Wang Guowei 王國維 argues, nor does it refer to "old books" as

Qian Mu 錢穆 states. To Nylan, the term simply means "old script," which might be used to indicate "the Warring States script form that evolved in the Ch'i-Lu region," "the canonical texts written in a pre-Ch'in script form," "any text written entirely in the particular pre-Ch'in script form known as *ku wen*," or "any text that included some sources that treat authoritative texts preserving older traditions as *ku wen*." Han scholars might be familiar or use these old script texts, but it does not mean that there were transmission lines with defenders. Therefore, it is even harder to imagine hostile debates directly derived from the new script and old script division.[55]

Michael Nylan also surveys four criteria for modern scholars to assign a Han scholar's affiliation to either the new or old script tradition: (1) literary evidence hinting his affiliation to old script lineage, (2) whether *gu xue* 古學, literally, "old learning," is mentioned as part of his training, (3) his attitude toward apocryphal texts, and (4) his attitude toward the "commentaries by chapter and verse" (*zhang ju* 章句). For the first criterion, Nylan argues that many scholars after approximately 100 BC mastered both so-called old script and new script classics, meaning that this criterion does not point to a clear-cut lineage line. As for *gu xue*, the term itself is vague, and it refers to ancient learning without indicating specific lineages. She also disputes the last two criteria since both putatively "old script" and "new script" scholars use apocryphal texts and the "chapter and verse" as a commentarial style.[56]

Nylan is not saying that we need better criteria to account for the new script and old script controversy. Instead, she is saying that the veracity of "new script" texts and "old script" texts was not the crux of contemporary scholarly controversies,[57] and that we face more complex intellectual endeavors than the theory of new/old script controversy can predict. She argues that only after abandoning the old model will we be able to think about the question of what "learning" meant in Han China, what it constituted, and how it was associated with economic and political situations.[58]

In his comprehensive study of Han political history, *Spring and Autumn Annals and the Way of Han: Studies on Politics and Political Culture in the Two Han Dynasties* (Chunqiu *yu "Han dao": liang Han zhengzhi yu zhengzhi wenhua yanjiu*《春秋》與"漢道"——兩漢政治與政治文化研究), Chen Suzhen 陳蘇鎮 no longer adopts the model of new/old script controversy. He argues that the study of old script texts, centered on the Zuo tradition and the *Rites of Zhou*, did not have any fundamental differences from the study of new script texts. In fact, in the Eastern Han dynasty, "the scholars of the study of old script" (*guwen xue jia* 古文學家) agreed with Gongyang scholars' many premises, especially rituals' central position in state policy (Gongyang scholars supposedly belong to the "new text" school).[59]

Chen Suzhen further identifies two camps in the *ru* group with different political philosophies. One emphasized "transforming the people's ethos by virtue" (*yi de hua min* 以德化民), the other "governing with rites" (*yi li wei zhi* 以禮為治). These two tendencies are responsible for forming the dynamics of political culture during the Han dynasty. They eventually combined with each other in the Eastern Han dynasty, becoming a political theory that took the Great Peace as its ideal and considered rites and laws as the means of achieving this ideal. Chen Suzhen, nevertheless, does not merely substitute the old dichotomy with his new one. He does not understand the political culture of the Han dynasty as a mix of several static sets of thought struggling for political dominance. Instead, he perceives Han political culture as a dialectical evolution.[60]

Appendix 4

The Assumptions of the Confucian Empire and Its Problems

Rather than expanding the contrast-debate model of intellectual conflict in the Han dynasty, many scholars have turned to the commonality among participants in intellectual disputes. From this perspective, "Confucianism" and its permeation of Han-dynasty thought has become the major preoccupation of their scholarship. In his *History of Chinese Philosophy*, Fung Yu-lan characterizes most of Chinese history, the period from Emperor Wu of Han to Kang Youwei, as the "period of the study of the Classics."[1] With their devotion to the classics, the Confucian school took over the Han empire. Fung Yu-lan calls this the "triumph of Confucianism."[2] That is to say, scholars who had different opinions on the classics in the contrast-debate model are now treated as a unified group under the name of Confucianism. Reacting to the "triumph of Confucianism," Japanese scholarship and American scholarship have developed their distinctive paths.

National Religion: Itano and Nishijima's Model

Many Japanese scholars have concentrated on the nationalization (*kokkyōka* 国教化) of Confucianism in Han China.[3] This research evolved from the study of Han-dynasty *jukyō* 儒教 (Confucianism) and *jugaku* 儒學 (the study of Confucianism).[4] In the first half of the twentieth century, the popular assumptions among Japanese scholars about Confucianism in Han China were still that Emperor Wu installed Confucianism as a national school of thought, and that Dong Zhongshu was the main advocate and architect of this undertaking.[5] Their main evidence in support of these assumptions was Emperor Wu's establishment of the five official positions associated with each Confucian classic, the "Five Classics Academicians."

However, since the late 1960s, scholars have started to rethink their assumptions about the emergence of Confucianism in Han China and its nationalization. For example, in 1967, Fukui Shigemasa 福井重雅 cast doubt on the establishment of the Five Classics Academicians and Dong Zhongshu as a crucial Confucian figure during Emperor Wu's time. He doubts the reliability of the main historical source *Han shu* 漢書 on this issue and thus the popular theory that Confucianism became dominant during Emperor Wu's reign.[6] Fukui's article has sparked many debates and discussions. No matter how strongly one might disagree with Fukui's own theory, the traditional theory of Confucianism as a national teaching has been challenged.[7]

Itano Chōhachi 板野長八 also challenged the old assumptions about the nationalization of Confucianism in his article from the 1970s, "The Establishment of Confucianism" ("Jukyō no kenkyū" 儒教の成立),[8] which is peppered with three words: supernatural (*jujutsu* 呪術), mysterious (*shinpi* 神秘), and extra-human (*chou-ningen* 超人間). He argues that Confucianism became important as a national religion during Emperor Guangwu's reign (r. AD 25–57), when Guangwu employed apocryphal texts to deify the emperor as a heavenly, supernatural being.[9] Other than simply seeing the acceptance of apocryphal texts as a tool for the ruling class as Gu Jiegang does,[10] Itano understands their acceptance as the result of previous intellectual and social developments. He thus explains why Guangwu may have chosen this strategy, and why it would have been acceptable to the contemporary literati. According to his theory, two developments in the Western Han dynasty eventually led to the promotion of apocrypha. One of them was the promotion of the emperor's power. Along with the diminishing of regional kings' power, the Western Han empire adopted filial piety as a moral ideal and used the *Classic of Filial Piety* to consolidate the emperor's authority.[11] The other development was the inclusion of the mysterious and superhuman dimension into Confucian teaching.[12] Texts like "The Commentary of the *Classic of Changes*" ("*Yi* zhuan" 易傳) and "The Grand Commentary on the *Book of Documents*" ("*Shangshu* dazhuan" 尚書大傳) are parts of this development. The aim of including this dimension was to give superhuman authority to the emperor.[13] During Guangwu's time, therefore, these two developments merged into one in apocryphal texts and hence led to the establishment of Confucianism as the national religion.[14]

Itano's study does share certain premises with previous scholarship. Although he does not believe that Dong Zhongshu managed to fully establish Confucianism during the Han dynasty, Itano still considers him a crucial advocate of it.[15] For Itano, Dong Zhongshu played a crucial role in the shift of emphasis from the human to the superhuman realm.[16] Itano argues that the ruling class's desire for political control is the primary factor that explains contemporary intellectual developments, which echoes Gu Jiegang's view.[17] However, Itano does not consider emperors the stick by which to measure the ruling class. Instead, he argues that the ruling class contained various camps, and the emperor was one camp unto himself, which was sometimes subject to the actions of others.[18] This is an insightful perspective because in this way one can focus on the people who adopted, transmitted, and reproduced intellectual traditions without reducing their complex motivations and ideas to the mere desire for reproducing power. While he examines the intellectual traditions of the Han dynasty, Itano does not fall into longwinded descriptions of court debates or the trap of the old/new script dichotomy. He instead points out a general shift in emphasis from the human to the superhuman, sketches how the shift took place, and shows how it is reflected in contemporary texts.

Nishijima Sadao 西嶋定生 argues that the establishment of Confucianism as the national religion and the tendency to emphasize the supernatural matured by Wang Mang's time.[19] The increasingly numerous Confucians in the government since Emperor Yuan's reign (49–33 BC) were responsible for the success of Confucianism. Nishijima offers several forms of evidence for these conclusions. He first points out that the Grand Chancellor (*chengxiang* 丞相) became the role responsible for keeping the balance of *yin* and *yang*, evidence of the increasing importance of supernatural phenomena to the political world. Second, he lists a series of ritual reforms of the late Western Han period based on what he calls Confucian standards and takes them as evidence of the nationalization of Confucianism. Third, he examines the mystic characteristics of the apocryphal texts, and their link to the emperor. This link was the result of the integration of the Confucian conceptualization of emperorship and popular "mysticism" (*shinpi shugi* 神秘主義). It grants mysterious authority to the emperor. Therefore, Nishijima argues, during his interregnum, Wang Mang enforced these ritual reforms and largely followed apocryphal texts, which led to the comprehensive institutionalization of Confucianism.[20]

There are several similarities between Itano's and Nishijima's theories. First, both of them are interested in finding when the nationalization of *jukyō* became complete in the Han dynasty. Second, whether explicitly or inexplicitly, they understand the term *jukyō* as "Confucian religion." Therefore, they both focus on sacrifices and ritual practices in the court, which are one of their major criteria for determining the time of the establishment of a Confucian state. Third, the apocryphal texts and their mystic characteristics play a major role in granting heavenly authority to the emperor. Fourth, these characteristics were not in the original teachings of Confucius but derived from popular belief at the end of the Western Han dynasty. Han Confucians appropriated them to consolidate the role of the emperor.

In contrast with the new/old script theory, the Itano-Nishijima model emphasizes developments and transitions instead of oppositions and conflicts. Itano especially argues that Confucianism's reorientation toward Heaven and its increasingly mystic character grew out of original Confucian teachings. This phenomenon, he argues, was a common tendency throughout the Western Han dynasty and eventually led to the nationalization of Confucianism. In their theory, the new and old script traditions become subject aspects of major transitions instead of the driving forces. This model also gives us a wider perspective from which to examine what was common among the different traditions of classical study, and what their broader, shared intellectual concerns were.

What Kind of Confucian Country and When: Fukui's Critique

As a radical skeptic of the victory of Confucianism during Emperor Wu's reign and Dong Zhongshu's role in it, Fukui Shigemasa has two major complaints about the Itano-Nishijima model. The first one is about their acceptance or "preservation" (*onzon* 溫存) of the old theory that Confucian officials took over the court during Emperor Wu's time, and Dong Zhongshu was the main figure pushing this project.[21] Based on his systematic studies on Dong Zhongshu and the setup of the Five Classics Academicians as official positions,[22] Fukui argues that scholars' impression of the comprehensive victory of Confucianism led by Dong Zhongshu in the Han court is due to bias from Ban Gu, and his work the *History of the Han*, the source that historians have relied upon most heavily.[23] Therefore, building their arguments solely or primarily upon this suspect foundation makes their model less convincing.

Fukui's second complaint concerns Itano and Nishijima's criteria for the establishment of a Confucian state. Both of them consider imperial sacrifices and other religious change as the major criteria for establishing the moment when the Confucian state came into full blossom. Fukui argues that the adoption of Confucian sacrificial or religious forms is the result of the establishment of a Confucian state rather than a sign of its coming to fruition. He points out that without enough Confucian scholars' advocacy and support in the court, the state would not have accepted these religious practices in the first place. Therefore, Fukui believes that the more interesting question is how Confucianism took over the court. He thus states that we need to examine the "officialization" (*kangakuka* 官學化) of Confucianism. He accordingly proposes his definition of *kangaku* 官學: "the only thought and education system that the state and officialdom officially advocate, protect, reward, and cherish, and which the officials and commoners must learn and support." Following this definition, he argues that the officialization of Confucianism happened between Emperor Xuan's reign (74–49 BC) and Emperor Yuan's period (49–33 BC).[24] The merit of Fukui's model is its emphasis on the embodiment of Confucianism in the persons and ideas of Han bureaucrats. Fukui warns us that without a certain degree of representation in the bureaucratic and political spheres, Confucian thought is just a bubble flowing randomly. Especially when we consider the establishment of a Confucian state, a key factor is the administrative and political structure of that.

Watanabe's Synthesis of the Creation of a Confucian Nation

Watanabe Yoshihiro 渡邊義浩 further polishes previous scholars' arguments on the Confucian nation and synthesizes them into a single perspective. In his book *State Control and Confucianism in the Later Han* (*Gokan kokka no shihai to Jukyō* 後漢国家の支配と儒教), he establishes four criteria that identify the Eastern Han dynasty as a Confucian state: the use of Confucian thought as political orthodoxy, an increase in the number of Confucians in officialdom, the use of Confucian thought as a means of control in specific sociopolitical occasions, and local acceptance of this control.[25]

The fourth criterion is not merely an adoption of previous scholarship; it is Watanabe's maneuver to reconcile imperial support of Confucian thought with the intermediate political structure between individuals and the imperial government, which was peculiar to the Eastern Han. Specifically, he argues that local powers (*zaichi seiryoku* 在地勢力) formed a cooperative community (*kyōdōtai* 共同体) with commoners in the Eastern Han, and the former was directly responsible for controlling the latter. The local acceptance of Confucian authority was the final step before the establishment of a Confucian nation.[26] Watanabe's synthesis is an attempt to show how people practiced Confucian thought in various social and political situations, and how it was suited to a particular social structure at a particular time.

From Itano to Fukui, then to Watanabe, the establishment of a Confucian state becomes a process divided into several phases. The number of stages increases, and the transition from one stage to another is portrayed in increasing detail.[27] This is a sign of specialization of the field. Nevertheless, despite different theories on what incidents complete the establishment of the Confucian state, they all agree that Han Confucianism was distinguished by the new bureaucratic recruitment system implemented during Emperor Wu's time, which increased the number of Confucian officials in government. From Wang Mang's interregnum to the early Eastern Han, Han Confucianism evolved to include apocryphal texts, which contained "mutant" (i.e., supernatural) Confucian doctrines.

After defining and redefining the Confucian state, people might ask a basic but crucial question: What is Confucianism? If, as Itano argues, Han Confucianism is a school of thought deviant from Confucius's original teachings, then can it still be called "Confucianism"? If political and official uses of the classics and the *Analects* can prove the existence of Confucianism, then is this "Confucianism" merely a collection of political sayings? Were the increasingly frequent references to the classics among the Han literati merely the result of accumulated habit? If not, does this phenomenon then necessary lead to a coherent social or intellectual unity that may be appropriately labeled "Confucianism"? If we cannot satisfactorily answer these questions, then jumping to the "victory of Confucianism" or the "establishment of a Confucian state" will not lead us any further. These are the questions that some Western scholars try to answer.

Confucianism: A Problematic Term

In 1938, Homer H. Dubs published "The Victory of Han Confucianism," in which he accepts the growing dominance of Confucianism in the Han dynasty, while challenging the assumption that Confucianism triumphed in Emperor Wu's time.[28] From late nineteenth to the early twentieth century, Marx Weber, Joseph R. Levenson, Homer Dubs,[29] and others centered Confucianism among other "isms" as the obstacle to achieving modernity for China. No matter whether their tone is orientalist or not, their perspectives are similar in at least one way: Confucianism took over China at some point in history, and since that moment, it has smothered China and prevented it from reaching modernity (i.e., the level of development in the Western world during the same time). In other words, they assumed that Confucianism (and other isms) was a stable if not completely static unity overshadowing most aspects of Chinese society throughout history. Since these scholars use the term "Confucianism" to generalize the many developments in Chinese history, it grew into a monster of a word, the meaning of which is too complex to mean anything solid.

In 1978, Nathan Sivin published a review on the perplexity caused by the use of the terms "Taoism" and "Confucianism" in the Western scholarship.[30] He points out scholars' careless use of the two words and their abuse as the scapegoats for China's perceived lack of modernity without any clarification of their meaning. Like the vague mystery of "Taoism," "Confucianism" became "a defensible one-word code for the hierarchic, bureaucratic, and bookish values that in traditional times were regularly invoked against change." It contains so many meanings that if we combine the possible "Confucians" together, "we would encounter everyone in traditional China who had the slightest claim to social or intellectual standing." Sivin warns us that without finding a place in society for people who formed particular doctrines, practices, and ways of thinking, using a vague label to refer to them does little for our understanding of their influence in Chinese history.[31]

Nicolas Zufferey further challenges the correspondence between "Confucianism" and *ru*.[32] Zufferey accepts "Confucianism" as a designation that refers to Confucius's immediate disciples and one or two generations after. Nevertheless, he argues, "Confucianism" and *ru* are two different things to ancient Chinese authors. The major literati of the early Western Han dynasty, according to his survey, belong to the group of *ru*, which is "not a well-structured group of Confucian thinkers" but rather "advocates of *wen* values such as civilization, of culture, of tradition, of ancient rituals, and of texts."[33] Therefore, his theory predicts that learners of classics are not necessarily followers of Confucius himself. Although many literati of the Han dynasty were immersed in the learning of the Five Classics, they were not Confucian, but *ru*. Therefore, following Michael Nylan, Zufferey argues that it is also problematic to call the texts Han literati advocated "Confucian Classics," because they were the common literary legacy from the ancients.[34]

Zufferey insightfully points out the incomparability of the correspondence between "Confucianism" and *ru*, for the latter is a much broader group than the former. His definition of "Confucianism" solves the question of why the English correspondence of *ru* contains Confucius's name.

However, if we correlate the group of *ru* to the people that are called *ru* in the primary sources, then for the Han dynasty specifically, we simply change the label from "Confucianism" to *ru*. This is not a bad start as long as we keep in mind that the term *ru* changed dramatically through time, and it might not refer to a single unit of people or organization at all.

Michael Nylan takes this principle one step further and extends her doubt to "the victory of Confucianism" and the "Han orthodox synthesis." In her "A Problematic Model: The Han 'Orthodox Synthesis,' Then and Now," Nylan questions several premises related to the "victory of Confucianism." She doubts that (1) the Confucians were a distinct group with a distinct ideology; (2) that the Han empire needed a single ruling orthodoxy; (3) that the state sponsorship of Confucian activities was consistent and effective; and (4) that the thought and practice led by the state was uniform and distinct. She further points out that "widely different receptions of the Han 'Confucian' canon were born from the widely varying interests and needs that individual persons brought to the Classics."[35] They are more suitably designated as "classicists."[36] In saying this, Nylan severs the link between the classics and Han "Confucians," a premise adopted by many Chinese scholars.

In his *Dong Zhongshu, a 'Confucian' Heritage and the "Chunqiu Fanlu,"* Michael Loewe presents a more radical view of Dong Zhongshu's significance and the validity of the term Confucianism. Loewe argues that Dong Zhongshu was a marginal figure in the court, and he never enjoyed a prestigious reputation or high position during his lifetime.[37] His reputation as a learned man and advocate of Confucius's teaching only grew slightly during the Eastern Han. Later scholars and historians did not consider Dong Zhongshu the leader of scholars in his time until the Tang dynasty (AD 618–907). Since then, especially due to the promotion of Song and Qing scholars, Dong Zhongshu has appeared to modern scholars as the main intellectual architect of Emperor Wu's reign and the crux of Han scholarly activities.[38] Loewe supports his doubts of Dong Zhongshu's role with a careful textual study of writings that people putatively attribute to Dong Zhongshu. According to Loewe, the *Luxuriant Dew of the Spring and Autumn Annals* (*Chunqiu fanlu* 春秋繁露), a main source scholars use to account for Dong Zhongshu's thought, is a collection of texts from different time periods, and none of these texts can be attributed to Dong Zhongshu with absolute certainty.[39] Among other writings, the three responses to Emperor Wu's rescripts are the most reliable reflection of Dong Zhongshu's thought, but they received very little attention from his contemporaries and subsequent generations.[40]

Michael Loewe's goal is not to point out that the victory of Han Confucianism lies in some factor besides the life and actions of Dong Zhongshu.⁴¹ Radically, he argues that there was no such coherent intellectual, philosophical, or social unity called "Confucianism."⁴² Similar to Nylan's theory, Loewe's theory is radically different from major Chinese and Japanese scholarship and those opponents of mainstream scholarship who were against the use of the term "Confucianism." He does not argue that "Confucianism" is not a proper name for the thought of the group of people whom we previously called "Confucian." He is questioning the existence of this group. He also disputes the idea that we can keep track of social and intellectual transitions in Han China by merely looking at the thought of those people whom we considered "Confucian" or whatever other label we choose to apply to this oft-studied group of scholars. In fact, Loewe's and Nylan's theories set future scholars free from not only the old script/new script dichotomy but also the demand that they reconcile Han scholars' thought with the phantom "Han Confucianism."⁴³ A question left is that without the label of Confucianism, what did those literati do in the Han dynasty, and can we see any other patterns other than the ambiguous "Confucian" one?

In *Witchcraft and the Rise of the First Confucian Empire*, Liang Cai tries to answer the question. She traces how the *ru* gained political power through Western Han official recruitments, and she argues that the power vacuum after the "witchcraft" (*wugu* 巫蠱) incident gave *ru* the opportunity to enter the Han court. Focused on political history, she emphasizes the importance of networking in promoting certain types of thought. Cai's work resembles many of Fukui's assumptions: both emphasize official recruitment, both link *ru* to the learning of the classics, and both attribute the making of the "Confucian empire" to Emperor Xuan.⁴⁴

However, Cai also brings the slippery terms "Confucian"/ *ru* as well as "Confucian empire" back to this already messy picture. While smashing the old myth about Confucians, she creates a new one:

> *Ru* were not those who merely took a class or two on Zhou culture or those who could recite a couple of sentences from the Five Classics as some of their contemporary officials might have been able to do. Instead, they were *ru* precisely because they made a living via their specialty in the old tradition, serving either as teachers or as professional ritualists in various occasions.⁴⁵

Does this mean that only the ones who could recite all the classics could be *ru* and could have the ability to decide the specific corpus of the classics? Was a *ru* not a *ru* anymore if he did not serve as a teacher or professional ritualist? What counted as a specialty in the old tradition, and did divinatory skills, medicine, or mastery of the text *Laozi* count? While Cai carves out a distinctive social space for *ru*, she defines the group too broadly. Most importantly, her use of the terms *ru* or Confucian conceals the diversity among the so-called *ru* as well as their agency to develop in different directions. In this sense, Sivin, Nylan, and Zufferey's warnings still hold.

Appendix 5

Apocryphal Texts

A History of Superstition and Adulation

The aforementioned contrast-debate model and political-oriented model are unable to satisfactorily contextualize the apocryphal texts (*chen wei* 讖緯), miscellaneous passages that are putative interpretations of the classics in the Han dynasty. They consider them either the ugly stepchild of the new script tradition, adulations conceived with political purposes in mind, or borrowings from vulgar traditions, such as that of the masters of methods (*fangshi* 方士).

In his 1926 study of Han apocrypha, "Apocrypha and the Learning of New and Old Script Classics" ("Weishu yu jing jin guwen xue" 緯書與經今古文學), Zhou Yutong argues that apocryphal texts are a hybrid of thought from classicists and masters of methods in the early Han dynasty.[1] The foundation of this hybrid is the thought of masters of *yin-yang* and Confucian numerology. The First Emperor of Qin 秦始皇 (r. 259–210 BC) and Emperor Wu were responsible for promoting masters of methods and thus led to this hybrid.[2] Zhou believes that the new script traditions are the precursor of the apocryphal texts.[3] Although old script schools had a chance to avoid this deviant trend, some members from old script traditions did manipulate apocryphal texts to chase political success.[4] Gu Jiegang and Chen Pan 陳槃 accept Zhou's theory of the origin of apocryphal texts.[5] Further developing this theory, Gu specifies that it was the Han emperors' preference for apocryphal texts and other prophecies that led to the dominance of those texts and prophecies. Chen focuses more on the thought of the masters of methods as a social group since the Warring States period.[6] Jack L. Dull sketches the line of apocrypha's development from Dong Zhongshu 董仲舒 to Jing Fang 京房 and Yi Feng 翼奉 in his doctoral dissertation.[7] He argues that through the development of "New Text Confucianism," people refined Dong's original idea to "fit the ruler into the cosmic shell." Liu Xiu 劉秀 (6 BC–AD 57), the founder of the Eastern Han, combined New Text Confucianism with the "vague and ill-defined tradition in the classics concerning diagrams and texts from various rivers." Therefore, apocryphal texts along with new script Confucianism became the ideological foundation of the Eastern Han dynasty.[8]

Yasui Kōzan 安居香山 also agrees that there is a close relationship between apocrypha and the new script tradition.[9] Yasui argues that the masters of methods manipulated this trend of thought to support certain political groups, such as those who supported Wang Mang's usurpation and Liu Xiu's ascendancy.[10] Based on his meticulous survey of the *Different Meanings of the Five Classics* (*Wujing yiyi* 五經疑義) by Xu Shen 許慎 (ca. AD 58–146), Hans van Ess argues that the differences between the new and old script traditions lay in their distinct political stances. What the apocryphal texts contain opposes the old script tradition's political point of view.[11] While downplaying the role of the masters of methods and the opposition between new and old script scholars, Chen Suzhen also emphasizes the interaction between apocryphal texts and the Gongyang tradition.[12]

Many scholars hold negative attitudes toward apocryphal texts because of their faith in modern science, their own ideological preference. In *A Comprehensive History of Chinese Thought* (*Zhongguo sixiang tongshi* 中國思想通史), apocryphal texts are described with the derogatory vocabulary of Marxist discourse, such as "superstition," or *mi xin* 迷信, and as "a mixture of theology and vulgar classicism" (*shenxue he yongsu jingxue de hunhe wu* 神學和庸俗經學的混合物).[13] Zhou Yutong 周予同 uses phrases like "deviant and chimerical thoughts" (*yaowang de sixiang* 妖妄的思想) and "foul, poisonous air" (*wuyan zhangqi* 烏煙瘴氣) to describe apocryphal texts, and he identifies a "superstitious thread" of which apocrypha is one element.[14] Chen Pan states that apocrypha is a "major collection of the adulteration and forgery" (*zha wei chengji zhi da jieji* 詐偽成績之大結集) by the masters of methods.[15]

Yasui also admits that the "superstitious" element exists in apocrypha and categorizes apocryphal texts with other types of divination in Chinese history, playfully labeling them as *itan* 異端, or "heterodox."[16] Zhong Zhaopeng 鐘肇鵬 draws the distinction between "classics" and "apocryphal texts," saying the former are historical documents and the latter are forged myths and hearsay.[17] The essence of the latter is "theological superstition," or *shenxue mixin* 神學迷信.[18] Renmin Press's newly published general history of the Qin and Han dynasties treats apocryphal texts as superstition and religious theology, deriding them as "vulgar and shabby," or *cusu bilou* 粗俗

鄙陋. In a related section of the book, the main topic becomes the struggles of some Han scholars against the "superstitious" apocrypha.[19] Some scholars even use this view to revise the division of new and old script schools. Robert P. Kramer, adopting Tjan Tjoe Som's theory, argues that the division between Han scholars regarding the application of apocryphal texts lay in the contrast between the "pursuit of baser motives," a process that Kramer argues "inflated this esoteric pseudoscience with endless explanations," and the rebellion against this "pernicious trend in classical studies" instead of the tension between the new script and old script camps.[20]

Scholars have attributed to apocryphal texts two major characteristics: "Supernatural (or its derogatory equivalent, 'superstitious')" and "politically oriented." The problem with the former is that "supernatural" and words similar to it usually assume a categorical dichotomy, which puts "rationality" and "causality" on one side, and "supernatural" on the other. However, "supernatural" did not exist as a category in early China; there is no division between the group that is "natural" and the one that is "supernatural" in the modern sense. Nor is it a case of conflict between "scientific" and "nonscientific" theories.[21] Certainly, Han scholars like Wang Chong 王充 might consider one theory true and dismiss the other as "bizarre," "false," or "hokum."[22] However, his judgment is rooted in his and his community's beliefs, and how they valued things based on their beliefs. He and other early Chinese thinkers did not exclusively adopt a working paradigm for understanding which theory contains nonphysical causality and which does not, if this paradigm is effective at all. Therefore, it is safer not to consider one intellectual trend more "natural" than another.

The Eastern Han imperial government did use apocryphal texts for political purposes. Nevertheless, as an action of persuasion, this move should result from the popularity of the ideas in these texts instead of the other way around. The question that remains is whence was their popularity derived? Yasui correctly points out that mysterious and other supernatural ideas were popular at the end of the Western Han dynasty. Nevertheless, we still need to further explain why the Eastern Han imperial house as well as literati appropriated apocryphal texts to supplement and interpret the classics. In other words, why were classics still the central concern of the literati? These questions urge us to go beyond "mysterious" and "supernatural."

Appendix 6

Chen, Wei, and Apocrypha

A Matter of Definition

Few classical Chinese corpora exist only in fragments, and unfortunately apocrypha are one of them. Facing a huge amount of fragments, we must identify what "apocrypha" indicates in the context of the Eastern Han dynasty. Around the first century AD, a corpus of texts appeared under the generic names *chen* 讖, *wei* 緯, or as a binome, *chenwei* 讖緯.[1] *Chen*, a seldom used word before the Han dynasty, indicates prophecies, either in words or images. *Wei* 緯, or "weft," derives its semantic meaning from weaving. In weaving, a warp sets up the frame based on which the woof is woven. Thus "warp," or *jing* 經, is borrowed to designate the classics because of its connotations of "foundation" and "constancy." The name "weft" accordingly claims to explicate, supplement, or elaborate the classics.[2] In addition, related to prophecies and prognostication, this corpus also includes a large amount of astrological information.[3]

Western scholars often use the word "apocrypha" to refer this corpus of texts.[4] Although conventional, the unqualified use of the term "apocrypha" can cause confusion.[5] "Apocrypha" appears most commonly in the context of biblical studies and carries four primary historical connotations. First, related to its etymological sense, "hidden things," "apocrypha" indicates esoteric and secret doctrines, particularly those of the Gnostic tradition. Second, since ecclesiastical writers such as Irenaeus (ca. AD 115–ca. 202) and Tertullian (ca. AD 160–ca. 225) opposed occult sciences in the Gnostic tradition, they used the term "apocrypha" pejoratively. This usage implied that the apocrypha were forged. Third, around the same time, some secretly transmitted books that were rejected by the Jewish synagogue authorities, but that were popular among the laity, were also called "apocrypha." That is to say, the term can indicate texts excluded or even banned from a canonical tradition. Fourth, in early Protestantism, it was used to designate texts that were neither canonical nor heretical.[6]

As the same valences suggests, *chenwei*'s history parallels that of "apocrypha" in the Judeo-Christian context. In the *chenwei* tradition, some texts appear to be "secret" (*mi* 秘) and written in a subtle (*yin* 隱) way so that only initiates could understand them.[7] We can detect the pejorative sense of *chenwei* from Zhang Heng's 張衡 (AD 78–139) complaint. Dissatisfied with their anachronistic and self-contradictory content, Zhang claimed that *chenwei* were not written by the sages, nor were they written in ancient times as they claimed. He believed that some people at the end of the Western Han made these texts to deceive others for profit. He thus proposed to ban the texts from commentarial traditions of classics.[8] Afterward, the imperial government implemented a series of bans on apocryphal texts. In AD 267, Emperor Wu 武 of the Western Jin 西晉 (AD 265–317) banned the *chenwei* with astrological information because rebels tended to manipulate these texts to claim political authority. From that time on, Southern Dynasties emperors occasionally issued bans against texts in the *chenwei* corpus. The deathblow came from Emperor Yang 煬 of the Sui 隋 dynasty in AD 593, whose ban, unlike earlier ones, was fully enforced. After this ban, most *chenwei* texts were lost.[9] Fragments of *chenwei* texts appeared in certain compilations, often in between works about the classics, even though other compilations did not consider them classics or legitimate commentaries. In the Qing dynasty, for example, some compilers of *chenwei* listed them under the category of classics, but they were more often put together under the name *weishu* 緯書, a subcategory separate from both the classics and other commentarial traditions.[10]

Despite these shared characteristics, there is a major difference between European apocrypha and *chenwei*, and it lies in the commentarial nature of *chenwei*. As Hans van Ess insightfully points out, while in biblical studies apocrypha are very different from commentaries, *chenwei* tend to be explications and interpretations of, or supplements to, the classics, rather than classics themselves.[11] They were not intended to be read as passages of the classics. Therefore, when "apocrypha" as a translation of the term *chenwei* appears in this book, it does not imply that the texts it refers to were once part of the classics.

We should also differentiate Han apocryphal texts from Chinese Buddhist apocrypha. In the latter case, "apocrypha" indicates Chinese Buddhist scriptures that their authors claimed were of foreign origin, but which are actually indigenous to China.[12] In this context, "apocrypha" is used in the sense of "forged scripture." While both are called "apocrypha," the two corpora served different communities in different periods. *Chenwei* was popular among literati groups in the first two centuries AD as a means of understanding the classics. More like the apocrypha of the Judeo-Christian tradition, the Chinese Buddhist apocrypha appeared to be scriptures, that is, teachings from the Buddha, popular among certain Buddhist communities in early medieval China.

Now what texts do the Han apocrypha contain? This is not easy to answer. Like many textual traditions, the core texts of the Eastern Han apocryphal corpus are rather stable, but supplementary or peripheral texts are sometimes included, sometimes not. The catalog of the imperial library in the *History of the Sui Dynasty* (*Suishu* 隋書), completed in AD 621, and a commentarial passage written by Li Xian 李賢 (AD 654–684) from the *History of the Later Han* (*Hou Han shu* 後漢書) count a similar number of chapters (*pian* 篇) for the so-called "seven apocrypha" (*qiwei* 七緯), which are categorized according to the seven classics, namely, the *Changes*, *Documents*, *Poetry*, *Rites*, the *Music*, the *Classic of Filial Piety*, and the *Annals*.[13] However, these two passages contradict each other concerning what the seven corresponding apocrypha were. Furthermore, the former also include texts considered apocryphal but that are outside the seven categories, such as the *Chart of the Yellow River* (*Hetu* 河圖) and the *Writing of the Luo River* (*Luoshu* 洛書), two titles originated from the *Changes*. The titles of these two texts never belonged to the corpus of the classics. It is even unclear what content is included in these two titles, for the two terms in the *Changes* do not appear as titles but rather describe the appearance of two particular omens "the chart of the Yellow River" and "the writing of the Luo River."

Our concern here is actually not so much which of these texts should be included in the apocryphal inventory, because we do not necessarily need a complete bibliography of Han apocrypha to explore the ideas therein. The major problem is rather that we might unwittingly include texts from after the Eastern Han.[14] Fortunately, generations of scholars, especially Yasui Kōzan 安居香山 and Nakamura Shōhachi 中村璋八, have made painstaking efforts to reconstruct apocryphal texts with critical textual studies. After consulting their works,[15] I have chosen to focus primarily on the seven apocrypha that correspond with the seven classics. I will also include fragments of texts that do not belong to these seven apocrypha if evidence shows that they are from the Eastern Han.[16]

Notes

Introduction

1. This corpus of texts is often referred to as the "Confucian classics." However, I have avoided using the terms "Confucian" and "Confucianism" loosely. By saying "Chinese classics," I indicate the corpus of texts incorporated in a collection edited by Ruan Yuan 阮元 in AD 1816. See appendix 1.

2. For how Yemeni judicial process relied on the Qur'an, see Brinkley Messick, *The Calligraphic State: Textual Domination and History in a Muslim Society* (Berkeley: University of California Press, 1993).

3. See ibid., and Anthony Grafton and Megan Williams, *Christianity and the Transformation of the Book: Origen, Eusebius, and the Library of Caesarea* (Cambridge: Harvard University Press, 2006), 178–232.

4. See appendixes 3 and 4.

5. Michael Nylan, "The *chin wen / ku wen* Controversy in Han Times," *T'oung Pao* 80.1–3 (1994): 83–145; Michael Loewe, "'Confucian' Values and Practices in Han China," *T'oung Pao* 98 (2012): 1–30.

6. See appendix 5.

7. Randall Collins, *The Sociology of Philosophies: A Global Theory of Intellectual Change* (Cambridge: Belknap Press of Harvard University Press, 1998), 21–56.

8. Randall Collins, *Interaction Ritual Chains* (Princeton: Princeton University Press, 2004), 3–4.

9. Collins, *The Sociology of Philosophies*, 23.

10. Collins, *Interaction Ritual Chains*, 10.

Chapter 1

1. See, for example, Bart D. Ehrman, *The Lost Gospel of Judas Iscariot: A New Look at Betrayer and Betrayed* (Oxford: Oxford University Press, 2006), 13–34; 85–98.

2. For a more elaborate review on the secondary literature, see appendix 1.

3. For the Han dynasty's overexpansion, see Michael Loewe, "The Former Han Dynasty," in *The Cambridge History of China, Vol. 1, The Ch'in and Han Empires, 211 B.C.–A.D. 220*, ed. Denis Twichett and Michael Loewe (Cambridge: Cambridge University Press, 1987), 179–97, esp. 104, 185. For more political events that reflect this transition, see Michael Loewe, *Crisis and Conflict in Han China, 104 BC to AD 9* (London: George Allen & Unwin, 1974), 139–43. Also see Qian Mu 錢穆, *Qin Han shi* 秦漢史 (Beijing: Sanlian, 2005), 201–07.

4. Ban Gu 班固, *Han shu* 漢書 (Beijing: Zhonghua, 1987), 75: 3157–58.

5. For a linguistic survey of the term "mandate," or *ming* 命 in early China, see David Schaberg, "Command and the Content of Tradition," in *The Magnitude of Ming: Command, Allotment, and Fate in Chinese Culture*, ed. Christopher Lupke (Honolulu: University of Hawai'i Press, 2005), 23–34; Michael Puett, "Following the Commands of Heaven: The Notion of *Ming* in Early China," in *The Magnitude of Ming*, 49–69, esp. 61–69.

6. *Han shu*, 75: 3153.

7. Ibid., 75: 3154.

8. Loewe, "The Former Han Dynasty," 179–97, esp. 104, 185. David W. Pankenier, "The Cosmo-Political Background of Heaven's Mandate," *Early China* 20 (1995): 121–76; and Herrlee G. Creel, *The Origins of Statecraft in China* (Chicago: University of Chicago Press, 1970), 81–100. For the view of the mandate of Heaven in early China in general, see Puett, "Following the Commands of Heaven," 49–69.

9. Michael Loewe insightfully points out the emphasis on omens and their relationship with Heaven's blessing in Emperor Xuan's reign. Loewe, "The Former Han Dynasty," 191.

10. Ibid., 190.

11. *Han shu*, 5: 224; 6: 164, 174, 185, 196, 245, 249, 253–54, 262, 263.

12. Ibid., 6: 245, 253–54.

13. For an introduction to the development of the Chinese cosmological synthesis and the importance of cosmological order for government, see Nathan Sivin's appendix "Evolution of the Chinese Cosmological Synthesis" in G. E. R. Lloyd and Nathan Sivin, *The Way and the Word: Science and Medicine in Early China and Greece* (New Haven: Yale University Press, 2002), 253–71.

14. Wei Xiang gained his high position from his success in political conflicts against the Huo family, the dominant clan from the reign of Emperor Zhao 昭 (87–74 BC) to the early reign of Emperor Xuan. See Loewe, *Crisis and Conflict in Han China*, 131–34.

15. *Han shu*, 74: 3147.

16. For a comprehensive study of the changes to the Imperial Chancellor's duties in the Western Han, see Kageyama Terukuni 影山輝國, "Kandai ni okeru saii to seiji: Saishō no saii sekinin o chūshin ni" 漢代における災異と政治——宰相の災異責任を中心に, *Shigaku zasshi* 90.8 (1981): 46–68.

17. *Han shu*, 74: 3139.
18. Ibid.
19. See Nathan Sivin, "State, Cosmos, and Body in the Last Three Centuries B.C.," *Harvard Journal of Asiatic Studies* 55.1 (1995): 5–37, esp. 14–16, 16–25.
20. This generalization follows ibid.
21. Many corpora of texts adopt this cosmology to explain the changes of the seasons and other meteorological phenomena such as "Yue ling 月令" in the *Record of Rites* and "Shize xun" 時則訓 in *Huainanzi* 淮南子. See *Liji zhengyi* 禮記正義, *j.* 16–17, in Ruan Yuan 阮元, ed., *Shisan jing zhushu* 十三經注疏 (Beijing: Zhonghua, 1980), 1379–84, and He Ning 何寧, *Huainanzi jishi* (Beijing: Zhonghua, 1998), 379–441. The idea of *yin* and *yang* also permeates military texts excavated from a tomb from Emperor Wu of the Han's time, located in Yinqueshan 銀雀山, Shandong Province. See Robin D. S. Yates, "The Yin-Yang Texts from Yinqueshan: An Introduction and Partial Reconstruction, with Notes on Their Significance in Relation to Huang-Lao Daoism," *Early China* 19 (1994): 74–144, esp. 77–80, 143.
22. *Han shu*, 56: 2500.
23. Lu Jia advanced a similar theory earlier: "Bad governance generates bad *qi*; bad *qi* generates disasters and bizarreness." See Lu Jia, "Ming jie" 明戒, in Wang Liqi 王利器, ed., *Xinyu jiaozhu* 新語校注 (Beijing: Zhonghua, 1986), 155.
24. *Han shu*, 56: 2502–03.
25. "Shuo gua" 說卦, *Yijing zhengyi*, in Ruan Yuan, ed., *Shisan jing zhushu*, 94. In a Mawangdui manuscript chapter called "Zhong" 衷, or "Kernel," the first half of the "Shuo gua" chapter is found. However, "Zhong" does not mention the seasonal changes or the correspondence between trigrams and creatures in the world. Instead, it elaborates on *yin* and *yang* and softness and firmness. For the Mawangdui text, see Ding Sixin 丁四新, *Chu zhushu yu Han boshu Zhou yi jiaozhu* 楚竹書與漢帛書周易校注 (Shanghai: Guji, 2011), 521–26, esp. 523, 525–26.
26. Some scholars call this type of theory "correlative thinking," such as John B. Henderson, *Development and Decline of Chinese Cosmology* (New York: Columbia University Press, 1984), 1–59, esp.14–18; A. C. Graham, *Disputers of the Tao: Philosophical Argument in Ancient China* (La Salle: Open Court, 1989), 319–70, esp. 358–70. Some even attribute it to a Huang-Lao 黃老 school of thought, such as John S. Major, *Heaven and Earth in Early Han Thought: Chapters Three, Four, and Five of the Huainanzi* (Albany: State University of New York Press, 1993), 35–38. I do not consider "correlative thinking" a way of thinking indigenous to Chinese culture. I follow Puett's systematic critique on this issue in his *To Become a God: Cosmology, Sacrifice, and Self-Divinization in Early China* (Cambridge: Harvard University Press, 2002), 145–200. I am also cautious in using the term "Huang-Lao," for, as Sivin points out, it is a vague term with contradictory definitions among scholars. See Nathan Sivin, "Old and New Daoisms," *Religious Studies Review* 36 (March 2010): 41–42.

27. *Han shu*, 74: 3139.

28. In comparing the Attached Statements with Lu Jia's understanding of the sages' duty, Puett insightfully picks up the nuance: "In the *xici zhuan* the sages are imitators; for Lu Jia they are responsible for the proper formation of the cosmos." See Puett, *To Become a God*, 250.

29. *Han shu*, 74: 3140.

30. An Zuozhang 安作璋 Xiong Tieji 熊鐵基, *Qin Han guanzhi shi gao* 秦漢官制史稿 (Jinan: Qilu, 2007), 28.

31. *Han shu*, 74: 3133, 3145; Sima Qian 司馬遷, *Shiji* 史記 (Beijing: Zhonghua, 1959), 112: 2949, 2953–54.

32. Edward L. Shaughnessy, *I Ching = The Classic of Changes, the First English Translation of the Newly Discovered Mawangdui Texts of I Ching* (New York: Ballantine Books, 1997), 1–13.

33. It is hard to determine exactly when this text was composed, but the oldest version of it we have was excavated from the Mawangdui site, located in Changsha 長沙, Hunan Province. For basic information about the Mawangdui corpus of the *Yijing*, see Shaughnessy, *I Ching*, 14–27. Edward L. Shaughnessy, basing his assessment on the Mawangdui version, dates the text to around 300 BC. See his "Xici zhuan de bianzhuan" 繫辭傳的編纂 in *Gushi guan yi* 古史觀異 (Shanghai: Guji, 2005), 294.

34. For an introduction to this passage and its dating, authorship, and textual issues, see Willard J. Peterson, "Making Connections: 'Commentary on the Attached Verbalizations' of the Book of Change," *Harvard Journal of Asiatic Studies* 42.1 (1982): 67–116. Based on the Shuihudi 睡虎地 excavation of this text, Peterson argues that the text existed, and it circulated to a certain degree beginning in the early years of the Western Han dynasty. See ibid., 76.

35. "Xici shang" 繫辭上, *Yijing zhengyi*, in Ruan Yuan ed., *Shisan jing zhushu*, j. 9, 82.

36. Peterson, "Making Connections," 85.

37. Ibid., 91.

38. Cf. Ikeda Shūzō, "Ryū Kō no gakumon to shisō" 劉向の學問と思想, *Tōhō gakuhō* 東方學報 50 (1978): 141.

39. Sivin, "Evolution of the Chinese Cosmological Synthesis," in *The Way and the Word*, 266–69, esp. 268.

40. *Han shu*, 88: 3598. For the translation of the title *boshi* 博士, I follow Loewe's rendering "Academician," which does not emphasize the erudition of books. See his "The Former Han Dynasty," 154, and also see Michael Nylan, "Textual Authority in Pre-Han and Han," *Early China* 25 (2001): 235–40.

41. *Han shu*, 8: 272; 88: 3600.

42. Ibid., 88: 3599.

43. See a fragment very similar to Wei Xiang's parallelism between trigrams and seasonal changes preserved in Ouyang Xiu 歐陽修, Song Qi, 宋祁, "Li zhi shang" 曆

志上, *Xin Tangshu* 新唐書 (Beijing: Zhonghua, 1975), 27a: 599. Also see Ma Guohan 馬國翰, ed., *Yuhan Shanfang jiyi shu* 玉函山房輯佚書 (Yangzhou: Guangling, 2005), 78.

44. In the Western Han dynasty, especially around Emperor Xuan's time, some scholars used the theory of *qi* to account for the dynamics of the correspondence. This is the so-called "trigram-*qi*" (*gua qi* 卦氣) theory. In this theory, the link between the trigrams or hexagrams and the Twenty-Four Solar Periods (*ershisi jie qi* 二十四節氣) is highlighted. See Michael Nylan and Nathan Sivin, "The First Neo-Confucianism: An Introduction to Yang Hsiung's 'Canon of Supreme Mystery' (*T'ai hsüan ching*, ca. 4 BC)," in Nathan Sivin, *Medicine, Philosophy and Religion in Ancient China: Researches and Reflections* (Brookfield: Variorum, 1995), 29–30. For a detailed study of Han scholars of the *Changes* and their various *gua qi* theories, see Richard J. Smith, *Fathoming the Cosmos and Ordering the World: The* Yijing *(*I Ching, *or* Classic of Changes*) and Its Evolution in China* (Charlottesville: University of Virginia Press, 2008), 57–88.

45. *Han shu*, 88: 3599. Meng Qing was not alone in this case. Sima Tan also considers the classics to have more information than can be mastered. See Sima Qian 司馬遷, "Tai shi gong zi xu" 太史公自序, *Shiji*, 3290.

46. Among the classics, the *Changes* has the reputation of including myriad situations in its text and thus being superior to the other classics. See "Yao" in Ikeda Tomoshisa, "Bo shu 'Yao' shi wen," *Guoji* Yi *xue yanjiu* 1 (1995): 45, and Liu Bin, *Bo shu "Yao" pian jiao shi* (Beijing: Guangming ribao, 2009), 160–70.

47. See, for example, "Yu cong yi" 語叢一, an excavated passage of the Warring States period from Guodian 郭店, Hubei Province: "《易》所以會天道人道也 (The *Changes* is that by which the way of Heaven is merged with that of humans)." See Liu Zhao 劉釗, *Guodian Chu jian jiao shi* 郭店楚簡校釋 (Fujian: Fujian renmin, 2003), 191. Also see the Mawangdui manuscript, "Yao" 要 (The gist [of the *Changes*]): "順於天地之心，此謂《易》道。(Following the heart of Heaven and Earth is the way of the *Changes*)." Zhang Zhenglang 張政烺, Li Ling 李零, ed., *Zhang Zhenglang lun* Yi *conggao* 張政烺論《易》叢稿 (Beijing: Zhonghua, 2011), 243.

48. *Han shu*, 9: 277.

49. The translation is adopted from Homer H. Dubs, trans., *The History of the Former Han Dynasty* (Baltimore: Waverly Press, 1938–1955), 2: 212.

50. Two concise introductions to the term "Great Peace" in the Daoist context are available: Max Kaltenmark, "The Ideology of the T'ai-p'ing ching," in *Facets of Taoism*, ed. Holmes Welch and Anna Seidel (New Haven: Yale University Press, 1979), 21–24; Barbara Hendrischke, *The Scripture on Great Peace: The* Taiping jing *and the Beginnings of Daoism* (Berkeley: University of California Press, 2007), 4–13. A concept similar to the Great Peace is the "Great Unity" (*datong* 大同). See Itano Chōhachi 板野長八, "*Raiki* no daidō" 禮記の大同, *Hokkaido Daigaku bungakubun kiyō* 5 (1956): 85–115. One major difference between these two concepts of the ideal society is that in *datong* the social relationships are impartial. For example, the text says that in the society of the Great Unity, people show affection not just

to their own son but to others' sons. See "Liyun" 禮運, *Liji zhengyi*, *j*. 21, in Ruan Yuan, ed., *Shisan jing zhushu*, 1414. The same cannot be said for the Great Peace.

51. Lu Jia, "Si wu" 思務, in Wang Liqi, ed., *Xinyu jiaozhu*, 168.
52. *Shiji*, 121: 3119.
53. *Han shu*, 58: 2514.
54. Ibid., 2518–19.
55. *Han shu*, 58: 2519–20.
56. *Han shu*, 72: 3062–63, 3065.
57. For an overview of Liu Xiang and his son Liu Xin's lives, see Michael Loewe, "Liu Xiang and Liu Xin," in *Chang'an 26 BCE: An Augustan Age in China*, ed. Michael Nylan and Griet Vankeerberghen (Seattle: University of Washington Press, 2015), 369–89.
58. *Han shu*, 36: 1933–34.
59. Ibid., 1934–37.
60. Ibid., 1941.
61. For similarities between Liu Xiang's and Dong Zhongshu's theories on omens, see Itano Chōhachi 板野長八, "Saiisetsu yori mita Ryū Kō to Ryū Kin" 災異說より見た劉向と劉歆, *Tōhō Gakkai sōritsu nijūgoshūnen kinen: tōhōgaku ronshū* 東方學會創立十五周年記念：東方學論集 (Tokyo: Tōhō Gakkai, 1972), 8. Cf. Tanaka Masami, *Ryōkan shisō no kenkyū* 兩漢思想の研究 (Tokyo: Kenbun Shuppan, 1986), 74–76.
62. *Han shu*, 36: 1942.
63. *Han shu*, 36: 1950.
64. As Emperor Xuan said. See this chapter, 12–13.
65. As Martin Kern and many others have shown, historically speaking Qin was not nearly as radical as Han scholars described. See Kern's *The Stele Inscriptions of Ch'in Shih-huang: Text and Ritual in Early Chinese Imperial Representation* (New Haven: American Oriental Society, 2000), and Yuri Pines, Lothar von Falkenhausen, Gideon Shelach, and Robin D. S. Yates, eds., *Birth of an Empire: The State of Qin Revisited* (Berkeley: University of California Press, 2014).
66. For example, Liu Xiang's contemporary Mei Fu 梅福 (fl. 16 BC–AD 8) explained how the Qin extinguished sagely rule: "The Qin practiced the way of extinction. They erased the traces of Confucius, eliminated the tracks of the Duke of Zhou, broke the Well-Field system (*jing tian* 井田), and got rid of the Five Rank system. Rites were abandoned, and music collapsed. Therefore, none of the people who desire to practice the Kingly Way can achieve it." *Han shu*, 67: 2912.
67. In the Han dynasty, only the Five Classics were extant. However, Han scholars still adopted phrases such as *liu jing* 六經 or *liu yi* 六藝 from the Warring States period, which included the *Music* when they referred to the corpus of the classics. In reasoning the significance of the classics, they also counted the *Music* in. Therefore, in this section, I use the phrase the "Six Classics" in order to better present Han scholars' verbatim, especially when their arguments under discussion contain the phrase the "Six Classics." I use the term "Five Classics" to indicate the actual corpus of texts discussed in the introduction. This, nevertheless, does not

necessarily mean that the "Six Classics" and "Five Classics" were different corpora of texts in Han literati's mind, nor did any Han scholar use the term "Six Classics" to promote or reconstruct the textual form of the *Music*.

68. Yang Xiong, "Wu bai" 五百, *Fa yan* 法言, in Wang Rongbao 汪榮寶, ed., *Fayan yishu* 法言義疏 (Beijing: Zhonghua, 1987), 11: 261.

69. See "Yu cong yi" 語叢一, Liu Zhao, *Guodian Chu jian jiao shi*, 191. For an extremely comprehensive summary of the parallelism in received texts of early China, see Fukui Shigemasa 福井重雅, *Kandai Jukyō no shiteki kenkyū* (Tokyo: Kyūko Shoin, 2005), 143–44. For a discussion of such parallelisms and order of the six texts' names, see Liao Mingchun 廖名春, "'Liu jing' cixu tanyuan" '六經'次序探源, *Lishi yanjiu* 2 (2002): 32–41.

70. Early Mohists, for example, largely based their argumentation on the *Documents*, *Poetry*, and *Annals* as the traces of ancient sage kings. See especially "Fei ming" 非命, *Mozi* 墨子, in Sun Yirang 孫詒讓, ed., *Mozi jian gu* 墨子間詁 (Beijing: Zhonghua, 2001), 266–83.

71. John B. Henderson, *Scripture, Canon, and Commentary: A Comparison of Confucian and Western Exegesis* (Princeton: Princeton University Press, 1991), 101–06.

72. "Quan xue" 勸學, Wang Tianhai 王天海, *Xunzi jiao shi* 荀子校釋 (Shanghai: Guji, 2005), 22–23.

73. As in "Yu cong yi," Liu Zhao, *Guodian Chu jian jiao shi*, 191.

74. Paul R. Goldin, *Confucianism* (Berkeley: University of California Press, 2011), 83.

75. In "Yao 要," a Mawangdui manuscript dating to the early Western Han dynasty, the conversation between Confucius and his disciple Zigong begins with a narration stating that Confucius became more and more interested in the *Changes*. Zigong questions him: "You taught me this the other day: When one's virtue is gone, he flees to divinities; when one's intelligence becomes distant from himself, he uses divination frequently." See Zhang Zhenglang, *Zhang Zhenglang lun Yi conggao*, 241.

76. Paul Rakita Goldin, "Xunzi and Early Han Philosophy," *Harvard Journal of Asiatic Studies* 67.1 (2006): 151. Also see Puett, *To Become a God*, 248–49.

77. Lu Jia 陸賈, "Dao ji" 道基, in Wang Liqi, ed., *Xinyu jiaozhu*, 18. Also see Puett, *To Become a God*, 253–54.

78. *Han shu*, 58: 2515. "Yu bei" 玉杯, in Su Yu 蘇輿, ed., *Chunqiu fanlu yizheng* 春秋繁露義證 (Beijing: Zhonghua, 1992), 1: 35–7. Also see Goldin, "Xunzi and Early Han Philosophy," 159–60.

79. *Han shu*, 58: 2515; Lu Jia, "Dao ji" 道基 and "Ben xing" 本行, *Xinyu jiaozhu*, 30, 142. Also see Goldin, "Xunzi and Early Han Philosophy," 165–66.

80. *Han shu*, 88: 3599.

81. This passage is preserved in Hou Cang's disciple Yi Feng's 翼奉 speech. *Han shu*, 75: 3172.

82. See Yan Shigu's 顏師古 commentary on the word *wuji* in *Han shu*, 75: 3173. The cycle goes through Daming 大明, Tianbao 天保, Caiqi 采芑, and Qifu 祈父 to Shiyue zhi jiao 十月之交 to correspond with Hai 亥, Mao 卯, Wu 午, You 酉,

and Xu 戌. For more information and a detailed explanation, see Zhang Fengqi 張峰屹, "Yi Feng *Shi* xue zhi 'Wu Ji' shuo kaoshi" 翼奉《詩》學之'五際'說考釋, *Zhengzhou daxue xuebao* 41.1 (2008): 125–28. There is also a handy diagram based on the reconstruction of the Five Contacts theory in Feng Haofei 馮浩菲, *Lidai* Shijing *lunshuo shuping* 歷代詩經論說述評 (Beijing: Zhonghua, 2003), 129. For this theory and other related ones in apocryphal traditions, see Cao Jianguo 曹建國, "*Shi* wei *sanji, sishi, wuji, liuqing* shuo tanwei"《詩》緯三基、四始、五際、六情說探微, *Wuhan Daxue xuebao* 59.4 (2006): 434–40.

83. As Xunzi would argue. See Goldin, *Confucianism*, 83.
84. Goldin, "Xunzi and Early Han Philosophy," 147.
85. *Han shu*, 75: 3154; 88: 3612.
86. Xiahou Sheng was promoted from Academician to Chamberlain for the Palace Revenues in 72 BC. *Han shu*, 19b: 800; 81: 3343. Xiahou Sheng was the Imperial Court Grandee (*guanglu dafu* 光祿大夫), a position usually reserved for the most seasoned scholars. Xiao Wangzhi became the Chamberlain for the Palace Revenues in 65 BC and Grandee Secretary from 59 to 56 BC.
87. *Han shu*, 81: 3332–33.
88. *Han shu*, 81: 3334.
89. *Han shu*, 81: 3343.
90. Yang Xiong, "Wu bai" 五百, in Wang Rongbao, ed., *Fayan yishu*, 8: 157.
91. See what Yang Xiong says about Zou Yan and Zhuangzi in "Wen dao" 問道, in Wang Rongbao, ed., *Fayan yishu*, 6: 134–35.
92. "Yang Huo" 陽貨, *Lunyu* 論語 (The *Analects*), Zhu Xi 朱熹 annotated, *Sishu zhangju jizhu* 四書章句集注 (Beijing: Zhonghua, 1983), *Lunyu jizhu*, 9: 178.
93. Yang Xiong, "Wu zi 吾子," in Wang Rongbao, ed., *Fayan yishu*, 4: 67.
94. Yang Xiong, "Gua jian," in Wang Rongbao, ed., *Fayan yishu*, 10: 222.
95. I follow Ikeda, who believes that Liu Xiang composed most of the "Seven Summaries," and that he incorporated his father's work and ideas into it in general. See Ikeda Shūzō, "Ryū Kō no gakumon to shisō," 119.
96. *Han shu*, 30: 1723.
97. Liu Xiang 劉向, "Xiu wen" 修文, in Xiang Zonglu 向宗魯, ed., *Shuiyuan jiaozheng* 說苑校證 (Beijing: Zhonghua, 1987), 504.
98. For a study of the *Changes* as in Liu Xiang and Liu Xin's philosophy, see Wang Feng 王風, "Liu Xin yu *Zhouyi* zui gao jingdian diwei de queli" 劉歆與《周易》最高經典地位的確立, in Jiang Guanghui 蔣廣輝, ed., *Zhongguo jingxue sixiang shi* 中國經學思想史 (Beijing: Zhongguo shehui kexue, 2010), 2: 313–35.
99. Cf. Ikeda Shūzō's mention of "organic unity" in his "Ryū Kō no gakumon to shisō," 122.
100. *Han shu*, 30: 1723.
101. Kuang Heng's anxiety in sticking to the classics in their right sense can be found in how he carried on the ritual reforms based on the prescription of the classics. *Han shu*, 73: 3123.

102. As mentioned in appendix 2 and argued in later chapters, I do not take the so-called "new script" and "old script" controversy as two unified and mutually exclusive groups who held their doctrines and diminished each other.

103. *Han shu*, 99a: 4110–11.

104. Dubs, *History of the Former Han Dynasty*, 3: 324.

105. *Han shu*, 24a: 1142.

106. For an introduction to the Well-Field system, see Fu Zhufu, "The Economic History of China: Some Special Problems," *Modern China* 7.1 (1981): 6–9. Jin Jingfang 金景芳 has a detailed study of the system before the Han dynasty. See his *Lun Jing Tian zhidu* 論井田制度 (Jinan: Qi Lu, 1982). For intensive studies on the Well-Field system as recorded in classical texts, see Hentona Tomokuni 辺土名朝邦, "Ka Kyu no seiden setsu" 何休の井田説, *Kwassui lonbunshū* 21 (1978): 35–49, and Kuwada Kōzō 桑田幸三, "*Moushi* seidensei no keizaishisō ni tsuite" 「孟子」井田制の経済思想について, *Hikone ronso* 154 (1972): 1–16. When it comes to topics about economic changes in Chinese history, Marxist scholars usually use words like "feudalism" in their works. I am cautious of using such terminology. For my reasons, I follow Li Feng, "'Feudalism' and Western Zhou China: A Criticism," *Harvard Journal of Asiatic Studies* 63.1 (2003): 115–44.

107. Hsu Cho-yun, *Han Agriculture: The Formation of Early Chinese Agrarian Economy (206 B.C.–A.D. 220)* (Seattle: University of Washington Press, 1980), 54–55, 65. For a comprehensive study of Wang Mang's reform, see Homer H. Dubs, "Wang Mang and His Economic Reforms," *T'oung Pao* 35.4 (1940): 219–65.

108. Michael Loewe, "Wang Mang, the Restoration of Han Dynasty, and Later Han," in *The Cambridge History of China, Vol. 1, The Ch'in and Han Empires, 221 B.C.–A.D. 220*, ed. Denis Twitchett and Michael Loewe (Cambridge: Cambridge University Press, 1987), 224–31.

109. *Han shu*, 36: 1967.

110. For a complete translation of the letter, see Loewe, "Liu Xiang and Liu Xin," 380–84.

111. *Han shu*, 36: 1968.

112. *Han shu*, 36: 1968–69.

113. *Han shu*, 36: 1969.

114. *Han shu*, 36: 1969–70.

115. *Han shu*, 36: 1970.

116. See Ban Gu's summary of Liu Xin's understanding of Zuo Qiuming and his tradition. In "Yiwen zhi" there is also a statement about the Zuo tradition probably written by Liu Xin. *Han shu*, 36: 1967; 30: 1715.

117. Zhang Zhenze 張震澤, ed., *Yang Xiong ji jiaozhu* 揚雄集校注 (Shanghai: Guji, 1993), 273. For a translation of these two letters between Yang Xiong and Liu Xin with an introduction to them, see David R. Knechtges, "The Liu Hsin / Yang Hsiung Correspondence on the *Fang Yen*," *Monumenta Serica* 33 (1977/78): 309–25. For the interaction between philology and the movement of restoring

antiquity, see Michael Nylan, *Yang Xiong and the Pleasures of Reading and Classical Learning in China* (New Haven: American Oriental Society, 2011), 103–25.

118. *Han shu*, 75: 3179.

119. This sentence is a quotation from the *Analects*, which in the context serves as an admonition against overreliance on the imperial harem. See *Lunyu*, 1:50.

120. *Han shu*, 75: 3193. *Yuan* indicates *tian zhi yuan ming* 天之元命 (the grand mandate of Heaven).

121. I do not take the received version of *Taiping jing* as the original text passed down from Gan Zhongke to Li Xun. Instead, I consider it a compilation from the Six Dynasties, though it does reflect many ideas popular in the Han dynasty. See Kaltenmark, "The Ideology of the T'ai-p'ing ching," 19–45, esp. 44–45.

122. *Han shu*, 75: 3192–94.

123. *Han shu*, 75: 3183, 3192–93.

124. This is mentioned in Jia Gongyan 賈公彥, "Xu *Zhouli* feixing" 序周禮廢興, in Ruan Yuan, ed., *Shisan jing zhushu*, 635.

125. *Han shu*, 75: 3192.

126. "Da zongshi" 大宗師, in Chen Guying 陳鼓應, *Zhuangzi jinzhu jinyi* 莊子今注今譯 (Beijing: Zhonghua, 1983), 168–70.

127. "Shanggu tianzhen lun" 上古天真論, Guo Aichun 郭靄春 annotated, *Huangdi neijing suwen jiaozhu yushi* 黃帝內經素問校註語釋 (Tianjin: Kexue jishu, 1981), 6–7.

128. "Quan yan xun" 詮言訓, in He Ning, *Huainanzi jishi*, 992.

129. *Han shu*, 75: 3191–92.

130. *Han shu*, 81: 3347.

131. Ikeda Shūzō, "Ryū Kō no gakumon to shisō," 139–42.

132. *Han shu*, 36: 1929.

133. *Han shu*, 36: 1950; 75: 3155. The similarity between Liu Xiang's *Discussion* and the *Tradition of Five Phases in the "Great Plan"* is mentioned in Ban Gu, "Wu xing zhi zhong zhi shang" 五行志, *Han shu*, 27b: 1353. Chen Kanli 陳侃理 argues that the *Tradition of Five Phases in the "Great Plan"* was written by Xiahou Shichang, Xiahou Sheng's master, and the text was circulated among a few of Xiahou Shichang's students such as Xiahou Sheng. See Chen Kanli, "'*Hong fan' wuxing zhuan* yu '*Hong fan*' zaiyi lun" 《洪範五行傳》與《洪範》災異論, *Guoxue yanjiu* 國學研究 26 (2010): 100.

134. Actually, Liu Xiang himself was well informed on each commentarial tradition, the Gongyang, Guliang, and Zuo. See Ikeda Shūzō, "Ryū Kō no gakumon to shisō," 127.

135. Liu Xin's own father, for example, preferred the Guliang tradition to the Zuo tradition. *Han shu*, 36: 1967. Kamada Tadashi 鎌田正 makes a thorough study on Liu Xiang and Liu Xin's scholarship on the *Annals*. He points out that both Liu Xiang and Liu Xin used the Gongyang, Guliang, and Zuo traditions extensively. Although he is considered a Guliang scholar, Liu Xiang actually relied on the Gongyang tradition more. See Kamada Tadashi, *Saden no seiritsu to sono*

tenkai 左傳の成立と其の展開 (Tokyo: Taishūkan shoten, 1992), 401–14. Kamada also points out Liu Xiang and Liu Xin's different theories on omens. While Liu Xiang and Dong Zhongshu interpreted omens more subjectively, Liu Xin established his delicate astrological system based on the Twelve Stations, or the *shier ci* 十二次. See ibid., 421–35. For the theory of the Twelve Stations, see Nathan Sivin, *Granting the Seasons: The Chinese Astronomical Reform of 1280, with a Study of Its Many Dimensions and a Translation of Its Records* (New York: Springer, 2009), 95–96.

136. *Han shu*, 75: 3155.

137. *Han shu*, 88: 3604.

138. *Han shu*, 8: 272; 30: 1706.

139. After Emperors Xuan and Yuan, interpretations of omens continued to be a fashion among many literati in the court. See Yang Shao-yun, "The Politics of Omenology in Chengdi's Reign," in *Chang'an 26 BCE: An Augustan Age in China*, ed. Michael Nylan and Griet Vankeerberghen (Seattle: University of Washington Press, 2015), 323–46.

140. *Han shu*, 84: 3421.

141. *Han shu*, 75: 3183.

142. Assuming we define "Confucianism" as a humanistic philosophy. See Goldin, *Confucianism*, 5.

Chapter 2

1. See Hou Wailu 侯外廬, Zhao Jibin 趙紀彬, Du Guoxiang 杜国庠, *Zhongguo sixiang tongshi* 中國思想通史 (Beijing: Renmin, 1957–1960), 225.

2. See Zhou Yutong 周予同, *Jingxue shi lunzhu xuanji* 經學史論著選集, second ed. (Shanghai: Shanghai renming, 1996), 40–41.

3. Chen Pan 陳槃, *Gu Chenwei yantao ji qi shulu jieti* 古讖緯研討及其書錄解題(Shanghai: Guji, 2009), 197–98.

4. For the naming and textual issues of this corpus, see appendixes 5 and 6.

5. Dubs, "Wang Mang and His Economic Reforms," 220. Also see Walter Scheidel, "The Monetary Systems of the Han and Roman Empires," in *Rome and China: Comparative Perspectives on Ancient World Empires*, ed. Walter Scheidel (New York: Oxford University Press, 2009), 150–54. Yü Ying-shih specifically points out that Wang Mang's measures for the creation of his ideal society did not benefit Wang Mang's supporters who were from the great families. These big clans thus initiated rebellions, which vitally contributed to the collapse of Wang Mang's rule. Yü Ying-shih 余英時, "Dong Han zhengquan zhi jianli yu shizu daxing zhi guanxi" 東漢政權之建立與士族大姓之關係, *Xinya xuebao* 2 (1965): 216–47, esp. 218. Differing from Yü Ying-shih, Hans Bielenstein believes that the two floods of the Yellow River and their aftermath led to a series of rebellions and thus the collapse of Wang Mang's reign. Hans Bielenstein, "Wang Mang, the Restoration of the Han Dynasty,

and Later Han," in *The Cambridge History of China, Vol. 1, The Ch'in and Han Empires, 221 B.C.–A.D. 220*, ed. Denis Twitchett and Michael Loewe (Cambridge: Cambridge University Press, 1987), 242–44.

6. For the name of the corpus and its textual traditions, see appendix 6.

7. Fan Ye 范曄, *Hou Han shu* 後漢書 (Beijing: Zhonghua, 1965), 35: 1201.

8. The four stars are Dubhe α, Merak β, Phecda γ, and Megrez δ. They form one of the twenty-eight celestial lodges, Kui 奎. Their Chinese names are Tianshu 天樞, Tianxuan 天璇, Tianji 天璣, and Tianquan 天權. As Sivin mentions, the meaning of this phrase is not entirely clear. See Sivin, *Granting the Seasons*, 214 note, 580.

9. See Feng Shi 馮時, *Zhongguo tianwen kaoguxue* 中國天文考古學 (Beijing: Zhongguo shehui kexue, 2007), 370–74.

10. This title appears in Ying Shao 應劭, "San huang" 三皇, in Wu Shuping 吳樹平, ed., *Fengsu tongyi jiaoshi* 風俗通義校釋 (Tianjin: Renmin, 1980), 1: 10.

11. *Chunqiu Shuo tici* 春秋說題辭, in Yasui Kozan 安居香山 and Nakamura Shōhachi 中村璋八, eds., *Weishu jicheng* 緯書集成 (Shijiazhuang: Hebei renmin, 1994), 856. The fragment is preserved in Li Fang 李昉 et al., eds., *Taiping yulan* 太平御覽 (Beijing: Zhonghua, 1960), 603: 2740b. Given part of the content, the title probably refers to explanations of the titles of the Five Classics. See *Weishu jicheng*, 854–58.

12. *Li ji mingzheng* 禮稽命徵, in Yasui and Nakamura, eds., *Weishu jicheng*, 507. The fragment is preserved in Li Fang et al., eds., *Taiping yulan*, 522: 2374b.

13. Goldin, *Confucianism*, 74.

14. *Shangshu zhong hou* 尚書中候, in Yasui and Nakamura, eds., *Weishu jicheng*, 399. This fragment is preserved in "Liyun 禮運," *Liji zhengyi* 禮記正義, *j.* 22, in Ruan Yuan, ed., *Shisan jing zhushu*, 1427.

15. "Xici" 繫辭 (Attached Statements), *Zhouyi zhengyi* 周易正義, *j.* 8, in Ruan Yuan, ed., *Shisan jing zhushu*, 86.

16. "Xici," *Zhouyi zhengyi*, *j.* 7, in Ruan Yuan, ed., *Shisan jing zhushu*, 83.

17. *Chunqiu Shuo tici*, in Yasui and Nakamura, eds., *Weishu jicheng*, 854. The passage is preserved in "Yi Gong" 隱公 (Duke Yin), *Chunqiu Gongyang zhuan zhushu*, *j.* 1, in Ruan Yuan, ed., *Shisan jing zhushu*, 2195.

18. Mencius and the author of the Gongyang tradition hold the former view. See "Teng Wen gong xia" 滕文公下, *Mengzi* 孟子, Zhu Xi annotated, *Sishu zhangju jizhu, Mengzi jizhu*, 6: 273; for the Gongyang tradition see "Ai Gong" 哀公 (Duke Ai), *Chunqiu Gongyang zhuan zhushu*, *j.* 28, in Ruan Yuan, ed., *Shisan jing zhushu*, 2354. Sima Qian holds the latter view. In Sima Qian's (ca. 145–ca. 86) letter to Ren An 任安 (fl. 91 BC), Confucius composed the *Annals* because he was unable to hold political positions. In this account, Sima Qian tries to tell Ren An that people compose their masterpieces when they are indignant and oppressed. See Ban Gu, "Sima Qian liezhuan" 司馬遷列傳, *Han shu*, 62: 2735.

19. *Chunqiu yan Kong tu* 春秋演孔圖, in Yasui and Nakamura, eds., *Weishu jicheng*, 578. The passage is preserved in "Ai Gong" 哀公 (Duke Ai), *Chunqiu Gongyang zhuan zhushu*, *j.* 28, in Ruan Yuan, ed., *Shisan jing zhushu*, 2354.

20. Ibid., 2353–54.

21. See Xu Yan's 徐彥 sub-commentary on this apocryphal passage, in ibid., 2354.

22. *Chunqiu yan Kong tu*, in Yasui and Nakamura, eds., *Weishu jicheng*, 578. The passage is preserved in "Ai Gong" 哀公 (Duke Ai), *Chunqiu Gongyang zhuan zhushu*, j. 28, Ruan Yuan ed., *Shisan jing zhushu*, 2354.

23. *Qian Kun zao du* 乾坤鑿度, in Yasui and Nakamura, eds., *Weishu jicheng*, 116–18. For the translation of its title, its content, and this text's relationship with *Cracking Open the Regularity of Qian*, see ibid., 74–75; Bent Nielsen, *A Companion to Yi Jing Numerology and Cosmology: Chinese Studies of Images and Numbers from Han (202 BCE–220 CE) to Song (960–1279 CE)* (London: RoutledgeCurzon, 2003), 304. The relationship between these two texts with similar titles is not completely clear. However, since the *Qian Kun zao du* has a section explaining the title *Qian zao du* and another section explaining the genealogy of the *Qian zao du* text, I consider it supplementary to the *Qian zao du*.

24. There is probably a textual corruption after the phrase "Gongsun shi" for two reasons. First, given the sentence structure proceeding "Gongsun shi," there should be another title coming after the name. Second, the first three names in the passage belong to one of the versions of the "Three Sovereigns" (*san huang* 三皇), and "Gongsun shi" indicates the Yellow Emperor, which is the first one of the "Five Emperors" (*wu di* 五帝). Therefore, it would be reasonable to expect other names from the "Five Emperors" group to show up after "Gongsun shi."

25. According to the anonymous commentary attached to this passage, Emperor Yan is another name for Shennong 神農. This combination of Fuxi, Sovereign Wa, and Shennong as the *san huang* can be found in the apocryphal text *Chunqiu yun doushu* 春秋運斗樞, preserved by Ying Shao 應劭 in *Fengsu tongyi*. See "San huang" 三皇, in Wu Shuping, ed., *Fengsu tongyi jiaozhi*, 1: 10. However, this is not the only version of *san huang*. For example, in *Baihu tong* 白虎通, there are two versions of *san huang*: Fuxi, Shennong, and Suiren 燧人 and Fuxi, Shennong, and Zhurong 祝融. See "Hao 號" (Titles), in Chen Li 陳立, ed., *Baihu tong shuzheng* 白虎通疏證 (Beijing: Zhonghua, 1994), 2: 49.

26. For *wu di*, see "Hao 號" (Titles), in Chen Li 陳立, ed., *Baihu tong shuzheng*, 2: 52.

27. "Hao" 號, in Chen Li 陳立, ed., *Baihu tong shuzheng*, 2: 45.

28. These historical kings were referred to as the "Three Kings" (*san wang* 三王), indicating the Xia, Shang, and Zhou dynasties, and the "Five Hegemons," dominant warlords in the Spring and Autumn period (770–476 BC). Together with the mythical figures mentioned previously, these two groups form one of the most popular historical narratives from the first century AD.

29. *Han shu*, 30: 1704.

30. *Cracking Open the Regularity of Qian and Kun*, in Yasui and Nakamura, eds., *Weishu jicheng*, 75–76.

31. It is not certain whether the word *mu* 目 here is supposed to be the more common word in that circumstance, *yue* 曰. I am inclined to take the word as *mu* based on the principle of *lectio difficilior*. Based on the commentary attached to it, *mu* can mean "to categorize" in *mingmu* 名目 (names and categories).

32. It is not clear what the *er* and *san* exactly refer to. It is plausible that the former indicates *yin* and *yang*, since they are the pair most commonly related to *qi*. *San* might refer back to the previous sentences, thus indicating Heaven, Earth, and *qi*. It might also indicate the realms of Heaven, Earth, and humans. The latter is called *san cai* 三材 in the "Shuo Gua" chapter of the *Changes*. "Shuo gua" 說卦, *Yijing zhengyi*, in Ruan Yuan, ed., *Shisan jing zhushu*, 94. Assuming that the human world derives from *qi*, these two readings of *san* are not mutually exclusive.

33. *Chunqiu yuanming bao* 春秋元命包, in Yasui and Nakamura, eds., *Weishu jicheng*, 590. The fragment is preserved in Ruan Yuan, ed., *Mao shi zhengyi* 毛詩正義, *j*. 16, *Shisan jing zhu shu*, 503.

34. 中舟 is probably a reversal of 舟中 due to the textual corruption.

35. *Chunqiu yuanming bao*, in Yasui and Nakamura, eds., *Weishu jicheng*, 592. The fragment is preserved in Ruan Yuan, ed., *Mao shi zhengyi*, *j*. 16, in Ruan Yuan, ed., *Shisan jing zhu shu*, 503.

36. *Chunqiu yuanming bao*, in Yasui and Nakamura, eds., *Weishu jicheng*, 592. The fragment is preserved in Qutan xida 瞿曇悉達 (Gautama Siddha), *Kaiyuan zhanjing* 開元占經 (Zhengzhou: Zhongzhou guji, 1994), 120: 814.

37. See chapter 2, 24–28. The sage kings are Huangdi 黃帝, Yao 堯, Shun 舜, Yu 禹, Tang 湯, King Wen 文王, King Wu 武王, the Duke of Zhou 周公, and Confucius.

38. Many passages about the physiognomic features of the sages can be found in *The Annals' Diagrams of Elaborating Confucius*, in Yasui and Nakamura, eds., *Weishu jicheng*, 574.

39. *Chunqiu yuanming bao*, in Yasui and Nakamura, eds., *Weishu jicheng*, 590. The fragment is preserved in Li Fang et al., eds., *Taiping yulan*, 79: 368b.

40. Taiwei is located at β (Vir), containing ten stars. See Sun Xiaochun and Jacob Kistemaker, *The Chinese Sky during the Han: Constellating Stars and Society* (Leiden: E. J. Brill, 1997), 152.

41. *Chunqiu yan Kong tu*, in Yasui and Nakamura, eds., *Weishu jicheng*, 576. The fragment is preserved in Li Fang et al., eds., *Taiping yulan*, 377: 1740a.

42. During the Han dynasty, one *chi* was theoretically equal to 23.1 cm. See the measurements shown on excavated measuring sticks and related discussions in Qiu Guangming 丘光明, Qiu Long 邱隆, and Yang Ping 楊平, *Zhongguo kexue jishu shi: Du liang heng juan* 中國科學技術史：度量衡卷 (Beijing: Kexue, 2001), 198–211.

43. *Wei* 圍 is an approximate unit for measuring the perimeter of objects. One *wei* can either stand for the perimeter of the circle made by the length from one's thumb to the index finger of the same hand or one's arm span. Here it is very likely that nine *wei* is measured the former way.

44. "Fei xiang" 非相, Wang Tianhai, *Xunzi jiao shi*, 162. In the passage, Xunzi uses the phrase *meng qi* 蒙倛 to describe Confucius's look. The phrase also refers to the masks exorcists wore in ceremonies to ward off demons. Therefore, the masks were supposed to be terrifying and undesirable even to ghosts. See Wang Tianhai's annotation no. 13 in ibid., 167.

45. Ibid., 161–62, 169.

46. Ibid., 159.

47. *Shangshu diming yan* 尚書帝命驗, in Yasui and Nakamura, eds., *Weishu jicheng*, 369. The fragment is preserved in Li Fang et al., eds., *Taiping yulan*, 82: 380b.

48. *Annals' Tallies of Corresponding to the Essence*, in Yasui and Nakamura, eds., *Weishu jicheng*, 741. The fragment is preserved in Li Fang et al., eds., *Taiping yulan*, 84: 396b.

49. *Chunqiu yuanming bao*, in Yasui and Nakamura, eds., *Weishu jicheng*, 591. The fragment is preserved in Xiao Ji 蕭吉, Nakamura Shōhachi 中村璋八 annotated, *Wuxing dayi* 五行大義 (Tokyo: Kyūko shoin, 1984), 5: 454.

50. *Chunqiu Han han zi* 春秋漢含孳, in Yasui and Nakamura, eds., *Weishu jicheng*, 815.

51. See the passage in *Shangshu diming yan*, in Yasui and Nakamura, eds., *Weishu jicheng*, 367. The fragment is preserved in Li Fang et al., eds., *Taiping yulan*, 533: 2418a and the commentary attached to it. The relationship between human emperors and these heavenly emperors is depicted by Zheng Xuan 鄭玄 in his commentary on the "Da zhuan" 大傳 in *Liji zhengyi*, in Ruan Yuan, ed., *Shisan jing zhushu*, 1506. Eastern Han emperors and literati tried to set up ceremonies based on a ritual system, which Watanabe and Ikeda Shūzō call the "six heavens" (*liu tian* 六天). See Watanabe Yoshihiro 渡邊義浩, "Sacrifices to Heaven in the Han and the Theory of Six Heavens," *Acta Asiatica* 98 (2010): 43–75, and Ikeda Shūzō 池田秀三, "Cheng Hsüan's Theory of Six Heavens and Ritual Scholarship during the Han," *Acta Asiatica* 98 (2010): 77–98.

52. For comprehensive collections of material concerning the sage kings' birth in apocryphal texts, see Gu Jiegang, *Zhongguo shanggu shi yanjiu jiangyi*, 273–79, and Xu Xingwu 徐興無, "Zuowei pifu de xuansheng suwang—chenwei wenxian zhong de Kongzi xingxiang yu sixiang" 作為匹夫的玄聖素王—讖緯文獻中的孔子形象與思想, *Gudian wenxian yanjiu* 古典文獻研究 11 (2008): 27–28.

53. For a summary of the use of the Five Phases and the evolution of this theory during the Han dynasty, see Michael Loewe, *The Men Who Governed Han China: Companion to A Biographical Dictionary of the Qin, Former Han and Xin Periods* (Leiden: Brill, 2011), 457–521, and *Divination, Mythology and Monarchy in Han China* (Cambridge: Cambridge University Press, 1995), 55–60.

54. "Feng shan shu" 封禪書, *Shiji*, 28: 1381; "Lü li zhi" 律曆志, *Han shu*, 21b: 1011–13.

55. Loewe, *Divination, Mythology and Monarchy in Han China*, 57, 94.

56. *Chunqiu baoqian tu* 春秋保乾圖, in Yasui and Nakamura, eds., *Weishu jicheng*, 806. The fragment is preserved in Li Fang et al., eds., *Taiping yulan*, 76: 355a.

57. *Xue qi* 血氣 here indicates people's physical vitalities in general. For the term and how the meaning of *xue* is different from "blood" in the modern sense, see Sivin, *Traditional Medicine in Contemporary China*, 46, 150–60.

58. *The Annals' Diagrams of Elaborating Confucius*, in Yasui and Nakamura, eds., *Weishu jicheng*, 581. The fragment is preserved in Li Fang et al., eds., *Taiping yulan*, 76: 355a.

59. For this reason, many modern scholars, especially Gu Jiegang 顧頡剛 (AD 1983–1980), have scorned the apocrypha, as if political motivations made apocrypha insincere forgeries with impure intellectual pursuits. See appendix 5.

60. See the section "The Six Classics: Complete and Fundamental" starting from 20.

61. *Han shu*, 11: 340.

62. "Three-seven," as in three multiplied by seven equals twenty-one. For the calendric foundation of this claim, see Liu Tseng-kuei, trans. Luke Habberstad, "Calendrical Computation Numbers and Han Dynasty Politics: A Study of Gu Yong's Three Troubles Theory," in *Chang'an 26 BCE: An Augustan Age in China*, ed. Michael Nylan and Griet Vankeerberghen (Seattle: University of Washington Press, 2015), 293–322, esp. 302–04.

63. *Han shu*, 51: 2372. It is not clear when Lu Wenshu said so.

64. *Han shu*, 85: 3465.

65. Ibid., 3468.

66. This calculation is based on Han people's concept of the establishment of the Han dynasty, such as the account in which Liu Bang was enthroned as Gaozu 高祖 in the first month of 202 BC in *Shiji* and *Han shu*. In the biography of Liu Bang, Sima Qian switches his way of addressing Liu Bang from Hanwang 漢王, or the "king of Han," to Gaozu in 202 BC. See Sima Qian, "Gaozu benji" 高祖本紀 (The biography of Gaozu), *Shiji*, 8: 378–79. A change of title also happens in Ban Gu's *Han shu*, although Ban Gu uses the word *di* 帝, or "the emperor," instead of Gaozu. See Ban Gu, "Gaozu ji" 高祖紀, *Han shu*, 1: 50–54.

67. *Han shu*, 99b: 4099, 4110–11.

68. Ibid., 4108–09.

69. Homer H. Dubs, trans., *History of the Former Han Dynasty: A Critical Translation with Annotations* (Baltimore: Waverly Press, 1938), 3: 281–82.

70. "Red" stands for the phase of fire in the theory of Five Phases, with which the Liu house corresponded. *Han shu*, 99b: 4113.

71. *Han shu*, 99b: 4105. This attribution of Five Phases can also be found in the "Lü li zhi" of *Han shu*.

72. The Red Eyebrow was a rebellious group that mainly contained peasants. The group received this name because the members painted their foreheads red to

distinguish themselves from the Han official troops. For their rebellion, see Bielenstein, "Wang Mang, the Restoration of the Han Dynasty, and Later Han," 243–54.

73. *Hou Han shu*, 13: 538.

74. *Hou Han shu*, 1a: 20; 11: 480.

75. The classical Chinese sentence by Gongsun Shu's wife is 朝聞道，夕死尚可, and the original sentence by Confucius from *Analects* is 朝聞道，夕死可矣. Whether she really said it or not, the expected audience of this account is literati with at least basic familiarity with the classics. *Hou Han shu*, 13: 535. "Li ren" 里仁, *Lunyu*, Zhu Xi annotated, *Sishu zhangju jizhu, lunyu jizhu*, 2: 71.

It seems like Gongsun Shu and his wife understood the person's prophecy quite well, but actually they have sharply different understandings of it. On another occasion, Gongsun Shu mentioned "twelve" as the number of Han emperors, which corresponds to the number of dukes in the *Annals*. Therefore, by saying "twelve as the time," Gongsun Shu perceivably understood it as the time when the Han had their twelve emperors. His wife, however, led by Gongsun Shu's question, considered "twelve" as a time span they would endure, which is probably longer than the period from morning to afternoon. Nevertheless, it is unclear how long the specific time span was in her mind. It might be twelve years, twelve months, twelve days, or even one day, given the 120 divisions of a day used beginning in Wang Mang's time. *Hou Han shu*, 13: 535; *Han shu*, 99a: 4094.

76. *Hou Han shu*, 13: 535.

77. *Han shu*, 99a–b: 4078–79, 4093–94, 4112–13.

78. *Hou Han shu*, 17: 645.

79. *Hou Han shu*, 1a: 1.

80. Ibid., 21.

81. Ibid., 21–22.

82. Ibid., 21.

83. *Hou Han shu*, 23: 798.

84. See, for example, *Han shu*, 56: 2500. According to the commentator Yan Shigu 顏師古, the account is from the new script version of "Tai Shi" 泰誓. This passage does not belong to the received version of the *Documents*. In an apocryphal text named *Shangshu zhong hou* 尚書中候, or the *Inner Observation of the Documents*, there is an elaborate form of the account, in which King Wu receives a white fish with a specific description of how to defeat Zhou 紂.

85. *Hou Han shu*, 13: 535.

86. This list includes eleven Liu emperors and Empress Lü, which is also an idea found in Ban Gu's historiography.

87. This understanding of the title is based on Zheng Xuan's 鄭玄 (AD 127–200) commentary on the title. See Yasui Kōzan and Nakamura Shōhachi, *Isho no kisoteki kenkyū* 緯書の基礎的研究 (Tokyo: Kokusho Kankōkai, 1976), 1089.

88. *Hou Han shu*, 13: 538.

89. Here the character *yi* 乙 is borrowed as *zha* 軋, meaning "to crush" or "to forge." Since *mao jin* can refer to metal, the metaphor is thus forging or crushing metal. See Li Xian's 李賢 commentary on the word *yi* in *Hou Han shu*, 13: 538.

90. The latter two titles were included later in the discourse of literati with *Hetu* and *Xiaojing* respectively preceding the titles. See Cao Chong's 曹充 (fl. AD 60) speech, where *Hetu kuo dixiang* 河圖括地象 is mentioned. See *Hou Han shu*, 35: 1201. The name *Xiaojing yuanshen qi* 孝經援神契 can be found in the "Jisi zhi 祭祀志" by Sima Biao 司馬彪 (AD 243–306), in *Hou Han shu zhi*, 9: 3200.

91. *Yuanshen qi* is mentioned too in *Baihu tongyi* 白虎通義. See Xianggang Zhongwen Daxue Zhongguo Wenhua Yanjiusuo 香港中文大學中國文化研究所, *Baihu tong zhuzi suoyin* 白虎通逐字索引, Xian Qin Liang Han guji zhuzi suoyin congkan 先秦兩漢古籍逐字索引叢刊 (Hong Kong: The Commercial Press, 1995), 432.

92. *Han shu*, 75: 3153. The sentence *gongsun bingyi li* 公孫病已立 can be read in several ways, and the English translation provided earlier is just one of them. It can also mean, for example, "The grandson of the duke will be established." *Gong* 公 in this context does not indicate "duke" as a rank title but is an honorific term indicating anyone significant.

93. *Han shu*, 8: 238.

94. Judging from the way Liu Xiu treated Gongsun Shu's quotes, it seems that the prophetic texts the latter used were familiar. Otherwise, it would be easier and more economical to deny the authenticity of the texts. In contrast, for example, Liu Xiu debunked Gongsun Shu's supposedly prophetic tattoo on his palm and warned him that he should not imitate Wang Mang's usurpation. Liu Xiu could have debunked Gongsun Shu's use of prophetic texts as well, but he didn't. See *Hou Han shu*, 13: 538.

95. *Han shu*, 99b: 4100; 99c: 4185.

96. For how great families invested their money in local society to gain authority in the early years of the Eastern Han, see Yü Ying-shih, "Dong Han zhengquan zhi jianli yu shizu daxing zhi guanxi," 207–16; Higashi Shinji 東晉次, *Gokan jidai no seiji to shakai* 後漢時代の政治と社會 (Nagoya: Nagoya Daigaku Shuppankai, 1995), 70–89; and Cui Xiangdong 崔向東, *Han dai haozu yanjiu* 漢代豪族研究 (Wuhan: Chongwen, 2003), 168–79.

97. Yang Lien-sheng 楊聯陞, "Dong Han de haozu" 東漢的豪族, *Qinghua xuebao* 4 (1936): 1011–16; Yü Ying-shih, "Dong Han zhengquan zhi jianli yu shizu daxing zhi guanxi," 213–16, 249–52.

98. Kimura Masao 木村正雄, *Chūgoku kodai nōmin hanran no kenkyū* 中國古代農民叛亂の研究 (Tokyo: Tōkyō Daigaku Shuppankai, 1979), 324–25, 332, 355. Yang Lien-sheng, "Dong Han de haozu," 1011–16. Also see Yü Ying-shih, "Dong Han zhengquan zhi jianli yu shizu daxing zhi guanxi," 238–39.

99. Yü Ying-shih, "Dong Han zhengquan zhi jianli yu shizu daxing zhi guanxi," 213–16.

100. Hirai Masashi 平井正士, "Kandai ni okeru Juka kanryō no kugesō he no shinjun" 漢代における儒家官僚の公卿層への浸潤, in Sakai Tado Sensei Koki Shukuga Kinen no Kai 酒井忠夫先生古稀祝賀記念の会, ed., *Rekishi ni okeru minū to bunka: Sakai Tadao Sensei koki shukuga kinen ronshū* 歴史における民衆と文化:酒井忠夫先生古稀祝賀記念論集 (Tokyo: Kokusho Kankōkai, 1982), 51–66. Xiao Wangzhi 蕭望之 is an example of a dominant scholar and high official with a local-gentry background. See Yü Ying-shih, "Dong Han zhengquan zhi jianli yu shizu daxing zhi guanxi," 214.

101. *Hou Han shu*, 13: 513. The Shanggong position, designated as higher than the Sangong 三公, or Three Ducal Ministers, specifically referred to Liu Xin's position, National Teacher. See Li Xian's commentary on Kui Xiao's position "Shi" in ibid.

102. *Hou Han shu*, 11: 481.

103. Based on *Hou Han shu*, they all declined it. Therefore, Gongsun Shu tried to murder them. The source is certainly from a biased perspective favoring Liu Xiu and the Eastern Han dynasty, but it does reflect how important these local classicists were for the warlords. See Fan Ye, "Duxing liezhuan" 獨行列傳, *Hou Han shu*, 81: 2666–69.

104. The *qi jing chen* 七經讖, or the apocrypha of the seven classics, were first mentioned in an event of 50 AD. In 56 AD, Liu Xiu, as Emperor Guangwu, announced apocryphal texts to All-under-Heaven. *Hou Han shu*, 1b: 84; 35: 1196.

105. This conjecture is based on Zhang Heng's complaint about apocryphal texts: contradictory accounts. He claimed that Jia Kui 賈逵 (AD 30–101) found more than thirty cases that contradicted each other. This contradiction is probably due to the compilation of isolated or heterogeneous texts. *Hou Han shu*, 59: 1912. This situation is sometimes as true, but less obvious, with other texts compiled through a relatively long period of time. In the *Documents*, for example, the characteristics of sage kings appear to be different from chapter to chapter. See Michael Nylan, *The Five "Confucian" Classics* (New Haven: Yale University Press, 2001), 136–39.

106. Cai Shaogong was the one who, in the last years of Wang Mang's rule, told Liu Xiu the prophecy that someone named Liu Xiu will become the next son of Heaven. In the conversation, people took the National Teacher, Liu Xin, who had already changed his name to "Liu Xiu" then, as the person in the prophecy. *Hou Han shu*, 15: 582.

107. See *Hou Han shu*, 15: 573, and Li Xian's commentary on the term *Zong qingshi*.

108. Ibid.

109. *Hou Han shu*, 15: 575. The National Academy was restored in AD 28. *Hou Han shu*, 1a: 40.

110. *Hou Han shu*, 79a: 2558; 79b: 2573. Part of Yin Min's job was to delete prophecies about Wang Mang in the prophetic corpus. For what I mean by "old text tradition," see page 103.

111. *Hou Han shu*, 35: 1196. The seven classics are probably the Five Classics plus *Music* and the *Classic of Filial Piety*. Li Xian's commentary on the words *qi jing* does not mention the *Classic of Filial Piety*, but the *Analects*.

112. *Hou Han shu*, 79a: 2558.

113. *Hou Han shu*, 28a: 961.

114. *Hou Han shu*, 1b: 84.

115. So far the most comprehensive study of Emperor Guangwu's *feng* and *shan* sacrifices is Xing Yitian 邢義田, "Donghan Guangwu di yu feng shan" 東漢光武帝與封禪 in his *Tianxia yi jia: Huangdi, Guanliao yu shehui* 天下一家: 皇帝、官僚與社會 (Beijing: Zhonghua, 2011), 177–201. For an introduction to the practices of *feng* and *shan* sacrifices in English, see Tiziana Lippiello, "On the Secret Texts of the Feng and Shan Sacrifices," *Annali di Ca' Foscari* 35.3 (1996): 399–406; and Hans Bielenstein, *The Restoration of the Han Dynasty, Vol. IV, The Government* (Stockholm: Museum of Far Eastern Antiquities, 1979), 163–83. For a translation of the record about Emperor Guangwu's *feng* and *shan* sacrifices called *Feng shan yi ji* 封禪儀記, or *Records of the Ceremonies of the Feng and Shan Sacrifices*, by Ma Dibo 馬第伯 (ca. first century AD) preserved in the commentary on Sima Biao's "Jisi zhi" 祭祀志, see Stephen Bokenkamp, "Record of the Feng and Shan Sacrifices," in *Religions of China in Practice*, ed. Donald S. Lopez Jr. (Princeton: Princeton University Press, 1996), 251–60.

116. See Zhang Shoujie's 張守節 commentary and how Emperor Wu practiced it in Sima Qian, "Fengshan shu" 封禪書, *Shiji*, 28: 1355, 1398.

117. *Shiji*, 28: 1355, 1384.

118. See Li Xian's commentary on the phrase "*feng shan* Taishan 封禪泰山" in Sima Biao, "Jisi shang," *Hou Han shu zhi* 後漢書志, in Fan Ye, *Hou Han shu*, 7: 3162.

119. For the purposes of the sacrifices and how the First Emperor did the *feng* and *shan* sacrifices, see Martin Kern, *The Stele Inscriptions of Ch'in Shih-huang: Text and Ritual in Early Chinese Imperial Representation* (New Haven: American Oriental Society, 2000), 112–18.

120. *Shiji*, 28: 1366–67; *Han shu*, 25a: 1201–02, 1205.

121. See Li Xian's quote from *Dongguan Han ji* in *Hou Han shu zhi*, 7: 3162.

122. *Hou Han shu zhi*, 7: 3161.

123. Ibid., 3162.

124. Ibid.

125. *Hou Han shu zhi*, 7: 3163, and Xing Yitian 邢義田, "Donghan Guangwu di yu feng shan" 東漢光武帝與封禪, 184–85.

126. *Hou Han shu zhi*, 7: 3169–70.

127. Ibid., 3165.

128. *Hou Han shu zhi*, 7: 3165.

129. *Hou Han shu zhi*, 7: 3165.

130. See Higashi's evaluation of the reign of Emperor Guangwu, Ming and Zhang 章 (r. AD 76–88) in *Gokan jidai no seiji to shakai*, 43–68.

Chapter 3

1. See examples in Annals' *Diagrams Elaborating Confucius* or *Contract for Assistance from Spirits of the* Classic of Filial Piety, in Yasui and Nakamura, eds., *Weishu jicheng*, 580–81, 992.
2. *Hou Han shu*, 2: 95.
3. *Hou Han shu*, 42: 1423–24.
4. *Hou Han shu*, 10a: 405.
5. Three scholars have made great contributions to the understanding of the image of Confucius as *xuan sheng* and *su wang* in apocryphal texts: Jack L. Dull, Yasui Kōzan 安居香山, and Xu Xingwu 徐興無. Dull points out Confucius's semi-divine nature and that Confucius was depicted as the uncrowned king to announce the rise of the Han dynasty and the creation of an ideal institution for the Han dynasty. Yasui Kōzan greatly emphasizes apocryphal texts as the product of the new script camp and the Gongyang tradition of the *Annals of Spring and Autumn*. He is extremely cautious about Confucius being the uncrowned king. Instead, adopting Pi Xirui's 皮錫瑞 theory, Yasui argues that, in apocryphal texts, Confucius narrated the principles of the uncrowned king for the new dynasty. Xu Xingwu also emphasizes Confucius's divine nature and argues that the idea that Confucius was the representative of the phase of water is due to the cycle of *tian tong* 天統, *di tong* 地統, and *ren tong* 人統 from *Chunqiu fanlu*. See Jack L. Dull, "A Historical Introduction to the Apocryphal (Ch'an-wei) Texts of the Han Dynasty," PhD thesis, University of Washington, 1966, 516–27; Yasui and Nakamura, *Isho no kisoteki kenkyū*, 152–170, esp. 160 and 166; Xu Xingwu, "Zuowei pifu de xuansheng suwang—chenwei wenxian zhong de Kongzi xingxiang yu sixiang," 21–42. For this observation in Han texts, see, for example, Mark Csikszentmihalyi, "Confucius and the *Analects* in the Hàn," in *Confucius and the* Analects*: New Essays*, ed. Bryan W. Van Norden (Oxford: Oxford University Press, 2002), 142–44.
6. I understand the *Way* to be a metaphysical concept defined as the generator of the world, but also that force which keeps everything moving in its own particular pattern. Here, it is also a normative concept—the ideal *way* a sage or emperor should behave. Different social roles have different ideal behaviors.
7. "Tian dao" 天道, in Chen Guying 陳鼓應, *Zhuangzi jinzhu jinyi* 莊子今注今譯 (Beijing: Zhonghua, 1983), 337.
8. Victor H. Mair, *Wandering on the Way: Early Taoist Tales and Parables of Chuang Tzu* (New York: Bantam Books, 1994), 120.
9. By saying "supreme," especially in this context, I mean that one achieves the state of *zhi ren* 至人, or the "ultimate man," whose mind "functions like a mirror. It neither sends off nor welcomes; it responds but does not retain. Therefore, he can triumph over things without injury" (至人之用心若鏡，不將不迎，應而不藏，故能勝物而不傷). See "Ying diwang" 應帝王, in Chen Guying, *Zhuangzi jinzhu jinyi*, 227. I quote the translation from Mair, *Wandering on the Way*, 71.

10. People who understand the Way but are in lower social positions in *Zhuangzi* might be a cook, fisherman, woodcutter, and so on. See Alan J. Berkowitz, *Patterns of Disengagement: the Practice and Portrayal of Reclusion in Early Medieval China* (Stanford: Stanford University Press, 2000), 27–29, in which he calls this kind of person the "wise rustic."

11. Also, if we consider the characteristics of the Way, "dark" can also be epithet of the Way. Accordingly, *su* can also indicate a characteristic of the Way as in *pu su* 樸素, or "raw and plain." See "Tian dao" 天道, in Chen Guying, *Zhuangzi jinzhu jinyi*, 337. According to the context, the author's intention seems to be to make multiple correspondences. Therefore, we should keep as many layers of meaning as possible.

12. I suspect that a problem arose in the word order of the title during transmission of the text. The alternative form of the title is *Chunqiu kong yan tu*, which makes more sense, since according to an entry in the text, the title alludes to the legend of Fu Xi 伏羲 making *ba gua* 八卦 and Confucius elaborating (*yan* 演) them. Therefore, I translate the title as "The Diagrams of the *Annals of Spring and Autumn* Deduced by Confucius," though I still keep the word order of the title used in Yasui and Nakamura's compilation and other literature. See *Chunqiu yan Kong tu*, in Yasui and Nakamura, eds., *Weishu jicheng*, 573.

13. *Chunqiu yan Kong tu*, in Yasui and Nakamura, eds., *Weishu jicheng*, 576. The fragment is preserved in the commentary on *Hou Han shu*, 40b: 1377.

14. See Gu Jiegang 顧頡剛, *Zhongguo shanggu shi yanjiu jiangyi* 中國上古史研究講義 (Beijing: Zhonghua, 1988), 238–41. For a handy chart of the summary of the mysterious births of the founder of the dynasties, see Xu, "Zuowei pifu de xuansheng suwang," 27–28.

15. As Mencius mentioned. See *Mengzi*, "Wan Zhang" 萬章, in Zhu Xi annotated, *Sishu zhangju jizhu, Mengzi jizhu*, 9: 309.

16. For the theory of "correlative thinking," see, for example, A. C. Graham, *Disputers of the Tao: Philosophical Argument in Ancient China* (La Salle: Open Court, 1989), 355. For an assessment of Graham's theory of correlative thinking and the history of this theory since Max Weber, see Puett, *To Become a God*, 16–17, 5–21.

17. *Xiao jing gou ming jue* 孝經鉤命決, in Yasui and Nakamura, eds., *Weishu jicheng*, 1011. Cf. Yasui's punctuation: 邱為制法，主黑綠不代蒼黃. The fragment is preserved in the commentary in "Qu li xia" 曲禮下, *Liji zhengyi*, *j*. 4, in Ruan Yuan, ed., *Shisan jing zhushu*, 1257.

18. *Chunqiu yan Kong tu*, in Yasui and Nakamura, ed., *Weishu jicheng*, 580. The fragment is preserved in the commentary in "Zhongyong" 中庸, *Liji zhengyi*, *j*. 52, in Ruan Yuan, ed., *Shisan jing zhushu*, 1628.

19. *Chunqiu yan Kong tu*, in Yasui and Nakamura, eds., *Weishu jicheng*, 579. The fragment is preserved in the commentary in "Yingong yuannian" 隱公元年, *Chunqiu Gongyang zhuan zhushu* 春秋公羊傳注疏, *j*. 1, in Ruan Yuan, ed., *Shisan jing zhushu*, 2195.

20. "Ba yi" 八佾, *Lunyu*, in Zhu Xi 朱熹 annotated, *Sishu zhangju jizhu*, *Lunyu jizhu*, 2: 68.

21. *Chunqiu yan Kong tu*, in Yasui and Nakamura, eds., *Weishu jicheng*, 579. The fragment is preserved in the commentary in "Yingong yuannian" 隱公元年, *Chunqiu Gongyang zhuan zhushu*, j. 1, in Ruan Yuan, ed., *Shisan jing zhushu*, 2195.

22. *Chunqiu yan Kong tu*, in Yasui and Nakamura, ed., *Weishu jicheng*, 578.

23. *Chunqiu yan Kong tu*, in Yasui and Nakamura, eds., *Weishu jicheng*, 580. The fragment is preserved in the commentary in Ban Gu 班固, "You tong fu 幽通賦," in Xiao Tong 蕭統 (AD 501–531), ed., *Wen xuan* 文選 (Beijing: Zhonghua, 1977), 14: 212b.

24. For example, Pi Xirui supported this argument. See Pi Xirui 皮錫瑞, *Jingxue tonglun* 經學通論 (Beijing: Zhonghua, 1954), preface, 1; chapter 4 "*Chun qiu*," 1.

25. For an explanation of the context of Mencius's statement and a discussion of the meaning of *zuo* 作, which is translated as "made" here, see Joachim Gentz, *Das Gongyang zhuan: Auslegung und Kanonisierung der Frühlingsund Herbstannalen (Chunqiu)* (Wiesbaden: Harrassowitz, 2001), 36–40.

26. "Teng Wengong xia" 滕文公下, *Mengzi*, Zhu Xi 朱熹 annotated, *Mengzi zhang ju* 孟子章句, *Sishu zhangju jizhu*, 272.

27. James Legge, *The Chinese Classics with a Translation, Critical and Exegetical Notes Prolegomena, and Copious Indexes, Vol. 1: Confucian Analects, The Great Learning, and the Doctrine of the Mean* (London: Trübner, 1961), 281–82.

28. *Shiji*, 129: 3297–98. For a discussion of the translation of the title *Shiji*, see Stephen Durrant, Wai-Yee Li, Michael Nylan, and Hans Van Ess, *The Letter to Ren An and Sima Qian's Legacy* (Seattle: University of Washington Press, 2016), 18–21, in which the title is translated as *Records of the Historian*. The authors in the book argue that for the *shi* part, it is ideal to keep the classical Chinese Taishi ling stead of translating it into "Grand Scribe" or "Grand Historian," for the duties of the position cover more than the two translations can render. While aware of this situation, I use "Grand Historian" because it is a good compromise between the classical Chinese name and how we modern readers perceive the text *Shiji*.

29. For more information about the subtlety of the praise and blame in the *Annals of Spring and Autumn*, see Nylan, *The Five "Confucian Classics,"* 263–65. For a comprehensive study on the Gongyang tradition in a Western language, see Gentz, *Das Gongyang zhuan*.

30. Yuri Pines, "Chinese History Writing between the Sacred and the Secular," in *Early Chinese Religion, Part I: Shang through Han (1250 BC–220 AD)*, ed. John Lagerwey and Marc Kalinowski (Leiden: Brill, 2009), 327. For how Confucius affects the exegesis of the Gongyang commentary as a supreme sage, and how this is related to the *weisheitlicher Sinn* (the sense of wisdom) in the *Dunkle Sprache* (the hidden speech), see Gentz, *Das Gongyang zhuan*, 72–75.

31. See the relevant section in the previous chapter. Also see Sarah Queen, *From Chronicle to Canon: The Hermeneutics of the* Spring and Autumn, *According*

to *Tung Chung-shu* (New York: Cambridge University Press, 1996), 119–26; Pines, "Chinese History Writing between the Sacred and the Secular," 332.

32. Dong Zhongshu tried to convince Emperor Wu by using this argument. See Ban Gu, "Dong Zhongshu liezhuan," *Han shu*, j. 56, 2509.

33. For examples from the early Western Han, the end of the Western Han, and the middle of the Eastern Han, respectively, see *Huainanzi* 淮南子, "Zhushu xun 主術訓"; *Shuiyuan* 說苑, "Gui de 貴德"; and *Shi Ming* 釋名, "Shi dian yi 釋典藝," in He Ning 何寧, *Huainanzi jishi* 淮南子集釋 (Beijing: Zhonghua, 1998), 9: 697; Xiang Zonglu 向宗魯, *Shuiyuan jiaozheng* 說苑校證 (Beijing: Zhonghua, 1987), 5: 95, and Bi Yuan 畢沅, *Shi Ming shuzheng bu* 釋名疏證補 (Beijing: Zhonghua, 2008), 6: 210.

34. Liu Xiang, "Gui de 貴德," in Xiang Zonglu, ed., *Shuiyuan jiaozheng*, 5: 95.

35. Jack L. Dull argues that Dong Zhongshu 董仲舒 connected the term "uncrowned king" to Confucius. By doing so, he further emphasizes the connection between the new script camp and the concept of Confucius being the "uncrowned king." However, as the quote from *Huainanzi* shows, the idea of the "uncrowned king" was not merely exclusive to the new script camp. See Dull, "A Historical Introduction to the Apocryphal (Ch'an-wei) Texts of the Han Dynasty," 28.

36. "Zhu shu xun," in He Ning, ed., *Huainanzi jishi*, 9: 697.

37. Due to textual variation, Ames adopts *xiao dao* 孝道 (the Way of filial piety) instead of *jiao dao* 教道 (Way of teaching). However, according to the context, the term used here has less to do with filial piety than with showing people what is right and wrong according to the *Annals of Spring and Autumn*. See Roger T. Ames, *The Art of Rulership: A Study of Ancient Chinese Political Thought* (Albany: State University of New York Press, 1994), 205.

38. Adapted from Ames, *The Art of Rulership*, 205.

39. Yasui and Nakamura, eds., *Weishu jicheng*, 1072.

40. Yasui and Nakamura, eds., *Weishu jicheng*, 1073. This is not exclusive to apocryphal texts. The author of the preface to *Zuo zhuan* 左傳, Du Yu 杜預 (AD 222–285), mentions and also criticizes the theory that Confucius is the uncrowned king and Zuo Qiuming is the plain minister. One may infer from this that the theory of Confucius being the uncrowned king and Zuo, the plain minister, was popular during his time to the extent that he needed to clarify this in his preface to the commentary on *Zuo Zhuan*. See Ruan Yuan, ed., *Shisan jing zhushu*, 1708.

41. Wang Chong 王充, "Chao qi" 超奇, *Lun heng* 13: 213.

42. Tian and An argue that apocryphal texts serve political conflicts. See Tian Changwu and An Zuozhang, eds., *Qin Han shi*, 647.

43. *Shiji*, 67: 2202–03.

44. Cheng Shude 程樹德, *Lunyu jishi* 論語集釋 (Beijing: Zhonghua, 1990), 742.

45. See the next pages. Also Fan Ning 范甯, an Eastern Jin 東晉 commentator on the *Analects*, commented on *wenxue* as follows: "by saying *wenxue*, it means he [Zixia] was good at the documents and works of the ancient kings." See Cheng Shude, *Lunyu jishi*, 744. Also, the term in the Western Han text *Yan tie lun* 鹽鐵論

indicates a group of people who majored in classics. See Wang Liqi 王利器, "Qian yan 前言," *Yan tie lun jiao zhu* 鹽鐵論校注 (Beijing: Zhonghua, 1992), 6–7. Wang specifically points out that the people described as *wenxue* are actually the intellectual descendants of Zixia's lineage. I would not go so far as to agree with him, since it is still unclear who belongs to the group of *wenxue* in *Yan tie lun*. However, I do agree with him to the extent that in the Han dynasty the term *wenxue* was already used to indicate the study of classics from the ancient sages and kings.

46. Cheng Shude, *Lunyu jishi*, 742.

47. "Wu du" 五蠹, Wang Xianshen 王先慎, ed., *Han Feizi jijie* 韓非子集解 (Beijing: Zhonghua, 1998), 19: 456.

48. "Cha chuan" 察傳, Wang Liqi 王利器, ed., *Lüshi chunqiu zhushu* 呂氏春秋注疏 (Chengdu: Bashu, 2002), 22: 2780–81.

49. Yang Zhaoming 楊朝明, ed., *Kongzi jiayu tongjie—fu chutu ziliao yu xiangguan yanjiu* 孔子家語通解—附出土資料與相關研究 (Taibei: Wanjuan lou, 2005), 433.

50. *Hou Han shu*, 44: 1500.

51. "Gongsun chou" 公孫丑, *Mengzi*, Zhu Xi annotated, *Sishu zhangju jizhu, Mengzi jizhu*, 3: 233–34.

52. Although in apocryphal texts, Confucius's major disciples' abnormal appearance is also a sign of their supremacy compared to ordinary people, Yan Yuan is the only person to whom one of the five phases is matched. See Yasui and Nakamura, eds., *Weishu jicheng*, 1069.

53. *Hou Han shu*, 37: 1255.

54. The specific year, which is referred to by *qi* 其, is unclear here.

55. The original story from the *Analects* goes as such: "Zi Xia asked, 'Her entrancing smile dimpling, her beautiful eyes glancing, and patterns of color upon plain silk.' What is the meaning of these lines [from the *Poetry*]." Confucius said, "The plain silk is there first. The colors come afterward." "Does the practice of the rites likewise come afterward?" Confucius said, "The person who raises me up is, you, Zixia. Only now can I discuss the *Poetry* with you." See "Bayi" 八佾, *Lunyu*, Zhu Xi annotated, *Lunyu zhang ju, Sishu zhangju jizhu, Lunyu jizhu*, 2: 63. The English translation is adapted from D. C. Lau, trans., *Confucius: The Analects* (Hong Kong: Chinese University Press, 2000), 21.

56. As Hsing I-tien insightfully points out, Han emperors were reluctant to compare the sages, for whether the Han dynasty had had a sage ruler was a sensitive issue among the literati. See Hsing I-tien 邢義田, "Qin Han huangdi yu '*shengren*'" 秦漢皇帝與"聖人," rev. version, in his *Tianxia yijia: Huangdi, guanliao yu shehui*, 73–82, esp. 78.

57. For a summary of the cases of auspicious omens in the Han dynasty, see Tiziana Lippiello, *Auspicious Omens and Miracles in Ancient China: Han, Three Kingdoms and Six Dynasties* (Sankt Augustin: Steyler Verlag, 2001), 40–51.

58. The most obvious examples would be the *Analects* 12.7–9; 13. 9. See Zhu Xi annotated, *Sishu zhangju jizhu, Lunyu jizhu*, 6: 137–38, 7: 143.

59. Michael Loewe, "The Conduct of Government and the Issues at Stake AD 57–167," in *The Cambridge History of China, Vol. 1, The Ch'in and Han Empires, 221 B.C.–A.D. 220*, ed. Denis Twitchett and Michael Loewe (Cambridge: Cambridge University Press, 1987), 293. For more information about Emperor Ming's reign, see the same chapter by Loewe, 292–97. Before Loewe, Qian Mu 錢穆 gave a similar description of Emperor Ming and argued that he was "fond of bureaucratic business" (*hao lishi* 好吏事). See Qian Mu 錢穆, *Guo shi dagang* 國史大綱 (Beijing: Shangwu, 1996), 1: 177.

60. Liu Xiu is famous for believing in and using apocrypha to legitimize his rule. Before Liu Xiu enthroned himself, the war between Liu Xiu and Gongsun Shu was not merely on the battlefield. Both were very aware of the information apocrypha conveyed, and they competed over their interpretations of apocryphal texts. See Lü Simian, *Qin Han shi* 秦漢史, *Lü Simian wenji* (Shanghai: Shanghai guji, 2005), 739.

61. *Hou Han shu* 2: 106.

62. *Hou Han shu* 2: 111. For a more detailed analysis of the political function of omens, see Loewe, *Divination, Mythology and Monarchy in Han China*, 94–97. For apocrypha used as a way to claim political legitimacy in general, see Lippiello, *Auspicious Omens and Miracles in Ancient China*, 56–65.

63. Fan Ye, *Hou Han shu*, 2: 83. Divine fungus is the translation of *zhi cao* 芝草, which were various kinds of mushrooms connected to immortality.

64. Wang Chong, "Qi shi" 齊世, *Lun heng*, 18: 294. Wang Chong does not believe the connection between the auspicious omens and good governance. However, he did not dispute the statement that there were indeed a large number of auspicious omens either. For Wang Chong's agenda in praising the Han dynasty, see Reinhard Emmerich, "Wang Chong's Praises for the Han Dynasty," *Monumenta Serica* 56 (2008): 117–48.

65. *Hou Han shu*, 2: 95; 42:1423–24; 10a: 405.

66. *Hou Han shu*, 2: 102, 109–10, 113–14; 42: 1427; 42: 1446–48.

67. *Hou Han shu*, 42: 1429; 2: 120, 42: 1444; 42: 1431.

68. *Hou Han shu*, 2: 113, 118. So far this is the earliest record of sacrificing to Confucius and his disciples. Also, iconographies of Confucius and his "seventy-two" disciples were found in Eastern Han dynasty tombs. See Huang Jinxing 黃進興, "'Shengxian'yu 'shengtu': ru jiao congsi zhi yu jidu jiao fengsheng zhi de bijiao" "聖賢"與"聖徒": 儒教從祀制與基督教封聖制的比較, *Zhongyang Yanjiu Yuan Lishi Yuyan Yanjiu Suo jikan* 71.3 (2000): 534–35.

69. For a detailed description of *taiping* by people of the Western Han dynasty, see *Han shi wai zhuan* 韓詩外傳 in Xu Weiyu 許維遹, ed., *Han shi waizhuan jishi* 韓詩外傳集釋 (Beijing: Zhonghua, 1980), 3: 102. For issues of dating, authorship, and authenticity of *Han shi wai zhuan*, see the entry of *Han shih wai chuan* 韓詩外傳 by James R. Hightower, in *Early Chinese Texts: A Bibliographical Guide*, ed. Michael Loewe (Berkeley: University of California Press, 1993), 125–28.

70. "Wang dao" 王道, in Su Yu, ed., *Chunqiu fanlu yizheng*, 4: 109. "The kings of Heaven" here refers to the Zhou kings. For a systematic dating and the authorship of every chapter of *Chunqiu fan lu*, see Michael Loewe, *Dong Zhongshu, a 'Confucian' Heritage and the* Chunqiu Fanlu (Leiden: Brill, 2011), esp. 335–41.

71. Yang Xiong 揚雄, "Wubai" 五百, *Fa yan*, 8: 261.

72. Wang Chong, "Xuan Han" 宣漢, *Lun heng*, 17: 295.

Chapter 4

1. See the section "An Abortive Path: Li Xun's Departure from the Classics" starting from 35.

2. *Hou Han shu*, 20b: 1076, 1083.

3. Paul Demiéville, "Philosophy and Religion from Han to Sui," in *The Cambridge History of China, Vol. 1, The Ch'in and Han Empires, 221 B.C.–A.D. 220*, ed. Denis Twitchett and Michael Loewe (Cambridge: Cambridge University Press, 1987), 816. For a general introduction to the movement, see ibid., 815–20.

4. *Hou Han shu*, 7: 316. For the cult of Laozi at court, see Rafe de Crespigny, "The Harem of Emperor Huan: A Study of Court Politics in Later Han," *Papers on Far Eastern History* 12 (1975): 34–42. For a detailed study on Emperor Huan's intellectual and political agenda, see Rafe de Crespigny, "Politics and Philosophy under the Government of Emperor Huan 159–168 A.D.," *T'oung Pao* 66.1–3 (1980): 41–83.

5. *Hou Han shu*, 8: 340. For an excellent study of the Hongdu Gate school, see David R. Knechtges, "Court Culture in the Late Eastern Han: The Case of the Hongdu Gate School," in *Interpretation and Literature in Early Medieval China*, ed. Alan K. L. Chan and Yuet-Keung Lo (Albany: State University of New York Press, 2010), 9–40.

6. These questions are raised by Knechtges and Howard L. Goodman's observation that a tendency of more versatile and polymath literati culture arose since the Eastern Han in their "Court Culture in the Late Eastern Han" and "Chinese Polymaths, 100–300 AD: The Tung-kuan, Taoist Dissent, and Technical Skills," *Asia Major* (third series) 18.1 (2005): 101–74, respectively.

7. In addition to other issues, Eastern Han emperors faced a more complex and balanced bureaucratic system than ever. See Hans Bielenstein, "The Institutions of Later Han," in *The Cambridge History of China, Vol. 1, The Ch'in and Han Empires, 221 B.C.–A.D. 220*, ed. Denis Twitchett and Michael Loewe (Cambridge: Cambridge University Press, 1987), 517–19.

8. For well-accepted views of the great families, see Patricia Ebrey, "The Economic and Social History of Later Han," in *The Cambridge History of China, Vol. 1, The Ch'in and Han Empires, 221 B.C.–A.D. 220*, ed. Denis Twitchett and Michael Loewe (Cambridge: Cambridge University Press, 1987), 626–48. One of

the most noticeable characteristics of Eastern Han politics is the great families and their influence in local society. For two classic studies about the great families in Eastern Han dynasty, see Yang Lien-sheng 楊聯陞, "Dong Han de haozu," 1007–63; Yü Ying-shih, "Dong Han zhengquan zhi jianli yu shizu daxing zhi guanxi," 209–80. While the former emphasizes great families' tremendous impact on Han economics and politics, the latter focuses on the fundamental role great families played in the establishment of the Eastern Han dynasty. Tada Kensuke 多田狷介, in comparison, studies how great families gained wealth and power in local society. See his *Kan Gi Shin shi no kenkyū* 漢魏晉史の研究 (Studies on the history of Han, Wei, and Jin) (Tokyo: Kyūko shoin, 1999), 3–48. For a comprehensive study of the Eastern Han great families, see Cui Xiangdong 崔向東, *Han dai haozu yanjiu* 漢代豪族研究 (Wuhan: Chongwen, 2003).

9. For the power of great families in Eastern Han society, see Ebrey, "The Economic and Social History of Later Han," 626–48. Tada argues that great families managed to occupy peasants' land and rented it back to them. The former landowners thus became tenant peasants and were left to the great families' mercy. These great families also rented their land, even though this was not their priority, to laborers from other localities. By doing so, they gained great power to control people who worked for them, essentially the local society. This phenomenon broke the direct link between the empire and the populace, and in turn compromised the empire's authority. See his *Kan Gi Shin shi no kenkyū*, 13–14.

10. For major scholarly activities held by the imperial house in the Eastern Han dynasty, see Rafe de Crespigny, "Scholars and Rulers: Imperial Patronage under the Later Han Dynasty," in *Han-Zeit: Festschrift für Hans Stumpfeldt aus Anlaß seines 65. Geburtstages*, ed. Michael Friedrich et al. (Wiesbaden: Harrassowitz, 2006), 57–77. I agree with de Crespigny that "the emperor of China was a focal point of religion, philosophy and scholarship," for the emperor was central in any sense from the perspective of almost everyone in the first two centuries AD. Nevertheless, he did not initiate intellectual transitions all the time, nor can we explain these transitions only by emperors' preferences.

11. Consult Qian Mu, *Guo shi dagang*, 156–58. In the chart, "b" in the parentheses indicates the elder brother of the empress or empress dowager, and "f" indicates the father of the empress or empress dowager.

12. Rafe de Crespigny has made a series of studies on the dynamics of Han, especially the Eastern Han recruitment system, see his "The Recruitment System of the Imperial Bureaucracy of Later Han," *Chung Chi Journal* 6.1 (1966): 67–78; "An Outline of the Local Administration of the Later Han Empire," *Chung Chi Journal* 7.1 (1967): 57–71; "Inspection and Surveillance Officials under the Two Han Dynasties," in *State and Law in East Asia: Festschrift Karl Bünger*, ed. Dieter Eikemeier and Herbert Franke (Wiesbaden: Otto Harrassowitz, 1981), 40–79; and "Recruitment Revisited: The Commissioned Civil Service of the Later Han," *Early Medieval China* 13–14.2 (2008): 1–47. For works with more case studies of recruit-

ment, see Fukui Shigemasa 福井重雅, *Kandai kanri tōyō seido no kenkyū* 漢代官吏登用制度の研究 (Tokyo: Sōbunsha, 1988) and Huang Liuzhu 黃留珠, *Qin Han shijin zhidu* 秦漢仕進制度 (Xi'an: Xibei Daxue, 1985). For a more comprehensive depiction of the recruitment system, see An Zuozhang and Xiong Tieji, *Qin Han guanzhi shi gao*, 796–910, and more recently, Chen Weisong 陳蔚松, *Handai kaoxuan zhidu* 漢代考選制度 (Wuhan: Hubei, 2002).

13. De Crespigny, "The Recruitment System of the Imperial Bureaucracy of Later Han," 71.

14. Ibid., 67.

15. See de Crespigny, "The Recruitment System of the Imperial Bureaucracy of Later Han," 69–70, esp. 68. For a groundbreaking study of the Eastern Han people who were recommended as *xiaolian* 孝廉, or Filial and Incorrupt, a major type of governmental recruitment, and their educational background, see Xing Yitian 邢義田, "Donghan Xiaolian de shenfen Beijing" 東漢孝廉的身份背景, in *Di er jie Zhongguo shehui jingji shi yantaohui lunwenji* 第二屆中國社會經濟史研討會論文集, ed. Xu Zhuoyun 許倬云 (Cho-yun Hsu), Mao Hanguang 毛漢光, and Liu Cuirong 劉翠溶 (Taipei: Hanxue Yanjiu ziliao ji fuwu zhongxin, 1983), 1–56. Also see Huang Liuzhu, *Qin Han shijin zhidu*, 81–157.

16. Michael Loewe, "The Structure and Practice of Government," in *The Cambridge History of China, Vol. 1, The Ch'in and Han Empires, 221 B.C.–A.D. 220*, ed. Denis Twitchett and Michael Loewe (Cambridge: Cambridge University Press, 1987), 464.

17. Hirai Masashi 平井正士 convincingly proves that from Emperor Xuan to Wang Mang's time, the number of high officials with training in the classics gradually increased. According to his statistics, from 87 BC to AD 5, the percentage of people with training in the classics increased from 9.2 percent to 28.6 percent. See his "Kandai ni okeru Juka kanryō no kugyōsō he no shinjun" 漢代に於ける儒家官僚の公卿層への浸潤, in *Rekishi ni okeru minshū to bunka: Sakai Tadao Sensei koki shukuga kinen ronshū* 歴史における民衆と文化: 酒井忠夫先生古稀祝賀記念論集, ed. Sakai Tadao Sensei Koki Shukuga Kinen no Kai 酒井忠夫先生古稀祝賀記念の会 (Tokyo: Kokusho Kankōkai, 1982), 51–65, esp. 55. In his 1985 study, Huang Liuzhu collects 307 cases of *xiaolian* from the Western and Eastern Han. He points out that among 234 cases that have specific mentioning of people's background, people with training in the classics (or in his original phrase, *rusheng* 儒生) and people with both training in the classics and local official experience (or in his original phrase, *ruli* 儒吏) occupy 32.1 percent and 13.2 percent, respectively. See Huang Liuzhu, *Qin Han shijin zhidu*, 142–44. For a handy list of these people including information on their background, see Fukui, *Kandai kanri tōyō seido no kenkyū*, 55–70. As Xing Yitian suggests, the training in the classics and knowledge about Han statutes were the two largest categories in requirements. See his "Donghan Xiaolian de shenfen beijing," 19.

18. For a detailed introduction to Han official and private educational systems, see Yu Qiding 俞啟定 and Shi Kecan 施克燦, *Zhongguo jiaoyu zhidu tongshi* 中國教

育制度通史, *Vol. 1, Xian Qin, Qin, Han* 先秦, 秦漢 (pre-Qin, Qin, Han) in *Zhongguo jiaoyu zhidu tongshi*, ed. Li Guojun 李國鈞 and Wang Bingzhao 王炳照 (Jinan: Shandong jiaoyu, 2000), 255–504. For the local official schools, see ibid., 384–93.

19. See appendix 2.

20. For more information about Academicians' income and careers, see Yu Qiding and Shi Kecan, *Zhongguo jiaoyu zhidu tongshi*, 331–37.

21. Bielenstein, *The Bureaucracy of Han Times*, 138–39.

22. Based on his statistics, Xing Yitian points out that the career path for *xiaolian* candidates was to begin as students of the classics, then becoming minor functionaries in local governments, and then *xiaolian*. See his "Donghan Xiaolian de shenfen beijing," 18–19.

23. As Xing Yitian points out, great political power and cultural privileges were generated from this master-disciple relationship. See his "Donghan Xiaolian de shenfen beijing," 15. For the outcome after studying at the National Academy, see Yu Qiding and Shi Kecan, *Zhongguo jiaoyu zhidu tongshi*, 354–58.

24. Yü Ying-shih, "Dong Han zhengquan zhi jianli yu shizu daxing zhi guanxi," 210–16. As Xing Yitian mentions, while wealth and authority were important, knowledge about the classics was a crucial factor in Eastern Han recruitment. See Xing Yitian, "Donghan Xiaolian de shenfen beijing," 11. Miranda Brown touches on the social relationship among supervisors and subordinates, and among colleagues as reflected in Eastern Han stelae. See her *The Politics of Mourning in Early China* (Albany: State University of New York Press, 2007), 86–94. For a detailed introduction to the relationship between the training in the classics, recommendations, and aspects of literati culture in this context, see Ichimura Sanjirō 市村瓚次郎, *Shina shi kenkyū* 支那史研究 (Tokyo: Shunjusha, 1939), 143–83.

25. For the role local gentry played in the Eastern Han, see Rafe de Crespigny, "Local Worthies: Provincial Gentry and the End of the Later Han," in *Das andere China: Festschrift für Wolfgang Bauer zum 65. Geburtstag*, ed. Helwig Schmidt-Glintzer (Wiesbaden: Harrassowitz, 1995), 533–58.

26. Xing Yitian, "Donghan Xiaolian de shenfen beijing," 18–19, 37.

27. One of the best case studies of these private schools is Yoshikawa Tadao's 吉川忠夫 close examination of Zheng Xuan's school. See his "Tei Gen no gakujuku" 鄭玄の學塾, in *Chūgoku kizokusei shakai no kenkyū* 中國貴族制社會の研究, ed. Kawakatsu Yoshio 川勝義雄 and Tonami Mamoru 礪波護 (Kyoto: Kyōto Daigaku Jinbun kagaku kenkyūjo, 1987), 321–59. Yoshikawa notices that increasing social mobility led to the flourishing of private schools, which in turn compromised the popularity of the National Academy. See ibid., 351.

28. The local schools can be roughly divided into "official" and "private," though the latter type usually needed permission from the local government. For many aspects of private schools in the Eastern Han, see Zhang Hequan 張鶴泉, "Donghan shidai de sixue" 東漢時代的私學, *Shixue jikan* 1 (1993): 54–59. Many official schools sponsored by local governments played a crucial role in providing

basic knowledge and literacy to local societies as well as training local officials and clerks. See Yu Qiding and Shi Kecan, *Zhongguo jiaoyu zhidu tongshi*, 379–99. I will not specifically discuss this type of school, since their curriculum often dealt with literacy, moral value, etiquette, and statutes. See ibid., 403–12. However, it is worth remembering that these local official schools provided the foundation for higher education.

29. For anecdotes about students bonding, see Yu Qiding and Shi Kecan, *Zhongguo jiaoyu zhidu tongshi*, 353.

30. Ibid., 343–46.

31. See Sahara Yasuo 佐原康夫, "Kandai no ichi ni tsute" 漢代の市について, *Shirin* 68.5 (1985): 33–71, esp. 44–46.

32. See Ma Duanlin's 馬端臨 (AD 1254–1323) study on this issue and a prototype of a recommendation letter preserved in his *Wenxian tongkao* 文獻通考. Ma Duanlin, "Xuexiao kao" 學校考, in *Wenxian tongkao* 文獻通考, ed. Shanghai Shifan Daxue Guji Yanjiu Suo 上海師範大學古籍研究所 and Huadong Shifan Daxue Guji Yanjiu Suo 華東師範大學古籍研究所 (Beijing: Zhonghua, 2011), 40: 1184. Also see Yu Qiding and Shi Kecan, *Zhongguo jiaoyu zhidu tongshi*, 337–42. Yu and Shi point out that while Western Han recruitment emphasized transmission lineage, it was no longer the case in the Eastern Han dynasty. See ibid., 338.

33. *Hou Han shu*, 79a: 2545.

34. *Han shu*, 36: 1968. We can find the grouping of the four traditions in the "Zan" 贊 part of the *Rulin zhuan* 儒林傳 in *Han shu*, in which case Ban Gu not only narrated the establishment of the four traditions during Emperor Ping's time, but also gave his explanation of the establishment. *Han shu*, 88: 3621. This has been pointed out by Michael Nylan, "The *chin wen/ku wen* Controversy in Han Times," *T'oung Pao* 80.1–3 (1994): 91–107. For a summary of Nylan's argument as well as its scholarly context, see appendix 3.

35. *Hou Han shu*, 3: 145.

36. *Hou Han shu*, 69b: 2573.

37. *Hou Han shu*, 53: 1746–8; 82a: 2717, and 67: 2201.

38. *Hou Han shu*, 82a: 2721, 2724.

39. For a family tradition of medical texts, see Nathan Sivin, "Text and Experience in Classical Chinese Medicine," in *Knowledge and the Scholarly Medical Traditions*, ed. Don Bates (Cambridge: Cambridge University Press, 1995), 177–204.

40. For a comprehensive study of the Kong family tradition and their lineage, see Huang Huaixin 黃懷信 et al., *Han Jin Kongshi jiaxue yu "weishu" gongan* 漢代孔氏家學與"偽書"公案 (Xiamen: Xiamen Daxue, 2011), esp. 36–38, 41–42, 53–58, 120–01, 131–56.

41. *Hou Han shu*, 37: 1255, 1257.

42. *Hou Han shu*, 45: 1517–23.

43. *Hou Han shu*, 54:1760, 1769, 1776, 1786.

44. *Hou Han shu*, 37: 1257, 1259.

45. *Hou Han shu*, 79b: 2571–2, 26: 893–94.

46. *Hou Han shu*, 44: 1500–01.

47. For more examples, Wa Dan's 洼丹 (29 BC–AD 41) family passed on the Meng tradition of the *Changes* for generations. After receiving the Yan 嚴 tradition of Gongyang from Fan Tiao 樊鯈 (?–AD 67), Zhang Ba 張霸 (fl. AD 89–106) passed it down to his son Zhang Kai 張楷 (AD 80–149), who formed a popular local academy in Hongnong. Qiao Xuan 橋玄 (AD 109–183) came from a family with a tradition of the *Rites*. Their tradition can be traced back to seven generations earlier, when his ancestor Qiao Ren 橋仁 (fl. 49 BC–AD 2) was a disciple of Dai De 戴德 (fl. 73–49 BC), the founder of the Younger Dai tradition. *Hou Han shu*, 79a: 2551; 36, 1242–43; 51: 1695.

48. Another possible pair is Liu Xin's favorite student, Kong Fen 孔奮 (fl. 13 BC–AD 36), who received the Zuo tradition from him, and his son Kong Jia 孔嘉 (ca. first century AD), the author of the *Explication of the Zuo* (*Zuoshi shuo* 左氏說). *Hou Han shu*, 36: 1217, 1224, 1234–39.

49. *Hou Han shu*, 31: 1098.

50. *Hou Han shu*, 36: 1224.

51. See chapter 3, 79.

52. *Hou Han shu*, 35: 1201–03.

53. *Hou Han shu*, 36: 1226–29.

54. *Hou Han shu*, 79b: 2582.

55. *Hou Han shu*, 37: 1249.

56. Huang Huaixin 黃懷信, *Han Jin Kong shi jia xue yu "weishu" gongan*, 138, 156.

57. Zhang Hequan points out several advantages of private schools, such as lower expectations regarding one's economic condition, no particular geographical requirement, and no requirement for age in his "Donghan shidai de sixue," 57–58. For the academic and economic requirements for students in general, see Yu Qiding and Shi Kecan, *Zhongguo jiaoyu zhidu tongshi*, 424–28. For details about examinations at the National Academy, see Yu Qiding and Shi Kecan, *Zhongguo jiaoyu zhidu tongshi*, 354–58.

58. They were more specifically known as the "minor nobles of the four surnames" (*sixing xiaohou* 四姓小侯): Fan 樊, Guo 郭, Yin 陰, and Ma 馬. For more information about the *sixing xiaohou*, see the commentary on the phrase in *Hou Han shu*, 2: 113.

59. *Hou Han shu*, 45: 1528.

60. *Hou Han shu*, 37: 1250.

61. *Hou Han shu*, 54: 1760–61.

62. *Hou Han shu*, 65: 2138.

63. For a very brief introduction to the organization of these schools, see Yu Qiding and Shi Kecan, *Zhongguo jiaoyu zhidu tongshi*, 417–24.

64. *Hou Han shu*, 79b: 2582–83.

65. For the management and pedagogy at private schools, especially that of Ma Rong, see Yu Qiding and Shi Kecan, *Zhongguo jiaoyu zhidu tongshi*, 432–35.

66. *Hou Han shu*, 35: 1207; 60a: 1972.

67. Yoshikawa Tadao, "Tei Gen no gakujuku," 341–51.

68. *Hou Han shu*, 35: 1207; 64: 2113.

69. Liu Zhen 劉珍 et al., Wu Shuping 吳樹平, ed., *Dongguan Han ji jiaozhu* 東觀漢記校注 (Beijing: Zhonghua, 2008), 13: 493.

70. Yoshikawa Tadao, "Tei Gen no gakujuku," 328–30.

71. *Hou Han shu*, 36: 1241–42.

72. For more information about Qianwei, see the section "The Spread of Apocryphal Texts."

73. Liu Zhen 劉珍 et al., Wu Shuping, ed., *Dongguan Han ji jiaozhu*, 13: 512. The measure word *duan* 端 for cloth, which is the equivalent of two *zhang*, only indicates length.

74. See Lin Ganquan, ed., *Zhongguo jingji tongshi: Qin Han jingji juan*, 571. For a more specialized study in the price of goods in Han China, especially in the northwestern regions, see Ding Bangyou 丁邦友, *Handai wujia xintan* 漢代物價新探 (Beijing: Shehui kexue, 2009).

75. Lin Ganquan, ed., *Zhongguo jingji tongshi: Qin Han jingji juan*, 575.

76. *Hou Han shu*, 37: 1249.

77. *Hou Han shu*, 76: 2458.

78. Also, Hou Jin 侯瑾 (fl. AD 190), a poor native of Dunhuang commandery, did hired labor during the day and used his spare time to read. *Hou Han shu*, 68: 2229; 80b: 2649.

79. Wang Jia 王嘉, *Shiyi ji* 拾遺記, *Siku quanshu*, vol. 1042 (Shanghai: Guji, 1987), 6: 344. Regarding Ren An's mother, see Chang Qu 常璩, "Xianxian shinü zong zan 先賢士女總贊, Ren Naiqiang 任乃強 annotated, *Huayang guo zhi jiaobu tuzhu* 華陽國志校補圖注 (Shanghai: Guji, 1987), 10b: 579.

80. A set of rules in *Guanzi* partly reflects Han people's expectations of how disciples should behave in daily life at school. See Li Xiangfeng 黎翔鳳 annotated, *Guanzi jiaozhu* 管子校注 (Beijing: Zhonghua, 2004), 1144–65. For the date of "Dizi zhi," I follow Luo Genze 羅根澤, who believes it as a work of the Western Han dynasty. For an introduction to authenticity, date, translations, and modern studies of *Guanzi*, see W. Allyn Rickett, "*kuan tzu* 管子," in *Early Chinese Texts: A Bibliographical Guide*, ed. Michael Loewe (Berkeley: University of California Press, 1993), 244–51. For the date of every single chapter of the *Guanzi*, see Luo Genze, "*Guanzi* tanyuan" 《管子》探源, in Luo Genze 羅根澤, *Luo Genze shuo zhuzi* 羅根澤說諸子 (Shanghai: Guji, 2001), 285–368. Luo's date of "Dizi zhi" is in ibid., 353–54.

81. See chart 1, 10.

82. *Hou Han shu*, 43: 1479. For the dress code of the mourning period, see, e.g., "Sangfu xiao ji" 喪服小記 and "Sang da ji" 喪大記, *liji zhushu*, j. 32, 44 and 45, in Ruan Yuan, ed., *Shisan jing zhushi*, 1494–97, 1571–85. For a more dramatic

case about Li Gu, where his students risked their life to pick up his corpse, see *Hou Han shu*, 63: 2088.

83. For more cases in which students or former subordinates practiced a three-year mourning period, projecting the deceased as their father, see Ichimura Sanjirō, *Shina shi kenkyū*, 177–79. As Washio mentions, the interrelationship Han promoted was based on the comparison to that of kinship. See Washio Yūkō 鷲尾祐子, "Zenkan no ninkan tōyō to shakaichitsujo" 前漢の任官登用と社会秩序 in *Chūgoku kodaishi ronsō dai 5 sū* 中國古代史論叢第5集, ed. Ritsumeikan Tōyō Shigakkai Chūgoku Kodaishi Ronsō Henshū Iinkai 立命館東洋史學會中國古代史論叢編集委員會 (Kyoto: Ritsumeikan Tōyō Shigakkai, 2008), 69. As Zhang Hequan mentions, their relationship between a teacher and a student is far more complex than teaching and receiving knowledge. In fact, he points out, they have the master and subordinate relationship. See his "Donghan shidai de sixue," 58–59, 31.

84. A letter written by Zhang Hong preserved in *Wu lu* 吳录, quoted by Pei Songzhi 裴松之 in the commentary of Chen Shou 陳壽, *Sanguo zhi* 三國志 (Beijing: Zhonghua, 1959), 46: 1106.

85. See the section "The Classicists and Prophets from Liu Xiu's Group," 72–74.

86. Yoshikawa Tadao authored a groundbreaking study on Yang Hou's 楊厚 apocryphal lineage in the Shu region: Yoshikawa Tadao 吉川忠夫, "Shoku ni okeru shin'i no gaku no dentō" 蜀における讖緯の學の傳統, in *Shin'i shisō no sōgōteki kenkyū* 讖緯思想の綜合的研究, ed. Yasui Kōzan (Tokyo: Kokusho kankōkai, 1984), 103–36. Based on Yoshikawa's research, Michael J. Farmer gives a resourceful portrayal of general intellectual trends of the Eastern Han in the Sichuan area. See his *The Talent of Shu: Qiao Zhou and the Intellectual World of Early Medieval Sichuan* (Albany: State University of New York Press, 2007), 15–30. While I have benefited greatly from their focus on lineage transmission, I will examine the dynamics between travel and the spread of knowledge.

87. *Hou Han shu*, 79b: 2573–75. According to John Lagerwey, the received version of the *Wu Yue Chunqiu* is at least an abridged version of Zhao Ye's original one. For more information about the received version of *Wu Yue Chunqiu* and its relation to Zhao Ye's original one, see John Lagerwey, "*Wu Yüeh ch'un ch'iu* 吳越春秋," in *Early Chinese Texts: A Bibliographical Guide*, ed. Michael Loewe (Berkeley: University of California Press, 1993), 473–76.

88. For a more complete transmission line from Yang Tong's father Yang Chunqing 楊春卿 to Qiao Zhou 譙周 (ca. AD 201–270), and Yang's family tradition, see Yoshikawa, "Shoku ni okeru shin'i no gaku no dentō," 106–18, 132.

89. *Hou Han shu*, 30a: 1048.

90. *Hou Han shu*, 79a: 2551; 82a: 2734.

91. Sima Biao, "Jun Guo wu" 郡國五, *Hou Han shu zhi*, 23: 3509.

92. *Hou Han shu*, 86: 2845; 48: 1607, 1614, and 79b: 2588. Ying Fen abridged materials from *Shiji*, *Han shu*, and *Han ji* 漢紀 to make a text called *Han*

shi 漢事 (Affairs of Han). His son, Ying Shao 應劭 was a famous scholar at the end of the Eastern Han and also the author of *Fengsu tong* 風俗通, or the *Comprehensive Meaning of Customs*.

93. *Hou Han shu*, 63:2073, and Xie Cheng 謝承, *Hou Han shu*, preserved in Li Xian's commentary in *Hou Han shu*, 63: 2073.

94. *Hou Han shu*, 82a: 2721.

95. Ibid.

96. *Hou Han shu*, 81: 2688–89.

97. *Hou Han shu*, 27: 934–35.

98. Ibid., 625.

99. *Hou Han shu*, 36: 1229–30.

100. Liu Zhen et al., Wu Shuping ed., *Dongguan Han ji jiaozhu*, 12: 451.

101. *Hou Han shu*, 36: 1228, 1233; 15: 573.

102. *Hou Han shu*, 36: 1228; 79b: 2555.

103. *Hou Han shu*, 79a: 2559–60, 2564.

104. *Hou Han shu*, 37: 1263.

105. For Eastern Han literati's increasing interest in *Laozi*, see Mark Laurent Asselin, *A Significant Season: Cai Yong (ca. 133–192) and His Contemporaries* (New Haven: American Oriental Society, 2010), 110–17.

106. For example, Zheng Xuan came to Ma Rong's attention when Ma Rong and his senior students discussed apocryphal texts. *Hou Han shu*, 35: 1207; 60a: 1972. Also, Ma Rong's disciple Lu Zhi transmitted *Huainanzi*, which suggests that Ma taught *Huainanzi* at his academy.

107. "Wu Rong bei 武榮碑," in Gao Wen 高文 annotated, *Han Bei jishi* 漢碑集釋 (Collected explanations of Han steles) (Kaifeng: Henan Daxue, 1997), 295. The original classical Chinese sentences and a literal translation are: 君諱榮，字含和。治《魯詩經韋君章句》。闕幘，傳講《孝經》、《論語》、《漢書》、《史記》、《左氏》、《國語》。(Lord Wu's first name is Rong, style name Hanhe. He worked on Master Wei's Chapter and Verse on the Lu tradition of the *Poetry*. Before capped, he transmitted and taught the *Classic of Filial Piety*, *Analects*, the *History of Han*, the *Grand Historian's Records*, the Zuo tradition, and the *Speeches of the States*.)

108. *Hou Han shu*, 49: 1629.

109. *Hou Han shu*, 60a: 1953, 1972. The original classical Chinese sentences and a literal translation are: 賈君精而不博，鄭君博而不精。既精既博，吾何加焉！(While Mr. Jia is refined but not comprehensive, Mr. Zheng's work is comprehensive but not refined. They are refined and comprehensive [together]. What can I add to their works?)

110. Ibid.

111. He is the author of Chunqiu *Zuoshi zhuanjie* 春秋左氏傳解. *Hou Han shu*, 79b: 2583.

112. The original classical Chinese sentences and a literal translation are: 吾久欲注，尚未了。聽君向言，多與吾同。今當盡以所注與君。(I have desired to comment but

have not finished it yet. I heard what you have just said. It is similar to mine. Now I should give all of which I commented to you.) Liu Yiqing 劉義慶, Liu Xiaobiao 劉孝標 annotated, Zhu Zhuyu 朱鑄禹, ed., "Wenxue" 文學 (Literariness), *Shishuo xinyu hui jiao ji zhu* 世說新語彙校集注 (Shanghai: Guji, 2002), 1: 171.

113. *Hou Han shu*, 49: 1629.

114. For the state of oral tradition, manuscript culture, and literacy around AD 1, see Nylan, *Yang Xiong and the Pleasures of Reading and Classical Learning in China*, 48–61.

115. For the rise of writing culture in the first three hundred years AD, see Inoue Susumu 井上進, *Chūgoku shuppan bunkashi: shomotsu sekai to chi no fūkei* 中國出版文化史―書物世界と知の風景 (Nagaya: Nagoya Daigaku Shuppankai, 2002), 31–58. For an introduction to manuscript culture from the Warring States period to the late Western Han, see Nylan, *Yang Xiong and the Pleasures of Reading and Classical Learning in China*, 32–47. Nylan correctly points out the transition from archives to library, and the crucial role it played in increasing accessibility to manuscripts. For studies of how Han paperwork worked in the Han bureaucratic system, see Tomiya Itaru 富谷至, *Bunsho gyōsei no kan teikoku: mokkan chikukan no jidai* 文書行政の漢帝國―木簡竹簡の時代 (Nagayo: Nagoya Daigaku Shuppankai, 2010).

116. For the communicative function of letters to keep social solidarity, see Patrizia Violi, "Letters," in *Discourse and Literature*, ed. Teun A. van Dijk (Amsterdam: Benjamins, 1985), 149–68. For a pioneering study of epistolary culture in early medieval China, see Antje Richter, "Beyond Calligraphy: Reading Wang Xizhi's Letters," *T'oung Pao* 96 (2011): 370–407.

117. For a pioneering study of paper's impact on Eastern Han scholarship, see Shimizu Shigeru 清水茂, "Kami no hatsumei to Gokan no gakufū" 紙の發明と後漢の學風, *Tōhōgaku* 79 (1990): 1–13. For information about the technology of papermaking, archeological evidence, and the issue of Cai Lun, see Tsien Tsuen-hsuin, *Chemistry and Chemical Technology*, vol. 5 of Joseph Needham, ed., *Science and Civilisation in China* (Cambridge: Cambridge University Press, 1985), 38–41, and more up-to-date, Pan Jixing 潘吉星, *Zhongguo zaozhi shi* 中國造紙史 (Shanghai: Renmin, 2009), 56–66, 112–29.

118. Michael Nylan points out that calligraphy as an art did not emerge from the distinctive features of the Chinese writing system but from changes in "high culture's attitude" in the late Eastern Han. See her "Calligraphy: The Sacred Test and Text of Culture," in *Character and Context in Chinese Calligraphy*, ed. Cary Y. Liu et al. (Princeton: Princeton University Art Museum, 1999), 19.

119. For reflections on making friends revealed by literary works of late Eastern Han literati, see Asselin, *A Significant Season*, 135–53. Miranda Brown also discusses friendship mentioned in Eastern Han stelae in her *The Politics of Mourning in Early China* (Albany: State University of New York Press, 2007), 94–96.

120. The dominance of imperial harem families and eunuchs marked the rest of the Eastern Han dynasty after Emperor Ming. See Qian Mu 錢穆, *Guo shi*

dagang 國史大綱 (Beijing: Shangwu, 1996), 156–68. For a comprehensive description of political conflicts among various parties, see Lü Simian, *Qin Han shi*, 263–82, 305–14. For a study of the imperial harem family during Emperor Huan's time, see Rafe de Crespigny, "The Harem of Emperor Huan: A Study of Court Politics in Later Han," *Papers on Far Eastern History* 12 (1975): 1–42. The major reason why eunuchs were involved in this situation is that younger emperors usually relied on them to fight against the imperial harem families. See Qian Mu's chart, in *Guo shi dagang*, 158. However, even when the eunuchs succeeded in helping the emperor to win the conflict temporarily, their special role in the bureaucracy prevented them from further celebrating their victory. This is probably why, in the eyes of literati, there were always eunuchs abusing their power. This illegitimate power of eunuchs is institutionally related to the emperor's centralized power. This is especially clear from a comparative perspective. See Maria H. Dettenhofer, "Eunuchs, Women, and Imperial Courts," in *Rome and China: Comparative Perspectives on Ancient World Empires*, ed. Walter Scheidel (New York: Oxford University Press, 2009), 83–99, esp. 98.

121. See Rafe de Crespigny, "Political Protest in Imperial China: The Great Proscription of Later Han," *Papers on Far Eastern History* 11 (1975): 3–15. Also see Qian Mu, *Guo shi dagang*, 176–84, and Lü Simian, *Qin Han shi*, 289, for a more detailed description. For the National Academy students' appeal to a sagely rule and ideal society, see Yoshikawa Tadao, "Tōko to gakumon," 72–79.

122. *Hou Han shu*, 59: 1897.

123. For Wang Fu and his work *Qianfu lun* 潛夫論, see Ch'en Ch'i-yün and Margaret Pearson, "*Ch'ien fu lun* 潛夫論," in *Early Chinese Texts: A Bibliographical Guide*, ed. Michael Loewe (Berkeley: University of California Press, 1993), 12–15. For a partial translation of *Qianfu lun*, textual studies, and a discussion of the genre *lun*, see Anne Behnke Kinney, *The Art of the Han Essay: Wang Fu's* Ch'ien-fu lun (Tempe: Arizona State University Center for Asian Studies, 1990). By comparing works of *lun* in the Han dynasty, Kinney correctly points out one of the main characteristics of the genre: "it comments on contemporary events and ideas, rather than leaning towards classical exegesis." See her summary on the characteristics of this genre, ibid., 90.

For a study of Wang Wu's attitude toward divination and the important role morality should play in it, see Anne Behnke Kinney, "Predestination and Prognostication in the *Ch'ien-fu lun*," *Journal of Chinese Religions* 19 (1991): 27–45.

124. *Hou Han shu*, 49: 1630; 52: 1722.

125. Dou Zhang was appointed to be a Gentleman Collating Books (Jiaoshu Lang 校書郎) in the Dongguan library in the early years of Yongchu's 永初 reign (AD 107–113); Ma Rong started with the same position in AD 110. Both Zhang Heng and Cui Yuan traveled to Luoyang. The former became the Grand Historian and stayed in Luoyang. The latter became famous after studying under Jia Kui. The only unclear case is Wang Fu, whose career was obscure in the primary sources. *Hou Han shu*, 23: 821, 52: 1722, and 59: 1940.

126. For the history and function of the Dongguan library in the Eastern Han dynasty, see Goodman, "Chinese Polymaths, 100–300 AD," 112–16.

127. Although they were friends, I did not link Dou Zhang, Zhang Heng, Cui Yuan, and Wang Fu together in chart 12 for the sake of readability.

128. A mature epistolary system for personal use in the Eastern Han was related to the great reliance on letters in the Han administrative system. See Kōmura Takeyiki, "Kandai bunsho giōsei ni okeru shoshin no ichizuke," 1–33.

129. Dou Zhang's style name.

130. The letter, originally from *Ma Rong ji* 馬融集 under the name "Yu Dou Boxiang shu 與竇伯向書" is preserved in Li Xian's commentary in *Hou Han shu*, 23: 821.

131. This is described in Ma Rong's letter in ibid.

132. David Pattinson points out that letters in the Han dynasty were not so much an exchange of intimate information between two individuals as part of public life, since letters were expected to be circulated. See David Pattinson, "Privacy and Letter Writing in Han and Six Dynasties China," in *Chinese Concepts of Privacy*, ed. Bonnie S. McDougall and Anders Hansson (Leiden: Brill, 2002), 97, 113, 118.

133. *Ming* is probably a wrong character for *mei* 每.

134. The letter is preserved in Lu Ji's 陸績 (AD 187–219) preface to the *Classic of Supreme Mystery*. See Yang Xiong 揚雄, Sima Guang 司馬光 annotated, Liu Shaojun 劉韶君, ed., *Tai xuan ji zhu* 太玄集注 (Beijing: Zhonghua, 1998), 229–30.

135. For an introduction to the text, its authenticity, editions, content, and modern scholarship, see Michael Nylan, "*T'ai hsüan ching* 太玄經," in *Early Chinese Texts: A Bibliographical Guide*, ed. Michael Loewe (Berkeley: University of California Press, 1993), 460–66. For a study of the significance of the *Supreme Mystery* in Han China and its reception in later times, see ibid., and Sivin, "The First Neo-Confucianism," 1–42.

136. For Zhang Heng's scholarly interest, see the next sections.

137. Marcel Mauss, E. E. Evans-Pritchard, trans., *The Gift: Forms and Functions of Exchange in Archaic Societies* (New York: Norton, 1967), 1–2, 46–62. For gift-giving and social networking based on "greeting tablets," or *ci* 刺 and *ye* 謁, found in excavated texts, see Maxim Korolkov, "'Greeting Tablets' in Early China: Some Traits of the Communicative Etiquette in Light of Newly Excavated Inscriptions," *T'oung Pao* 4–5 (2012): 295–348.

138. This assumption is from the use of the word *zhi* 贄, a gift one gentleman gave to the another during visiting. See Fan Ye's use of this word and Li Xian's commentary in *Hou Han shu*, 52: 1732. Another example comes from an anecdote of Tai Tong 臺佟 (fl. AD 76–84) in *Hou Han shu*, 83: 2770.

139. *Hou Han shu*, 80a: 2617.

140. Yu Shinan 虞世南, *Beitang shuchao* 北堂書鈔, in *Tangdai sida leishu* 唐代四大類書, ed. Dong Zhian 董治安 (Beijing: Qinghua, 2003), 104: 439c.

141. This assumption is also based on the fact that in many cases paper was used for letters in the Eastern Han. Paper nevertheless was probably still expensive compared to wooden and bamboo slips, since after all the book was a gift.

142. For a comprehensive evaluation of Ma Rong's life and scholarship, see Ikeda Shūzō 池田秀三, "Ba Yū shiron" 馬融私論, *Tōhō gakuhō* 52 (1980): 243–84.

143. Cheng Nanzhou, *Dong Han shidai zhi* Chunqiu Zuoshi xue, 197.

144. Liu Zhen et al., Wu Shuping, ed., *Dongguan Han ji jiaozhu*, 12: 451.

145. *Hou Han Shu*, 60a: 1953. *Jia* 家 is an extremely perplexing word in the field of early China. For generations of debates on this word and relevant issues, see what is, so far, the most comprehensive review, Li Rui 李銳, "*Liujia, jiuliu yu baijia*: Xifang Hanxue jie xiangguan yanjiu shuping" 六家，九流與百家—西方漢學界相關研究述評, *Zhongguo xueshu* 30 (2011): 371–413. For a study that reflects contemporary Western scholars' consensus on this issue, see Kidder Smith, "Sima Tan and the Invention of Daoism, 'Legalism,' 'et cetera,'" *Journal of Asian Studies* 62.1 (2003): 129–56. I follow most scholars' understanding that Sima Tan and most Han writers used *jia* in a way to divide different kinds of thought without necessarily considering them as philosophical lineages or schools with traceable transmission lines. In this case specifically, the word *jia* simply indicates works by various ancient masters such as Han Feizi, Mozi, among others.

146. *Hou Han shu*, 24: 859. *Jianwu zhuji* was later incorporated into the *Dongguan Han ji* 東觀漢記. For the process of incorporation and information about the *Dongguan Han ji*, see Hans Bielenstein and Michael Loewe, "*Tung kuan Han chi* 東觀漢記," in *Early Chinese Texts: A Bibliographical Guide*, ed. Michael Loewe (Berkeley: University of California Press, 1993), 471–72, and Goodman, "Chinese Polymaths, 100–300 AD," 116–22.

147. As the source says: "*bo guan qun ji* 博觀群籍" ([He] broadly read numerous texts). *Hou Han shu*, 24: 862.

148. Ibid. For an introduction to the *Jiu zhang suanshu*, see Christopher Cullen, "*Chiu chang suan shu*" 九章算術, in *Early Chinese Texts: A Bibliographical Guide*, ed. Michael Loewe (Berkeley: University of California Press, 1993), 16–23. According to the received version, the text provides arithmetic problems and answers framed in daily activities, such as agricultural field mensuration, harvests, salaries, and taxes. Ma Xu's contemporary Zheng Zhong was also interested in the text, and he explicated it. See ibid., 16–18.

149. The original classical Chinese phrase is *bo tong jingji* 博通經籍. In *Hou Han shu*, *jingji* can mean both "texts of classics" and the genetic term for "texts" based on context. I read it here as the latter meaning, since Ma Rong was interested in making commentary on many texts besides classics. *Hou Han shu*, 60a: 1953.

150. *Hou Han shu*, 80a: 2617.

151. *Hou Han shu*, 60a: 1972, 79a: 2554, 79b: 2577.

152. Ikeda Shūzō points out that Ma Rong had the tendency to systematize the classics. See his "Ba Yū shiron," 274.

153. Ma Rong did take Deng Zhi's 鄧騭 (?–AD 121) job offer in order to save his own life, and he claimed that his choice went along with Laozi and Zhuangzi's teaching. *Hou Han shu*, 60a: 1954. Nevertheless, there is no extant allusion to Ma Rong's attitude toward these texts. However, we can get a better understanding of some of them by at least examining how his contemporaries viewed them. For example, Gao You 高誘 (fl. AD 205), a disciple of Ma Rong's student Lu Zhi, continued his teacher's commentary of *Huainanzi*. In the preface to it, he mentioned that previous worthy men and erudite scholars used this work to "test," or *yan* 驗, the classics and their commentaries. See "Xu mu 敘目," in He Ning, ed., *Huainanzi jishi*, 6. For "Li sao," in his preface to *Chuci zhangju* 楚辭章句, Wang Yi 王逸 (ca. AD 89–158) argues that the general idea of "Li sao" is based on the Five Classics, and that is why it is so magnificent (夫《离骚》之文，依托五经以立义焉). See Wang Yi's preface to "Li Sao" in Hong Xingzu 洪興祖 annotated, *Chuci Buzhu* 楚辭補註 (Beijing: Zhonghua, 1983), 1: 49. For the most recent study of "Li sao" and Wang Yi's commentary, especially about why he wrote this commentary and how the commentary fit into the Later Han exegetical context, see Gopal Sukhu, *The Shaman and the Heresiarch: A New Interpretation of the* Li sao (Albany: State University of New York Press, 2012), 5–8, 39–70. For a study of commentarial traditions of the Han as reflected in Wang Yi's work and the Han's interest in commenting on the Chu lyrics in general, see Kominami Ichirō 小南一郎, "O Itsu *Soji shoku* omegutte: Kandai shoku no gaku no i sokumon" 王逸「楚辭章句」をめぐって―漢代章句の學の一側面, *Tōhō gakuhō* 63 (1991): 61–114. For Han scholars' studies of the *Huainanzi*, see Ikeda Shūzō 池田秀三, "Kandai no Enangaku: Ryū Kō to Kyo Shin" 漢代の淮南學―劉向と許慎, *Chūgoku shisōshi kenkyū* 11 (1988): 1–27.

154. For the Cui family's literature tradition, see Wu Guimei 吳桂美, *Haozu shehui de wenxue zheguang: Dong Han jiazu wenxue shengtai toushi* 豪族社會的文學折光―東漢家族文學生態透視 (Haerbin: Heilongjinang renmin, 2008), 125–71.

155. *Hou Han shu*, 52: 1703–04.

156. The original classical Chinese for the last two parts is *gujin xungu baijia zhi yan* 古今訓詁百家之言, literally meaning "ancient and contemporary [works of] explanations of words and words of the hundred experts." See *Hou Han shu*, 52: 1708.

157. He was as reputable as famous writers like Ban Gu and Fu Yi 傅毅 (ca. ?–AD 90). See *Hou Han shu*, 52: 1708.

158. By "four," "four directions" is meant. See Li Xian's commentary on this word in *Hou Han shu*, 52: 1719. For the fragments of this work, see Yan Kejun 嚴可均, ed., *Quan Hou Han wen* 全後漢文, *quan shanggu sandai Qin Han Sanguo Liuchao wen* 全上古三代秦漢三國六朝文 (Beijing: Zhonghua, 1958), 44: 713–14.

159. *Hou Han shu*, 52: 1718.

160. Ibid., 1162. For all the received literary works of Cui Yin, see Yan Kejun, ed., *Quan Hou Han wen*, 44: 711–16. Wu Guimei provides lists of the Cui

family members' received works, in which we can clearly see the disappearance of their commentarial tradition. See Wu, *Haozu shehu de wenxue zheguang*, 135–36.

161. *Hou Han shu*, 52: 1722.

162. *Zhi* 执 is cognate to *shi* 势, indicating the shape of characters coming out of this writing style. The title as "Cao shu shi" instead of "Cao shu zhi," is listed in Fang Xuanling 房玄齡 et al., *Jin shu* 晉書 (Beijing: Zhonghua, 1974), 36: 1066.

163. *Hou Han shu*, 64: 2122–23. For "Grass writing" as a fashion in calligraphy and literati culture, see other examples from Emperor Ming's time, such as *Hou Han shu*, 14: 557; 80b: 2652; and 65: 2144. For an introduction to *cao shu*, Chinese calligraphy as a type of art, and its relation to manuscript and printing culture in imperial China, see Frederick W. Mote *et al.*, *Calligraphy and the East Asian Book*, ed. Howard L. Goodman (Boston: Shambhala, 1989), 35–95. For the Grass writing style in Han administrative documents as part of the development of calligraphy, see Tomiya, *Bunsho gyōsei no kan teikoku*, 141–71. Bai Qianqi particularly points out that calligraphy was in circulation via letters in the Eastern Han. See his "Chinese Letters: Private Words Made Public," in *The Embodied Image: Chinese Calligraphy from the John B. Elliot Collection*, ed. Robert E. Harrist and Wen C. Fong (Princeton: The Art Museum, Princeton University, 1999), 381.

164. *Jin shu*, 36: 1066.

165. See Cui Yuan, "Xu zhen 序箴," Yan Kejun, ed., *Quan Hou Han wen*, 45: 717.

166. See Cui Yuan's other admonitions and particularly the frequent references to the Qin dynasty in Yan Kejun, ed., *Quan Hou Han wen*, 45: 717–18.

167. *Hou Han shu*, 52: 1724.

168. See Cui Yuan's extant inscriptions in Yan Kejun, ed., *Quan Hou Han wen*, 45: 719.

169. Michael Nylan, "Toward an Archaeology of Writing: Text, Ritual, and the Culture of Public Display in the Classical Period (475 B.C.E.–220 C.E.)," in *Text and Ritual in Early China*, ed. Martin Kern (Seattle: University of Washington Press, 2005), 26–30, 33.

170. See Zhang Heng's large number of literary works, especially rhapsodies, in Yan Kejun, ed., *Quan Hou Han wen*, 52–54: 759–70. For a comprehensive evaluation of Zhang Heng's rhapsodies, see Gong Kechang 龔克昌, *Han fu yanjiu* 漢賦研究 (Ji'nan: Shandong wenyi, 1990), 231–60. For a translation of Zhang Heng's famous pieces praising the Eastern Han, "Er Jing fu" 二京賦, two rhapsodies about Chang'an and Luoyang, the capital of Western and Eastern Han, respectively, see David R. Knechtges, trans., *Wen xuan or Selections of Refined Literature* (Princeton: Princeton University Press, 1982), 1: 47–148; 181–309. For discussions about these two works together with Ban Gu's similar rhapsodies, "Liang du fu 兩都賦," see E. R. Hughes, *Two Chinese Poets: Vignettes of Han Life and Thought* (Princeton: Princeton University Press, 1960), 221–66. While I agree with Hughes that Ban Gu and Zhang Heng's works express their praise on achievements of the Han dynasty,

I do not believe that Zhang Heng was "Scripture centric" or a "theologian," for Zhang Heng's broad erudition included designing experimental devices, rejection of apocryphal texts, and interest in history. See ibid., 259–60.

171. *Hou Han shu*, 59: 1909. For a brilliant reconstruction of Zhang Heng's seismoscope, see André Wegener Sleeswyk and Nathan Sivin, "Dragons and Toads: The Chinese Seismoscope of A.D. 132," *Chinese Science* 6 (1983): 1–19. Yan Kejun, ed., *Quan Hou Han wen*, 52–55: 759–79.

172. *Hou Han shu*, 59: 1897.

173. Supervisor of the Internuncios is a position to assist at imperial ceremonies and with sending messages. See Bielenstein, *The Bureaucracy of Han Times*, 26.

174. *Hou Han shu*, 80a: 2617.

175. *Hou Han shu*, 59: 1940; 80a: 2617. "Zhang Heng liezhuan" 張衡列傳 puts the project of composing the *Records of the Han* around 107 to AD 113, while "Wenyuan liezhuan" 文苑列傳 places it at AD 120. I follow the latter record, since the former also mentions that Liu Zhen and Liu Taotu died soon thereafter, but other biographies mention Liu Zhen after AD 113. See, for example, *Hou Han shu*, 78: 2513. Also, it seems that, between the two projects that Empress Dowager Deng initiated, Emperor An also initiated a project of editing the classics and official commentarial traditions and chose a eunuch, Cai Lun 蔡倫 (AD 61–121), to supervise this project.

176. For Zhang Heng's excitement to work at Dongguan again, see his letter to Tejin, "Yu Tejin shu" 與特近書, in Yan Kejun, ed., *Quan Hou Han wen*, 54: 773. For what Penglai 蓬萊 means in that letter, see how Zhang's contemporaries referred to Dongguan library in *Hou Han shu*, 23: 821–22.

177. *Hou Han shu*, 59: 1940.

178. Ibid., 1285.

179. Yang Xiong, *Tai xuan ji zhu*, 230. I collated it with another version from Fan Ye, "Zhang Heng liezhuan," *Hou Han shu*, 59: 1897–98. The parts of the text that are missing in the *Tai Xuan ji zhu* are bracketed.

180. The version in *Hou Han shu* is *zuo zhe* 作者 instead of *zuo xing zhe* 作興者. Here it indicates authors. See *Hou Han shu*, 59: 1897.

181. The logic behind this is not obvious to me. Zhang Heng's theory seems to me an allusion to Confucius and his *Annals*. From the beginning of the Spring and Autumn period (722 BC) in the *Annals* to Confucius's death (479 BC), there were 243 years. His work *Annals* became popular in the Han dynasty, which is 206 BC, 273 years later. If this is true, Zhang Heng read the numbers rather roughly.

182. Michael Nylan insightfully points out that Yang Xiong's *Mystery* was a further step from writing commentaries on the *Changes*. See her *The Canon of Supreme Mystery by Yang Hsiung: A Translation with Commentary of the* T'ai Hsüan Ching (Albany: State University of New York Press, 1993), 8. Gong Kechang points out Zhang Heng's use of doctrines in the classics to compose and judge rhapsodies. Gong sees this as an obstacle for the independence of literature. See Gong Kechang,

Han fu yanjiu, 236–37. To me, this is exactly Zhang Heng's project of carrying the spirit of the classics in contemporary writing, which eventually led to the "the self-consciousness of literature," or *wenxue zijue* 文學自覺, as discussed in ibid., 335–50.

183. Collins, *The Sociology of Philosophies*, 790.

184. Ibid.

185. *Hou Han shu*, 54: 1790, 70: 2279. As mentioned by Wu Guimei, literary composition increased significantly at the end of the Eastern Han. See Wu, *Haozu shehu de wenxue zheguang*, 220–21.

186. The phrase to describe their relationship is usually *xiang you shan* 相友善 (to consider each other friends) or *xiang hao* 相好 (to be affectionate with each other). This is extremely observable particularly around Guo Tai in chart 12, where I used single black lines to represent this relationship. See *Hou Han shu*, 67: 2217; 68: 2227.

187. See, for example, *Hou Han shu*, 68, 2225, 2229–30, 2230, 2232. For more material relevant to "discussion," see Liu Jigao 劉季高, *Dong Han Sanguo shiqi de tanlun* 東漢三國時期的談論 (Shanghai: Guji, 1999). While Liu Jigao distinguishes *tanlun* from *qingtan* 清談 (pure talk), I see them as homogeneous. Both of them took the form of personal conversations. However, in the late Eastern Han, the topics of conversation were not specific to metaphysical or ontological issues.

188. See Zheng Xuan's experience on this. *Hou Han shu*, 35: 2111.

Chapter 5

1. See the section "An Abortive Path: Li Xun's Departure from the Classics" of the first chapter, starting on 35.

2. *Hou Han shu*, 20b: 1076, 1083.

3. Demiéville, "Philosophy and Religion from Han to Sui," 816. For a general introduction to the movement, see ibid., 815–20.

4. *Hou Han shu*, 7: 316. For the cult of Laozi at court, see de Crespigny, "The Harem of Emperor Huan: A Study of Court Politics in Later Han." For a detailed study on Emperor Huan's intellectual and political agenda, see de Crespigny, "Politics and Philosophy under the Government of Emperor Huan 159–168 A.D."

5. *Hou Han shu*, 8: 340. For an excellent study of the Hongdu Gate school, see Knechtges, "Court Culture in the Late Eastern Han."

6. See, for example, Chen Chi-yun (陳啟雲), *Hsün Yüeh (A.D. 148–209): The Life and Reflections of an Early Medieval Confucian* (Cambridge: Cambridge University Press, 1975), esp. 30–65; his "Confucian, Legalist, and Taoist Thought in Later Han," in *The Cambridge History of China, Vol. 1, The Ch'in and Han Empires, 221 B.C.–A.D. 220*, ed. Denis Twitchett and Michael Loewe (Cambridge: Cambridge University Press, 1987), 766–807, and Yü Ying-shih, "Individualism and the Neo-Taoist Movement in Wei-Chin China," in *Individualism and Holism*, ed. Donald J. Munro (Ann Arbor: University of Michigan Press, 1985), 121–55.

7. See, for example, Chen Chi-yun, "Confucian, Legalist, and Taoist thought in Later Han," 786–802. Notice the term Chen coins, "Taoist-Confucian," reflects a rather rigid distinction between Confucianism and Daoism common among twentieth-century scholarship. Barbara Hendrischke touches on the root of the *Scripture of the Great Peace* in the Han dynasty intellectual context. See her "The Place of the *Scripture on Great Peace* in the Formation of Taoism," in *Religion and Chinese Society, Volume I: Ancient and Medieval China*, ed. John Lagerwey (Hong Kong: The Chinese University Press, 2004), 249–78.

8. In Ted Robert Gurr's words, the discontent is from "a perceived discrepancy between men's value expectations and their value capabilities." See Ted Robert Gurr, *Why Men Rebel* (Princeton: Princeton University Press, 1970), 13. For discontent in the form of literary works, see Asselin, *A Significant Season*, 54–107.

9. De Crespigny, "Political Protest in Imperial China," 3.

10. Ibid., 8.

11. For political conflicts in Emperor Huan's reign and their consequences, see de Crespigny, "The Harem of Emperor Huan."

12. As de Crespigny mentions, many officials made alliances with eunuchs and imperial harem families such as the Liang without necessarily being stigmatized. See de Crespigny, "Political Protest in Imperial China: The Great Proscription of Later Han," 4, 13.

13. Ibid., 12–13, 23. *Hou Han shu*, 56: 2169.

14. De Crespigny points out that the proscription between AD 169 to 184 broke the literati's hope for reforms and their belief in the Han dynasty. De Crespigny, "Political Protest in Imperial China," 27, 30–34, 35–36.

15. Besides studying the content of his commentaries, Qing scholars already started studying Zheng Xuan, and they usually had three foci: the life of Zheng, his various writings including commentaries, treatises, and letters, and his school especially his disciples. For example, Zheng Zhen's 鄭珍 work representatively reflects such a perspective. See his *Zheng xue lu* 鄭學錄, *Xuxiu siku quanshu* 續修四庫全書 (Shanghai: Guji, 1999), 515: 1–56. Qing scholars were particularly interested in the chronicle of Zheng Xuan's life. See, for example, Chen Zhan 陳鱣, *Zheng jun jinian* 鄭君紀年; Sun Xingyan 孫星衍, *Zheng Sinong nianpu* 鄭司農年譜; and Shen Kepei 沈可培, *Zheng Kangcheng nianpu* 鄭康成年譜, among others, in Guojia Tushuguan, ed., *Han Wei Jin mingren nianpu* 漢魏晉名人年譜 (Beijing: Beijing Tushuguan, 2004), 1: 427–62, 463–554, and 555–622, respectively. Modern scholars such as Zhang Shunhui 張舜徽 and Wang Liqi 王利器 followed this tradition. See Zhang Shunhui, *Zheng xue cong zhu* 鄭學叢著 (Jinan: Qi Lu, 1984), and Wang Liqi, *Zheng Kangceng nianpu* 鄭康成年譜 (Jinan: Qi Lu, 1983). Modern scholarship also piles up on the textual study of Zheng Xuan's commentaries, such as John Makeham, "The Earliest Extant Commentary on *Lunyu: Lunyu Zheng shi zhu*," *T'oung Pao* 83 (1997): 260–99; Yang Tianyu's 楊天宇 *Zheng Xuan Sanli zhu yanjiu* 鄭玄三禮註研究 (Tianjin: Renmin, 2007). However, few scholars pay major attention to Zheng Xuan's larger

agenda in general or his close relationship to apocryphal texts. Two scholarly works made tremendous contributions to these two areas respectively: Mashima Junichi 間嶋潤一, *Jō Gen to* Shurai: *Shū no taihei kokka no kōsō* 鄭玄と「周礼」: 周の太平國家の構想 (Tokyo: Meiji Shoin, 2010), and Lü Kai 呂凱, *Zheng Xuan zhi chenwei xue* 鄭玄之讖緯學 (Taipei: Commercial Press, 1982).

16. At the time such positions tended to be the property of families. *Hou Han shu*, 35: 1207. For more information about Zheng Xuan's family background, see Li Qian's commentary in ibid., 1207, which quotes from *Zheng Xuan bie zhuan* 鄭玄別傳.

17. *Hou Han shu*, 35: 1207. As for Zheng Xuan's knowledge of the *Documents*, see He Ruyue and Michael Nylan, "On a Han-era Postface (Xu 序) to the Documents," *Harvard Journal of Asiatic Studies* 75.2 (2015): 400. Also see appendix 3 in this volume for a fuller picture of Nylan's argument.

18. *Hou Han shu*, 35: 1207.

19. This list is the Five Classics plus the *Analects* and often, but not always, the *Classic of Filial Piety*. See, for example, *Hans shu*, 30: 1703–19, and the commentary in *Hou Han shu*, 60b: 1990.

20. For another case that shows Yellow Turbans' disastrous impact on local society, see Michael J. Farmer, "The Three Chaste Ones of Ba: Local Perspectives on the Yellow Turban Rebellion on the Chengdu Plain," *Journal of the American Oriental Society* 125.2 (2005): 191–202.

21. *Hou Han shu*, 35: 1209–10.

22. Ibid.

23. Ibid., 813.

24. *Hou Han shu*, 35: 2111.

25. See Wang Chong, for example, "Xie duan 謝短," and "Bie tong 別通," Huang Hui 黃暉, ed., *Lun heng jiaoshi* 論衡校釋 (Beijing Zhonghua, 1990), 12: 554–78, and 13: 590–605.

26. *Hou Han shu*, 35: 1207–08.

27. Wang Jia 王嘉, *Shiyi ji* 拾遺記, *Siku quanshu*, vol. 1042 (Shanghai: Guji, 1987), 6: 344.

28. See the section "Liu Xin's Approach to the Original Classics," 30–35.

29. Collins, *The Sociology of Philosophies*, 65.

30. Zheng Xuan's "Liuyi lun" 六藝論 is a lost text. Scholars such as Yan Kejun compiled the fragments of this text together in his *Quan Hou Han wen*, 84: 925–28. For a comprehensive textual study of different scholars' compilation of "Liuyi lun," see Zeng Shengyi 曾聖益, "Zheng Xuan 'Liuyi lun' shi zhong jijiao" 鄭玄《六藝論》十種輯斠, *Guoli Zhongyang Tushuguan Taiwan Fenguan guan kan* 國立中央圖書館臺灣分館館刊 4.1 (1997): 70–93. For an elaborate commentary on the fragments of the "Liuyi lun," see Pi Xirui 皮錫瑞, *"Liuyi lun" shuzheng* 六藝論疏證, *Xuxiu Siku quanshu* 續四庫全書, vol. 171 (Shanghai: Guji, 1995–2002). This work was first published in 1899.

31. Zheng Xuan, "Liuyi lun," in Yan Kejun, ed., *Quan Hou Han wen*, 84: 926.
32. Zheng Xuan, "Liuyi lun," in Yan Kejun, ed., *Quan Hou Han wen*, 84: 927.
33. Ibid., 927.
34. Zheng Xuan, "*Shi* pu Xu" 詩譜序, in Yan Kejun, ed., *Quan Hou Han wen*, 84: 9276.
35. Zheng Xuan, "Liuyi lun," in Yan Kejun, ed., *Quan Hou Han wen*, 84: 927.
36. Similar disparagement existed among learners of the classics since Xunzi's time, calling each other *suru* 俗儒 (vulgar classicist) as opposed to a true classicist. However, here we are dealing with the dichotomy between *ru* 儒 (classicist) and *tongren* 通人 (erudite), which could be found in Wang Chong's writing. Wang clearly stated that the knowledge beyond the classics defined a *tongren*, which in turn was superior to that of a *ru*. See Wang Chong, "Bie tong," *Lun heng*, 13: 590–605.
37. For example, in the compiled fragments of the "Discussion of the Six Arts," he quotes apocryphal texts twice. Zheng Xuan, "Liuyi lun," in Yan Kejun, ed., *Quan Hou Han wen*, 84: 927.
38. Zheng Xuan, "Liuyi lun," in Yan Kejun, ed., *Quan Hou Han wen*, 84: 928.
39. Jia Gongyan 賈公彥, "Xu *Zhouli* fei xing" 序周禮廢興, *Zhouli zhushu*, in Ruan Yuan, ed., *Shisan jing zhushi*, 636. For Zheng Xuan's understanding of how the Duke of Zhou brought the Great Peace, see Mashima Junichi's 間嶋潤一 very elaborate study, *Jō Gen to* Shurai: *Shū no taihei kokka no kōsō*. While Mashima mainly focuses on how the text *Rites of Zhou* is related to the Great Peace brought by the Duke of Zhou, based on Zheng Xuan's commentaries, I am more interested in finding out how Zheng Xuan thought about rites in general and how he applied them to the contemporary world.
40. "Li qi" 禮器, *Liji zhushu*, *j*. 23, in Ruan Yuan, ed., *Shansan jing zhushu*, 1435.
41. Ibid.
42. Confucius's saying in Zheng Xuan's commentary is originally from "Wei zheng" 為政, *Lunyu*, Zhu Xi annotated, *Sishu zhangju jizhu*, *Lunyu jizhu*, 1: 59.
43. See page 1440 and also Zheng's commentary of "Li yun" 禮運, *Liji zhushu*, *j*. 22, in Ruan Yuan, ed., *Shansan jing zhushu*, 1426.
44. Ibid., *j*. 23, in Ruan Yuan, ed., *Shansan jing zhushu*, 1435. The "Li yun" 禮運 text mentions that after following Heaven, auspicious animals such as phoenixes, dragons, and turtles will appear. Zheng Xuan comments: 功成而太平。陰陽氣和而致象物 (The accomplishment is achieved, and then it was the Great Peace. The *yin* and *yang qi* are in harmony, so they attract objects alike.) See "Li qi," *Liji zhushu*, *j*. 24, in Ruan Yuan, ed., *Shansan jing zhushu*, 1440.
45. "Li qi," *Liji zhushu*, *j*. 23, in Ruan Yuan, ed., *Shansan jing zhushu*, 1435.
46. The word *cheng* here is derived from *cheng* 成, meaning "completion" or "self-perfection." This is why in the context Zheng Xuan compared *zhi* 至, meaning "arrival," "extreme," and "perfection" to *cheng*.
47. "Li qi," *Liji zhushu*, *j*. 23, in Ruan Yuan, ed., *Shansan jing zhushu*, 1431.
48. "San zheng" 三正, in Chen Li, ed., *Baihu tong shuzheng*, 8: 360.

49. "Li qi," *Liji zhushu, j.* 24, in Ruan Yuan, ed., *Shansan jing zhushu*, 1440.
50. Ibid.
51. Ibid.
52. See Wang Yi's preface to "Li Sao" in Hong Xingzu 洪興祖 annotated, *Chuci Buzhu* 楚辭補註 (Beijing: Zhonghua, 1983), 1: 49.
53. Yoshikawa mentions that while advocating the return to the original meaning of the Gongyang tradition, He Xiu is not actually a faithful follower of the original tradition. Influenced by the intellectual trend at the National Academy in the 160s, He had his innovative reading of the Gongyang tradition, especially his "Three Eras," or *sanshi* 三世. See Yoshikawa Tadao 吉川忠夫, "Tōko to gakumon: tokuni Ka Kyu no ba'ai" 黨錮と學問—とくに何休の場合, *Tōyōshi kenkyū* 35.3 (1976): 425–26, 429, 432.
54. For an elaborate biography of He Xiu's life, see Huang Pumin 黃樸民, *He Xiu ping zhuan* 何休評傳 (Nanjing: Nanjing daxue, 1998), 1–62.
55. Wang Jia, *Shiyi ji*, 6: 343.
56. *Han shu*, 88: 3617.
57. See Zhang Heng's group in the previous chapter.
58. He Xiu, preface to the Gongyang tradition of the *Annals*, *Chunqiu Gongyang zhushu* 春秋公羊注疏 (Commentaries and Sub-commentaries on the Gongyang Tradition of the *Annals*), in Ruan Yuan, ed., *Shansan jing zhushu*, 2190.
59. Confucius's words in this passage are from Xiaojing *Gouming jue* 孝經鉤命決 and preserved in *Chunqiu Gongyang zhushu* 春秋公羊注疏, *Shisan jing zhushu*, in Ruan Yuan, ed., 2190.
60. He Xiu's commentary, *Chunqiu Gongyang zhuan zhushu*, in Ruan Yuan, ed., *Shisan jing zhushu, j.* 28, 2352.
61. *Han shu*, 30: 1723. See chapter 1, 24–28.
62. *Han shu*, 36: 1967.
63. He Xiu's commentary, *Chunqiu Gongyang zhuan zhushu, j.* 1, in Ruan Yuan, ed., *Shisan jing zhushu*, 2200.
64. Ibid.
65. Ibid.
66. Ibid.
67. Henderson, *Scripture, Canon, and Commentary*, 89.
68. Rising Peace, or *shengping* 升平, was used differently by He Xiu's contemporaries. In his *A Comprehensive Meaning of Customs*, or *Fengsu tongyi* 風俗通義, for example, Ying Shao uses it interchangeably with the term *taiping* 太平, or the Great Peace. In the narration, Ying Shao first quotes a passage in which *shengping* is mentioned. Later on in this narration, he paraphrases the passage and substitute the term *shengping* with *taiping*. See "Zheng shi 正失," Ying Shao 應劭, Wang Liqi 王利器 annotated, *Fengsu tong yi jiaozhu* 風俗通義校注 (Beijing: Zhonghua, 1981), 2: 94, 99.
69. *Chunqiu Gongyang zhuan zhushu, j.* 28, in Ruan Yuan, ed., *Shisan jing zhushu*, 2352.
70. Ibid., 2352–53.

71. He Xiu compared the *qilin* as the symbolic creature of the Great Peace, or *taiping zhi shou* 太平之獸, to the sage Confucius, thus the capture and final death of the *qilin* represented Heaven's sign for the death of Confucius. See *Chunqiu Gongyang zhuan zhushu*, in Ruan Yuan, ed., *Shisan jing zhushu*, *j.* 28, 2353. Li Wai-yee notes a diverse historiography behind different narratives of this incident, namely, the Gongyang, Guliang, and Zuo traditions, and *Shiji*. See her *The Readability of the Past in Early Chinese Historiography* (Cambridge: Harvard University Press, 2007), 411–21.

72. *Chunqiu Gongyang zhuan zhushu*, *j.* 28, in Ruan Yuan, ed., *Shisan jing zhushu*, 2353.

73. Zhou represents the virtue of wood according to the Five Phases.

74. See page 70.

75. Ibid.

76. He Xiu, preface to the Gongyang tradition of the *Annals*, *Chunqiu Gongyang zhushu* 春秋公羊注疏, *Shansan jing zhushu*, in Ruan Yuan, ed., 2191.

77. *Hou Han shu*, 79b: 2583.

78. See the case of our next section's hero Xiang Kai 襄楷 in the passage from Sima Biao 司馬彪, *Jiuzhou chunqiu* 九州春秋, cited by Pei Songzhi in Chen Shou, *Sanguo zhi*, 1: 4.

79. Collins points out opposition as a distinctive pattern in intellectual competitions and innovation in *The Sociology of Philosophies*, 137.

80. For example, *Hou Han shu*, 30b: 1056, 1060.

81. *Chunqiu Gongyang zhuan zhushu*, *j.* 28, in Ruan Yuan, ed., *Shisan jing zhushu*, 2353.

82. For more instances of He Xiu following his predecessors' theories, particularly Dong Zhongshu's interpretation of calamities, Jing Fang's theory, and citing from apocryphal texts, see Huang Zhaoji 黃肇基, *Handai Gongyang xue zaiyi lilun yanjiu* 漢代公羊學災異理論研究 (Taipei: Wenjin, 1998), 189–224, esp. 216–17.

83. Despite the complicated textual issues and dating problems, many modern scholars seek to reveal the thought in the text, such as Lin Fu-shih (林富士), Taiping jing de shenxian guannian"《太平經》的神仙觀念, *Zhongyang Yanjiu Yuan Lishi Yuyan Yanjiu Suo jikan* 80.2 (2009): 217–63; "Shi lun *Taiping jing* de zhuzhi yu xingzhi" 試論《太平經》的主旨與性質, *Zhongyang Yanjiu Yuan Lishi Yuyan Yanjiu Suo jikan* 69.2 (1998): 205–44; and "Shi lun *Taiping jing* de jibing guannian" 試論《太平經》的疾病觀念, *Zhongyang Yanjiu Yuan Lishi Yuyan Yanjiu Suo jikan* 62.2 (1993): 225–63. Lin's "Shi lun *Taiping jing* de zhuzhi yu xingzhi" is particularly focused on the overall perspective and agenda of the *Scripture*. He points out the strong political orientation in the *Scripture*. See Lin, "Shi lun *Taiping jing* de zhuzhi yu xingzhi," 205. Wang Ping 王平 and Jiang Shoucheng 姜守誠 did a monograph-length study on the *Scripture*. The former explores the political agenda and philosophical system inside the text, and the latter is focused on what the *Scripture* says about human beings' life span. See Wang Ping, Taiping jing *yanjiu*《太平經》研究 (Taipei:

Wenjin, 1995), and Jiang Shoucheng, Taiping jing *yanjiu*: *Yi shengming wei zhongxin de zonghe kaocha*《太平經》研究—以生命為中心的綜合考察. Beijing: Shehui kexue wenxian, 2007. Compared to Chinese scholars who more or less treat the *Scripture* as a coherent unity, Western scholars in general are more cautious about the received version of the *Scripture* and treat the received version as an accumulation of various layers throughout history. See Hendrischke, *The Scripture on Great Peace*, 1–54, and Kristofer Schipper, "1. B. 6 The *Taiping jing*," in *The Taoist Canon: A Historical Companion to the* Daozang, ed. Kristofer Schipper and Franciscus Verellen (Chicago: University of Chicago Press, 2004), 1: 277–80; Hendrischke, *The Scripture on Great Peace*, 31–38; and Kaltenmark, "The Ideology of the T'ai-p'ing ching," 10–45. Many Japanese scholars explore the *Scripture* within the context of the Six Dynasties' intellectual world. See, for example, Ōfuchi Ninji 大淵忍爾, *Shoki no dōkyō: Dōkyōshi no kenkyū sono ichi* 初期の道教—道教史の研究其の一 (Tokyo: Sōbunsha, 1991), 77–136; and Kamitsuka Yoshiko 神塚淑子, *Rikuchō Dōkyō shisō no kenkyū* 六朝道教思想の研究 (Tokyo: Sōbunsha, 1999), 301–58. However, none of them work on the relationship between the classics and the *Scripture*.

84. *Hou Han shu*, 30b: 1080, 1083. For a study on Xiang Kai and the text he presented, see Oyanagi Shigeta 小柳司氣太, "*Go Kan jo* Jō Kai den no *Taihei shōryō sho* ni tsuite" 後漢書襄楷傳の太平清領書について, in *Kuwabara Hakushi kanreki kinen Tōyōshi ronsō* 東洋史論叢, ed. Kuwabara Hakushi Kanreki Kinen Shukugakai 桑原博士還曆記念祝賀會 (Kyoto: Kōbundō, 1930), 141–71. There is much controversy on whether and to what extent the *Taiping qingling shu* and *Taiping jing* are the same text. See the next section for more information.

85. *Hou Han shu*, 30b: 1083.

86. For Xun Shuang, and the Xun family as an extremely well-known literatus family in late Eastern Han, see Chen Chi-yun (陳啟雲), *Hsün Yüeh (A.D. 148–209): The Life and Reflections of an Early Medieval Confucian* (Cambridge: Cambridge University Press, 1975), 27–29, 66–83.

87. *Hou Han shu*, 30b: 1085.

88. For an introduction to the Yellow Turban rebellion, see Howard S. Levy, "Yellow Turban Religion and Rebellion at the End of the Han," *Journal of the American Oriental Society* 76 (1956): 214–27; and B. J. Mansvelt Beck, "The Fall of Han," in *The Cambridge History of China, Vol. 1, The Ch'in and Han Empires, 221 B.C.–A.D. 220*, ed. Denis Twitchett and Michael Loewe (Cambridge: Cambridge University Press, 1987), 325–40. Levy does not stress the difference between various religious groups. The Yellow Turbans, for example, were actually very distinctive from Zhang Lu's 張魯 religious community in Sichuan. For information on Zhang Lu's group, which was later labeled as Celestial-Master Daoism, see Howard L. Goodman, "Celestial-Master Taoism and the Founding of the Ts'ao-Wei Dynasty: The Li Fu Document," *Asia Major* 7.1 (1994): 5–33. For the religious background of the Yellow Turban rebellion, see Akizuki Kan'ei 秋月觀暎, "Kōkinnoran no shūkyōsei: Taiheidō tono kanren o chūshin toshite" 黄巾の亂の宗教性：太平道教法との關連を

中心として, *Tōhōshi kenkyū* 15.1 (1956): 43–56. Akizuki insightfully points out the relationship between the rapid growth of the Yellow Turbans with their healing methods and several outbreaks of epidemics in the second half of the second century AD China. See ibid., 51–53. For the meaning of "yellow turban" and the Yellow Turbans' slogans, see Fang Shiming 方詩銘, "Huangjin qiyi xianqu yu wu ji yuanshi Daojiao de guanxi: jian lun *Huangjin yu Huangshenyue zhang*" 黃巾起義先驅與巫及原始道教的關係—兼論 '黃巾' 與 '黃神越章, *Lishi yanjiu* 3 (1993): 3–13; and Liu Zhaorui 劉昭瑞, "Lun *Huangshen yue zhang*: jian tan Huangjin kouhao de yiyijixiangguan wenti" 論'黃神越章'—兼談黃巾口號的意義及相關問題, *Lishi yanjiu* 1 (1996): 125–32. While his study on terms like "*yellow turban*" is helpful here, I am cautious about Fang's general theory, which assumes that a group of people evolved from *wu* to a popular religion worshiping the Yellow Emperor in the Eastern Han and then to the Yellow Turban religion. I do not see such a specific group in a sociological sense existing through the Eastern Han, but hints of small groups and communities allying or competing with each other. Wang Yucheng's 王育成 study on excavated stamps with *huangshen* 黃神 inscribed on them and other inscriptions testifies to the existence of multiple religious communities in the Eastern Han. See Wang Yucheng 王育成, "Dong Han tiandi shizhe lei daoren yu Daojiao qiyuan" 東漢天帝使者類道人與道教起源, *Daojia wenhua yanjiu* 16 (1999): 181–203, esp. 203. For a more updated introduction to the relevant issues and some of the archeological objects mentioned earlier, see T. H. Barrett, "Religious Change under Eastern Han and Its Successors," in *China's Early Empires: A Re-appraisal*, ed. Michael Nylan and Michael Loewe (Cambridge: Cambridge University Press, 2010), 430–48.

89. *Hou Han shu*, 30b: 1085. Ōfuchi Ninji tries to make the link between the *Scripture* and Zhang Jiao's practices. However, information on the latter is too scarce to make any concrete conclusions. See his *Shoki no dōkyō*, 77–136, esp. 136.

90. The Ming dynasty Daoist Canon is a compilation of Daoist scriptures from AD 1444. It contains most of the earliest received versions of Daoist scriptures.

91. As Tang Zhangru 唐長孺 mentions, the *Scripture of the Great Peace*, the *Writing of the Great Peace*, and the received version of the *Scripture of the Great Peace* are not identical. One of the most obvious differences is that while the received version of the *Scripture of the Great Peace* promotes the color red, Zhang Jue and his group promoted yellow. See Tang Zhangru, "Taiping dao yu Tianshi dao" 太平道與天師道, in *Tang Zhangru wencun* 唐長孺文存 (Shanghai: Guji, 2006), 735–38.

92. See, for example, Tang Yongtong 湯用彤, "Du *Taiping jing* shu suo jian" 讀《太平經》書所見, *Guoxue jikan* 5.1 (1933): 16–17. Chen Guofu 陳國符, *Daozang yuanliu kao* 道藏源流考 (Examinations of the Origins of the Daoist Canon) (Shanghai: Zhonghua, 1949), 82–83, Fukui Kōjun 福井康順, *Dōkyō no kisoteki kenkyū* 道教の基礎的研究 (Tokyo: Shoseki Bunbutsu Ryūtsūkai, 1958), 214–54; Kobayashi Masayoshi 小林正美, *Chūgoku no Dōkyō* 中國の的道教 (Tokyo: Sōbusha, 1998), 43–45.

93. See Kristofer Schipper, "1. B. 6 The *Taiping jing*," in *The Taoist Canon: A Historical Companion to the* Daozang, ed. Kristofer Schipper and Franciscus

Verellen (Chicago: University of Chicago Press, 2004), 1: 277–80; Hendrischke, *The Scripture on Great Peace*, 31–38.

94. See Kaltenmark, "The Ideology of the T'ai-p'ing ching," 10–45, esp. 44–45.

95. For the relationship between different Great Peace texts, see Oyanagi, "*Go Kan jo* Jō Kai den no *Taihei shōryō sho* ni tsuite," 141–71; Ōfuchi Ninji 大淵忍爾, "*Taiheikyō* no rareki ni tsuite" 太平經の來歷について, *Tōyō gakuhō* 東洋學報 27.2 (1940): 100–24; Wang Ming 王明, "Lun *Taiping jing* de chengshu shidai he zuozhe" 論《太平經》的成書時代和作者, in his *Daojia he Daojiao sixiang yanjiu* 道家和道教思想研究 (Beijing: Zhongguo shehui kexue, 1984), 183–200; and Grégoire Espesset, "The Date, Authorship, and Literary Structure of the *Great Peace Scripture Digest*," *Journal of the American Oriental Society* 133.2 (2013): 321–52, and "Editing and Translating the *Taiping Jing* and the Great Peace Textual Corpus," *Zhongguo Wenhua Yanjiusuo xuebao* 48 (2008): 469–86.

96. Ge Hong 葛洪, "Ming ben" 明本, in Wang Ming 王明 annotated, *Baopuzi neipian jiaoshi* 抱樸子內篇校釋 (Beijing: Zhonghua, 1985), 10: 184–85.

97. Yan Zhitui 顏之推, "Mian xue" 勉學, Wang Liqi 王利器 annotated, *Yashi jiaxun jijie* 顏氏家訓集解 (Beijing: Zhonghua, 1993), 3: 157, 165.

98. The categorization of Daoist scriptures, the Three Caverns (*san dong* 三洞), exemplifies this tendency. It includes scriptures from three traditions, namely, the Shangqing 上清 (Supreme Purity), Lingao 靈寶 (Sacred Treasures), and Sanhuang 三皇 (Three Sovereigns) traditions. While the compiler claimed the Shangqing tradition the most supreme one, he considerably valued and included scriptures from other traditions. See Ōfuchi Ninchi 大淵忍爾, "The Formation of the Taoist Canon," in *Facets of Taoism*, ed. Holmes Welch and Anna Seidel (New Haven: Yale University Press, 1979), 253–68. For the formation of the Three Caverns in the Six Dynasties, and especially the agenda of the compiler Lu Xiujing 陸修靜 (AD 406–477), see "Lu Xiujing, Buddhism, and the First Daoist Canon," in *Culture and Power in the Reconstitution of the Chinese Realm, 200–600*, ed. Scott Pearce, Audrey Spiro, and Patricia Ebrey (Cambridge: Harvard University Press, 2001), 181–99.

99. See Yoshikawa Tadao 吉川忠夫, "Shinjin to kakumei" 真人と革命, in his *Rikuchō seishinshi no kenkyū* 六朝精神史の研究 (Kyoto: Dōhōsha, 1986), 85–105, esp. 85–89. As Yoshikawa mentions, when Cao Pi 曹丕 was inaugurated as the emperor of the Wei dynasty, his officials still most frequently compared him to a "sage." However, the occasional mentioning of the term "perfected man" indicates the growing popularity of the term in the political realm. See "Shinjin to kakumei," 89. For the socio-intellectual context of the Cao family's acceptance of the "perfected man," see Jiang Sheng 姜生, "Cao Cao yu yuanshi Daojiao" 曹操與原始道教, *Lishi yanjiu* 歷史研究 1 (2011): 22–23. For more information about the "perfected man" in the Cao family's ascendancy, see Howard L. Goodman, *Ts'ao P'i Transcendent: The Political Culture of Dynasty-Founding in China at the End of the Han* (Seattle: Scripta Serica, 1998), 37, and 122–44. For the relationship between the Cao family and the cult of Celestial Masters, see ibid., 71–87, and Goodman's "Celestial-Master

Taoism and the Founding of the Ts'ao-Wei Dynasty: The Li Fu Document," *Asia Major* 7.1 (1994): 5–33.

100. See Anna Seidel, "Imperial Treasures and Taoist Sacraments: Taoist Roots in the Apocrypha," in *Tantric and Taoist Studies in Honour of R. A. Stein*, ed. Michel Strickmann, *Mélanges chinois et bouddhiques* 21 (1983): 291–371.

101. See Li Yangzheng 李養正, "*Taiping jing* yu yinyang wuxing shuo, Daojia, ji chenwei zhi guanxi" 《太平經》與陰陽五行說、道家及讖緯之關係, *Daojia wenhua yanjiu* 15 (1999): 89–106. Xiao Dengfu 蕭登福 makes a more comprehensive study of this topic. See Xiao Dengfu, *Chenwei yu Daojiao* 讖緯與道教 (Taipei: Wenjin, 2000). I am cautious about the method behind Li and Xiao's observations. For example, Li and Xiao both claim that there is a relationship between apocryphal texts and the *Scripture* because both corpora mention the theory of the Five Phases. Since the theory of the Five Phases was still popular for the whole span of imperial China, there is no reason to believe that the *Scripture* directly adopted the theory from apocryphal texts. I also disagree with Xiao's statement "some apocryphal texts can even be read as Daoist texts; their influence on Daoism is both direct and obvious." Ibid., 66. Xiang does not say what particular Daoist texts apocryphal texts resemble, and Xiao does not provide evidence to prove that any Daoist text was written by referring to apocrypha. Among other issues, Yasui Kōzan points out the idea of "revolution," or *kakumei* 革命, was shared by apocrypha and rebels at the end of the Eastern Han. See his "Dōkyō no seiritsu to shin'i shisō" 道教の成立と讖緯思想, in *Dōkyō to shūkyō bunka* 道教と宗教文化, ed. Akizuki Kan'ei 秋月觀暎 (Tokyo: Hirakawa Shuppansha, 1987), 45–54.

102. As Seidel's title suggests.

103. Wang Ming 王明, ed., *Taiping jing he jiao* 太平經合校 (Beijing: Zhonghua, 1960), 1: 4; 35: 34.

104. Wang Ming, ed., *Taiping jing he jiao*, 40: 76.

105. Adapted from Hendrischke, *The Scripture on Great Peace*, 181.

106. Wang Ming, ed., *Taiping jing he jiao*, 51: 190.

107. Ibid., 70: 277.

108. See chapter 1, 26–27.

109. Wang Ming, ed., *Taiping jing he jiao*, 41: 86.

110. Adapted from Hendrischke, *The Scripture on Great Peace*, 199.

111. Wang Ming, ed., *Taiping jing he jiao*, 41: 86.

112. Adapted from Hendrischke, *The Scripture on Great Peace*, 199.

113. Michael Puett insightfully points out how the authors of *Huainanzi* tried to make their text appear to be timeless: "the *Huainanzi* will endure because it alone is based upon a proper understanding of the natural world." See his *The Ambivalence of Creation: Debates Concerning Innovation and Artifice in Early China* (New York: Cambridge University Press, 2000), 159–60.

114. Liu An, "Yao lue" 要略, in He Ning, ed., *Huainanzi jishi*, 21: 1463. I consulted the translation from John S. Major *et al.*, trans., *The Huainanzi: A Guide to the Theory and Practice of Government in Early Han China* (New York: Columbia

University Press, 2010), 867. Modern scholars agree that Liu An's text was presented to persuade young Emperor Wu on various political and moral issues, so that Liu An could gain political advantages as well as establish his intellectual authority. For why Liu An compiled this text, and how this text fit into the political and intellectual environment of his time, see Major *et al.*, *The Huainanzi*, 7–13, and more elaborately, Griet Vankeerberghen, *The* Huainanzi *and Liu An's Claim to Moral Authority* (Albany: State University of New York Press, 2001), 1–61.

115. The original classical Chinese sentence and the literal translation are 若劉氏之書，觀天地之象，通古今之事 (As for Liu's text, [it has] observed the phenomena of Heaven and Earth, and comprehended ancient and present affairs). Compare to John Major *et al.*, *The Huainanzi*, 867, in which Sarah A. Queen and Judson Murray put "we have" as the subject of the sentence to avoid subject-verb disagreement.

116. Liu An, "Yao lue" 要略, in He Ning, ed., *Huainanzi jishi*, 21: 1462–63. Compare to Major *et al.*, *The Huainanzi*, 867. Queen and Murray understand the subject of the sentence as "we," the compilers of the text.

117. As his contemporaries called him: "Xu Shen, the incomparable in [the learning] of the Five Classics (五經無雙許叔重)." *Hou Han shu*, 79b: 2588.

118. For Han scholars' commentaries on *Huainanzi*, see Gao You's "Xu mu" 序目 (An introduction to the chapters), in He Ning, ed., *Huainanzi jishi*, 4–6, and Charles Le Blanc, "*Huai nan tzu* 淮南子," in *Early Chinese Texts: A Bibliographical Guide*, ed. Michael Loewe (Berkeley: University of California Press, 1993), 190–91.

119. Gao You 高誘, "Xu mu" 序目, in He Ning, ed., *Huainanzi jishi*, 6.
120. Ibid., 5.
121. Wang Ming, ed., *Taiping jing he jiao*, 41: 86.
122. Adapted from Hendrischke, *The Scripture on Great Peace*, 199.

Conclusion

1. For example, among other liturgical texts, Liu Xiujing 陸修靜 (406–477 AD) wrote about the proper manners and etiquette for attending lectures on certain scriptures. See his *Dongxuan liingbao zhai shuo guang zhu jie fa deng zhuyuan yi* 洞玄靈寶斋說光燭戒罰燈祝願儀, in *Zhengtong Daozang* 正統道藏 (The Zhengtong Daoist Canon) (Beijing: Wenwu, 1988), 9: 824–26.

2. See, for example, *Sanguo zhi*, 26: 722.

3. Luo Xinhui 羅新慧 gives a succinct study of the concept of the mandate of Heaven and its changes from the beginning of the Zhou dynasty to the late Warring States period. See her "Zhoudai tianming guannian de fazhan yu shanbian" 周代天命觀念的發展與嬗變, *Lishi yanjiu* 歷史研究 2012. 5: 4–18. Also see David W. Pankenier, "The Cosmo-Political Background of Heaven's Mandate," *Early China* 20 (1995): 121–76, and Herrlee G. Creel, *The Origins of Statecraft in China* (Chicago: University of Chicago Press, 1970), 81–100.

4. See Graham, *Disputers of the Tao*, 13–15, 45–47, 113–17, 215–35, 267–85; Yuri Pines, *Foundations of Confucian Thought: Intellectual Life in the Chunqiu Period, 722–453 B. C. E.* (Honolulu: University of Hawai'i Press, 2002), 136–63; Pines, *Envisioning Eternal Empire: Chinese Political Thought of the Warring States Era* (Honolulu: University of Hawai'i Press, 2009), 13–111.

5. "Li yun," *Liji zhengyi*, in Ruan Yuan, ed., *Shisan jing zhushu, j.* 21, 1414.

6. One exception is from "Zhongni yan ju" 仲尼燕居, in which Confucius stated that the rites and music could rectify the world so that "All-under-Heaven would be greatly peaceful (*tianxia tai ping* 天下太平)." See *Liji zhengyi*, in Ruan Yuan, ed., *Shisan jing zhushu, j.* 50, 1615.

7. For the meaning of this term and how it is applied, I follow Collins, *The Sociology of Philosophies*, 793–99.

8. For traveling in the ancient world, especially the reasons for traveling, see Lionel Casson, *Travel in the Ancient World* (Baltimore: Johns Hopkins University Press, 1994), 76–85. Zhang Cong provides a full picture of Song dynasty literati's traveling culture. See his *Transformative Journeys: Travel and Culture in Song China* (Honolulu: University of Hawai'i Press, 2011), esp. 180–206.

9. See, for example, Cui Yin's inscriptions made for chariots in Yan Kejun, *Quan Hou Han wen*, 44: 715.

10. These lines are from "Konghou yao" 箜篌謠, included in Lu Qinli 逯欽立, ed., *Xian Qin Han Wei Jin Nanbei chao shi* 先秦漢魏晉南北朝詩 (Beijing: Zhonghua, 1983), 287.

11. Sun Ji 孫機, *Handai wuzhi wenhua ziliao tushuo* 漢代物質文化資料圖說 (Shanghai: Guji, 2008), 330.

12. For papermaking techniques, see Sun Ji, *Handai wuzhi wenhua ziliao tushuo*, 330–32.

13. *Hou Han shu*, 78: 1697.

14. For two classic studies of the study of mystery, see Tang Yongtong 湯用彤, *Wei Jin Xuanxue lun gao* 魏晉玄學論稿 (Shanghai: Shanghai guji, 2001); and Etienne Balazs, "Nihilistic Revolt or Mystical Escapism: Currents of Thought in China during the Third Century A.D.," in *Chinese Civilization and Bureaucracy*, trans. H. M. Wright (New Haven: Yale University Press, 1964), 226–54. For the scholarship on the intellectual trends in the third and fourth centuries in general, see Yü Ying-shih 余英時, "Han Jin zhi ji shi zhi xin zijue yu xin sichao" 漢晉之際士之新自覺與新思潮, in *Zhongguo zhishi jieceng shi lun* 中國知識階層史論 (Taipei: Lianjing, 1980), 205–327, and "Individualism and the Neo-Taoist Movement in Wei-Chin China," in *Individualism and Holism*, ed. Donald J. Munro (Ann Arbor: University of Michigan Press, 1985), 121–55. Yü particularly emphasizes literati's realization of their own identity and several social activities linked to that realization. Chen Jo-shui 陳弱水 emphasizes transition toward inwardness and abstractness among the Wei and Jin dynasty literati, who became more and more interested in liberating and nurturing innate human nature as well as cosmogony based on the *Changes*, *Laozi*, and the *Supreme Mystery*.

See his "Han Jin zhiji de mingshi sichao yu Xuanxue tupo" 漢晉之際的名士思潮與玄學突破, in *Zhongguo shi xinlun: Sixiang shi fence* 中國史新論—思想史分冊, ed. Chen Jo-shui (Taipei: Zhongyang Yanjiu Yan; Lianjin, 2012), 170–250, esp. 221–29 and 229–42. Ge Zhaoguang 葛兆光 points out how the knowledge preserved in Buddhism and Daoism stimulated intellectual incorporation and debates in medieval China. My dissertation is focused on how knowledge in Buddhism and Daoism could be stimulating. I argue that that was exactly the tendency of broad learning that led to further incorporation of knowledge. See Ge Zhaoguang, "Zhou Kou heyi bu an: Zhonggu Fojiao, Daojiao dui Rujia zhishi shijie de kuochong yu tiaozhan" 周孔何以不言?—中古佛教、道教對儒家知識世界的擴充與挑戰, in Chen Jo-shui, ed., *Zhongguo shi xinlun: Sixiang shi fence* 中國史新論—思想史分冊, 251–81.

15. For a detailed portray of *qingtan*, see Tang Yiming, "The Voice of Wei-Jin Scholars: A Study of 'Qingtan'" (PhD dissertation, University of Columbia, 1991). For a snapshot of the content in the pure discussions, see Richard B. Mather, "The Controversy over Conformity and Naturalness during the Six Dynasties," *History of Religions* 9.2/3 (November 1969–February 1970): 160–80.

16. *Sanguo zhi*, 38: 973–74.

17. Hui Jiao 慧皎, "Yi jing" 譯經, in Tang Yongtong 湯用彤, ed., *Gao seng zhuan* 高僧傳 (Beijing: Zhonghua, 1992), 1: 27.

18. See Ge Hong and Yan Zhitui's attitude toward the classics in chapter 5, 161–162, and 179.

Appendix 1

1. Ruan Yuan 阮元, ed., *Shisan jing zhushu* 十三經注疏 (Beijing: Zhonghua, 1980), 1–2.

2. For an introduction to the chronological versions of this text and their content, see Nylan, *The Five "Confucian Classics,"* 202–52.

3. For the textual issues and different images of sage kings in different chapters of the text, see Nylan, *The Five "Confucian Classics,"* 120–67.

4. For the formation and the use of poems in the text, see Nylan, *The Five "Confucian Classics,"* 72–119.

5. For a summary of the content of the *Rites* corpus, see Nylan, *The Five "Confucian Classics,"* 168–201.

6. For some important concepts and the historical significance of the *Spring and Autumn Annals* and the three commentarial traditions, see Nylan, *The Five "Confucian Classics,"* 253–306.

7. People from different time periods of Chinese history might have different understandings of what should be "classics." Nevertheless, the "classics" (with various names, such as "Liu yi" 六藝, or "Jia bu" 甲部) as a bibliographical category has existed since the Western Han dynasty in Liu Xiang's 劉向 "Qi lüe" 七略, or

the "Seven Summaries." See Yu Jiaxi 余嘉錫, *Mulu xue fawei* 目錄學發微 (Beijing: Zhonghua, 2007), chart following 174.

8. For example, Gu Yanwu 顧炎武 (AD 1613–1682) argues that the learning of the Classics is the learning of the principle, but after 150 years of intellectual development, Zhang Xuecheng 章學誠 (AD 1738–1801) argues that the learning of the Classics is the learning of history. See Yü Ying-shih, "Zhang Xuecheng Versus Dai Zhen: A Study in Intellectual Challenge and Response in Eighteenth-Century China," in *Chinese Language, Thought, and Culture*, ed. Philip J. Ivanhoe (Chicago: Open Court, 1996), 127–38.

9. *Han shu*, 30: 1712.

10. *Han shu*, 30: 1719.

11. Benjamin Elman, *A Cultural History of Civil Examinations in Late Imperial China* (Berkeley: University of California Press, 2000), 736–37.

12. For how the Dao learning was added in the civil examination system of the Yuan, see Elman, *A Cultural History of Civil Examinations in Late Imperial China*, 37–38.

13. For the proportion of questions concerning the Four Books that appear in the civil examinations from Yuan to the Qing, see Elman, *A Cultural History of Civil Examinations in Late Imperial China*, 734–37.

14. See *Siku quanshu zongmu tiyao* 四庫全書總目提要, "Jing bu, Xiao xue" 經部小學, Yong Rong 永瑢 et al., *Siku quanshu zongmu* 四庫全書總目 (Beijing: Zhonghua, 1965), 338.

15. The other titles in this section include *Wujing za yi* 五經雜議 and *Dizi zhi* 弟子職. See "Yi wen zhi," in *Han shu*, 1718.

Appendix 2

1. I capitalize "New Script" and "Old Script" when I refer to Qing dynasty scholars' understanding of the transmission lines of the old and new script texts. They considered that two separate and hostile groups transmitted each of the two texts, and they labeled them with the names "New Script" and "Old Script." Thus, I capitalize the terms to preserve the connotation of social grouping. Throughout the book, I use "new script" and "old script" to refer to the relevant concepts in the previous scholarship, especially *jinwen* 今文 and *guwen* 古文, respectively. For my own conception of the issue, see 105.

2. Qian Mu 錢穆, *Zhongguo jin sanbai nian xueshu shi* 中國近三百年學術史 (Taipei: Taiwan shangwu, 1966), 9–10.

3. Ibid., 25.

4. Ibid., 28–29, 31.

5. Ibid., 133. The "Dao" Gu Yanwu mentions here is in the context of Zhu Xi and the Dao learning. For a definition of Dao learning, the Dao in this context,

and other relevant terms, see, for example, Peter Bol, *Neo-Confucianism in History* (Cambridge: Harvard University Press, 2008), 78–79.

6. Bol, *Neo-Confucianism in History*, 134.

7. See the entry "Han ren zhu jing" 漢人注經, in Gu Yanwu 顧炎武, *Ri zhi lu* 日知錄 (Shanghai: Guji, 2006), 1487–92, esp. 1487.

8. Qian Mu, *Zhongguo jin sanbai nian xueshu shi*, 134.

9. Jiang Fan 江藩, *Guochao Hanxue shicheng ji* 國朝漢學師承記 (Beijing: Sanlian, 1998), 6.

10. Ibid., 7–8.

11. See Luo Jianqiu 羅檢秋, *Qianjia yilai Hanxue chuantong de yanbian yu chuancheng* 乾嘉以來漢學傳統的衍變與傳承 (Beijing: Renming daxue, 2006), 9. Gu Yanwu specifically says that the Han commentaries have their own advantages and disadvantages and any given commentary might have mistakes. Gu Yanwu, *Ri zhi lu*, 453.

12. Luo Jianqiu, *Qianjia yilai Hanxue chuantong de yanbian yu chuancheng*, 11; Luo Zhitian 羅志田, "Fangfa cheng le xueming: Qingdai kaoju heyi cheng xue" 方法成了學名：清代考據何以成學, *Wenyi yanjiu* 2 (2010): 24–31.

13. For example, Dai Zhen was expected and pressured by his contemporaries to produce philological works. See Yü Ying-shih 余英時, *Lun Dai Zhen yu Zhang Xuecheng: Qingdai zhongqi xueshu sixiangshi yanjiu* 論戴震與章學誠——清代中期學術思想史研究 (Beijing: Sanlian, 2000), 107–27.

14. Jiao Xun 焦循, *Diao gu ji* 雕菰集 (Taipei: Taiwan shangwu, 1966), 215.

15. By using "Changzhou school" in the sense of an academic school, I follow Benjamin A. Elman's designation of "school." See his *Classicism, Politics, and Kinship: The Ch'ang-chou School of New Text Confucianism in Late Imperial China* (Berkeley: University of California Press, 1990), 4–5.

16. Luo Jianqiu, *Qianjia yilai Hanxue chuantong de yanbian yu chuancheng*, 12.

17. For more geographical information about the Changzhou school, see Elman, *Classicism, Politics, and Kinship*, xxxiii.

18. Many people from the Liu family, Zhuang's most important affiliated family, also belong to the Changzhou school. See ibid., 37–48, 59–73.

19. Ibid., 172.

20. Ibid., 171.

21. For a brief summary of Qing scholars' evaluation of the old script sections of the *Book of Documents*, see Edward L. Shaughnessy's chapter "*Shangshu* 尚書 (*Shu ching* 書經)," *Early Chinese Texts: A Bibliographical Guide*, ed. Michael Loewe (Berkeley: University of California Press, 1993), 383–85. For a study of the textual formation of the *Book of Documents*, see Michael Nylan, *The Five "Confucian Classics*," 127–36. For Yan Ruoqu's methodology and his contemporaries' attitude toward the authenticity of the *Documents*, see Lin Qingzhang 林慶彰, *Qing chu de qun jing bianwei xue* 清初的群經辨偽學 (Shanghai: Huadong shifan, 2011), 146–250.

22. I am certainly not denying the possibility of Wang Su as a forger, but I do not accept this theory as definite. I see this issue mainly as Qing scholars' attempt to explaining why the chapters in the *Book of Documents* are not consistent. For scholars' changing evaluation of Wang Su as the forger, see Yu Wanli 虞萬里, "Yi Ding Yan Shangshu *yu lun* wei zhongxin kan Wang Su weizao *Guwen Shangshu zhuan* shuo: cong kending dao fouding hou zhi sikao" 以丁晏《尚書餘論》為中心看王肅偽造《古文尚書傳》說—從肯定到否定後之思考, *Zhongguo wen zhe yanjiu jikan* 中國文哲集刊 37 (2010): 131–52.

23. Elman, *Classicism, Politics, and Kinship*, 171, 196–97.

24. For Liu's scholarly orientation, see Qian Mu, *Zhongguo jin sanbai nian xueshu shi*, 526–32. For a detailed study on Zhuang Cunyu, Liu Fenglu, and the Changzhou "New Script" school, see Elman, *Classicism, Politics, and Kinship*, 186–256.

25. Ruan Yuan did not include Zhuang Cunyu's work in the *Huang qing jing jie* 皇清經解 because Zhang did not use "evidential research" methods. However, that is no longer a problem for Liu's work. See Elman, *Classicism, Politics, and Kinship*, 221–22.

26. Elman, *Classicism, Politics, and Kinship*, 229.

27. Ibid., 250. For Liu's attitude toward Liu Xin's forgery of the Zuo tradition, see Liu Fenglu, Chunqiu Zuo zhuan *kao zheng* 春秋左傳考證, *Huang Qing jing jie* 皇清經解, vol. 1295 (Gengshen bu kan ben, 1860), 6a.

Appendix 3

1. For a study of Pi Xirui's work and detailed book review on Pi Xirui's *A History of the Learning of Classics*, see Wu Yangxiang 吳仰湘, "Pi Xirui *Jingxue lishi* yanjiu" 皮錫瑞《经学历史》研究, *Jingxue yanjiu luncong* 经学研究论丛 14 (2006): 1–52.

2. Pi Xirui 皮錫瑞, *Jingxue lishi* 經學歷史 (Beijing: Zhonghua, 2004), 41.

3. Ibid., 45.

4. Ibid., 54.

5. Ibid., 55.

6. Ibid., 100.

7. Ibid., 101.

8. Ibid., 105.

9. Ibid., 6–7. For the Changzhou school's overall attitude toward Confucius and the Duke of Zhou, see Elman, *Classicism, Politics, and Kinship*, 228.

10. Elman, *Classicism, Politics, and Kinship*, 9–11. For a survey of the Yangzhou school tradition, especially from Liu Wenqi 劉文淇 (AD 1789–1854) to his great-grandson, Liu Shipei 劉師培 (AD 1884–1919), see Zhang Shunhui 張舜徽, *Qing dai Yangzhou xueji* 清代揚州學記 (Wuhan: Huazhong shifan daxue, 2005), 160–202. For Yu Yue's attitude toward the classics, see Luo Jianqiu, *Qianjia yilai Hanxue chuantong de yanbian yu chuancheng*, 260–62. For a study of the Yangzhou school's

academic disciplines and their relationship with other schools, see Feng Qian 冯乾, "Qing dai Yangzhou xuepai xueshu yuanyuan kaobian" 清代扬州学派学术渊源考辨, *Jingxue yanjiu luncong* 经学研究论丛15 (2008): 163–92. The author argues that the Yangzhou school derived from Dai Zhen's 戴震 (AD 1724–1777) Wan school (*Wan pai* 皖派). See ibid., 169.

11. Li Xueqin 李學勤 argues that Liao Ping was largely responsible for coining the strict opposition between the New and Old Script schools. He mentions that Liao Ping used Xu Shen's 許慎 *Wujing yiyi* 五經疑義 as his major evidence for the opposition. However, as Li Xueqin's examples show, the strict opposition did not exist in Xu Shen's work. See Li Xueqin 李學勤, "'Jin Gu xue kao' yu *Wujing yiyi*"《今古學考》與《五經異義》, in Zhang Dainian 張岱年 et al., *Guoxue jinlun* 國學今論 (Shenyang: Liaoning jiaoyu, 1995), 125–35. For a study of Liao Ping's preference to the Gongyang tradition and his attitude toward Liu Xin, see Zhao Pei 赵沛, *Liao Ping Chunqiu xue yanjiu* 廖平春秋学研究 (Chengdu: Bashu, 2007), 130–38, 164–74, 187–205.

12. As Liu's mentor, Zhang Binglin 章炳麟 (AD 1869–1936) holds a similar view. Zhang believes that only a strict transmission process could pass down the complex philological information of the classics from generation to generation. See Zhang Taiyan, "Jin guwen bian yi" 今古文辨義, in Fu Jie 傅傑, ed., *Zhang Taiyan xueshu shi lunji* 章太炎學術史論集 (Kunming: Yunnan, 2008), 455–61, esp. 460. For Zhang Binglin and his school's influence in the early twentieth century, see Sang Bing 桑兵, *Wan Qing Minguo de xueren yu xueshu* 晚清民國的學人與學術, 225–52.

13. See Liu Shipei 劉師培, "Han dai guwen xue bianwu" 漢代古文學辨誣, in *Zuoan wai ji* 左盦外集, *Liu Shipei Quanji* 劉師培全集 (Beijing: Zhonggong Zhongyang Dangxiao, 1997), 178–97. For a summary of Liu Shipei's dissatisfaction with Kang Youwei's perspective, see Li Fan 李帆, "Liu Shipei dui Kang Youwei bianfa lilun de jingxue bonan" 劉師培對康有為變法理論的經學駁難, *Jinyang xue kan* 4 (2010): 76–80.

14. Liu Shipei, "Han dai guwen xue bianwu," 178.

15. Ibid., 181.

16. Ibid., 184.

17. Ibid., 186–88.

18. Ibid., 190.

19. Liu Shipei 劉師培, "Xi Han jinwen xue duo cai Zou Yan shuo kao" 西漢今文學多采鄒衍說考, in *Zuoan ji* 左盦集, *Liu Shipei Quanji*, 31–33.

20. The supporters of the old script classics do not necessarily use the same method to justify the authenticity of these texts. For example, Sun Yirang 孫詒讓 (AD 1848–1908) wrote that the Qin burning of books destroyed the *Rites of Zhou*, but people rediscovered this text from the wall of Confucius's family house. Liu Xin did make his own commentary and explanation of this text for Wang Mang's interest. However, Liu Xin neither forged the text, nor was his commentary an intentional misinterpretation of it. See Sun Yirang 孫詒讓, *Zhouli zhengyi* 周禮正義 (Beijing: Zhonghua, 1987), 2–3.

21. Ma Zonghuo 馬宗霍, *Zhongguo jingxue shi* 中國經學史 (Shanghai: Shanghai shudian, 1984), 41–42. Ma Zonghuo focuses on four pairs of concepts in the chapter about Han classicism, namely, old script versus new script (*guwen/jinwen* 古文/今文), area of Qi versus of Lu (Qi/Lu 齊/魯), teaching models versus lineage models (*shi fa / jiafa* 師法/家法), and official learning versus private learning (*guan xue / si xue* 官學/私學). See *Zhongguo jingxue shi*, 35.

22. Ibid., 45.

23. Ibid., 50.

24. Ibid., 46.

25. Ibid., 58–60. Differing from Ma Zonghuo, Pi Xirui believes the confusion of the transmission lines led to this scholasticism. Pi Xirui, *Jingxue lishi*, 89–90.

26. The article was first published in 1925, with the title "Jing jin, guwen zhi zheng jiqi yi tong" 經今古文之爭及其異同. See Zhou Yutong 周予同, "Jing jin, guwen xue" 經今古文學, in *Jingxue shi lunzhu xuanji* 經學史論著選集 (Shanghai: Shanghai renmin, 1996), 1.

27. See the list Zhou Yutong makes in ibid., 9.

28. Xu Fuguan 徐復觀, "Zhongguo jingxue shi de jichu" 中國經學史的基礎, in *Xu Fuguan jingxue shi liang zhong* 徐復觀經學史兩種 (Shanghai: Shanghai shudian, 2005), 58–133.

29. This model becomes almost a cliché; for example, see Song Yanping 宋豔萍, *Gongyang xue yu Handai shehui* 公羊學與漢代社會 (Beijing: Xueyuan, 2010), 135. Many other scholars, such as Feng Youlan 馮友蘭 and Tang Yongtong 湯用彤, also accept this view. For these scholars' view and its relation to their political agenda, see Hans van Ess, "The Old Text / New Text Controversy: Has the 20th Century Got It Wrong?" *T'oung Pao* 80.1–3 (1994): 146–70. There are also revisionist views on the new/old script controversy. For example, Huang Zhangjian 黃彰健 argues that Liu Xin's promotion of the old script classics was purely academic, but Wang Mang's was to serve for his usurpation. See his *Jing jin gu wen wenti xinlun* 經新古文問題新論 (Taipei: Taiwan shangwu, 1982), 770.

30. This book is a reprint of the 2001 Fujian Renmin Press's *Zhongguo jingxue shi*, edited by Wu Yannan 吳雁南, Qin Xueqi 秦學頎, and Li Yujie 李禹階. See their *Zhongguo jingxue shi* 中國經學史 (Fuzhou: Fujian renmin; Beijing: Renmin, 2010), 99–104, 107–24.

31. See for example, Qian Mu 錢穆, "Liu Xiang Xin fuzi nianpu" 劉向歆夫子年譜, in *Liang Han jingxue jin gu wen ping yi* 兩漢經學今古文平議 (Beijing: Shangwu, 2001), 104–07, 118–19. For Qian Mu's discontent with Kang Youwei's theory and his historiography in general, see Li Fan 李帆, "Cong 'Liu Xiang Xin fuzi nianpu' kan Qian Mu de Shixue linian" 從《劉向歆父子年譜》看錢穆的史學理念, *Shixue shi yanjiu* 118.2 (2005): 46–54.

32. Ibid., 151–52.

33. Ibid., 150.

34. Ibid., 119.

35. Ibid., 5–6.

36. For the background on why Qian Mu wrote this work and for reviews of this work, especially those of Gu Jiegang 顧頡剛, Qian Xuantong 錢玄同, and Hu Shi 胡適, see Liu Wei 劉巍, "'Liu Xiang Xin fuzi nianpu' de xueshu Beijing yu chushi fanxiang"《劉向歆父子年譜》的學術背景與初始反響, *Lishi yanjiu* 3 (2001): 45–64.

37. For an insightful study of Gu Jiegang's historiography, see Laurence A. Schneider, "From Textual Criticism to Social Criticism: The Historiography of Ku Chieh-kang," *The Journal of Asian Studies* 28.4 (1969): 771–88. For a more comprehensive study of Gu Jiegang and his role in the field of Chinese history in China, see Schneider, *Ku Chieh-kang and China's New History: Nationalism and the Quest for Alternative Traditions* (Berkeley: University of California Press, 1971).

38. Gu Jiegang 顧頡剛, *Qin Han de fangshi yu rusheng* 秦漢的方士與儒生 (Shanghai: Guji, 1998.), 4.

39. Ibid., 4–5. Also see Schneider, "From Textual Criticism to Social Criticism," 781.

40. The book started with an outline of a class in 1933, and it was published in 1935, entitled *Handai xueshu shi lue* 漢代學術史略 by Yaxiya 亞細亞 Press. The book was revised and republished with the title *Qin Han de fangshi yu rushing*. Gu Jiegang, *Qin Han de fangshi yu rusheng*, 6–7, 9–11.

41. Ibid., 6–7.

42. Ibid., 8–9.

43. For previous scholars' influence on Gu Jiegang, especially Kang Youwei and Cui Shu 崔述 (AD 1740–1816), and how Gu Jiegang accommodated their scholarship, see Schneider, "From Textual Criticism to Social Criticism," 775–81.

44. The latter is thus the "parasite of the ruling class," as Schneider translates. See ibid., 783, 785.

45. Though he considers it polluted by the thought of the masters of methods.

46. Schneider, "From Textual Criticism to Social Criticism," 786.

47. Xu Fuguan, "Zhongguo jingxue shi de jichu," 163.

48. Wu Yannan et al., eds., *Zhongguo jingxue shi* 中國經學史 (Fuzhou: Fujian renmin; Beijing: Renmin, 2010), 107.

49. Gu Jiegang, *Qin Han de fangshi yu rusheng*, 6–7, 9–11, 116–17.

50. See Nishijima Sadao, "The Economic and Social History of Former Han," in *The Cambridge History of China Vol. 1, The Ch'in and Han Empires, 221 B.C.–A.D. 220*, ed. Denis Twitchett and Michael Loewe (Cambridge: Cambridge University Press, 1987), 627–28; and Ebrey, "The Economic and Social History of Later Han," in the same volume, 628.

51. Ebrey, "The Economic and Social History of Later Han," 122.

52. Ibid., 123.

53. Michael Nylan, "The *chin wen / ku wen* Controversy in Han Times," *T'oung Pao* 80.1–3 (1994): 83–145.

54. Ibid., 86, 136. Liu Lizhi 劉立志 gives a more comprehensive and systematic review of modern scholars' theories of *guwen*. See his *Han dai Shijing xue shi lun* 漢代《詩經》學史論 (Beijing: Zhonghua, 2007), 71–83.

55. Michael Nylan, "The *chin wen / ku wen* Controversy in Han Times," 90, 93, 95, 117–22.

56. Ibid., 108–15.

57. After Nylan, more and more scholars question the seamless transmission of classics and the contrast-debate model in general. See, for example, Wang Baoxuan 王葆玹, "Jin, guwen jingxue zhi zheng jiqi yiyi" 今、古文經學之爭及其意義, in Jiang Guanghui 姜廣輝, ed., *Zhongguo jingxue sixiang shi* 中國經學思想史 (Beijing: Zhongguo shehui kexue, 2003), 2: 554–89; Liu Lizhi, *Han dai* Shijing *xue shi lun*, 130–31.

58. Nylan, "The *chin wen/ku wen* Controversy in Han Times," 117, 134.

59. See Chen Suzhen 陳蘇鎮, Chunqiu *yu "Han dao": liang Han zhengzhi yu zhengzhi wenhua yanjiu*《春秋》與"漢道"——兩漢政治與政治文化研究 (Beijing: Zhonghua, 2011), 617.

60. Ibid., 1, 617.

Appendix 4

1. Fung Yu-lan, *A History of Chinese Philosophy*, trans. Derk Bodde, second edition (Princeton: Princeton University Press, 1952–1953), 403.

2. Ibid., 400–07, esp. 403.

3. For a detailed literature review of this issue, see Fukui Shigemasa 福井重雅, "Jukyō no kangakuka o meguru gakusetsu kenkyō ryakushi" 儒教の官學化をめぐる學說研究略史, in *Kandai Jukyō no shiteki kenkyū: Jukyō no kangakuka o meguru teisetsu no saikentō* 漢代儒教の史的研究:儒教の官學化をめぐる定說の再檢討 (Tokyo: Kyūko Shoin, 2005), 23–96.

4. Some Japanese scholars use the word *jukyō* as "Confucian teaching," others as "Confucian religion." See Watanabe Yoshihiro 渡邊義浩, "Nihon ni okeru 'jukyō no kokkyōka' o meguru kenkyū ni tsuite" 日本における「儒教の国教化」おめぐる研究について, in Watanabe Yoshihiro 渡邊義浩, ed., *Ryō Kan no Jukyō to seiji kenryoku* 両漢の儒教と政治權力 (Tokyo: Kyūko shoin, 2005), 258–60. I use "Confucianism" as a more general word to translate the terms in these Japanese publications.

5. See, for example, Shigezawa Toshirō 重沢俊郎, "Dōchūjo kenkyū" 董仲舒研究, in *Shū Kan shisō kenkyū* 周漢思想研究, 1943, 143–265. This is still the most popular view held by most Chinese scholars and many Western scholars. For a summary of Western scholars who hold this view, see the appendix Michael Loewe includes in his *Dong Zhongshu, a 'Confucian' Heritage and the* Chunqiu Fanlu, 6–18. The view is too common among Chinese scholars for me to list their names here.

6. Fukui Shigemasa 福井重雅, "Jukyō seiritsu shijo no nisan no mondai: gokyō hakase no secchi to Dōchūjo no jiseki ni kansuru gigi" 儒教成立史上の二三の問題——五経博士の設置と董仲舒の事跡に關する疑義, *Shigaku zasshi* 76.1 (1967): 1–34.

7. For a summary of different theories on Confucianism as a national teaching or religion, see Watanabe Yoshihiro, "Nihon ni okeru 'jūkyō no kokkyōka' o meguru kenkyū ni tsuite," 264–69.

8. Itano Chōhachi 板野長八, "Jukyō no kenkyū" 儒教の成立, in *Jukyō seiritsushi no kenkyū* 儒教成立史の研究 (Tokyo: Iwanami Shoten, 1995), 493–527. It was first published in *Iwanami kōza sekai rekishi* 岩波講座世界歴史 4 (1970).

9. Ibid., 494, 526.

10. Itano does agree that Confucianism is a tool for the emperor and officials to control the commoners. See ibid., 493.

11. Ibid., 501.

12. Itano believes that this dimension is not part of Confucius's original teachings, but a result of compromise. See ibid., 508.

13. Ibid., 504.

14. Itano has a more elaborate study specifically on the importance of apocryphal texts for the establishment of Confucianism as a national religion, see his "Toshin to jukyō no seiritsu (1)" 図讖と儒教の成立（一）, *Shigaku zasshi* 84.2 (1975): 125–73; "Toshin to jukyō no seiritsu (2)" 図讖と儒教の成立（二）, *Shigaku zasshi* 84.3 (1975): 283–99.

15. Itano, "Jukyō no kenkyū," 496–97.

16. Ibid., 516.

17. Ibid., 493.

18. See Itano's theory about the emergence of prophecy at the end of the Western Han dynasty and Wang Mang's enthronement. Ibid., 522–24.

19. Nishijima Sadao 西嶋定生, *Shin Kan teikoku* 秦漢帝國 (Tokyo: Kōdansha, 1975), 344.

20. Ibid., 306–11, 311–22, 325–27.

21. Fukui, "Jukyō no kangakuka o meguru mondaiten" 儒教をめぐる官學化をめぐる問題點, *Kandai Jukyō no shiteki kenkyū*, 98–100, esp. 100.

22. Fukui, "Gokyō hakase no kenkyū" 五經博士の研究 and "Dōchūjo no kenkyū" 董仲舒の研究, *Kandai Jukyō no shiteki kenkyū*, 111–260, 261–414.

23. Ibid., 515–18.

24. Ibid., 13, 102–03, 104–06.

25. Watanabe Yoshihiro 渡邊義浩, *Gokan kokka no shihai to Jukyō* 後漢国家の支配と儒教 (Tokyo: Yūzankaku Shuppan, 1995), 37–38.

26. Ibid., 22–23, 31.

27. See Watanabe's handy summary in his *Gokan ni okeru "Jukyō kokka" no seiritsu* 後漢における「儒教國家」の成立 (Tokyo: Kyūko shoin, 2009), 21–25.

28. Homer H. Dubs, "The Victory of Han Confucianism," *Journal of the American Oriental Society* 58 (1938): 435–49.

29. Homer H. Dubs, "The Failure of the Chinese to Produce Philosophic Systems," *T'oung pao* 26 (1929): 96–109.

30. Nathan Sivin, "On the Word 'Taoist' as a Source of Perplexity, with Special Reference to the Relations of Science and Religion in Traditional China," *History of Religious* 17.4 (1978): 303–30.

31. Ibid., 308–10, 314–17, 327.

32. Nicolas Zufferey, *To the Origins of Confucianism: The* Ru *in Pre-Qin Times and during the Early Han Dynasty* (Bern: Peter Lang, 2003).

33. Ibid., 368, 370–71.

34. Ibid., 372. Zufferey follows Michael Nylan on this issue. See her "A Problematic Model: The Han 'Orthodox Synthesis,' Then and Now," in *Imagining Boundaries: Changing Confucian Doctrines, Texts, and Hermeneutics*, ed. Kai-wing Chow et al. (Albany: State University of New York Press, 1999), 19, 37.

35. Nylan, "A Problematic Model," 18, 25.

36. See Nylan, *The Five "Confucian Classics,"* 2.

37. Loewe, *Dong Zhongshu*, 75.

38. Ibid., 64–65, 67, 74–75.

39. Ibid., 192, 226–27, 212. I adopt Michael Loewe's view on this. Chinese scholars such as Zhong Zhaopeng 鐘肇鵬 and Chen Suzhen take *Chunqiu fanlu* as Dong Zhongshu's authentic writing. This leads to a radically different understanding of the intellectual development of the Han dynasty from mine. Cf. Zhong, *Chen wei lun lue* 讖緯論略 (Shenyang: Liaoning jiaoyu, 1991), 127; and Chen, Chunqiu yu "Han dao," 159–206, 617.

40. Loewe, *Dong Zhongshu*, 182; 338.

41. Ibid., 338.

42. Ibid., 36–37, 40.

43. I am certainly not arguing that Han scholars' thought or philosophy have nothing to do with Confucius, Mencius, or any other Warring States–period philosophers, nor do I believe that we can ignore the links and relationships between Han scholars and their predecessors. What I mean here is that future scholars do not need to begin their research on Han scholars with the sentence "This individual's philosophy deviates from Confucius's original teaching by . . ."

44. Liang Cai, *Witchcraft and the Rise of the First Confucian Empire* (Albany: State University of New York Press, 2014), 77–112, 135–51, 187–97.

45. Cai, *Witchcraft and the Rise of the First Confucian Empire*, 189–90.

Appendix 5

1. Zhong Zhaopeng 鐘肇鵬 also holds this view. He states that the foundation of apocrypha is the classics, and the essence of it is theological superstition. *Chen wei lun lue*, 2.

2. Zhou Yutong, *Jingxue shi lunzhu xuanji*, 52.

3. Ibid., 57.

4. Ibid., 58. Lü Simian 呂思勉 holds a similar view on this issue. See his *Qin Han shi* 秦漢史 (Shanghai: Shanghai guji, 2005), 741–42.

5. Chen Pan argues that the masters of methods forged documents and put them under the titles *River Chart* (*He tu* 河圖) and *Luo Writing* (*Luoshu* 洛書). See his *Gu Chenwei yantao ji qi shulu jieti* 古讖緯研討及其書錄解題 (Shanghai: Guji, 2009), 108–11.

6. Ibid. "Zhanguo Qin Han jian fangshi kao lun" 戰國秦漢間方士考論, 179–254.

7. Dull, "A Historical Introduction to the Apocryphal (Ch'an-wei) Texts of the Han Dynasty," 428–29.

8. Ibid., 427, 430–33.

9. Yasui and Nakamura, *Isho no kisoteki kenkyū*, 72, 104.

10. Ibid., 104–05.

11. Van Ess, "The Apocryphal Texts of the Han Dynasty and the Old Text/New Text Controversy," 56.

12. Chen Suzhen, *"Chunqiu" yu "Han dao,"* 414, 454.

13. See Hou Wailu 侯外廬, Zhao Jibin 趙紀彬, Du Guoxiang 杜国庠. *Zhongguo sixiang tongshi* 中國思想通史 (Beijing: Renmin, 1957–1960), 225.

14. See Zhou Yutong, *Jingxue shi lunzhu xuanji*, 40–41.

15. Chen Pan, *Gu Chenwei yantao ji qi shulu jieti*, 197–98.

16. Yasui Kōzan 安居香山, *Isho to Chūgoku no shinpi shisō* 緯書と中国の神秘思想 (Tokyo: Hirakawa Shuppansha, 1988), 2, 11.

17. Zhong Zhaopeng, *Chen wei lun lue*, "Introduction," 5.

18. Ibid., 2.

19. See Tian Changwu 田昌五 and An Zuozhang 安作璋, ed., *Qin Han shi* 秦漢史 (Beijing: Renmin, 2008), 647–58.

20. See Robert P. Kramer, "The Development of Confucian Schools," in *The Cambridge History of China, Vol. 1, The Ch'in and Han Empires, 221 B.C.–A.D. 220*, ed. Denis Twitchett and Michael Loewe, 763; Tjan Tjoe Som, trans., *Po Hu T'ung: The Comprehensive Discussions in the White Tiger Hall* (Leiden: E. J. Brill, 1949–1952), 1: 141–43.

21. This is just the same as China's Western counterpart. See Dale B. Martin, *Inventing Superstition: From the Hippocratics to the Christians* (Cambridge: Harvard University Press, 2004), 11–13.

22. Or in his own word, *wang* 妄. See Wang Chong 王充, "Dui zuo" 對作, *Lun heng* 論衡 (Shanghai: Shanghai renmin, 1974), 29: 445.

Appendix 6

1. So far the most comprehensive study on the generic name of apocryphal texts is Chen Pan, *Gu Chenwei yantao ji qi shulu jieti*, 148–71. In the study, Chen

Pan convincingly points out that the many names, such as *chen*, *wei*, *tuchen* 圖讖, *tuwei* 圖緯, are largely interchangeable during the Eastern Han dynasty.

2. Ibid., 141–48.

3. See, for example, *Chunqiu wei* 春秋緯, in Yasui and Nakamura, eds., *Weishu jicheng*, 912–42.

4. This convention probably started from Tjan Tjoe Som (曾珠森), trans., *Po Hu T'ung*, 100, and Dull, "A Historical Introduction to the Apocryphal (Ch'an-wei) Texts of the Han Dynasty," 5–6.

5. For a defense of "apocrypha" as the translation of *chenwei* texts, see Hans van Ess, "The Apocryphal Texts of the Han Dynasty and the Old Text New Text Controversy," *T'oung Pao* 85.1–3 (1999): 31–36.

6. Wilhelm Schneemelcher, ed., *New Testament Apocrypha*, trans. R. McL. Wilson (Philadelphia: Westminster Press, 1962–1963), 14–15. Cf. John J. Collins, "Apocrypha," in *Encyclopedia of Early Christianity*, ed. Everett Ferguson et al. (New York: Garland, 1990), 61–62. I use the word "canonical" to designate a standard but not necessarily fixed category of scriptures accepted by certain communities. For various understanding of the word "canon," see Lee Martin McDonald, *Forgotten Scriptures: The Selection and Rejection of Early Religious Writings* (Louisville: Westminster John Knox Press, 2009), 14–31.

7. *Kong Qiu mi jing* 孔丘秘經 was a good example of this. See *Hou Han shu*, 30a: 1043. Also see Yasui and Nakamura, *Isho no kisoteki kenkyū*, 152.

8. See Zhang's biography in *Hou Han shu*, 59: 1897–98. For more information, see Tanaka Masami 田中麻紗巳, *Gokan Shisō no tankyū* 後漢思想の探究 (Tokyo: Kenbun Shuppan, 2003), 83–93.

9. Yasui, *Isho no kisoteki kenkyū*, 261–63.

10. See, for example, Ma Guohan, ed., *Yuhan Shanfang jiyi shu*, 11–12.

11. Van Ess, "The Apocryphal Texts," 36.

12. Robert E. Buswell Jr., "Introduction: Prolegomenon to the Study of Buddhist Apocryphal Scriptures," in *Chinese Buddhist Apocrypha*, ed. Robert E. Buswell Jr. (Honolulu: University of Hawai'i Press, 1990), 1.

13. *Hou Han shu*, 82a: 2721–22. Wei Zheng 魏徵 et al., eds., "Jingji zhi" 經籍志, *Sui shu* 隋書 (Beijing: Zhonghua, 1973), 32: 940–41. Also see Chen Pan's reading of these two passages, *Gu Chenwei yantao ji qi shulu jieti*, 149–71.

14. Two major yardsticks for dating are the theory of the Five Phases in Generation (*wuxing xiang sheng* 五行相生) and the promotion of the Liu 劉 family as the current recipient of the mandate of Heaven. It is certainly true that later dynasties also used the theory of the Five Phases in Generation, and that the rulers of the kingdom of Shu 蜀 (AD 221–263) and the Song 宋 dynasty (AD 420–479) carried the surname of Liu. The intensive employment of the two characteristics, especially combined, still seems to be peculiar to the early Eastern Han dynasty. See Gu Jiegang 顧頡剛, *Zhongguo shanggu shi yanjiu jiangyi* 中國上古史研究講義 (Beijing: Zhonghua, 1988), 270, 291–94.

15. Nakamura Shōhachi has completed the most thorough textual studies and transmission histories thus far of fragments under every single title that can possibly be considered an apocryphal text. Yasui and Nakamura also give the most complete compilation of apocryphal texts. I will mainly rely on their compilation and constantly refer to Nakamura's textual studies. See Yasui and Nakamura, *Isho no kisoteki kenkyū*, 475. Chen Pan examines fragmented texts whose titles contain the names *Hetu* or *Luoshu* and explicates the titles. See Chen Pan, *Gu Chenwei yantao ji qi shulu jieti*, 257–548.

16. Therefore, I will draw a much smaller pool of apocryphal texts from Yasui Kōzan and Nakamura Shōhachi's compilation, but I certainly do not reject the possibility that these texts were included in apocryphal tradition. This restricted scope might narrow the pool of sources I can use, but hopefully it will help to avoid anachronisms.

Bibliography

Akizuki Kan'ei 秋月觀暎. "Kōkinnoran no shūkyōsei: Taiheidō tono kanren o chūshin toshite 黄巾の亂の宗教性：太平道教法との關連を中心として (The Religious Connotation of the Rebellions of the Yellow Turbans: Focus on the Relationship with the Teaching of the Way of the Great Peace). *Tōhōshi kenkyū* 15.1 (1956): 43–56.

An Zuozhang 安作璋 Xiong Tieji 熊鐵基. *Qin Han guanzhi shi gao* 秦漢官制史稿 (A Manuscript of the History of Qin and Han's Bureaucratic System). Jinan: Qilu, 2007.

Asselin, Mark Laurent. *A Significant Season: Cai Yong (ca. 133–192) and His Contemporaries*. New Haven: American Oriental Society, 2010.

Baihu tongyi 白虎通義 (Comprehensive Meaning from the White Tiger Hall). Chen Li 陳立, ed., *Baihu tong shuzheng* 白虎通疏證 (Commentaries on the *Comprehensive Meaning from the White Tiger Hall*). Beijing: Zhonghua, 1994.

Bai Qianqi. "Chinese Letters: Private Words Made Public." In *The Embodied Image: Chinese Calligraphy from the John B. Elliot Collection*, ed. Robert E. Harrist and Wen C. Fong, 380–99. Princeton: The Art Museum, Princeton University, 1999.

Balazs, Etienne. "Nihilistic Revolt or Mystical Escapism: Currents of Thought in China during the Third Century A.D." In *Chinese Civilization and Bureaucracy*, trans. H. M. Wright, 226–54. New Haven: Yale University Press, 1964.

Ban Gu 班固. *Han shu* 漢書 (History of the Han). Beijing: Zhonghua, 1987.

Barbieri-Low, Anthony J. "Craftsman's Literacy: Uses of Writing by Male and Female Artisans in Qin and Han China." In *Writing and Literacy in Early China: Studies from the Columbia Early China Seminar*, ed. Li Feng and David Prager Branner, 370–99. Seattle: University of Washington Press, 2011.

Bielenstein, Hans. *The Restoration of the Han Dynasty*. 4 vols. Stockholm: Museum of Far Eastern Antiquities, 1953–1979.

———. *The Bureaucracy of Han Times*. Cambridge: Cambridge University Press, 1980.

———. "Wang Mang, the Restoration of the Han Dynasty, and Later Han." In *The Cambridge History of China, Vol. 1, The Ch'in and Han Empires, 221 B.C.–*

A.D. 220, ed. Denis Twitchett and Michael Loewe, 223–90. Cambridge: Cambridge University Press, 1987.

———. "The Institutions of Later Han." In *The Cambridge History of China, Vol. 1, The Ch'in and Han Empires, 221 B.C.–A.D. 220*, ed. Denis Twitchett and Michael Loewe, 491–519. Cambridge: Cambridge University Press, 1987.

Bodde, Derk. "The Chinese Cosmic Magic Known as Watching for the Ethers." In *Studia Serica Bernhard Karlgren dedicata: Sinological Studies Dedicated to Bernhard Karlgren on His Seventieth Birthday, October Fifth, 1959*, 14–35. Copenhagen: E. Munksgaard, 1959.

Bokenkamp, Stephen. "Record of the Feng and Shan Sacrifices." In *Religions of China in Practice*, ed. Donald Lopez Jr., 251–60. Princeton Readings in Religions. Princeton: Princeton University, 1996.

———. "Lu Xiujing, Buddhism, and the First Daoist Canon." In *Culture and Power in the Reconstitution of the Chinese Realm, 200–600*, ed. Scott Pearce, Audrey Spiro, and Patricia Ebrey, 181–99. Cambridge: Harvard University Press, 2001.

Bol, Peter. *Neo-Confucianism in History*. Cambridge: Harvard University Press, 2008.

Brashier, K. E. *Ancestral Memory in Early China*. Cambridge: Harvard University Press, 2011.

———. *Public Memory in Early China*. Cambridge: Harvard University Press, 2014.

Brokaw, Cynthia J., and Kai-wing Chow, eds. *Printing and Book Culture in Late Imperial China*. Berkeley: University of California Press, 2005.

Brown, Miranda. *The Politics of Mourning in Early China*. Albany: State University of New York Press, 2007.

Buswell, Robert E., Jr., ed. *Chinese Buddhist Apocrypha*. Honolulu: University of Hawai'i Press, 1990.

Cai Liang. "In the Matrix of Power: A Study of the Social and Political Status of Confucians (*Ru* 儒) in the Western Han Dynasty (206 BCE–8 CE)." PhD thesis, Cornell University, 2007.

———. "'Who Said, 'Confucius Composed Chunqiu'? The Genealogy of the 'Chunqiu' Canon in the Pre-Han and Han Periods." *Frontiers of History in China* 5.3 (2010): 363–85.

———. "Excavating the Genealogy of Classical Studies in the Western Han Dynasty (206 BCE–8 CE)." *Journal of American Oriental Society* 131.3 (2011): 371–94.

———. *Witchcraft and the Rise of the First Confucian Empire*. Albany: State University of New York Press, 2014.

Cao Jianguo 曹建國. "*Shi* wei *sanji, sishi, wuji, liuqing* shuo tanwei《詩》緯三基、四始、五際、六情說探微" (An Exploration of the Theory of Three Bases, Four Beginnings, Five Contacts and of Six Emotions in the *Book of Poetry* Apocrypha). *Wuhan Daxue xuebao* 59.4 (2006): 434–40.

Casson, Lionel. *Travel in the Ancient World*. Baltimore: Johns Hopkins University Press, 1994.

Chang Qu 常璩. Ren Naiqiang 任乃強 annotated. Huayang guo zhi jiaobu tuzhu 華陽國志校補圖注 (Collations, Supplements, and Illustrations of the *Gazetteer of the State of Huayang*). Shanghai: Guji, 1987.

Chen Chi-yun 陳啟雲. *Hsün Yüeh (A.D. 148–209): The Life and Reflections of an Early Medieval Confucian*. Cambridge: Cambridge University Press, 1975.

Chen Guofu 陳國符. *Daozang yuanliu kao* 道藏源流考 (Examinations of the Origins of the Daoist Canon). Shanghai: Zhonghua, 1949.

Chen Jo-shui (Chen Ruoshui) 陳弱水. "Han Jin zhiji de mingshi sichao yu Xuanxue tupo" 漢晉之際的名士思潮與玄學突破 (The Intellectual Trend for Literati and the Breakthrough of the Study of Darkness in between the Han and Jin Dynasties). In *Zhongguo shi xinlun: Sixiang shi fence* 中國史新論—思想史分冊 (New Perspectives on Chinese History: The Volume on Intellectual History), ed. Chen Ruoshui, 170–250. Taipei: Zhongyang Yanjiu Yan; Lianjing, 2012.

Chen Kanli 陳侃理. "'*Hong fan' wuxing zhuan* yu '*Hong fan*'zaiyi lun"《洪範五行傳》與《洪範》災異論 (The *Tradition of Five Phases in the "Great Plan"* and the Omenology of the "Great Plan"). *Guoxue yanjiu* 國學研究 26 (2010): 89–112.

———. "Jing Fang de *Yi* yinyang zaiyi lun" 京房的《易》陰陽災異論 (Jing Fang's Theory of the *Changes* of *yin-yang* and Omens). *Lishi yanjiu* 6 (2011): 70–85.

Chen Pan 陳槃. *Gu Chenwei yantao ji qi shulu jieti* 古讖緯研討及其書錄解題 (Studies of Ancient Apocryphal Texts and Explanations on the Titles of Them). Shanghai: Guji, 2009.

Chen Shou 陳壽. *Sanguo zhi* 三國志 (The History of the Three Kingdoms). Beijing: Zhonghua, 1959.

Chen Suzhen 陳蘇鎮. "Han dao, wangdao, tiandao: Dong Zhongshu *Chunqiu* gongyang shuo xintan" 漢道、王道、天道—董仲舒《春秋》公羊說新探 (The Way of Han, of the King and of Heaven: A New Exploration of Dong Zhongshu's Gongyang Study). *Guoxue yanjiu* 國學研究 2 (1994): 313–37.

Chen Suzhen 陳蘇鎮. "*Chunqiu* yu '*Han dao*': Dong Zhongshu '*yi de hua min*' shuo zaitan"《春秋》與"漢道"—董仲舒"以德化民"說再探 (The *Spring and Autumn Annals* and the "Way of Han": A Reexamination of Dong Zhongshu's Theory of Transforming [the Ethos of] People by Virtue). *Guoxue yanjiu* 國學研究 4 (1997): 39–62.

Chen Suzhen 陳蘇鎮. Chunqiu *yu "Han dao": liang Han zhengzhi yu zhengzhi wenhua yanjiu* 《春秋》與"漢道"—兩漢政治與政治文化研究 (*Spring and Autumn Annals* and the Way of Han: Studies on Politics and Political Culture in the Two Han Dynasties). Beijing: Zhonghua, 2011.

Chen Yan 陳雁. "Donghan Wei Jin shiqi Ying, Ru, Nanyang diqu de sixue yu youxue" 東漢魏晉時期潁汝、南陽地區的私學與遊學 (Private Learning and Traveling to Learn in Yinghuan, Runan and Nanyang Regions from the Eastern Han to Jin). *Wen shi zhe* 1 (2000): 71–75.

Chen Weisong 陳蔚松. *Handai kaoxuan zhidu* 漢代考選制度 (The Recruitment System of the Han Dynasties). Wuhan: Hubei, 2002.

Cheng, Dennis Chi-hsiung. "Interpretations of *yang* (陽) in the *Yijing* Commentarial Traditions." *Journal of Chinese Philosophy* 35.2 (2008): 219–34.

Cheng Nanzhou 程南洲. *Dong Han shidai zhi* Chunqiu Zuoshi xue 東漢時代之春秋左氏學 (The study of the Zuo tradition of *Annals* in the Eastern Han). Shanghai: Huadong Shifan, 2011. (Reprint of Cheng's 1978 dissertation.)

Chow, Kai-wing, et al., eds. *Imagining Boundaries: Changing Confucian Doctrines, Texts, and Hermeneutics*. Albany: State University of New York Press, 1999.

Chung, Eva Yuen-wah. "A Study of the 'Shu' (Letters) of the Han Dynasty (206 B.C.–A.D. 220)." PhD dissertation, University of Washington, 1982.

Chunqiu fanlu 春秋繁露. Su Yu 蘇與, ed. *Chunqiu fanlu yizheng* 春秋繁露義證. Beijing: Zhonghua, 1992.

Collins, Randall. *The Credential Society: An Historical Sociology of Education and Stratification*. New York: Academic Press, 1979.

———. *The Sociology of Philosophies: A Global Theory of Intellectual Change*. Cambridge: Belknap Press of Harvard University Press, 1998.

———. *Interaction Ritual Chains*. Princeton: Princeton University Press, 2004.

Creel, Herrlee G. *The Origins of Statecraft in China*. Chicago: University of Chicago Press, 1970.

de Crespigny, Rafe. "The Recruitment System of the Imperial Bureaucracy of Later Han." *Chung Chi Journal* 6.1 (1966): 67–78.

———. "An Outline of the Local Administration of the Later Han Empire." *Chung Chi Journal* 7.1 (1967): 57–71.

———. *Official Titles of the Former Han Dynasty as Translated and Transcribed by H. H. Dubs*. Oriental Monograph Series 2. Canberra: Australian National University, Centre of Oriental Studies, 1967.

———. "Prefectures and Population in South China in the First Three Centuries AD." *Bulletin of the Institute of History and Philology* 40.1 (1968): 139–54.

———. "Political Protest in Imperial China: The Great Proscription of Later Han." *Papers on Far Eastern History* 11 (1975): 3–15.

———. "The Harem of Emperor Huan: A Study of Court Politics in Later Han." *Papers on Far Eastern History* 12 (1975): 1–42.

———. "The Second Year of Yen-hsi: Notes to the Han Chronicle of A.D. 159." *Journal of the Oriental Society of Australia* 10.1–2 (1975): 7–25.

———. *Portents of Protest in the Later Han Dynasty: The Memorials of Hsiang K'ai to Emperor Huan*. Canberra: Australian National University Press, 1976.

———. "Politics and Philosophy under the Government of Emperor Huan 159–168 A.D." *T'oung Pao* 66.1–3 (1980): 41–83.

———. "Inspection and Surveillance Officials under the Two Han Dynasties." In *State and Law in East Asia: Festschrift Karl Bünger*, ed. Dieter Eikemeier and Herbert Franke, 40–79. Wiesbaden: Otto Harrassowitz, 1981.

———. "Local Worthies: Provincial Gentry and the End of the Later Han." In *Das andere China: Festschrift für Wolfgang Bauerzum 65.Geburtstag*, ed. Helwig Schmidt-Glintzer, 533–58. Wolfenbütteler Forschungen 62. Wiesbaden: Harrassowitz, 1995.

———. "South China in the Han Period." In *Ancient Chinese and Southeast Asian Bronze Age Cultures*, ed. F. David Bulbeck and Noel Barnard, 2: 759–68. Taipei: SMC, 1996–1997.

———. *A Biographical Dictionary of Later Han to the Three Kingdoms (23–220 AD)*. Handbuch der Orientalistik IV. 19. Leiden: Brill, 2006.

———. "Scholars and Rulers: Imperial Patronage under the Later Han Dynasty." In *Han-Zeit: Festschrift für Hans Stumpfeldt aus Anlaßseines 65. Geburtstages*, ed. Michael Friedrich et al., 57–77. Lun Wen: Studien zur Geistesgeschichte und Literatur in China 8. Wiesbaden: Harrassowitz, 2006.

———. "Recruitment Revisited: The Commissioned Civil Service of the Later Han." *Early Medieval China* 13–14.2 (2008): 1–47.

———. *Five over Luoyang: A History of the Later Han Dynasty 23–220 AD*. Leiden: Brill, 2016.

Cui Xiangdong 崔向東. *Han dai haozu yanjiu* 漢代豪族研究 (A Study on Han Great Families). Wuhan: Chongwen, 2003.

Demiéville, Paul. "Philosophy and Religion from Han to Sui." In *The Cambridge History of China, Vol. 1, The Ch'in and Han Empires, 221 B.C.–A.D. 220*, ed. Denis Twitchett and Michael Loewe, 808–72. Cambridge: Cambridge University Press, 1987.

Dettenhofer, Maria H. "Eunuchs, Women, and Imperial Courts." In *Rome and China: Comparative Perspectives on Ancient World Empires*, ed. Walter Scheidel, 83–99. New York: Oxford University Press, 2009.

Di Giacinto, Licia. *The* Chenwei *Riddle: Time, Star, and Heroes in Apocrypha*. Gossenberg: Ostasien Verlag, 2013.

Ding Bangyou 丁邦友. *Handai wujia xintan* 漢代物價新探 (New Explorations on Prices in the Han). Beijing: Shehui kexue, 2009.

Ding Sixin 丁四新. *Chu zhushu yu Han boshu* Zhou yi *jiaozhu* 楚竹書與漢帛書周易校注 (Chu Bamboo Manuscript and Han Silk Manuscript Versions of the *Changes of Zhou* with Annotations and Collations). Shanghai: Guji, 2011.

Dubs, Homer H. "The Failure of the Chinese to Produce Philosophic Systems." *T'oung pao* 26 (1929): 96–109.

———. "The Victory of Han Confucianism." *Journal of the American Oriental Society* 58 (1938): 435–49.

———. "Wang Mang and His Economic Reforms." *T'oung Pao* 35.4 (1940): 219–65.

———, trans. *History of the Former Han Dynasty: A Critical Translation with Annotations*. 3 vols. Baltimore: Waverly Press, 1938.

Dull, Jack L. "A Historical Introduction to the Apocryphal (Ch'an-wei) Texts of the Han Dynasty." PhD dissertation, University of Washington, 1966.

Ebrey, Patricia. "The Economic and Social History of Later Han." In *The Cambridge History of China, Vol. 1, The Ch'in and Han Empires, 221 B.C.–A.D. 220*, ed. Denis Twitchett and Michael Loewe, 608–48. Cambridge: Cambridge University Press, 1987.

Elman, Benjamin A. *Classicism, Politics, and Kinship: The Ch'ang-chou School of New Text Confucianism in Late Imperial China*. Berkeley: University of California Press, 1990.

———. *A Cultural History of Civil Examinations in Late Imperial China*. Berkeley: University of California Press, 2000.

Espesset, Grégoire. "Editing and Translating the *Taiping Jing* and the Great Peace Textual Corpus." *Zhongguo Wenhua Yanjiusuo xuebao* 48 (2008): 469–86.

———. "The Date, Authorship, and Literary Structure of the *Great Peace Scripture Digest*." *Journal of the American Oriental Society* 133.2 (2013): 321–52.

van Ess, Hans. "The Old Text / New Text Controversy: Has the 20th Century Got It Wrong?" *T'oung Pao* 80.1–3 (1994): 146–70.

———. "The Apocryphal Texts of the Han Dynasty and the Old Text / New Text Controversy." *T'oung Pao* 85.1–3 (1999): 29–64.

Fang Shiming 方詩銘. "Huangjin qiyi xianqu yu wu ji yuanshi Daojiao de guanxi: jian lun *Huangjin yu Huangshenyue zhang*" 黃巾起義先驅與巫及原始道教的關係——兼論'黃巾'與'黃神越章' (The Pioneer of Yellow Turban Rebellion and Its Relationship with *wu* and Proto-Daoism with [the Term] *Yellow Turban* and *Huangshenyue zhang*). *Lishi yanjiu* 3 (1993): 3–13.

Fang Xuanling 房玄齡, et al. *Jin shu* 晉書 (A History of Jin). Beijing: Zhonghua, 1974.

Farmer, J. Michael. "The Three Chaste Ones of Ba: Local Perspectives on the Yellow Turban Rebellion on the Chengdu Plain." *Journal of the American Oriental Society* 125.2 (2005): 191–202.

———. *The Talent of Shu: Qiao Zhou and the Intellectual World of Early Medieval Sichuan*. Albany: State University of New York Press, 2007.

Feng Haofei 馮浩菲. *Lidai* Shijing *lunshuo shuping* 歷代詩經論說述評 (Summary and Comments on Theories of the *Book of Poetry* through Imperial China). Beijing: Zhonghua, 2003.

Feng Qian 冯乾. "Qing dai Yangzhou xuepai xueshu yuanyuan kaobian" 清代扬州学派学术渊源考辨 (An Examination of the Qing Dynasty Yangzhou School and Its Origin). *Jingxue yanjiu luncong* 经学研究论丛 15 (2008): 163–92.

Feng Shi 馮時. *Zhongguo tianwei kaoguxue* 中國天文考古學 (Chinese Archaeological Astronomy). Beijing: Zhongguo shehui kexue, 2007.

Ferguson, Everett, *et al.*, eds. *Encyclopedia of Early Christianity*. New York: Garland, 1990.

Fu Jie 傅傑, ed. *Zhang Taiyan xueshu shi lunji* 章太炎學術史論集 (A Collection of Zhang Taiyan's Works on the History of Chinese Scholarship). Kunming: Yunnan, 2008.

Fu Zhufu. "The Economic History of China: Some Special Problems." *Modern China* 7.1 (1981): 3–30.

Fuehrer, Bernhard. "The Court Scribe's *Eikon Psyches*: A Note on Sima Qian and His Letter to Ren An." *Asian and African Studies* 6.2 (1997): 170–83.

Fukui Kōjun 福井康順. *Dōkyō no kisoteki kenkyū* 道教の基礎的研究 (Basic Studies of Daoism). Tokyo: Shoseki Bunbutsu Ryūtsūkai, 1958.

Fukui Shigemasa 福井重雅. "Jukyō seiritsu shijo no nisan no mondai: gokyōhakase no secchi to Dōchūjo no jiseki ni kansuru gigi" 儒教成立史上の二三の問題——五経博士の設置と董仲舒の事跡に關する疑義 (Few Questions about the History of the Establishment of Confucianism: Doubts about the Opening of the Position of Five Classics Erudite and Dong Zhongshu's Deeds). *Shigaku zasshi* 史學雜誌 76.1 (1967): 1–34.

———. *Kandai kanri tōyō seido no kenkyū* 漢代官吏登用制度の研究 (Studies of Han Governmental Recruitment System). Tokyo: Sōbunsha, 1988.

———. *Kandai Jukyō no shiteki kenkyū: Jukyō no kangakuka o meguru teisetsu no saikentō* 漢代儒教の史的研究：儒教の官學化をめぐる定説の再檢討 (A Historical Study of Confucianism during the Han Dynasties: A Reexamination of the Standard Theory of the Transformation of Confucianism into the Official Learning). Tokyo: Kyūko Shoin, 2005.

Fung Yu-lan (1895–1990). *A History of Chinese Philosophy*, second edition. Trans. Derk Bodde. 2 vols. Princeton: Princeton University Press, 1952–1953.

Gao Jiyi 郜積意. "Liu Xin zhi xue ji houshi de pingjia" 劉歆之學及後世的評價 (The Scholarship of Liu Xin and the Evaluation from Later Generations). *Guoxue yanjiu* 國學研究 19 (2007): 289–333.

Gao Wen 高文 annotated. *Han Bei jishi* 漢碑集釋 (Collected Explanations of Han Steles). Kaifeng: Henan Daxue, 1997.

Ge Hong 葛洪. Wang Ming 王明 annotated. *Baopuzi neipian jiaoshi* 抱樸子內篇校釋 (Annotations and Collations of the *Inner Chapters of the Master Who Embraces Simplicity*). Beijing: Zhonghua, 1985.

Ge Zhaoguang 葛兆光. "Zhou Kou heyi bu an: Zhonggu Fojiao, Daojiao dui Rujia zhishi shijie de kuochong yu tiaozhan" 周孔何以不言？——中古佛教、道教對儒家知識世界的擴充與挑戰 (Why Did the Duke of Zhou and Confucius Not Mention It: Medieval Buddhism and Daoism's Expansion and Challenges on the Confucian World of Knowledge). In Chen Jo-shui, ed., *Zhongguo shi xinlun: Sixiang shi fence* 中國史新論——思想史分冊 (New Perspectives on Chinese History: The Volume on Intellectual History), 251–81. Taipei: Lianjing, 2012.

Goldin, Paul Rakita. "Xunzi and Early Han Philosophy." *Harvard Journal of Asiatic Studies* 67.1 (2006): 135–66.

———. *Confucianism*. Berkeley: University of California Press, 2011.

———, ed. *Routledge Handbook of Early Chinese History*. Abingdon: Routledge, 2018.

Goodman, Howard L. "Celestial-Master Taoism and the Founding of the Ts'ao-Wei Dynasty: The Li Fu Document." *Asia Major* 7.1 (1994): 5–33.

———. *Ts'ao P'i Transcendent: The Political Culture of Dynasty-Founding in China at the End of the Han*. Seattle: Scripta Serica, 1998.

———. "Chinese Polymaths, 100–300 AD: The Tung-kuan, Taoist Dissent, and Technical Skills." *Asia Major* (third series) 18.1 (2005): 101–74.

Grafton, Anthony, and Megan Williams. *Christianity and the Transformation of the Book: Origen, Eusebius, and the Library of Caesarea.* Cambridge: Harvard University Press, 2006.

Graham, A. C. *Disputers of the Tao: Philosophical Argument in Ancient China.* LaSalle: Open Court, 1989.

Grieder, Jerome B. *Intellectuals and the State in Modern China: A Narrative History.* New York: Free Press, 1981.

Guanzi. Li Xiangfeng 黎翔鳳 annotated. Guanzi *jiaozhu* 管子校注 (Collations and Annotations of the *Guanzi*). Beijing: Zhonghua, 2004.

Gu Jiegang 顧頡剛. *Zhongguo shanggu shi yanjiu jiangyi* 中國上古史研究講義 (Lectures on the History of Early China). Beijing: Zhonghua, 1988.

———. *Qin Han de fangshi yu rusheng* 秦漢的方士與儒生. Shanghai: Guji, 1998.

Gu Mingyuan 顧明遠, et al., eds. *Zhongguo jiaoyu daxi* 中國教育大系 (A great Compilation of Chinese Education), vol. 2., *Lidai jiaoyu zhidu kao* 歷代教育制度考 (Examinations on Educational Systems in History). *Zhongguo jiaoyu daxi.* Wuhan: Hubei jiaoyu, 2004.

Gurr, Ted Robert. *Why Men Rebel.* Princeton: Princeton University Press, 1970.

Guwen yuan 古文苑 (The Garden of Ancient Texts). Ed. Qian Xizuo 錢熙祚. Taipei: Taibei shangwu, 1968.

Gu Yanwu 顧炎武. *Ri zhi lu* 日知錄 (The Record of the Daily Knowing). In Huang Rucheng 黃汝成, ed., *Ri zhi lu jishi* 日知錄集釋 (A Collective Commentary on *The Record for the Daily Knowing*). 3 vols. Shanghai: Guji, 2006.

Han Fei 韓非. Wang Xianshen 王先慎 annotated. *Han Feizi jijie* 韓非子集解 (A Collected Explication of the *Han Feizi*). Beijing: Zhonghua, 1998.

Henderson, John B. *Development and Decline of Chinese Cosmology.* New York: Columbia University Press, 1984.

———. *Scripture, Canon, and Commentary: A Comparison of Confucian and Western Exegesis.* Princeton: Princeton University Press, 1991.

Hendrischke, Barbara. "The Place of the *Scripture on Great Peace* in the Formation of Taoism." In *Religion and Chinese Society, Volume I: Ancient and Medieval China*, ed. John Lagerwey, 249–78. Hong Kong: The Chinese University Press, 2004.

———. *The Scripture on Great Peace: The* Taiping jing *and the Beginnings of Daoism.* Daoist Classics 3. Berkeley: University of California Press, 2007.

He Ning 何寧. *Huainanzi jishi* 淮南子集釋 (Collected Interpretations of the *Huainanzi*). Beijing: Zhonghua, 1998.

Hentona Tomokuni 辺土名朝邦. "Ka Kyu no seiden setsu" 何休の井田説 (He Xiu's Theory of the Well-Field System). *Kwassui lonbunshū* 21 (1978): 35–49.

Higashi Shinji 東晉次. "Gokan jidai no senkyo to sahoushakai" 後漢時代の選舉と地方社會 (Selections and Recruitment of the Eastern Han Dynasty and Local Society). *Tōyōshi kenkyū* 46.2 (1987): 33–60.

———. *Gokan jidai no seiji to shakai* 後漢時代の政治と社會 (Eastern Han Politics and Society). Nagoya: Nagoya Daigaku Shuppankai, 1995.

Hihara Toshikuni 日原利国. *Kandai Shisō no kenkyū* 漢代思想の研究 (Studies on Thought in the Han Dynasty). Tokyo: Kenbun Shuppan, 1986.

Hirai Masashi 平井正士. "Kandai ni okeru Juka kanryō no kugyōsō he no shinjun" 漢代に於ける儒家官僚の公卿層への浸潤 (The Permeation of the Confucian Officials into the High Official Level in the Han Dynasty). In *Rekishi ni okeru minshū to bunka: Sakai Tadao Sensei koki shukuga kinen ronshū* 歴史における民衆と文化: 酒井忠夫先生古稀祝賀記念論集, ed. Sakai Tadao Sensei Koki Shukuga Kinen no Kai 酒井忠夫先生古稀祝賀記念の会, 51–65. Tokyo: Kokusho Kankōkai, 1982.

Hong Xingzu 洪興祖 annotated. *Chuci Buzhu* 楚辭補註 (A Supplementary Commentary of the Chu Lyrics). *Zhongguo gudian wenxue jinben congshu* 中國古典文學基本叢書. Beijing: Zhonghua, 1983.

Hsu, Cho-yun. *Han Agriculture: The Formation of Early Chinese Agrarian Economy (206 B.C.–A.D. 220)*. Ed. Jack L. Dull. Han Dynasty China 2. Seattle: University of Washington Press, 1980.

Huan Tan 桓譚. Zhu Qianzhi 朱謙之, ed. *Xin jiben Huan Tan Xin lun* 新輯本桓譚新論 (Newly Collected Version of Huan Tan's *New Discussions*). Beijing: Zhonghua, 2009.

Huangdi neijing 黃帝內經. Guo Aichun 郭靄春 annotated. *Huangdi neijing suwen jiaozhu yushi* 黃帝內經素問校註語釋 (Annotations and Collations of *Yellow Emperor's Inner Canon*). Tianjin: Kexue jishu, 1981.

Huang Huaixin 黃懷信. *Han Jin Kongshi jiaxue yu "weishu" gongan* 漢代孔氏家學與"偽書"公案 (The Family Tradition of the Kong in Han and Jin and the Controversial Case about the "Forged Book"). Xiamen: Xiamen Daxue, 2011.

Huang Liuzhu 黃留珠. *Qin Han shijin zhidu* 秦漢仕進制度 (Systems of Qin and Han Governmental Recruitment). Xi'an: Xibei Daxue, 1985.

Huang Zhangjian 黃彰健. *Jing jin gu wen wenti xinlun* 經新古文問題新論 (New Discussion on the Issue of New and Old Script Classics). *Zhongyang Yanjiu Yuan Lishi Yuyan Yanjiu Suo zhuankan zhi qishijiu* 中央研究院歷史語言研究所專刊之七十九. Taipei: Taiwan shangwu, 1982.

Huang Zhaoji 黃肇基. *Handai Gongyang xue zaiyi lilun yanjiu* 漢代公羊學災異理論研究 (A Study of the Theory of Calamities in the Gongyang Traditions of the Han Dynasty). Taipei: Wenjin, 1998.

Hucker, Charles O. *A Dictionary of Official Titles in Imperial China*. Stanford: Stanford University Press, 1985.

Hughes, E. R. *Two Chinese Poets: Vignettes of Han Life and Thought*. Princeton: Princeton University Press, 1960.

Hui Dong 惠棟. Zheng Wangeng 鄭萬耕, ed. *Zhouyi shu* 周易述 (Explanations of the *Classic of Changes of Zhou*). Beijing: Zhonghua, 2007.

Hui Jiao 慧皎. Tang Yongtong 湯用彤, ed. *Gao seng zhuan* 高僧傳 (Biographies of Eminent Monks). Beijing: Zhonghua, 1992.

Ichimura Sanjirō 市村瓚次郎. *Shina shi kenkyū* 支那史研究 (Studies on Chinese History). Tokyo: Shunjusha, 1939.

Inoue Susumu 井上進. *Chūgoku shuppan bunkashi: shomotsu sekai to chi no fūkei* 中國出版文化史――書物世界と知の風景 (A History of Publishing Culture: The World of Books and the Intellectual Landscape). Nagaya: Nagoya Daigaku Shuppankai, 2002.

Inoue Wataru 井上亘. "Kandai no shofu: Chūgoku kodai ni okeru jōhōkanri gijutsu" 漢代の書府――中國古代における情報管理技術 (Han Dynasty Text Storage: Techniques of Information Management in Ancient China). *Tōyō gakuhō* 87.1 (2005): 1–35.

Ikeda Shūzō 池田秀三. "Ryū Kō no gakumon to shisō" 劉向の學問と思想 (The Scholarship and Thought of Liu Xiang). *Tōhō gakuhō* 東方學報 50 (1978): 109–90.

———. "Ba Yū shiron" 馬融私論 (Private Opinions on Ma Rong). *Tōhō gakuhō* 52 (1980): 243–84.

———. "Kandai no Enangaku: Ryū Kō to Kyo Shin" 漢代の淮南學――劉向と許慎 (Studies of *Huainanzi* in the Han Dynasties: Liu Xin and Xu Shen). *Chūgoku shisōshi kenkyū* 11 (1988): 1–27.

———."Kieta Sashi setsu no nazo: Gokan Sashigaku no keisei tokushitsu" 消えた左氏說の謎――後漢左氏學の形成特質 (The Riddle of the Disappearance of the Zuo Tradition: The Characteristics of the Formation of the Learning of the Zuo in the Eastern Han). *Nihon Chūgoku Gakkai hō* 日本中國學會報 54 (2002): 16–31.

———. "Cheng Hsüan's Theory of Six Heavens and Ritual Scholarship during the Han." *Acta Asiatica* 98 (2010): 77–98.

Ikeda Tomoshisa 池田知久. "Bo shu 'Yao' shi wen" 帛書《要》釋文 (A Transcription and Interpretation of the Silk Manuscript "Yao"). *Guoji Yi xue yanjiu* 1 (1995): 40–05.

Itano Chōhachi 板野長八. "*Raiki* no daidō" 禮記の大同 (The Great Equality in the *Records of Rites*). *Hokkaido Daigaku bungakubun kiyō* 5 (1956): 85–115.

———. "Saiisetsu yori mita Ryū Kō to Ryū Kin" 災異說より見た劉向と劉歆 (Liu Xiang and Liu Xin from the Perspective of Their Theory of Omens). In *Tōhō Gakkai sōritsu nijūgoshūnen kinen: tōhōgaku ronshū* 東方學會創立十五周年記念：東方學論集, 1–15. Tokyo: Tōhō Gakkai, 1972.

———."Toshin to jukyō no seiritsu (1)" 図讖と儒教の成立（一）(Apocryphal Texts and the Establishment of Confucianism, 1). *Shigaku zasshi* 史學雜誌 84.2 (1975): 125–73.

———. "Toshin to jukyō no seiritsu (2)" 図讖と儒教の成立（二）(Apocryphal Texts and the Establishment of Confucianism, 2). *Shigaku zasshi* 史學雜誌 84.3 (1975): 283–99.

———. *Jukyō seiritsushi no kenkyū* 儒教成立史の研究. Tokyo: Iwanami Shoten, 1995.

Ivanhoe, Philip J., ed. *Chinese Language, Thought, and Culture: Nivison and His Critics*. Chicago: Open Court, 1996.

Jensen, Lionel M. *Manufacturing Confucianism: Chinese Traditions and Universal Civilization*. Durham: Duke University Press, 1997.

Jiang Fan 江藩. *Guochao Hanxue shicheng ji* 國朝漢學師承記 (The Record of the Learning of Han's Transmission Lineage in Our Dynasty). In *Hanxue shicheng ji (wai er zhong)* 漢學師承記（外二種）(The Record of the Learning of Han's Transmission Lineage with Two Other Works), ed. Qian Zhongshu 钱锺书, 1–180. *Zhongguo jindai xueshu mingzhu* 中國近代學術名著. Beijing: Sanlian, 1998.

———. *Guochao Hanxue yuanyuan ji* 國朝宋學淵源記 (The Record of the Learning of Song's Origin in Our Dynasty). In *Hanxue shicheng ji (wai er zhong)*. *Zhongguo jindai xueshu mingzhu*, ed. Qian Zhongshu 钱锺书, 181–231. Beijing: Sanlian, 1998.

Jiang Guanghui 姜廣輝, ed. *Zhongguo jingxue sixiang shi* 中國經學思想史 (An Intellectual History of the Learning of Classics). 2 vols. Beijing: Zhongguo shehui kexue, 2003.

Jiang Sheng 姜生. "Cao Cao yu yuanshi Daojiao" 曹操與原始道教 (Cao Cao and Proto-Daoism). *Lishi yanjiu* 歷史研究 2011.1: 4–24.

Jiang Shoucheng 姜守誠. *Taiping jing yanjiu: Yi shengming wei zhongxin de zonghe kaocha* 《太平經》研究——以生命為中心的綜合考察 (A Study of the *Scripture of the Great Peace*: A Comprehensive Examination Centered on Life). Beijing: Shehui kexue wenxian, 2007.

Jiao Xun 焦循. *Diao gu ji* 雕菰集 (The Collection of Carving the Gu Millet). Congshu jicheng 叢書集成 vols. 581–84. Taipei: Taiwan shangwu, 1966.

Jin Fagen 金發根. "Dong Han danggu renwu de fenxi" 東漢黨錮人物的分析 (An Analysis of Partisans in the Eastern Han). *Zhongyang yanjiuyuan lishi yuyan yanjiusuo jikan* 34 (1963): 505–58.

Jin Jingfang 金景芳. *Lun Jing Tian zhidu* 論井田制度 (Discussions of the Well-Field System). Jinan: Qi Lu, 1982.

Jugel, Ulrike. *Politische Funktion und soziale Stellung der Eunuchen zur späteren Hanzeit (25–220 n. Chr.)*. Münchener Ostasiatische Studien 15. Wiesbaden: Steiner, 1976.

Kageyama Terukuni 影山輝國. "Kandai ni okeru saii to seiji: Saishō no saiisekinin o chūshin ni" 漢代における災異と政治——宰相の災異責任を中心に (Disasters and Politics in the Han Dynasty: The Grand Chancellor's Responsibility for Disasters). *Shigaku zasshi* 90.8 (1981): 46–68.

Kaltenmark, Max. "The Ideology of the T'ai-p'ing ching." In *Facets of Taoism*, ed. Holmes Welch and Anna Seidel, 19–52. New Haven: Yale University Press, 1979.

Kamada Tadashi 鎌田正. *Saden no seiritsu to sono tenkai* 左傳の成立と其の展開 (The Establishment and Development of the Zuo Tradition). Tokyo: Taishūkan shoten, 1963, 1992 reprint.

Kamitsuka Yoshiko 神塚淑子. *Rikuchō Dōkyō shisō no kenkyū* 六朝道教思想の研究. Tokyo: Sōbunsha, 1999.

Kern, Martin. "Religious Anxiety and Political Interest in Western Han Omen Interpretation: The Case of the Han Wudi Period (141–87 B.C.)." *Studies in Chinese History* 10 (2000): 1–31.

———. *The Stele Inscriptions of Ch'in Shih-huang: Text and Ritual in Early Chinese Imperial Representation*. American Oriental Series 85. New Haven: American Oriental Society, 2000.

Kimura Masao 木村正雄. *Chūgoku kodai nōmin hanran no kenkyū* 中國古代農民叛亂の研究 (Studies on Peasant Revolts in Ancient China). Tokyo: Tokyo Daigaku Shuppankai, 1979.

Kinney, Anne Behnke. "Predestination and Prognostication in the *Ch'ien-fu lun*." *Journal of Chinese Religions* 19 (1991): 27–45.

Knechtges, David R. "The Liu Hsin / Yang Hsiung Correspondence on the *Fang Yen*." *Monumenta Serica* 33 (1977/78): 309–25.

———. "Liu Kun, Lu Chen, and Their Writings in the Transition to the Eastern Jin." *Chinese Literature: Essays, Articles, Reviews* 28 (2006): 1–66.

———. "Court Culture in the Late Eastern Han: The Case of the Hongdu Gate School." In *Interpretation and Literature in Early Medieval China*, ed. Alan K. L. Chan and Yuet-Keung Lo, 9–40. Albany: State University of New York Press, 2010.

Knechtges, David R., trans. *Wen xuan or Selections of Refined Literature*. 3 vols. Princeton: Princeton University Press, 1982–1996.

Kobayashi Masayoshi 小林正美. *Chūgoku no Dōkyō* 中國の的道教 (Chinese Daoism). Tokyo: Sōbusha, 1998.

Kogachi Ryuichi 古勝隆一. "Gokan Gi Shin chūshaku sho no jobun" 後漢魏晉注釋書の序文 (Prefaces to Han, Wei, and Jin Commentaries on Books). *Tōyōshi kenkyū* 73 (2002): 1–48.

Kominami Ichirō 小南一郎. "O Itsu *Soji shoku* omegutte: Kandai shoku no gaku no i sokumon" 王逸「楚辭章句」をめぐって—漢代章句の學の一側面 (Wang Yi's *Verses and Sentences on the Lyrics of Chu*: An Aspect of Han Learning of Verses and Sentences). *Tōhō gakuhō* 63 (1991): 61–114.

Kōmura Takeyiki 高村武幸. "Kandai bunsho giōsei ni okeru shoshin no ichizuke" 漢代文書行政における書信の位置付け (The Position of Letters in the Han Administration of Documents). *Tōhō gakuhō* 91.1 (2009): 1–33.

Korolkov, Maxim. " 'Greeting Tablets' in Early China: Some Traits of the Communicative Etiquette in Light of Newly Excavated Inscriptions." *T'oung Pao* 4–5 (2012): 295–348.

Ku, Mei-kao. *A Chinese Mirror for Magistrates: The Hsin-yü of Lu Chia*. Canberra: Australian National University, 1988.

Kudō Motoo 工藤元男. *Suikochi Shinkan yori mita Shindai no kokka to shakai* 睡虎地秦簡よりみた秦代の國家と社會 (The State and Society of Qin as Seen in Shuihudi Bamboo Manuscripts). Tokyo: Sōbunsha, 1998.

Kuwada Kōzō 桑田幸三. "*Moushi* seidensei no keizaishisō ni tsuite" 「孟子」井田制の経済思想について (A Study on the Economic Thought of the Well-Field System in *Mencius*). *Hikone ronso* 154 (1972): 1–16.

Lagerwey, John, ed. *Religion and Chinese Society, Volume I: Ancient and Medieval China*. Hong Kong: The Chinese University Press, 2004.

Lagerwey, John, and Marc Kalinowski, eds. *Early Chinese Religion, Part I: Shang through Han (1250 BC–220 AD)*. Leiden: Brill, 2009.

Legge, James. *The Chinese Classics, with a Translation, Critical and Exegetical Notes, Prolegomena, and Copious Indexes*. 5 vols. Hong Kong: Hong Kong University Press, 1970.

Levy, Howard S. "Yellow Turban Religion and Rebellion at the End of the Han." *Journal of the American Oriental Society* 76 (1956): 214–27.

Lewis, Mark Edward. "The *feng* and *shan* Sacrifices of Emperor Wu of the Han." In *State and Court Ritual in China*, ed. Joseph P. McDermott, 50–80. Cambridge: Cambridge University Press, 1999.

———. "Gift Circulation and Charity in the Han and Roman Empires." In *Rome and China: Comparative Perspectives on Ancient World Empires*, ed. Walter Scheidel, 121–36. New York: Oxford University Press, 2009.

Li Fan 李帆. "Cong 'Liu Xiang Xin fuzi nianpu' kan Qian Mu de Shixue linian" 從《劉向歆父子年譜》看錢穆的史學理念 (Qian Mu's Historiography as Reflected in His "The Chronicle of Liu Xiang and His Son Liu Xin"). *Shixue shi yanjiu* 118.2 (2005): 46–54.

———. "Liu Shipei dui Kang Youwei bianfa lilun de jingxue bonan" 劉師培對康有為變法理論的經學駁難 (Liu Shipei's Dispute of Kang Youwei's Theory of Reform concerning the Learning of Classics). *Jinyang xue kan* 4 (2010): 76–80.

Li Fang 李昉, et al., eds. *Taiping yulan* 太平御覽 (Imperial Readings of the Taiping Reign). Beijing: Zhonghua, 1960.

Li Feng. "'Feudalism' and Western Zhou China: A Criticism." *Harvard Journal of Asiatic Studies* 63.1 (2003): 115–44.

Li Rui 李銳. "*Liujia, jiuliu yu baijia*: Xifang Hanxue jie xiangguan yanjiu shuping" 六家，九流與百家—西方漢學界相關研究述評 (The Six *jia*, Nine *liu* and Hundred *jia*: A Review on Relevant Scholarship in Western Sinology). *Zhongguo xueshu* 30 (2011): 371–413.

Li, Wai-yee. *The Readability of the Past in Early Chinese Historiography*. Cambridge: Harvard University Press, 2007.

Li Xueqin 李學勤. "'Jin gu xue kao' yu *Wujing yiyi*"《今古學考》與《五經異義》("An Examination of New and Old Learning" and *Different Meanings of Five Classics*). In *Guoxue jinlun* 國學今論 (Present Discussions of Sinology), ed. Zhang Dainian 張岱年 et al., 125–35. Shenyang: Liaoning jiaoyu, 1995.

Li Yangzheng 李養正. "*Taiping jing* yu yinyang wuxing shuo, Daojia, ji chenwei zhi guanxi"《太平經》與陰陽五行說、道家及讖緯之關係 (The *Scripture of the Great Peace* and Its Relationship with the Theory of the Five Phases, Daoism, and Apocrypha). *Daojia wenhua yanjiu* 15 (1999): 89–106.

Liang Weixian 梁韋弦. *Han Yi guaqi xue yanjiu* 漢易卦氣學研究 (A Study of the Trigram-*qi* Theory in the Han [Learning of] *Changes*). Jinan: Qilu, 2007.

Liao Mingchun 廖名春. "'Liu jing' cixu tanyuan" '六經'次序探源 (An Exploration of the Origin of the Arrangements of Six Classics' Titles). *Lishi yanjiu* 2 (2002): 32–41.

———."Shi lun boshu 'Zhong' de pianming he zishu" 試論帛書《衷》的篇名和字數 (A Tentative Discussion on the Title and the Number of Characters of "Zhong"). *Zhouyi yanjiu* 55.5 (2002): 3–9.

Lin Fu-shih 林富士. "Shi lun *Taiping jing de jibing guannian*" 試論《太平經》的疾病觀念 (A Tentative Discussion on the Concept of Diseases in the *Scripture of the Great Peace*). *Zhongyang Yanjiu Yuan Lishi Yuyan Yanjiu Suo jikan* 62.2 (1993): 225–63.

———. "Shi lun *Taiping jing* de zhuzhi yu xingzhi" 試論《太平經》的主旨與性質 (A Tentative Discussion on the Main Points and Nature of the *Scripture of the Great Peace*). *Zhongyang Yanjiu Yuan Lishi Yuyan Yanjiu Suo jikan* 69.2 (1998): 205–44.

———. "*Taiping jing* de shenxian guannian"《太平經》的神仙觀念 (The Concept of Immortals in the *Scripture of the Great Peace*). *Zhongyang Yanjiu Yuan Lishi Yuyan Yanjiu Suo jikan* 80.2 (2009): 217–63.

Lin Ganquan 林甘泉, ed. *Zhongguo jingji tongshi: Qin Han jingji juan* 中國經濟通史——秦漢經濟卷 (A Complete Economic History of China: The Volume of Qin and Han). *Zhongguo jingji tongshi*. Beijing: Jingji ribao, 1999.

Lin Qingzhang 林慶彰. *Qing chu de qun jing bianwei xue* 清初的群經辨偽學 (The Study of Classics' Authenticity in the Early Qing). Shanghai: Huadong shifan, 2011.

Lippiello, Tiziana. "On the Secret Texts of the Feng and Shan Sacrifices." *Annali di Ca' Foscari* 35.3 (1996): 399–406.

———. *Auspicious Omens and Miracles in Ancient China: Han, Three Kingdoms and Six Dynasties.* Sankt Augustin: Steyler Verlag, 2001.

Liu Bin 劉彬. *Bo shu "Yao" pian jiao shi* 帛書《要》篇校釋 (A Collation and Interpretation of the Chapter "Yao" in the Silk Manuscript of the *Yijing*). Beijing: Guangming ribao, 2009.

Liu Fenglu 劉逢祿. Zhen Gao Huang *ping* 箴膏肓評. In Ruan Yuan 阮元, ed. *Huang Qing jing jie* 皇清經解, vol. 1296. Guangdong: Gengshen bu kan ben, 1860.

———. Chunqiu Zuo zhuan *kao zheng* 春秋左傳考證 (The Evidential Examination of the Zuo Tradition of the *Spring and Autumn Annals*). In Ruan Yuan 阮元, ed. *Huang Qing jing jie* 皇清經解, vols. 1294–95. Gengshen bu kan ben, 1860.

Liu Jigao 劉季高. *Dong Han Sanguo shiqi de tanlun* 東漢三國時期的談論 (Discussions in the Eastern Han and the Three Kingdoms Periods). Shanghai: Guji, 1999.

Liu Lizhi 劉立志. *Han dai* Shijing *xue shi lun* 漢代《詩經》學史論 (Discussions on the History of the Han Learning of the *Book of Poetry*). Beijing: Zhonghua, 2007.

Liu Shipei 劉師培. *Liu Shipei Quanji* 劉師培全集 (The Complete Collection of Liu Shipei). Beijing: Zhonggong Zhongyang Dangxiao, 1997.

Liu Wei 劉巍. "'Liu Xiang Xin fuzi nianpu' de xueshu Beijing yu chushi fanxiang"《劉向歆父子年譜》的學術背景與初始反響 (The Academic Background of "The Chronicle of Liu Xiang and His Son Liu Xin" and People's Review). *Lishi yanjiu* 3 (2001): 45–64.

Liu Xiang 劉向. Xiang Zonglu 向宗魯, ed. *Shuiyuan jiaozheng* 說苑校證 (Collations of the *Garden of Persuasion*). Beijing: Zhonghua, 1987.

Liu Yiqing 劉義慶. Liu Xiaobiao 劉孝標 annotated. Zhu Zhuyu 朱鑄禹, ed., *Shishuo xinyu hui jiao ji zhu* 世說新語彙校集注 (A Collected Collation and Annotations of *A New Account of Tales of the World*). Shanghai: Guji, 2002.

Liu Zhao 劉釗. *Guodian Chu jian jiao shi* 郭店楚簡校釋 (Collations and Interpretations of Guodian Bamboo Manuscripts). Fujian: Fujian renmin, 2003.

Liu Zhaorui 劉昭瑞. "Lun *Huangshen yue zhang*: jian tan Huangjin kouhao de yiyijixiangguan wenti" 論'黃神越章'—兼談黃巾口號的意義及相關問題 (A Discussion on *Huangshen yue zhang* with the Meaning of Yellow Turban's Slogan and Relevant Issues). *Lishi yanjiu* 1 (1996): 125–32.

Liu Zhen 劉珍, et al. Wu Shuping 吳樹平, ed. *Dongguan Han ji jiaozhu* 東觀漢記校注 (Collations of *The Dongguan Records of Han*). Beijing: Zhonghua, 2008.

Lloyd, G. E. R., and Nathan Sivin. *The Way and the Word: Science and Medicine in Early China and Greece*. New Haven: Yale University Press, 2002.

Loewe, Michael. *Crisis and Conflict in Han China, 104 BC to AD 9*. London: George Allen & Unwin, 1974.

———. "The Former Han Dynasty." In *The Cambridge History of China, Vol. 1, The Ch'in and Han Empires, 221 B.C.–A.D. 220*, ed. Denis Twitchett and Michael Loewe, 103–22. Cambridge: Cambridge University Press, 1987.

———. *Divination, Mythology and Monarchy in Han China*. University of Cambridge Oriental Publications 48. Cambridge: Cambridge University Press, 1995.

———. *The Men Who Governed Han China: Companion to* A Biographical Dictionary of the Qin, Former Han and Xin Periods. Leiden: Brill, 2011.

———. *Dong Zhongshu, a 'Confucian' Heritage and the* Chunqiu Fanlu. Leiden: Brill, 2011.

Loewe, Michael, ed. *Early Chinese Texts: A Bibliographical Guide*. Berkeley: Society for the Study of Early China; Institute of East Asian Studies, University of California, Berkeley, 1993.

Lue Xinhui 羅新慧. "Zhoudai tianming guannian de fazhan yu shanbian" 周代天命觀念的發展與嬗變 (The Developments and Changes of the Concept "Mandate of Heaven" of the Zhou Dynasty). *Lishi yanjiu* 歷史研究 5 (2012): 4–18.

Lu Jia 陸賈. Wang Liqi 王利器, ed. *Xinyu jiaozhu* 新語校注 (Collations and Commentaries on the *New Speeches*). Beijing: Zhonghua, 1986.

Lü Kai 呂凱. *Zheng Xuan zhi chenwei xue* 鄭玄之讖緯學 (Zheng Xuan's Study of Apocrypha). Taipei: Commercial Press, 1982.

Lu Qinli 逯欽立, ed. *Xian Qin Han Wei Jin Nanbei chao shi* 先秦漢魏晉南北朝詩 (Poems from Pre-Qin, Han, Wei, Jin, and Northern and Southern Dynasties). Beijing: Zhonghua, 1983.

Lü Simian 呂思勉. *Qin Han shi* 秦漢史. *Lü Simian wenji*. Shanghai: Shanghai guji, 2005.

Lu Zongli. *Power of the Words: Chen Prophecy in Chinese Politics, AD 265–618*. Oxford: Peter Lang, 2003.

Lunyu 論語. Zhu Xi 朱熹 annotated. *Sishu zhangju jizhu* 四書章句集注 (Collected Commentaries on the Paragraphs and Verses of the Four Books). Beijing: Zhonghua, 1983.

Luo Genze 羅根澤. *Luo Genze shuo zhuzi* 羅根澤說諸子 (Luo Genze Explaining Various Masters). Shanghai: Guji, 2001.

Luo Jianqiu 羅檢秋. *Qianjia yilai Hanxue chuantong de yanbian yu chuancheng* 乾嘉以來漢學傳統的衍變與傳承 (The Evolvement and Transmission of the Tradition of the Learning of Han since Qianjia Reign). *Guojia Qing shi bianzuan weiyuanhui yanjiu congkan* 國家清史編纂委員會研究叢刊. Beijing: Renming daxue, 2006.

Luo Zhitian 羅志田. "*Gushi bian* de xueshu he sixiang Beijing: Shu Luo Xianglin shaoweirenzhi de yi pian jiuwen" 《古史辨》的學術和思想背景——述羅香林少為人知的一篇舊文 (The Academic and Intellectual Background of *Critiques of Ancient History*: On One of Luo Xianglin's Old Papers That Is Rarely Known). *Shehui kexue zhanxian 2 (*2008): 110–15.

———. "Fangfa cheng le xueming: Qingdai kaoju heyi cheng xue" 方法成了學名：清代考據何以成學 (Methodology Becoming the Name of a Field: How Evidential Research Became a Field in the Qing Dynasty). *Wenyi yanjiu 2 (*2010): 24–31.

Lupke, Christopher, ed. *The Magnitude of* Ming: *Command, Allotment, and Fate in Chinese Culture*. Honolulu: University of Hawai'i Press, 2005.

Ma Duanlin 馬端臨. Shanghai Shifan Daxue Guji Yanjiu Suo 上海師範大學古籍研究所 and Huadong Shifan Daxue Guji Yanjiu Suo 華東師範大學古籍研究所, eds. *Wenxian tongkao* 文獻通考 (General History of Institutions and Critical Examination of Documents and Studies). Beijing: Zhonghua, 2011.

Ma Guohan 馬國翰, ed. *Yuhan Shanfang jiyi shu* 玉函山房輯佚書 (The Jade Sack Mountain House's Collections of Lost Books). 5 vols. Yangzhou: Guangling, 2005.

Ma Zonghuo 馬宗霍. *Zhongguo jingxue shi* 中國經學史 (A History of the Learning of Chinese Classics). Shanghai: Shanghai shudian, 1984.

Major, John S. *Heaven and Earth in Early Han Thought: Chapters Three, Four, and Five of the Huainanzi*. SUNY series in Chinese Philosophy and Culture. Albany: State University of New York Press, 1993.

Major, John S., et al., trans. *The Huainanzi: A Guide to the Theory and Practice of Government in Early Han China*. Translations from the Asian Classics. New York: Columbia University Press, 2010.

Makeham, John. "The Earliest Extant Commentary on *Lunyu*: *Lunyu Zheng shi zhu*." *T'oung Pao* 83 (1997): 260–99.

Martin, Dale B. *Inventing Superstition: From the Hippocratics to the Christians*. Cambridge: Harvard University Press, 2004.

Mashima Junichi 間嶋潤一. *Jō Gen to Shurai: Shū no taihei kokka no kōsō* 鄭玄と「周礼」：周の太平國家の構想 (Zheng Xuan and the *Rites of Zhou*: The Imagination of the State of the Great Peace of Zhou). Tokyo: Meiji Shoin, 2010.

Mather, Richard B. "The Controversy over Conformity and Naturalness during the Six Dynasties." *History of Religions* 9.2/3 (November 1969–February 1970): 160–80.

Mauss, Marcel. *The Gift: Forms and Functions of Exchange in Archaic Societies*. Trans. E. E. Evans-Pritchard. New York: Norton, 1967.

McDonald, Lee Martin. *Forgotten Scriptures: The Selection and Rejection of Early Religious Writings*. Louisville: Westminster John Knox Press, 2009.

Mengzi 孟子 (*Mencius*). Zhu Xi 朱熹 annotated. *Sishu zhangju jizhu* 四書章句集注 (Collected Commentaries on the Paragraphs and Verses of the Four Books). Beijing: Zhonghua, 1983.

Messick, Brinkley. *The Calligraphic State: Textual Domination and History in a Muslim Society*. Berkeley: University of California Press, 1993.

Mote, Frederick W., et al. *Calligraphy and the East Asian Book*. Ed. Howard L. Goodman. Boston: Shambhala, 1989.

Mozi 墨子. Sun Yirang 孫詒讓, ed., *Mozi jian gu* 墨子間詁 (Inquiries and Interpretations on *Mozi*). Beijing: Zhonghua, 2001.

Nielsen, Bent. *A Companion to Yi jing Numerology and Cosmology: Chinese Studies of Images and Numbers from Han (202 BCE–220 CE) to Song (960–1279 CE)*. London: RoutledgeCurzon, 2003.

Nishijima Sadao 西嶋定生. *Shin Kan teikoku* 秦漢帝國 (The Qin and Han Empires). Tokyo: Kōdansha, 1974.

Nylan, Michael. *The Canon of Supreme Mystery by Yang Hsiung: A Translation with Commentary of the* T'ai Hsüan Ching. Albany: State University of New York Press, 1993.

———. "The *chin wen/ku wen* Controversy in Han Times." *T'oung Pao* 80.1–3 (1994): 83–145.

———. "A Problematic Model: The Han 'Orthodox Synthesis,' Then and Now." In *Imagining Boundaries: Changing Confucian Doctrines, Texts, and Hermeneutics*, ed. Kai-wing Chow et al., 17–56. Albany: State University of New York Press, 1999.

———. "Calligraphy: The Sacred Test and Text of Culture." In *Character and Context in Chinese Calligraphy*, ed. Cary Y. Liu *et al.*, 16–77. Princeton: Princeton University Art Museum, 1999.

———. *The Five "Confucian Classics."* New Haven: Yale University Press, 2001.

———. "Toward an Archaeology of Writing: Text, Ritual, and the Culture of Public Display in the Classical Period (475 B.C.E.–220 C.E.)." In *Text and Ritual in Early China*, ed. Martin Kern, 3–49. Seattle: University of Washington Press, 2005.

———. *Yang Xiong and the Pleasures of Reading and Classical Learning in China*. American Oriental Series 94. New Haven: American Oriental Society, 2011.

Nylan, Michael, and Michael Loewe, eds. *China's Early Empires: A Re-appraisal*. Cambridge: Cambridge University Press, 2010.

Nylan, Michael, and Nathan Sivin. "The First Neo-Confucianism: An Introduction to Yang Hsiung's 'Canon of Supreme Mystery' (*T'ai hsüan ching*, ca. 4 B.C.)." In *Medicine, Philosophy and Religion in Ancient China: Researches and Reflections*, ed. Nathan Sivin, 1–42. Brookfield: Variorum, 1995.

Nylan, Michael, and He Ruyue. "On a Han-era Postface (*Xu* 序) to the *Documents*." *Harvard Journal of Asiatic Studies* 75.2 (2015): 377–426.

Nylan, Michael, and Griet Vankeerberghen, eds. *Chang'an 26 BCE: An Augustan Age in China*. Seattle: University of Washington Press, 2015.

Ōfuchi Ninji 大淵忍爾. "*Taiheikyō* no raireki ni tsuite" 太平經の來歷について (The Origin of the *Scripture of the Great Peace*). *Tōyō gakuhō* 東洋學報 27.2 (1940): 100–24.

———. *Shoki no dōkyō: Dōkyōshi no kenkyū sono ichi* 初期の道教——道教史の研究其の一 (Early Daoism: A Study of the History of Daoism). Tokyo: Sōbunsha, 1991.

Ouyang Xiu 歐陽修, Song Qi 宋祁. *Xin Tangshu* 新唐書 (A New History of Tang). Beijing: Zhonghua, 1975.

Oyanagi Shigeta 小柳司氣太. "*Go Kan jo Jō Kai den no Taihei shōryō sho* ni tsuite" 後漢書裏楷傳の太平清領書について (The *Writing of the Great Peace with Blue-Green Headings* in the Biography of Xiang Kai from the *History of Later Han*). In *Kuwabara Hakushi kanreki kinen Tōyōshi ronsō* 東洋史論叢, ed. Kuwabara Hakushi Kanreki Kinen Shukugakai 桑原博士還曆記念祝賀會, 141–71. Kyoto: Kōbundō, 1930.

Pan Jixing 潘吉星. *Zhongguo zaozhi shi* 中國造紙史 (A History of Papermaking in China). Shanghai: Renmin, 2009.

Pankenier, David W. "The Cosmo-Political Background of Heaven's Mandate." *Early China* 20 (1995): 121–76.

Pattinson, David. "Privacy and Letter Writing in Han and Six Dynasties China." In *Chinese Concepts of Privacy*, ed. Bonnie S. McDougall and Anders Hansson, 97–118. Sinica Leidensia 55. Leiden: Brill, 2002.

Peterson, Willard J. "Making Connections: 'Commentary on the Attached Verbalizations' of the Book of Change." *Harvard Journal of Asiatic Studies* 42.1 (1982): 67–116.

Pi Xirui 皮錫瑞. *Jingxue lishi* 經學歷史 (A History of the Learning of Classics). Zhou Yutong 周予同 annotated. Beijing: Zhonghua, 2004.

———. "*Liuyi lun" shuzheng* 六藝論疏證 (Explications of "Discussion of the Six Arts"). *Xuxiu Siku quanshu* 續四庫全書. Vol. 171. Shanghai: Guji, 2002.

Pines, Yuri. *Foundations of Confucian Thought: Intellectual Life in the Chunqiu Period, 722–453 B.C.E.* Honolulu: University of Hawai'i Press, 2002.

———. *Envisioning Eternal Empire: Chinese Political Thought of the Warring States Era*. Honolulu: University of Hawai'i Press, 2009.

———. "Chinese History Writing between the Sacred and the Secular." In *Early Chinese Religion, Part I: Shang through Han (1250 BC–220 AD)*, ed. John Lagerwey and Marc Kalinowski, 315–40. Leiden: Brill, 2009.

Pines, Yuri, Lothar von Falkenhausen, Gideon Shelach, and Robin D. S. Yates, eds. *Birth of an Empire: The State of Qin Revisited*. Berkeley: University of California Press, 2014.
Poo, Mu-chou. "How to Steer through Life: Negotiating Fate in the *Daybook*." In *The Magnitude of* Ming: *Command, Allotment, and Fate in Chinese Culture*, ed. Christopher Lupke, 107–25. Honolulu: University of Hawai'i Press, 2005.
Puett, Michael J. *The Ambivalence of Creation: Debates concerning Innovation and Artifice in Early China*. New York: Cambridge University Press, 2000.
———. *To Become a God: Cosmology, Sacrifice, and Self-Divinization in Early China*. Cambridge: Harvard University Press, 2002.
———. "Following the Commands of Heaven: The Notion of *Ming* in Early China." In *The Magnitude of* Ming: *Command, Allotment, and Fate in Chinese Culture*, ed. Christopher Lupke, 49–69. Honolulu: University of Hawai'i Press, 2005.
Qian Mu 錢穆. *Zhongguo jin sanbai nian xueshu shi* 中國近三百年學術史 (A History of Chinese Scholarship of the Most Recent Three Hundred Years). *Daxue congshu* 大學叢書. 2 vols. Taipei: Taiwan shangwu, 1966.
———. *Guo shi dagang* 國史大綱 (Outlines of Chinese History). Xiuding ben. Third edition. 2 vols. Beijing: Shangwu, 1996.
———. "Liu Xiang Xin fuzi nianpu" 劉向歆夫子年譜 (The Chronicle of Liu Xiang and His Son Liu Xin). In *Liang Han jingxue jin gu wen ping yi* 兩漢經學今古文平議 (The Evaluation and Examination of the Han Dynasties' Old and New Script Tradition in the Learning of Classics), 1–179. Beijing: Shangwu, 2001.
———. *Qin Han shi* 秦漢史 (A History of Qin and Han). *Qian Mu zuopin xilie*. Beijing: Sanlian, 2005.
Qian Zhongshu 钱锺书, ed. *Hanxue shicheng ji (wai er zhong)* 漢學師承記（外二種）(The Record of the Learning of Han's Transmission Lineage with Two Other Works). *Zhongguo jindai xueshu mingzhu* 中國近代學術名著. Beijing: Sanlian, 1998.
Qiu Guangming 丘光明, Qiu Long 邱隆, and Yang Ping 楊平. *Zhongguo kexue jishu shi: Du liang heng juan* 中國科學技術史：度量衡卷 (Chinese History of Science: The Volume of Measurement). Lu Jiaxi 盧嘉錫, ed., *Zhongguo kexue jishu shi*. Beijing: Kexue, 2001.
Queen, Sarah A. *From Chronicle to Canon: The Hermeneutics of the* Spring and Autumn, *According to Tung Chung-shu*. Cambridge Studies in Chinese History, Literature and Institutions. New York: Cambridge University Press, 1996.
Qutan xida 瞿曇悉達 (Gautama Siddha). *Kaiyuan zhanjing* 開元占經 (Classic of Astrology from Kaiyuan Reign). Zhengzhou: Zhongzhou guji, 1994.
Richter, Antje. "Beyond Calligraphy: Reading Wang Xizhi's Letters." *T'oung Pao* 96 (2011): 370–407.
Ruan Yuan 阮元, ed. *Shisan jing zhu shu* 十三經注疏. Beijing: Zhonghua, 1980.

Sahara Yasuo 佐原康夫. "Kandai no ichi ni tsute" 漢代の市について (Markets in the Han Dynasties). *Shirin* 68.5 (1985): 33–71.

Sakai Tado Sensei Koki Shukuga Kinen no Kai 酒井忠夫先生古稀祝賀記念の会, ed. *Rekishi ni okeru minū to bunka: Sakai Tadao Sensei koki shukuga kinen ronshū* 歴史における民衆と文化：酒井忠夫先生古稀祝賀記念論集. Tokyo: Kokusho Kankōkai, 1982.

Sang Bing 桑兵. *Wan Qing Minguo de xueren yu xueshu* 晚清民國的學人與學術 (Scholars and Scholarship in Late Qing and the Republic Period). Beijing: Zhonghua, 2008.

Schaberg, David. "Command and the Content of Tradition." In *The Magnitude of Ming: Command, Allotment, and Fate in Chinese Culture*, ed. Christopher Lupke, 23–48. Honolulu: University of Hawai'i Press, 2005.

Scheidel, Walter. "The Monetary Systems of the Han and Roman Empires." In *Rome and China: Comparative Perspectives on Ancient World Empires*, ed. Walter Scheidel, 137–207. New York: Oxford University Press, 2009.

Schipper, Kristofer, and Franciscus Verellen, eds. *The Taoist Canon: A Historical Companion to the* Daozang. 3 vols. Chicago: University of Chicago Press, 2004.

Schneemelcher, Wilhelm, ed., R. McL. Wilson, trans. *New Testament Apocrypha*. Second edition. 2 vols. Philadelphia: Westminster Press, 1962–1963.

Schneider, Laurence A. "From Textual Criticism to Social Criticism: The Historiography of Ku Chieh-kang." *The Journal of Asian Studies* 28.4 (1969): 771–88.

———. *Ku Chieh-kang and China's New History: Nationalism and the Quest for Alternative Traditions*. Berkeley: University of California Press, 1971.

Seidel, Anna. "Imperial Treasures and Taoist Sacraments: Taoist Roots in the Apocrypha." In *Tantric and Taoist Studies in Honour of R. A. Stein*, ed. Michel Strickmann. *Mélanges chinois et bouddhiques* 21 (1983): 291–371.

Shaughnessy, Edward L. *Before Confucius: Studies in the Creation of the Chinese Classics*. Albany: State University of New York Press, 1997.

———. *I Ching = The Classic of Changes, the First English Translation of the Newly Discovered Mawangdui Texts of I Ching*. New York: Ballantine Books, 1997.

Shaughnessy, Edward L. (Xia Hanyi 夏含夷). *Gushi guan yi* 古史觀異 (Observing Oddness in Ancient History). Shanghai: Guji, 2005.

Shields, Anna M. *One Who Knows Me: Friendship and Literary Culture in Mid-Tang China*. Cambridge: Harvard University Press.

Shigezawa Toshirō 重沢俊郎. "Kinko bungaku no honshitsu" 今古文學の本質 (The Essence of Old and New Script Learning). *Shinagaku* 支那學 9-4 (1939): 669–97.

Shimizu Shigeru 清水茂. "Kami no hatsumei to Gokan no gakufū" 紙の發明と後漢の學風 (The Invention of Paper and Scholarly Trends of the Eastern Han). *Tōhōgaku* 79 (1990): 1–13.

Sima Qian 司馬遷. *Shiji* 史記 (Records of the Grand Historian). Beijing: Zhonghua, 1987.

Sivin, Nathan. "On the Word 'Taoist' as a Source of Perplexity, with Special Reference to the Relations of Science and Religion in Traditional China." *History of Religions* 17.4 (1978): 303–30.

———. *Traditional Medicine in Contemporary China: A Partial Translation of a Revised Outline of Chinese Medicine (1972), with an Introductory Study on Change in Present-Day and Early Medicine*. Science, Medicine, and Technology in East Asia 2. Ann Arbor: Center for Chinese Studies, University of Michigan, 1987.

———. "State, Cosmos, and Body in the Last Three Centuries B.C." *Harvard Journal of Asiatic Studies* 55.1 (1995): 5–37.

———."Text and Experience in Classical Chinese Medicine." In *Knowledge and the Scholarly Medical Traditions*, ed. Don Bates, 177–204. Cambridge: Cambridge University Press, 1995.

———. *Granting the Seasons: The Chinese Astronomical Reform of 1280, with a Study of Its Many Dimensions and a Translation of Its Records*. New York: Springer, 2009.

———. "Old and New Daoisms." *Religious Studies Review* 36 (March 2010): 31–50.

Sleeswyk, André Wegener, and Nathan Sivin. "Dragons and Toads: The Chinese Seismoscope of A.D. 132." *Chinese Science* 6 (1983): 1–19.

Smith, Kidder. "Sima Tan and the Invention of Daoism, 'Legalism,' 'et cetera.'" *Journal of Asian Studies* 62.1 (2003): 129–56.

Smith, Richard J. *Fathoming the Cosmos and Ordering the World: The* Yijing *(*I Ching, or Classic of Changes*) and Its Evolution in China*. Richard Lectures for 1999. Charlottesville: University of Virginia Press, 2008.

Song Yanping 宋豔萍. *Gongyang xue yu Handai shehui* 公羊學與漢代社會 (The Gongyang Tradition and Han Society). Beijing: Xueyuan, 2010.

Studia Serica Bernhard Karlgren Dedicata: Sinological Studies Dedicated to Bernhard Karlgren on his Seventieth Birthday, October Fifth, 1959. Copenhagen: E. Munksgaard, 1959.

Sukhu, Gopal. *The Shaman and the Heresiarch: A New Interpretation of the* Li sao. Albany: State University of New York Press, 2012.

Sun Ji 孫機. *Handai wuzhi wenhua ziliao tushuo* 漢代物質文化資料圖說 (Illustrated Explanations of the Material Culture of the Han Dynasty). Shanghai: Guji, 2008.

Sun Xiaochun and Jacob Kistemaker. *The Chinese Sky during the Han: Constellating Stars and Society*. Sinica Leidensia 38. Leiden: E. J. Brill, 1997.

Sun Yirang 孫詒讓. Zhouli *zhengyi* 周禮正義 (The *Rectification of the Meaning of* Rites of Zhou). Beijing: Zhonghua, 1987.

Swidler, Ann. *Talk of Love*. Chicago: University of Chicago Press, 2001.

Tada Kensuke 多田狷介. *Kan Gi Shin shi no kenkyū* 漢魏晉史の研究 (Studies on the History of Han, Wei, and Jin). Tokyo: Kyūko shoin, 1999.

Takeda Tokimasa 武田時昌. "Kei Bou no saiisetsushisō" 京房の災異思想 (Jing Fang's Thought on Omens). In *Igaku kenkyū ronsō: Yasui Kōzan Hakushi tsuitō* 緯學

研究論叢：安居香山博士追悼, ed. Nakamura Shōhachi 中村璋八, 66–84. Tokyo: Hirakawa Shuppansha, 1993.

Tanaka Masami 田中麻紗巳. *Ryōkan shisō no kenkyū* 兩漢思想の研究 (Studies on the Thought of Han Dynasties). Tokyo: Kenbun Shuppan, 1986.

———. "*Shunjū Ukuyō Kaiko* Isho Kanren Kashio『春秋公羊解詁』緯書関連個所" (Cases Relevant to Apocryphal Texts in *Interpretations of the Gongyang Tradition of* the Annals). In *Igaku kenkyū ronsō: Yasui Kōzan Hakushi tsuitō* 緯學研究論叢：安居香山博士追悼, ed. Nakamura Shōhachi 中村璋八, 43–65. Tokyo: Hirakawa Shuppansha, 1993.

———. *Gokan Shisō no tankyū* 後漢思想の探究 (Explorations of the Thought of the Eastern Han Dynasty). Tokyo: Kenbun Shuppan, 2003.

Tang Yiming. "The Voice of Wei-Jin Scholars: A Study of 'Qingtan.'" PhD dissertation, Columbia University, 1991.

Tang Yongtong 湯用彤. "Du *Taiping jing* shu suo jian" 讀《太平經》書所見 (Notes from Reading the *Scripture of the Great Peace*). *Guouxe jikan* 5.1 (1933): 7–38.

Tang Yongtong 湯用彤. *Wei Jin Xuanxue lun gao* 魏晉玄學論稿 (A Draft of Discussions of the Wei and Jin Dark Learning). Penglai Ge congshu 蓬萊閣叢書. Shanghai: Shanghai guji, 2001.

Tang Zhangru 唐長孺. "Taiping dao yu Tianshi dao" 太平道與天師道 (The Cult of the Great Peace and the Cult of the Celestial Masters). In *Tang Zhangru wencun* 唐長孺文存, ed. Zhu Lei 朱雷 and Tang Gangmao 唐剛卯, 733–66. Shanghai: guji, 2006.

Tjan Tjoe Som 曾珠森, trans. *Po Hu T'ung: The Comprehensive Discussions in the White Tiger Hall*. 2 vols. Sinica Leidensia 6. Leiden: E. J. Brill, 1949–1952.

Tomiya Itaru 富谷至. *Bunsho gyōsei no kan teikoku: mokkan chikukan no jidai* 文書行政の漢帝國——木簡竹簡の時代 (Document Administration of the Han Dynasty: The Era of Wooden and Bamboo Slips). Nagayo: Nagoya Daigaku Shuppankai, 2010.

Tse W. K. Wicky. *The Collapse of China's Later Han Dynasty, 25–200 CE: The Northwest Borderlands and the Edge of Empire*. Abingdon: Routledge, 2018.

Tsien Tsuen-hsuin. *Chemistry and Chemical Technology, Vol. 5*. Ed. Joseph Needham, *Science and Civilisation in China*. Cambridge: Cambridge University Press, 1985.

Twitchett, Denis, and Michael Loewe, eds. *The Cambridge History of China, Vol. 1, The Ch'in and Han Empires, 221 B.C.–A.D. 220*. Cambridge: Cambridge University Press, 1987.

Uchino Kumaichirō 内野熊一郎. *Kansho keishogaku no kenkyū* 漢初經書學の研究 (A Study of the Learning of Classics in the Beginning of the Han Dynasty). Tokyo: Shimi zu shotn, 1948.

Ueda Sanae 上田早苗. "Gokan makki no jōyō no gōzoku 後漢末期の襄陽の豪族" (Great Families of Xiangyang at the End of Eastern Han). *Tōyōshi kenkyū* 28.4 (1970): 283–305.

Vankeerberghen, Griet. *The* Huainanzi *and Liu An's Claim to Moral Authority*. SUNY series in Chinese Philosophy and Culture. Albany: State University of New York Press, 2001.
Violi, Patrizia. "Letters." In *Discourse and Literature*, ed. Teun A. van Dijk, 149–68. Amsterdam: Benjamins, 1985.
Wang Aihe. *Cosmology and Political Culture in Early China*. New York: Cambridge University Press, 2000.
Wang Chong 王充. *Lun heng* 論衡 (Doctrines Evaluated). Shanghai: Shanghai renmin, 1974; Huang Hui 黃暉, ed., *Lun heng jiaoshi* 論衡校釋 (Collations and Explanations of *Doctrines Evaluated*). Beijing: Zhonghua, 1990.
Wang Jia 王嘉. *Shiyi ji* 拾遺記 (Records of Left-Out Stories). In *Siku quanshu*, vol. 1042, 311–64. Shanghai: Guji, 1987.
Wang Liqi 王利器. *Zheng Kangcheng nianpu* 鄭康成年譜 (A Chronicle of Zheng Kangcheng). Jinan: Qi Lu, 1983.
———. "Chenwei wu lun" 讖緯五論 (Five Issues on Apocrypha). In Zhang Dainian 張岱年 et al., *Guoxue jinlun* 國學今論 (Present Discussions of Sinology), 125–35. Shenyang: Liaoning jiaoyu, 1995.
———, ed. Lü Buwei 呂不韋. Lüshi chunqiu *zhushu* 呂氏春秋註疏 (Commentaries and Sub-Commentaries on *Lushi chunqiu*). 4 vols. Chengdu: Bashu Shushe, 2002.
Wang Ming 王明, ed. *Taiping jing he jiao* 太平經合校 (A Combined Collation of the *Scripture of the Great Peace*). Beijing: Zhonghua, 1960.
———. *Daojia he Daojiao sixiang yanjiu* 道家和道教思想研究 (Studies on Philosophical and Religious Daoism). Beijing: Zhongguo shehui kexue, 1984.
Wang Ping 王平. Taiping jing *yanjiu* 《太平經》研究 (A Study of the *Scripture of the Great Peace*). Taipei: Wenjin, 1995.
Wang Tianhai 王天海. *Xunzi jiao shi* 荀子校釋 (Collations and Interpretations of *Xunzi*). Shanghai: Guji, 2005.
Wang Yucheng 王育成. "Dong Han tiandi shizhe lei daoren yu Daojiao qiyuan" 東漢天帝使者類道人與道教起源 (The Envoy-of-the-Heavenly-Emperor Type of Masters of Dao in the Eastern Han and the Origin of Daoism). *Daojia wenhua yanjiu* 16 (1999): 181–203.
Washio Yukō 鷲尾祐子. "Zenkan no ninkan tōyō to shakaichitsujo" 前漢の任官登用と社会秩序 (Official Recruitment and Social Order in the Western Han). In *Chūgoku kodaishi ronsō dai 5 sū* 中國古代史論叢第5集 (Collected Discussions on Ancient Chinese History, vol. 5), ed. Ritsumeikan Tōyō Shigakkai Chūgoku Kodaishi Ronsō Henshū Iinkai 立命館東洋史學會中國古代史論叢編集委員會, 32–72. Kyoto: Ritsumeikan Tōyō Shigakkai, 2008.
Watanabe Yoshihiro 渡邊義浩. *Gokan kokka no shihai to Jukyō* 後漢国家の支配と儒教 (State Rule and Confucianism in the Later Han). Tokyo: Yūzankaku Shuppan, 1995.

———. "Nihon ni okeru 'jukyō no kokkyōka' o meguru kenkyū ni tsuite" 日本における「儒教の国教化」おめぐる研究について (Japanese Study of the Nationalization of the Confucian Teaching or Religion). In *Ryō Kan no Jukyō to seiji kenryoku* 両漢の儒教と政治権力 (Confucianism in the two Han dynasties and political power), ed. Watanabe Yoshihiro 渡邊義浩, 253–86. Tokyo: Kyūko shoin, 2005.

———. *Gokan ni okeru "Jukyōkokka" no seiritsu* 後漢における「儒教國家」の成立. Tokyo: Kyūko shoin, 2009.

———. "Sacrifices to Heaven in the Han and the Theory of Six Heavens." *Acta Asiatica* 98 (2010): 43–75.

———, ed. *Ryō Kan no Jukyō to seiji kenryoku* 両漢の儒教と政治権力 (Confucianism in the Two Han Dynasties and Political Power). Tokyo: Kyūko shoin, 2005.

Wei Zheng 魏徵, et al., eds. *Sui shu* 隋書 (History of Sui). Beijing: Zhonghua, 1973.

Welch, Holmes, and Anna Seidel, eds. *Facets of Taoism*. New Haven: Yale University Press, 1979.

Wu Guimei 吳桂美. *Haozu shehui de wenxue zheguang: Dong Han jiazu wenxue shengtai toushi* 豪族社會的文學折光——東漢家族文學生態透視 (The Refraction of Literature in the Society of Great Families: An Exploration of Eastern Han families' Ecological System of Literature). Haerbin: Heilongjinang renmin, 2008.

Wu Yannan 吳雁南, Qin Xueqi 秦學頎, and Li Yujie 李禹階, eds. *Zhongguo jingxue shi* 中國經學史 (A History of the Study of the Classics). Fuzhou: Fujian renmin; Beijing: Renmin, 2010.

Wu Yangxiang 吳仰湘. "Pi Xirui *Jingxue lishi* yanjiu" 皮锡瑞《经学历史》研究 (A Study on Pi Xirui's *A History of the Learning of Classics*). *Jingxue yanjiu luncong* 经学研究论丛 14 (2006): 1–52.

Xiang Jinwei 向晉衛. *Baihu tongyi sixiang de lishi yanjiu*《白虎通義》思想的歷史研究 (A Historical Study of the Thought in the *Comprehensive Meanings of the White Tiger Pavillion*). Beijing: Renmin, 2007.

Xianggang Zhongwen Daxue Zhongguo Wenhua Yanjiusuo 香港中文大學中國文化研究所 (The Chinese University of Hong Kong Institute of Chinese Studies). *Baihu tong zhuzi suoyin* 白虎通逐字索引 (A Concordance to the *Baihu tong*). Xian Qin Liang Han guji zhuzi suoyin congkan 先秦兩漢古籍逐字索引叢刊. Hong Kong: The Commercial Press, 1995.

Xiao Dengfu 蕭登福. *Chenwei yu Daojiao* 讖緯與道教 (Apocrypha and Daoism). Taipei: Wenjin, 2000.

Xiao Ji 蕭吉. Nakamura Shōhachi 中村璋八 annotated. *Wuxing dayi* 五行大義 (Significant Meaning of the Five Phases). Tokyo: Kyūko shoin, 1984.

Xiao Tong 蕭統 (501–31 A.D.), ed. *Wen xuan* 文選 (Selections of Literature). Beijing: Zhonghua, 1977.

Xing Yitian 邢義田. "Donghan Xiaolian de shenfen Beijing" 東漢孝廉的身份背景 (The Background of People Who Were Appointed as Filial Pious and Uncorrupted in the Eastern Han). In *Di er jie Zhongguo shehui jingji shi yantaohui lunwenji* 第二屆中國社會經濟史研討會論文集 (A Collection of Papers from the Second

Conference of Chinese Social and Economic History), ed. Hu Zhuoyun 許
倬云 (Cho-yun Hsu), Mao Hanguang 毛漢光, and Liu Cuirong 劉翠溶, 1–56.
Taipei: Hanxue Yanjiu ziliao ji fuwu zhongxin, 1983.
———. *Qin Han shi lun gao*秦漢史論稿 (Drafts on Discussions about the History
of Qin and Han). Taibei: Dongda tushu, 1987.
———. *Di bu ai bao: Handai de jiandu* 地不愛寶—漢代的簡牘 (The Earth Does Not
Love Treasure: Bamboo and Wooden Slips of the Han). Beijing: Zhonghua,
2011.
———. *Tianxia yi jia*: *Huandi, Guanliao yu shehui* 天下一家: 皇帝、官僚與社會 (All-
under-Heaven as the Same Family: Emperors, Officials and Society). *Qin Han
shi lunzhu xilie*. Beijing: Zhonghua, 2011.
Xu Fuguan 徐復觀. *Liang Han sixiang shi* 兩漢思想史 (An Intellectual History of the
Western and Eastern Han). 2 vols. Shanghai: Huadong shifan daxue, 2001.
———. *Xu Fuguan jingxue shi liang zhong* 徐復觀經學史兩種 (Two Works on the
History of the Classics by Xu Fuguan). Shanghai: Shanghai shudian, 2005.
Xu Xingwu 徐興無. "Zuowei pifu de xuansheng suwang—chenwei wenxian zhong
de Kongzi xingxiang yu sixiang" 作為匹夫的玄聖素王—讖緯文獻中的孔子形象與
思想 (The black Sage and Uncrowned King as a Commoner: The Image and
Thought of Confucius in Apocryphal Texts). *Gudian wenxian yanjiu* 古典文
獻研究 11 (2008): 21–42.
———. "Apocrypha and Literary Rhetoric of the Han, Wei, and Six Dynasty
Periods." Trans. Scott Davis. *Journal of Chinese Literature and Culture* 3.1
(2016): 137–74.
Yan Kejun 嚴可均, ed. *Quan shanggu sandai Qin Han Sanguo Liuchao wen* 全上古三
代秦漢三國六朝文 (A Comprehensive Collection of Great Antiquity, the Three
Dynasties, Qin, Han, the Three Kingdoms, and Six Dynasties Prose). 4 vols.
Beijing: Zhonghua, 1958.
Yan Zhitui 顏之推. Wang Liqi 王利器 annotated. *Yashi jiaxun jijie* 顏氏家訓集解 (Com-
piled Annotations of the *Yan Family Instructions*). Beijing: Zhonghua, 1993.
Yang Lien-sheng 楊聯陞. "Dong Han de haozu" 東漢的豪族 (Great Families in the
Eastern Han Dynasty). *Qinghua xuebao* 4 (1936): 1007–63.
Yang Tianyu 楊天宇. *Zheng Xuan Sanli zhu yanjiu* 鄭玄三禮註研究 (Studies on Zheng
Xuan's Commentaries of the Three *Rituals*). Tianjin: Renmin, 2007.
Yang Xiong 揚雄. Sima Guang 司馬光 annotated. Liu Shaojun 劉韶君, ed., *Tai xuan
ji zhu* 太玄集注 (A Collected Annotation of the *Classic of Supreme Mystery*).
Beijing: Zhonghua, 1998.
———. Wang Rongbao 汪榮寶, ed., *Fayan yishu* 法言義疏 (An Explication of the
Standard Sayings). Beijing: Zhonghua, 1987.
Yasui Kōzan 安居香山. "Dōkyōno seiritsu to shin'ishisō" 道教の成立と讖緯思想 (The
Establishment of Daoism and the Thought of Apocrypha). In *Dōkyo to shūkyō
bunka* 道教と宗教文化 (Daoism and Religious Culture), ed. Akizuki Kan'ei 秋
月觀暎, 45–60. Tokyo: Hirakawa Shuppansha, 1987.

———. *Isho to Chūgoku no shinpi shisō* 緯書と中国の神秘思想 (Apocryphal Texts and Chinese Mysterious Thought). Tokyo: Hirakawa Shuppansha, 1988.

Yasui Kōzan 安居香山 and Nakamura Shōhachi 中村璋八. *Isho no kisoteki kenkyū* 緯書の基礎的研究. Tokyo: Kokusho Kankōkai, 1976.

Yasui Kozan 安居香山 and Nakamura Shōhachi 中村璋八 eds. *Weishu jicheng* 緯書集成. Shijiazhuang: Hebei renmin, 1994.

Yates, Robin D. S. "The Yin-Yang Texts from Yinqueshan: An Introduction and Partial Reconstruction, with Notes on Their Significance in Relation to Huang-Lao Daoism." *Early China* 19 (1994): 74–144.

———. "Soldiers, Scribes, and Women: Literacy among the Lower Orders in Early China." In *Writing and Literacy in Early China: Studies from the Columbia Early China Seminar*, ed. Li Feng and David Prager Branner, 229–69. Seattle: University of Washington Press, 2011.

Ying Shao 應劭. Wu Shuping, ed. *Fengsu tongyi jiaozhi* 風俗通義校釋 (Collations and Explanations of the *Comprehensive Meaning of Customs*). Tianjin: Renmin, 1980.

Yong Rong 永瑢 et al. *Siku quanshu zongmu* 四庫全書總目 (The Catalog of the *Complete Library of the Four Treasures*). Beijing: Zhonghua, 1965.

Yoshikawa Tadao 吉川忠夫. "Tōko to gakumon: tokuni Ka Kyu no ba'ai" 黨錮と學問—とくに何休の場合 (The Proscription of Partisanship and Scholarship: Especially the Case of He Xiu). *Tōyōshi kenkyū* 35.3 (1976): 414–46.

———. "Shoku ni okeru shin'i no gaku no dentō" 蜀における讖緯の學の傳統 (Traditions of Apocryphal Learning in the Shu Region). In *Shin'i shisō no sōgōteki kenkyū* 讖緯思想の綜合的研究, ed. Yasui Kōzan, 103–36. Tokyo: Kokusho kankōkai, 1984.

———. *Rikuchō seishinshi no kenkyū* 六朝精神史の研究 (Studies of the Six Dynasties' Intellectual World). Second edition. Kyoto: Dōhōsha, 1986.

———. "Tei Gen no gakujuku" 鄭玄の學塾 (Zheng Xuan's School). In *Chūgoku kizokusei shakai no kenkyū* 中國貴族制社會の研究 (Studies on the aristocratic society of China), ed. Kawakatsu Yoshio 川勝義雄 and Tonami Mamoru 礪波護, 321–59. Kyoto: Kyoto Daigaku Jinbun kagaku kenkyūjo, 1987.

Yu Jiaxi 余嘉錫. *Mulu xue fawei* 目錄學發微. Beijing: Zhonghua, 2007.

Yu Qiding 俞啟定 and Shi Kecan 施克燦. *Zhongguo jiaoyu zhidu tongshi* 中國教育制度通史 (A Complete History of the Chinese Educational System), *Vol. 1, Xian Qin, Qin, Han* 先秦、秦漢 (Pre-Qin, Qin, Han). Eds. Li Guojun 李國鈞 and Wang Bingzhao 王炳照. *Zhongguo jiaoyu zhidu tongshi*. Jinan: Shandong jiaoyu, 2000.

Yu Shinan 虞世南. *Beitang shuchao* 北堂書鈔 (Excerpts from Books in the Northern Hall). In *Tangdai sida leishu* 唐代四大類書, ed. Dong Zhian 董治安. Beijing: Qinghua, 2003.

Yü Ying-shih 余英時. "Dong Han zhengquan zhi jianli yu shizu daxing zhi guanxi" 東漢政權之建立與士族大姓之關係 (The Establishment of the Eastern Han and Its Relationship with Big Clans). *Xinya xuebao* 2 (1965): 209–80.

———. "Han Jin zhi ji shi zhi xin zijue yu xin sichao" 漢晉之際士之新自覺與新思潮 (The New Self-Realization and Trend of Literati). *Zhongguo zhishi jieceng shi lun* 中國知識階層史論 (Discussions of the History of Chinese Intelligentsia), 205–327. Taipei: Lianjing, 1980.

———. "Individualism and the Neo-Taoist Movement in Wei-Chin China." In *Individualism and Holism*, ed. Donald J. Munro, 121–55. Ann Arbor: University of Michigan Press, 1985.

———. "Zhang Xuecheng versus Dai Zhen: A Study in Intellectual Challenge and Response in Eighteenth-Century China." In *Chinese Language, Thought, and Culture: Nivison and His Critics*, ed. Philip J. Ivanhoe, 85–112. Chicago: Open Court, 1996.

———. *Lun Dai Zhen yu Zhang Xuecheng: Qingdai zhongqi xueshu sixiangshi yanjiu* 論戴震與章學誠——清代中期學術思想史研究 (Discussions on Dai Zhen and Zhang Xuecheng: Studies on the Intellectual History of Scholarship in the Mid-Qing). Beijing: Sanlian, 2000.

Yu Wanli 虞萬里. "Yi Ding Yan Shangshu *yu lun* wei zhongxin kan Wang Su weizao *Guwen Shangshuzhuan* shuo: cong kending dao fouding hou zhi sikao" 以丁晏《尚書餘論》為中心看王肅偽造《古文尚書傳》說——從肯定到否定後之思考 (Examining the Theory of Wang Su Forging the *Old Script Book of Documents and Its Commentary* by Focusing on Ding Yan's *Leftover Discussion on the Book of Documents*: A Pondering on the [Changing Attitude] from Accepting to Negating It). *Zhongguo wen zhe yanjiu jikan* 中國文哲集刊 37 (2010): 131–52.

Zeng Shengyi 曾聖益. "Zheng Xuan 'Liuyi lun' shi zhong jijiao" 鄭玄《六藝論》十種輯斠 (Compilations and Evaluation of Ten Editions of Zheng Xuan's "Discussions of the Six Arts"). *Guoli Zhongyang Tushuguan Taiwan Fenguan guan kan* 國立中央圖書館臺灣分館館刊 4.1 (1997): 70–93.

Zhang Cong. *Transformative Journeys: Travel and Culture in Song China*. Honolulu: University of Hawai'i Press, 2011.

Zhang Dainian 張岱年 et al. *Guoxue jinlun* 國學今論 (Present Discussions of Sinology). Shenyang: Liaoning jiaoyu, 1995.

Zhang Fengqi 張峰屹. "Yi Feng *Shi* xue zhi 'Wu Ji' shuo kaoshi" 翼奉《詩》學之'五際'說考釋 (An Examination and Explanation of the Five Contacts in Yi Feng's Study of the *Book of Poetry*). *Zhengzhou daxue xuebao* 41.1 (2008): 125–28.

Zhang Hequan 張鶴泉. "Donghan shidai de sixue" 東漢時代的私學 (Private Teachings in the Eastern Han). *Shixue jikan* 1 (1993): 54–59.

———. "Donghan shidai de youxue fengqi jiqi yingxiang" 東漢時代的遊學風氣及其影響 (The Fashion of Traveling to Learn in the Eastern Han and Its Impact). *Qiushi xuekan* 2 (1995): 104–09.

———. "Donghan guli wenti shitan" 東漢故吏問題試探 (A Tentative Exploration on the Issue of Former Subordinates in the Eastern Han). *Jilin Daxue shehui kexue xuebao* 5 (1995): 8–14.

Zhang Shunhui 張舜徽. *Zheng xue cong zhu* 鄭學叢著 (Collected Works of the Study of Zheng). Jinan: Qi Lu, 1984.

———. *Qing dai Yangzhou xueji* 清代揚州學記 (The Record of the Yangzhou School in the Qing Dynasty). Wuhan: Huazhong shifan daxue, 2005.

Zhang Zhenze 張震澤, ed. *Yang Xiong ji jiaozhu* 揚雄集校注 (Yang Xiong's Work with Annotations and Collations). Shanghai: Guji, 1993.

Zhang Zhenglang 張政烺. Li Ling 李零, ed., *Zhang Zhenglang lun* Yi *conggao* 張政烺論《易》叢稿 (Zhang Zhenglang's manuscripts on the *Changes*). Beijing: Zhonghua, 2011.

Zhao Lu 趙璐. "To Become Confucius: Political Legitimacy and Han Apocryphal Texts in the Case of Emperor Ming (r. A.D. 58–75)." *Asia Major* 28.1 (2015): 115–44.

———. "Representations of Confucius in Apocrypha of the First Century CE." In *A Concise Companion to Confucius*, ed. Paul R. Goldin, 75–92. Chichester: Wiley-Blackwell, 2017.

Zhao Pei 趙沛. *Liao Ping Chunqiu xue yanjiu* 廖平春秋學研究 (A Study of Liao Ping's Theory of the *Spring and Autumn Annals*). Chengdu: Bashu, 2007.

Zheng Zhen 鄭珍. *Zheng xue lu* 鄭學錄 (A Record of Zheng Xuan's Scholarship). *Xuxiu siku quanshu* 續修四庫全書, vol. 515. Shanghai: Guji, 1999.

Zhengtong Daozang 正統道藏 (The Zhengtong Reign Daoist Canon). Beijing: Wenwu, 1988.

Zhong Zhaopeng 鐘肇鵬. *Chen wei lun lue* 讖緯論略 (A Brief Discussion on Apocrypha). Shenyang: Liaoning jiaoyu, 1991.

Zhou Yutong 周予同. *Jingxue shi lunzhu xuanji* 經學史論著選集. Second edition. Shanghai: Shanghai renming, 1996.

Zufferey, Nicolas. *To the Origins of Confucianism: The* Ru *in Pre-Qin Times and during the Early Han Dynasty*. Schweizer Asiatische Studien: Monographien 43. Bern: Peter Lang, 2003.

Index

Academicians (*boshi* 博士), 220n40
  See also Chen Shi; Fan Ying; Guo Tai; Hongdu Gate school; Li Ying; National Academy; private schools; Xue Han; Zheng Xuan
Analects (*Lunyu* 論語):
  and the corpus of classics (*jing*), 181
  Gongsun Shu's wife's paraphrasing of it, 67, 233n75
Annals:
  and Han intellectual communities, 171
  Liu Xiang and Liu Xin's reliance on three traditions of, 226n135
  See also Gongyang tradition of the *Spring and Autumn Annals*; Guliang tradition of the *Spring and Autumn Annals*; qilin
apocryphal texts (*chenwei* 讖緯):
  abnormal appearance of Confucius's major disciples, 241n52
  background information, xx, 281n1
  and Confucius as *su wang* (the "uncrowned king"), 80, 85–88, 237n5
  and Confucius as *xuan sheng* ("dark sage"), 80, 88
  and Daoism, 162–163, 169
  and Emperor Guangwu's legitimation of Han rule, 50, 195, 200, 235n105
  and Emperor Ming's affirmation of Han rule, 93–94
  fragments celebrating the legitimacy of the Liu family, 79
  Han apocryphal texts differentiated from Chinese Buddhist apocrypha, 214–215
  and Heaven's active role in the formation of the classics, 52–53
  on the origin of sage kings, 60
  sage kings compared to heavenly emperors in, 62–63
  seven apocrypha (*qi jing chen* 七經讖) corresponding to the seven classics (*qi jing* 七經), 215, 235n105
  "superstitious" elements associated with, xvi, 210–211, 280n1
  and the term *chenwei*, 讖緯, 213–215
  textual genealogy employed by, 56
  titles and their structure, 50–51, *51t1*
apocryphal texts (*chenwei* 讖緯)—means of transmission:
  and the Academy, 107
  within families of, 112
apocryphal texts (*chenwei* 讖緯)—titles:
  Chunqiu baoqian tu 春秋保乾圖 (*Annals of Cherishing the Qian*), *51t1*, 62, 232nn56–57

313

apocryphal texts (*chenwei* 讖緯)—titles (*continued*)
  Chunqiu gan jing fu 春秋感符 (*Annals' Tallies Corresponding to the Essence*), *51t1*, 231n49
  Chunqiu Shuo tici 春秋說題辭 (*Annals' explications of Words in Titles*), *51t1*, 52, 53, 228n11, 228n17
  Chunqiu yan Kong tu 春秋演孔圖 (*Annals' Diagrams Elaborating Confucius*), *51t1*, 54–55, 62, 82, 228n19, 229n22, 230n38, 232n58, 238nn12–13
  Chunqiu yuanming bao 春秋元命包 (*Annals' Inclusion of the Primary Mandate*), 58–59, 230n33, 230nn35–36, 230n39, 230n41, 231n49
  Chunqiu yun dou shu, 春秋運斗樞, 51, 228n14, 229n25
  Hetu Chifu fu 河圖赤伏符 (*Red Hidden Tally of the River Chart*), *51t1*, 67–68, 70, 76
  Hetu huichang fu 河圖會昌符 (*Tally of Meeting with Prosperity*), *51t1*, 75, 76–77
  Hetu kuo dixiang 河圖括地象 (*Inclusive Images of Earth of the River Chart*), *51t1*, 69–70, 234n90
  Hetu lu yun fa 河圖錄運法 (*Recorded Rule for the Movement of Mandate of the River Chart*), *51t1*, 69, 70
  Hetu ti Liu yu 河圖提劉予 (*Bestowal to the Promoted Liu of the River Chart*), *51t1*
  Li ji mingzheng 禮稽命徵 (*Rites' Examinations of the Omens of the Mandate*), *51t1*, 52, 228n12
  Qian Kun zao du 乾坤鑿度 (*Cracking Open the Regularity of Qian and Kun*), *51t1*, 56–58, 229n23
  Qian zao du 乾鑿度 (*Cracking Open the Regularity of Qian*), 56, 229n23
  Shangshu diming yan 尚書帝命驗 (*Documents' Verification of Emperors' Mandate*), 231n47
  Shangshu xuanji qian 尚書琁機鈐 (*Key to the Heavenly Pivot in the Book of Documents*), 50–52, *51t1*, 228n8
  Shangshu zhong hou 尚書中候 (*Inner Observation of the Documents*), *51t1*, 52–53, 233n84
  Xiaojing yuanshen qi (*Tally for Assistance from Spirits of the Classic of Filial Piety*), *51t1*, 70, 234n90, 237n1
area of Qi versus of Lu (Qi/Lu 齊/魯), and Ma Zonghuo's 馬宗霍 discussion of Han classicism, 276n21
auspicious omens:
  auspicious animals appearing after following heaven, 262n44
  and Emperor Xuan, 4–5, 218n9
  phoenixes (*fenghuang* 鳳凰), 5, 58–59
  sweet dew (*ganlu* 甘露), 5
  See also Chart of the Yellow River (*Hetu* 河圖); *qilin*; Writing of the Luo River (*Luoshu* 洛书)

Ban Gu 班固, and the First Emperor's sacrifice, 75
Bing Ji 丙吉, on *yin* and *yang* balance as the job of the highest Han officials, 5–8
Biographies of Significant Women (*Lie nü zhuan* 列女傳), and Ma Rong's academy, 122
Book of Documents (*Shangshu* 尚書):
  and the corpus of classics (*jing*), 20, 181

the Huan 桓 family and the Ouyang tradition of, 107, *108chart 7*
See also official learning
Brown, Miranda, 246n24
Buddhism:
and the classics, xv, 179, 271n14
Han apocryphal texts differentiated from Chinese Buddhist apocrypha, 214–215

Changes of Zhou (*Zhou yi* 周易):
and the corpus of classics (*jing*), 181
and divination in the Eastern Zhou, 9
Emperor Xuan's promotion of it, 21–23
transmission of, 107, *108–109charts 7–8*
triagrams associated with the four seasons, 7, 219n26, 219nn26–27
Xunzi's exclusion of it from his list of classics, 21
Changes of Zhou (*Zhou yi* 周易)—Jing 京 tradition of:
and Cui Yuan, 130
and the fourteen commentarial traditions of the National Academy, 105
Changes of Zhou (*Zhou yi* 周易)—Liang 梁 tradition of, and the fourteen commentarial traditions of the National Academy, 105
Changes of Zhou (*Zhou yi* 周易)—Meng 孟 tradition of:
and the fourteen commentarial traditions of the National Academy, 105
transmission of, *108chart 7*, 248n47
Changes of Zhou (*Zhou yi* 周易)—Shi 施 tradition of, and the fourteen commentarial traditions of the National Academy, 105

Changzhou 常州 school, 186–187, 189–190, 273n18
chapter and verse commentaries (*zhang ju* 章句):
and affiliation with the new or old script tradition, 196
by Huan Yu for Emperor Ming, 92
textual corruption associated with, 163–164
Zixia as the initiator of, 91, 196
Chart of the Yellow River (*Hetu* 河圖):
and the corpus of classics, 215
revelation of, 52–53, 144–145, 166
Chen Chi-yun 陳啟雲, 260n7
Chen Jo-shui (Chen Ruoshui) 陳弱水, 270–271n14
Chen Pan 陳槃, 209, 210, 281n1, 281n5, 283n15
Chen Shi 陳寔, 106, 120, *121chart 11*, *127chart 12*, 135
Chen Suzhen, 195
on Dong Zhongshu's relationship to the *Chunqiu Fanlu*, 280n39
Classic of Filial Piety (*Xiaojing* 孝經):
and the corpus of classics (*jing*), 181
and the "seven classics" (*qi jing* 七經), 73
and Wu Rong's intellectual repertoire, 122, 251n107
Classic of Poetry (*Shijing* 詩經):
and the corpus of classics (*jing*), 181
and the fourteen commentarial traditions of the National Academy, 105
Han 漢 family tradition of, 73, 106, 107, *109chart 8*, 118–119
and Wu Rong's intellectual repertoire, 122
Younger Dai 小戴 tradition, 105, 248n47

classics *jing* 經:
  as a bibliographical category, 271–272n7
  and Buddhism, 178
  and the civil examinations, 104, 175–176, 182–183, 245n17, 246n22, 246n22, 246n24, 272n13
  and the dynamic between scholars, the classics, intellectual innovations, and political reality, xvii, 2–3, 71–72, 175–179, 235n103
  Han transmitters of, xv, xviii–xix
  and "heart" emphasized by Zhang Heng, 134
  and *jing xue* 經學 ("the study of classics"), 182, 272n8
  and local gentries, 71–72, 175
  reliance on the Great Peace in the late Western Han, xx
  and understanding the Kingly way, 35
  See also seven classics (*qi jing* 七經)
classics *jing* 經—*Six Classics*:
  establishment as a corpus of texts, 20–21, 73, 222–223n67
  and He Xiu, 151, 153
  Hou Cang on cosmological order found in them, 22–23
  Kuang Heng's view of, 25–28
  and Zhang Heng, 73, 132–133
classics *jing* 經—*Thirteen Classics*:
  inventory of, 181–183
  Zheng Xuan's commentaries in, 140
  See also *Book of Documents* (*Shangshu* 尚書); *Changes of Zhou* (*Zhou yi* 周易); *Classic of Poetry* (*Shijing* 詩經); *Rites of Zhou* (*Zhouli* 周禮)
Collins, Randall:
  interaction ritual chains theory (IR theory), xvii–xviii, 143
  on the mind of a 'sophisticated' intellectual, 134
  on opposition, 264n79
Confucianism:
  and nationalization (*kokkyōka* 国教化), 200–204, 279n7
  refuted as a label by Michael Loewe, 207
  and the term *jukyō*, 278n4
Confucius, 237n5
  Annals composed by:
    Mencius on, 53–54, 228n18
    and the role of Heaven, 53–54, 238n14
    Sima Qian on, 228n18
  and the Kong 孔 family of Qufu, 曲阜, 107
  and the *qilin*, 54, 84, 87, 156–157, 264n71
  as *su wang* (the "uncrowned king"), 80, 85–88, 237n5, 240n35
  as *xuan sheng* ("dark sage"), 80, 88, 237n5
  Xunzi's description of, 59–60, 231n44
contrast-debate model, Nylan's critique of, 189, 278n57
de Crespigny, Rafe, 244n10, 244–245n12, 252–253n120, 260n12, 260n14
Cui Yuan 崔瑗:
  family background and writing by, 130–132
  letters exchanged with Zhang Heng, 126, 128
  and the traveling culture of literati, 126, 253n125

Ding Kuan, 丁寬, 10chart 1, 41chart 4, 43chart 5, 44chart 6
documents. *See Book of Documents* (*Shangshu* 尚書)
Dong Zhongshu 董仲舒:
  on achieving Great Peace, 14–15

and Confucius as *su wang* ("uncrowned king"), 240n35
Luxuriant Dew of the Spring and Autumn Annals (*Chunqiu fanlu*), 206
omens interpreted by, 226–227n135
theory of *qi* of, 7
Dou Zhang 竇章, 126, 253n125
Dubs, Homer H., 204
Du Fu 杜撫, *109chart 8*, 118–119
Dull, Jack L.:
on Confucius as *su wang* ("uncrowned king"), 237n5, 240n35
on the development of apocrypha texts, 209

Eastern Han dynasty:
and the dominance of imperial harem families and eunuchs, 252–253n120
emperors, *100t4*
writing culture, 102–103, 124, 178, 252n115, 252n117
See also Emperor An; Emperor Guangwu; Emperor Huan; Emperor Jing; Emperor Ming
Elman, Benjamin A.:
on the Changzhou school, 186
designation of a "school," 273n15
emperors:
ages and reign years of Eastern Han Emperors, *100t4*
centrality of, 173–174, 244n10
heavenly emperors, 60
Emperor Ai 哀, 30, 36–37, 45, 64
Emperor An 安, 107, *114chart 10*
Emperor Cheng 成 of Han (Liu Au), 17, 107, 112
and Li Xun's astrological expertise, 45
and the National Academy, 104
project to collect scattered books, 33, 39

Emperor Guangwu 光武 (Liu Xiu 劉秀):
apocryphal texts used to legitimize his rule, 50, 195, 200, 235n105, 242n60
feng 封 and *shan* 禪 sacrifices, 74–78, 236n115
and Gongsun Shu, 69–71
mandate to rule claimed by, 66
Emperor Huan 桓:
sacrifices to, Laozi, 子老, 99, 137
Scripture of the Great Peace presented to (AD 166), 99, 137, 159–160
Emperor Jing, paper use during his reign, 178
Emperor Ling 靈:
Hongdu Gate school established by, 99, 134, 137
and Xiang Kai, 160
Emperor Ming (Liu Yang 劉陽), 242n242
Huan Rong as his teacher, 107
political image of Zixia, 92, 95–96, 98
political legitimacy of Han rule affirmed by, 93–95
emperors, *See also* Five Phases in Generation (*wuxing xiang sheng* 五行相生)
Emperor Shun, 107, *114chart 10*, 120, 160
Emperor Wu of the Han:
feng 封 and *shan* 禪 sacrifices, 75
masters of methods promoted by, 209
Emperor Xuan 宣:
anxiety over understanding Heaven's will, 11–12, 22, 45
Changes promoted by, 21–23
and Emperor Yuan, 12–13
and Gongsun Shu's prophecies, 3–4, 70
Gongyang tradition of the *Annals* promoted by, 21

Emperor Xuan 宣 *(continued)*
  sensitivity to omens, 4–5, 218n9
Emperor Yuan, and Emperor Xuan,
  12–13
Emperor Zhang 章:
  and Cui Yuan, 98, 130
  Huan Yan as his teacher, 107,
    114chart 10
  textual lord-minister relationship
    during his reign, 89
van Ess, Hans, 210, 214
Evidential Research (Kao Ju 考據),
  186, 274n25

families:
  Han family tradition of the *Poetry*,
    73, 106, *109chart 8*, 118–119
  literati families, 107
  and old text traditions, 106–113
  ordinary or poor families and
    education, 117
  wealthy local gentries, 71–72, 175,
    234n96, 243–244n8, 244n9
  See also Huan 桓 family; imperial
    harem families; Kong 孔 family of
    Qufu 曲阜; Liu 劉 family; Meng
    孟 family; Yang 楊 family; Yuan
    袁 family
Fan Ying 樊英, 106, 120, *121chart 11*,
  127chart 12
Fang Shiming 方詩銘, 265–266n88
Farmer, J. Michael, 250n86, 261n20
first emperor. *See* Yellow Emperor
First Emperor of Qin 秦始皇:
  feng 封 and *shan* 禪 sacrifices, 75,
    236n119
  masters of methods promoted by,
    209
Five Phases in Generation (*wuxing
  xiang sheng* 五行相生), 93
  as a yardstick for dating dynasties,
    282n14

  and relationship between apocryphal
    texts and the *Scripture*, 268n101
  and succession by conquest
    (*xiangshèng* 相勝), 60–61, *61t2*
  and succession by generation
    (*xiangshēng* 相生), 60–61, *61t3*,
    65, 82
friends *xiang you shan* 相友善, 135,
  252n119, 259n186
Fu Qian 服虔:
  and Zheng Xuan, 鄭玄, *121chart 11*,
    123
  Zuo commentary on the *Annals* by,
    123
Fu Xi 伏羲:
  and Confucius, 189n9
  *Cracking Open the Regularity of Qian
    and Kun* attributed to, 56
  legend in the *Chunqiu yan Kong tu*,
    52, 238n14
  and the succession by generation
    (*xiangsheng* 相生), *61t3*
Fukui Shigemasa 福井重雅:
  criticism of Itano Chōhachi, 202
  on the victory of Confucianism
    during Emperor Wu's reign and
    Dong Zhongshu's role in it, 200,
    202

Ge Gong 葛龔, 128
Ge Hong 葛洪, attitude toward the
  classics, 161–162, 179
generative succession. *See* Five Phases
  in Generation
gift giving:
  and Ge Gong and Cui Yuan's
    friendship, 128
  and social networking, 254n137
  and the word *zhi* 贄, 254n138
Gong Chong 宮崇, 160
Gong Kechang 龔克昌, on Zhang
  Hen's rhapsodies, 258–259n182

Index

Gongsun Bingyi 公孫病已, 3–4, 70
Gongsun Hong, 公孫弘, 13–14, 171
Gongsun Shu 公孫述:
   Analects paraphrased by his wife, 67, 70, 233n75
   classical references used to support his mandate to rule, 69–72
   mandate to rule claimed by, 66–67
   occupation of Shu, 66
Gongyang tradition of the *Spring and Autumn Annals* (*Chunqiu Gongyang zhuan* 春秋公羊傳):
   and apocryphal texts, 210
   and Confucius's association with the *qilin*, 54, 156–157
   and Confucius's composition of the *Annals*, 228n18
   and the corpus of classics (*jing*), 181
   and Emperor Wu, 21
   and Emperor Xuan, 21
   and Liu Xiang 劉向, 226n135
   and the new script camp, 237n5
   Yan 顏 tradition of, 107, *109chart 8*, 248n47
Goodman, Howard L., 243n6
Great Peace (*taiping* 太平):
   and the imagination of an ideal society, 2, 13–15
   and the *qilin*, 264n71
   qilin as the symbolic creature of, 264n71
   religious movement led by, 99, 137, 159–160
   and Rising Peace (*shengping* 升平), 263
   sage kings associated with, 14, 24–26, 28–29
   Zheng Xuan's construction of, 145–150
Guliang tradition of the *Spring and Autumn Annals* (*Chunqiu Guliang zhuan* 春秋穀梁傳):

   and the corpus of classics (*jing*), 181
   and Liu Xiang, 劉向, 226n135
Guo Tai 郭太, *127chart 12*, 135, 259n186
Gurr, Ted Robert, 260n8
gu xue 古学 ("old learning"), 196

Han emperors:
   legitimacy of, 93
   Liu Bang's enthronement as Gaozu, 64, 232n66
Han Feizi 韓非子:
   and the intellectual history of the Eastern Han, 137
   mystical sugestions for rulers, 173
   and the word *jia,* 家, 255n145
He Xiu 何休:
   Confucius compared to the *qilin* by, 156–157, 264n71
   debate with Zheng Xuan, 142–143, 146, 152, 159, 169, 188
   and the Gongyang tradition, 138, 151–159, 176, 187, 263n53
   and the term Rising Peace (*shengping* 升平), 263
Henderson, John B., 155, 219n26
Hendrischke, Barbara, 161, 260n7
Hirai Masashi, 平井正士, 244n17
Hongdu Gate school (*Hongdu men xue* 鴻都門学), 99, 134, 137
Hou Cang 后蒼:
   chart of his disciples, *19chart 2*
   Han dynasty tied the Kingly Way by, 3, 18
   Six Classics used to connect Heaven to the human realm by, 22–23
   teaching of the *Rites and Annals* received from Meng Qing, 22, 39
Hsing I-tien 邢義田. *See* Xing Yitian
Huainanzi. *See Master Huainan* (*Huainanzi* 淮南子)

Huan 桓 family, *114chart 10*
  as high officials, 113, 115
  the imperial family taught the
    classics by, 107
  influence at court, 119
  and the Ouyang tradition of the
    Documents, *108chart 7*
Huan Tan 桓譚, 74
Huan Yu 桓郁:
  and Emperor Ming, 92–93, 95
  and Emperor Zhang, 107
Huang-Lao, 黃老, 219n26

Ikeda Shūzō 池田秀三:
  on Liu Xiang's composition of the
    "Seven Summaries," 224n95
  on "organic unity," 224n37
  on the "six heavens" (*liu tian* 六天),
    231n51
imperial harem families:
  Huan Rong as a tutor for, 113
  and power struggles, 125, 226n119,
    252–253n120, 260n12
Inner Canon of the Yellow Emperor
  (*Huangdi neijing* 黃帝內經), 38
Itano Chōhachi 板野長八:
  on the emergence of prophecy,
    279n18
  Fukui Shigemasa's criticism of, 202
  on the importance of apocryphal
    texts, 279n14
  nationalization of Confucianism
    challenged by, 200–202, 204,
    279n10, 279n12

jia 家:
  and *baijia* 柏家, 129, 142, 256n156
  used as a term by Sima Tan,
    255n145
Jia Kui 賈逵:
  on contradictory accounts in
    apocryphal texts, 235n105

as Cui Yuan's teacher, 130, 253n125
and the Elder Xiahou tradition, 110
and the Old Texts Tradition,
  111chart 9
and the Zuo tradition, 110,
  121chart 11, 123, *127chart 12*
Jiao Xun 焦循, criticism of evidential
  research, 186
Jiang Shoucheng 姜守誠, *264–265n83*
jinwen 今文 texts:
  introduced, xv–xvi
  See also new script and old script
    controversy

Kaltenmark, Max, 161
Kamada Tadashi 鎌田正, on Liu Xiang,
  226–227n135
Kang Youwei 康有為, theory that Liu
  Xin forged the old script classics,
  190
  and Gu Jiegang's views, 194
  Liu Shipei's dissatisfaction with,
    275n13
  Qian Mu's refutation of, 192–193
Kimura Masao 木村正雄, 71
Kinney, Anne Behnke, 253n123
Kong 孔 family of Qufu 曲阜, and the
  Yan 嚴 tradition of the Gongyang
  Annals, 107, *108chart 7*
Kramer, Robert P., 211
Kuang Heng 匡衡, *41chart 4*, *43chart
  5*, *44chart 6*
  and Hua Cang, *19chart 2*, 24–25
  on the the classics and the Kingly Way,
    25–28, 46, 51, 171, 224n101

Lagerwey, John, 250n87
Laozi 老子, Emperor Huan's sacrifices
  to, 99, 137
Laozi 老子:
  and Ma Rong's academy, 122,
    252n256

mystical suggestions for rulers found in, 173
and the root of second-century Daoist movements, xvi
letter writing:
Dou Zhang's correspondence with Ma Rong, 126
and gift giving, 128, 254n138
and intellectual discussions and debates, 126, 128, 177–178
Levy, Howard S., 265n88
Li Xun:
astrological expertise of, 45
promotion of the *Scripture of the Great peace*, 57
Li Ying 李膺, *127chart 12*, 135, 139
Liu An 劉安:
Master Huainan compiled by, 166
and the *Zhen zhong hongbao yuan mishu* ?中鴻苑秘書, 39
Lin Fu-shih 林富士, *264–265n83*
Liu 劉 family, as recipient of the mandate of Heaven, and Succession by Generation, 65–67, 282n14
Liu Fenglu 劉逢祿:
attitude toward Liu Xin's forgery of the Zuo tradition, 189, 190, 274n27
and the Gongyang tradition, 187
impact of his understanding of Han classicism, 187–188
Liu Jigao, 劉季高, 259n186
Liu Jing 劉荊, 94
Liu Qiang 劉彊, 79, 94
Liu Shipei 劉師培:
dissatisfaction with Kang Youwei's perspective, 275n13
and Gu Jiegang's criticism of the new and old tradition, 194
and Ma Zonghuo's theory of the dichotomy of official learning and private learning, 191

theory of the old script classics' transmission line, 190–191
and the Yangzhou tradition, 190, 274n20
and Zhang Binglin, 275n12
Liu Xiang 劉向:
on achieving the Great Peace, 17–18
Han dynasty tied to the Kingly Way by, 3, 18
intellectual breadth of, 39, *40chart 3*, 42, 226n134, 226n135
Kamada Tadashi 鎌田正 on, 226–227n135
"Seven Summaries" by, 26–27, 224n95
theory of *qi*, 16
Liu Xin 劉歆:
astrological system based on the Twelve Stations, 226–227n135
intellectual breadth of, 39, *40chart 3*, 42, 57, 226n135
Liu Xin 劉歆—and the old script classics:
and Liu Fenglu's views of his forgery of the Zuo tradition, 189, 190, 274n27
See also Kang Youwei 康有為, theory that Liu Xin forged the old script classics
Liu Xiu 劉秀. *See* Emperor Guangwu 光武
Loewe, Michael, 218n9
on *boshi* as "Academician," 220n40
on Dong Zhongshu's marginal role at court, 206
on Dong Zhongshu's relationship to the *Chunqiu Fanlu*, 278n5, 280n39
major ways to claim legitimacy of a monarchy identified by, 93
unity called "Confucianism" refuted by, xvi, 207

Lu Jia 陸賈:
  on bad *qi,* 219n23
  classics linked to Heaven by, 22, 220n28
  Great Peace outlined in his *New Speeches* (*Xin yu* 新語), 13, 16
    Hou Cang's views contrasted with, 23
Lu Zhi 盧植, 116, 121chart 11, 127chart 12
  and the *Huainanzi,* 167, 251n106, 252n256
lun 論 (discourse):
  as a classical genre, 253n123
  tanlun 談論 and *qingtan* ("pure discussions"), 135n187, 178, 259n186
  See also *Analects* (*Lunyu* 論語)

Ma Rong 馬融, and the traveling culture of literati, 101, 125–129
Ma Rong 馬融—academy of:
  and Laozi, 122, 252n256
  transmission of knowledge, *121chart 11*
Ma Zonghuo 馬宗霍, *Zhongguo jingxue shi* 中國經學史:
  and and Qian Mu's discussion of the contrast-debate model, 192
  four pairs of concepts discussed regarding Han classicism in, 276n21
  and Gu Jiegang's theories about the evolution of Han classicism, 194
  Pi Xirui's views compared with, 191
Master Huainan (*Huainanzi* 淮南子):
  compilation by Liu An 劉安, 166
  and Confucius as *su wang* ("uncrowned king"), 240n35
  and Ma Rong's academy, 122, 167, 251n106, 252n256
  "perfected men" and "sages" as terms in, 38

  "way of teaching" (*jiao dao* 教道) mentioned in, 87, 95, 240n37
measurements:
  chi, 尺, 230n42
  mu, 畝, 29
  wei, 圍, 230n43
Mencius 孟子:
  on Confucius's composing the *Annals,* 53–54, 228n18
  and the corpus of classics (*jing*), 181
  Well-Field system depicted in, 29
Meng 孟 family, Meng Xi, 孟喜, 9
Meng Qing 孟卿:
  on the classics having more information than can be mastered, 11, 221n45
  and Hou Cang and his disciples, *19chart 2,* 22, 39
  and the transmission line of the *Changes,* *10chart 1,* 11, 39
Meng 孟 tradition of the *Changes.* See *Changes of Zhou* (*Zhou yi* 周易)
Meng Xi 孟喜:
  scholarship of, 11
  and the transmission line of the *Changes,* 9, *10chart 1,* 11, 39

Nakamura Shōhachi 中村璋八, compilation of apocryphal texts by, 79, 215, 283nn15–16
National Academy (*Taixue* 太學):
  the Han court's attempts to monopolize authority over it, 172
  protest in AD 166 at, 106, 125, 135
  rise and fall of, 104–105
  and the transmission of apocryphal texts, 106
  See also official learning; official learning and private learning dichotomy

new script and old script controversy (*jin gu wen zhi zheng* 今古文之爭), and the identification of the original classics, 28

new script *jinwen* 今文. *See* old script versus new script (*guwen/jinwen* 古文/今文) texts

Nishijima Sadao, 西嶋定生, 201–202

Nylan, Michael:
  on calligraphy as an art, 252n118
  critique of the contrast-debate model, 189, 278n57
  on cultural display by the Han government, 131–132
  and the four traditions in the "Zan" 贊 part of the *Rulin zhuan* 儒林傳 in Han shu, 247n34
  on the link between classics and Han "Confucians," 205–208
  on manuscript culture, 252n115
  old script and new script controversy questioned by, xvi, 195–196
  on Yang Xiong's *Mystery*, 258n182

official learning 官學:
  the "Elder Xiahou" (Da Xiahou 大夏侯) tradition of *Documents* identified as, 42, 45, 105
  the "Younger Xiahou" (Xiao Xiahou 小夏侯) tradition of *Documents* identified as, 42, 45, 105
  See also National Academy; recruitment of the Han bureaucracy

official learning and private learning dichotomy (*guan xue/si xue* 官學/私學), and Ma Zonghuo 馬宗霍's discussion of Han classicism, 191, 276n21

Ōfuchi Ninji 大淵忍爾, 266n89

old script *guwen* 古文 transmission lineages:
  introduced, xv–xvi
  Liu Shipei's view of, 190
  Zhang Binglin's view of, 275n12
  See also new script and old script controversy

old script versus new script (*guwen/jinwen* 古文/今文) texts:
  and the Changzhou school, 186–187
  and chapter and verse commentaries (*zhang ju* 章句), 196
  introduced, xv–xvi
  and Ma Zonghuo's 馬宗霍 discussion of Han classicism, 276n21
  partisanship not fundamental to it, 42, 122
  Qing dynasty framework on the origin of the controversy, 185–188

paper as a writing material, 128–129, 255n141
  and Han dynasty scholarship, 102–103, 252n115, 252n117
  and traveling culture, 124–125, 178

paradox and intellectual dissimilarity, xxiWording okay?
  and He Xiu and Zheng Xuan, 159
  and Li Xun's and Liu Xin's arguments about the Kingly way, 37

partisans (*dang ren* 黨人), *127chart 12*
  and the Academy, 106, 125, 135
  and Eastern Han bureaucracy, 122, 125
  and the old script/new script controversy, 42, 122
  See also Yellow Turban (Huangjin 黃巾) rebellion

Pattinson, David, 254n132

perfected men (*zhenren* 真人):
  as agents of the *Scripture of the Great Peace*, 38, 57, 162, 167–169, 176

perfected men (*zhenren* 真人) *(continued)*
    eclecticism of, 168–170
    in the *Inner Canon of the Yellow Emperor*, 38
    in the *Master Huainan*, 38
    in the *Zhuangzi*, 38
Pi Xirui 皮錫瑞:
    assumption that Han scholars strictly followed their masters' teaching, 191
    and Confucius's role in writing and compiling the Six Classics, 189–190
    and Gu Jiegang's theories about the evolution of Han classicism, 194
    Old Script and New Script distinction accepted by, 189–190
    on the origins of Han scholasticism, 191, 276n25
    and Qian Mu's discussion of the contrast-debate model, 192
Pines, Yuri, 86
Poetry. See *Classic of Poetry* (*Shijing* 詩經)
private schools:
    and career options for scholars, 116, 118
    financial support of, 116
    official schools distinguished from, 246–247n28
    and students from ordinary or poor families, 117
Puett, Michael J.:
    on "correlative thinking," 219n26
    on the *Huainanzi*, 268n113
    on Lu Jia's understanding of the sages' duty, 220n28

qi 氣:
    Dong Zhongshu's theory of deviant *qi* (*xie qi* 邪氣), 7
    Liu Xiang's theory of, 16
    Lu Jia 陸賈 on bad *qi*, 219n23
    and oppositional aspects of yin and yang, 6–7
    Wei Xiang's theory of the balance of *yin* and *yang*, 5–8
Qian Mu 钱穆:
    description of Emperor Ming, 242n242
    and the old and new script dichotomy, 192–193, 196
qilin 麒麟, 14
    as a common narrative in the *Annals*, 55, 85, 156
    and Confucius, 54, 84, 156–157, 264n71

recruitment of the Han bureaucracy:
    and the civil examinations, 104, 175–176, 182–183, 245n17, 246n22, 246n22, 246n24, 272n13
    and the flourishing of local academies, xx, 13–14
Red Eyebrow (Chimei 赤眉), 66, 71, 232–233n72
Rising Peace (*shengping* 升平), and Great Peace (*taiping* 太平), 263
Rites. See *Rites of Zhou* (*Zhouli* 周禮)
Rites of Zhou (*Zhouli* 周禮)—Yan 嚴 and Yan 嚴 tradition of:
    and the establishment of Great Peace, 146–150
    and the fourteen commentarial traditions of the National Academy, 105
Ruan Yuan 阮元, exclusion of Zhuang Cunyu's work from the *Huang qing jing jie*, 274n25
Ruan Yuan 阮元, as the general editor of the *Thirteen Classics with Commentaries and Sub-Commentaries* (*Shisan jing zhushu*), 181
    and cosmological order based on balancing *yin* and *yang*, 219n21

ru 儒/*tongren* 通人 (erudite) dichotomy, 262n36
  and Zheng Xuan's treatment by guests at a banquet, 142, 168

sage kings:
  loss and deterioration of ancient traditions invented by, 131
  recovery of their lost Kingly Way, 20, 26
sage kings compared to heavenly emperors:
  and *xue qi* (physical vitalities), 62, 232n57
  Xunzi's objection to the comparison, 59–63
  Zheng Xuan's depiction of, 231n51
sages (*shengren* 聖人), and Han emperors, 241n56
Schipper, Kristofer, 160
Scripture of the Great Peace (*Taiping jing*), xxi
  dating of, 160–162
  and imagined transmission lines of Daoism, 138, 162–163, 169–170
  presentation to Emperor Huan, 99, 137, 159–160
  presentation to Emperor Shun, 160
  relationship to apocryphal texts, 162–164, 268n101
  scholarly exploration of its thought, 264–265n83
  Writing of the Great Peace with Blue-Green Headings as an alternative name for, 160
  and the Yellow Turban rebellion, 160, 266n91
Seidel, Anna, 162
seven classics (*qi jing* 七經), 73, 236n111
  and the seven apocrypha (*qi jing chen* 七經讖), 215, 235n105

Shi Dan 師丹, Well-Field system promoted by, 29
Shiji 史記 (Records of the Grand Historian). *See* Sima Qian 司馬遷
Sima Qian 司馬遷:
  on Confucius's composing the *Annals*, 86, 87, 228n18
  on the First Emperor's sacrifice, 75
  Liu Bang addressed as Gaozu rather than Hanwang 漢王 by, 232n66
Sima Tan 司馬談:
  on the classics having more information than can be mastered, 221n45
  jia 家 used as a term by, 255n145
Sivin, Nathan:
  on the "Heavenly Pivot" 天樞, 228n8
  on the term "Huang-Lao," 219n26
  on the terms "Taoism" and "Confucianism" in Western scholarship, 205
succession by generation (*xiangsheng* 相生). *See* Five Phases in Generation

taiping 太平. *See* Great Peace
Tang Zhangru 唐長孺, 266n91
teaching models versus lineage models (*shi fa*/*jiafa* 師法/家法), and Ma Zonghuo' 馬宗霍 discussion of Han classicism, 276n21
Thirteen classics. *See classics jing* 經
Tian Wangsun 田王孫:
  and Meng Xi, 11
  and the transmission line of the *Changes*, 9, 10chart 1, 41chart 4, 43chart 5, 44chart 6
Tjan Tjoe Som 曾珠森, 211, 282n4
tongren 通人 the "man with comprehensive knowledge":
  and the new *jing*, 168
  See also ru 儒/*tongren* 通人 (erudite) dichotomy

traveling culture:
   and private schools, 116, 143, 172, 246n27
   and the social life of Eastern Han scholars, 124–125, 128, 177, 253n125
   See also letter writing

Wang Chong, 97, 242n64
Wang Fu, and the traveling culture of literati, 126
Wang Ji 王吉:
   and moral cultivation, 15, 172
   and the transmission line of the *Changes*, 10*chart 1*
Wang Mang 王莽:
   classics as crucial in the sociopolitical realm of his time, 72, 103
   knowledge of the *Changes*, 107, 109*chart 8*
   and Liu Xin, 39, 67, 187, 193–194, 210
   and the old text traditions, *111chart 9*, 120, 177, 193, 195
   on the Three-Seven Predicament, 65–66
   usurpation of the Han empires, 49, 67, 187, 193–194, 210
   Well-Field system promoted by, 29–30, 46–47, 147
   and the Zuo tradition of the *Annals*, 120, *121chart 11*, 193–194
Wang Ping 王平, *264–265n83*
Wang Su 王肅:
   evaluation of him as a forger, 182, 274n22
   plan for the Great Peace, 46–47
   on Zixia's talent in reading ancient texts, 91
Watanabe Yoshihiro 渡邊義浩:
   on Confucianism as a national teaching or religion, 203–204, 279n7
   on the "six heavens" (*liu tian* 六天), 231n51
Wei Xiang 魏相, on *yin* and *yang* balance and harmonious *qi*, 5–8
Well-Field (*jing tian* 井田) system, 225n106
   and the Kingly Way, 29–30, 46–47, 147, 222n66
Writing of the Great Peace with Blue-Green Headings (*Taiping qingling shu* 太平清領書). *See Scripture of the Great Peace* (*Taiping jing*)
Writing of the Luo River (*Luoshu* 洛书):
   and the corpus of classics, 215
   revelation of, 53, 144–145, 166
Wu Rong, 武榮, 122, 251n107

Xiahou Jian 夏侯建:
   network of scholars he associated with, *19chart 2*, *41chart 4*, *43chart 5*, *44chart 6*
   "Younger Xiahou" (Xiao Xiahou 小夏侯) tradition of *Documents* founded by, 42
Xiahou Sheng 夏侯勝:
   network of scholars he associated with, *19chart 2*, 39, *41chart 4*, 110
   position at court, 24, 224n86
   and Xiao Wangzhi, 18, 24
Xiang Kai 襄楷, 99, 137, 159–160
Xiao Wangzhi 蕭望之:
   local-gentry background of, 235n100
   network of scholars he associated with, *19chart 2*, 39, *41chart 4*, 42, *43chart 5*
   position at court, 24, 224n86
   and Xiahou Sheng, 18, 24
Xing Yitian 邢義田 (Hsing I-tien), 邢義田, 241n56, 245n17, 246n22, 246n23, 246n24

Xu Fang 徐防:
  background of, 107, *109chart 8*
  on Zixia as the inventor of *zhang jua* ("study of chapter and verse"), 91, 196
Xu Xingwu 徐興無, on Confucius as *xuan sheng* and *su wang*, 237n5
xuanji 琁機, "Heavenly Pivot" 天樞 as the meaning of, 50, 228n8
Xue Han 薛漢, 73, 106, *109chart 8*, 118–119
Xunzi 荀子:
  Confucius's appearance described by, 59–60, 231n44
  and Emperor Xuan's court, 22
  Heaven viewed as separate from the human realm by, 23, 59, 62, 149
  moral cultivation of individuals as central to, 21–22, 46, 150, 172
  view of the rites, 52
    Zheng Xuan's views of proper rites distinguished from, 149
  Yellow Emperor described by, 59

Yang 楊 family:
  and the Huan family, 107, *108chart 7*, *114chart 10*, 250n88
  influence at court, 119
Yang Xiong 揚雄:
  on the Great Peace, 96
  letters exchanged with Liu Xin, 225–226n117
  and Liu Xin, 35, 74
  on recovering the Kingly Way from sages's writing, 20, 26
  Supreme Mystery by:
    writing commentaries on the *Changes* compared with, 258n182
    Zhang Heng's promotion of it, 128, 176
Yangzhou tradition, 190, 274n20

Yan Zhitui 顏之推, attitude toward the classics, 161–162, 179
Yasui Kōzan 安居香山:
  compilation of apocryphal texts by, 79, 215, 283nn15–16
  on Confucius as *su wang* ("uncrowned king"), 237n5
  on the idea of "revolution" (*kakumei* 革命) in the Eastern Han, 268n101
  on the relationship between apocrypha and the new script tradition, 210, 237n5
  on the "superstitious" element in apocrypha, 210, 211
Yellow Emperor 黃帝, and the Five Phases, *61t2*, *61t3*
Yellow Turban (Huangjin 黃巾) rebellion, 160, 261n20, 265–266n88, 266n91
Yijing 易經. See *Changes of Zhou* (*Zhou yi* 周易)
Ying Shao, and the terms Great Peace (*taiping* 太平) and Rising Peace (*shengping* 升平), 263
Yoshikawa Tadao, 吉川忠夫, 246n27, 250, 263n53
Yuan 袁 family:
  imperial family taught the classics by, 107
  influence at court, 118
  and the transmission of the classics, *108chart 7*, 135
Yuan Gu 轅固, *19chart 2*, 24, *41chart 4*, *43chart 5*, *44chart 6*
Yuan Zhao 袁紹, *108chart 7*, 172
  and Zheng Xuan, 141, 142, 143, 146
Yü Ying-shih, 余英時, 270n14

Zhang Ba 張霸, *109chart 8*, 116, 248n47

Zhang Heng 張衡:
  and bans against the *chenwei* corpus, 214
  on contradictory accounts found in apocryphal texts, 235n105
  division of the Han dynasty into two two-hundred year periods, 133–134, 258n181
  project of carrying the spirit of the classics in contemporary writing, 134, 258–259n182
  and the traveling culture of literati, 101, 125–126
  letter to Cui Yuan, 126, 128
  on Yang Xiong's *Supreme Mystery*, 176
Zhang Hequan 張鶴泉, 248n57, 250n83
Zhang Jue 張角, 160, 266n91
Zhang Shanfu 轅固, 張山柎, *19chart 2*, *41chart 4*, 42, *43chart 5*, *44chart 6*
Zhang Yu 張禹, *10chart 1*, 39, *40chart 3*, *41chart 4*, 42, *43chart 5*, *44chart 6*
Zheng Xuan 鄭玄:
  commentaries on the classics by, 123, 138, 140–141
  on the construction of Great Peace, 145–150
  debate with He Xiu, 142–143, 146, 152, 159, 169, 188
  "Li yun," 禮運, 262n44
  relationship between human emperors and heavenly emperors, 231n51
  and the *ru* 儒/*tongren* 通人 (erudite) dichotomy
Zheng Xuan 鄭玄—school of:
  financial support of his school, 116
  pedagogical techniques at, 116
  transmission of knowledge, *121chart 11*, 123
Zhong Zhaopeng 鐘肇鵬, 210, 280n1, 280n39
Zhou Kan 周堪:
  and Emperor Xuan, 18
  network of scholars he associated with, *19chart 2*, 39, *41chart 4*, *43chart 5*, *44chart 6*
Zhuangzi 莊子:
  and the intellectual history of the Eastern Han, 137
  "perfected men" as a term in, 38
  and the root of second-century Daoist movements, xvi
  xuan sheng and *su wang* as terms in, 80–81, 85
Zixia 子夏:
  in the *Analects*, 90, 241n55
  as Confucius's advanced disciple, 53, 55, 89–91
  Emperor Ming's political image of him, 92, 95–96, 98
  as the initiator of the study of *zhang ju*, 91
  Wang Liqi on his lineage, 241n45
  Wang Su 王肅 on his talent in reading ancient texts, 91
Zufferey, Nicolas, on the correspondence between "Confucianism" and *ru*, 205–206
Zuo tradition of the *Spring and Autumn Annals* (*Chungqiu Zuo zhuan* 春秋左傳):
  and the corpus of classics (*jing*), 181
  transmission of, *40chart 3*
  and Wu Rong's intellectual repertoire, 122

www.ingramcontent.com/pod-product-compliance
Lightning Source LLC
Chambersburg PA
CBHW030000240426
43672CB00007B/762